The Wampas Baby Stars

ALSO BY ROY LIEBMAN
AND FROM MCFARLAND

Musical Groups in the Movies, 1929–1970 (2009)

*From Silents to Sound: A Biographical Encyclopedia
of Performers Who Made the Transition to Talking Pictures*
(1998; paperback 2009)

*Silent Film Performers: An Annotated Bibliography
of Published, Unpublished and Archival Sources
for Over 350 Actors and Actresses* (1996)

The Wampas Baby Stars

A Biographical Dictionary, 1922–1934

ROY LIEBMAN

McFarland & Company, Inc., Publishers
Jefferson, North Carolina, and London

The present work is a reprint of the illustrated case bound edition of The Wampas Baby Stars: A Biographical Dictionary, 1922–1934, *first published in 2000 by McFarland.*

LIBRARY OF CONGRESS CATALOGUING-IN-PUBLICATION DATA

Liebman, Roy.
　The Wampas baby stars : a biographical dictionary, 1922–1934 / by Roy Liebman.
　　　p.　　cm.
　　Includes bibliographical references and index.

　　ISBN 978-0-7864-4061-0
　　softcover : 50# alkaline paper ∞

　　1. Motion picture actors and actresses — United States — Biography — Dictionaries.　2. Actresses — United States — Biography — Dictionaries.　3. Western Associated Motion Picture Advertisers (Organization)　I. Title.
PN1998.2.L53　　2009
791.43′028′092273 — dc21
　[B]　　　　　　　　　　　　　　　　　　　　　　　　00-42722

British Library cataloguing data are available

©2000 Roy Liebman. All rights reserved

No part of this book may be reproduced or transmitted in any form or by any means, electronic or mechanical, including photocopying or recording, or by any information storage and retrieval system, without permission in writing from the publisher.

On the cover: Kathryn McGuire

Manufactured in the United States of America

McFarland & Company, Inc., Publishers
　Box 611, Jefferson, North Carolina 28640
　　www.mcfarlandpub.com

To Janine, Marissa, Dennis and Hannah.
You're all stars to me!

Acknowledgments

Eugene Vazzana and Billy Doyle, both authors of very useful silent film necrologies, provided me with generous assistance in furnishing otherwise hard to find dates. Roi A. Uselton brought the Wampas Baby Stars back from obscurity, however briefly, with his February 1972 article in *Films in Review*.

Contents

Acknowledgments vii
Introduction 1
The Baby Star Roster, Year by Year 7

The Wampas Baby Stars 13

Appendix A: Wampas "Drop-Outs" 215
Appendix B: Presidents of Wampas 217
Appendix C: Wampas Baby Miscellany 219
Appendix D: Rivals and Successors to Wampas 223
Sources 237
Index 239

INTRODUCTION

It may be difficult to believe in this hard-nosed era of Hollywood megabuck deals, runaway star power, and political correctness that there could ever have been a group of actresses known as Wampas (or WAMPAS) Baby Stars. The name sounds positively risible today and invariably elicits a puzzled "Huh?" from all but the cognoscenti.

From 1922 to 1934 there were almost 150 young actresses who proudly bore the designation — especially in its mid- to late-1920s heyday — and it was a much sought-after honor to be so designated. In the days before Academy Awards, it was a signal recognition, and many actresses who became major stars were first recognized in this way.

The idea for the Baby Star promotion sprang from the organization known as the Western Associated Motion Picture Advertisers, founded in 1920 by professional publicists in the film industry. (It is sometimes misidentified as the Western Association of Motion Picture Advertisers.) Ray Leek was the first president. It became known to one and all by the acronym WAMPAS and was recognized as such by its own members. It was also widely, although unofficially, spelled in lowercase letters (and frequently was misspelled in either case as "Wampus"). The lowercase form is used throughout this book.

The Wampas Constitution reads in part: "The WAMPAS founders were animated by a spirit of fraternity and cooperation. Their aims were both social and professional. Their objectives ... were to foster comradeship, promote the ethics of the profession and encourage cooperation among the members." These noble aims were to be observed in the breach later on.

The constitution further went on to say that Wampas should engender "in every member an ever-present consciousness of his responsibility to the profession he publicizes, the industry he represents and *to the public whose tendencies, thoughts and impulses he is such a factor in forming and directing*" (italics not in original). One way that this august group of opinion makers met such a weighty obligation became clear in 1921. It involved, as did so much in the Hollywood of its day, a parade of (mostly) pretty girls.

The idea was conceived to select 13 young women with potential star power and to publicize them to a fare-thee-well. The future stars were to be known as the Wampas Baby Stars; the "Baby" not meaning infants but rather "junior" stars. At first, the organization's desire to publicize Wampas, rather than the actresses, was undoubtedly at the forefront. Its members may not have been prepared for what followed. The studios realized the inherent promotional value of this hoopla and gave the idea their enthusiastic blessing. The concept took off and became wildly popular.

The term "starlet" was apparently not in general use in those times. Whether any of the young hopefuls objected to being dubbed "Baby Stars" is not recorded. It is more likely that they were greatly excited to be distinguished from the innumerable others striving to make a breakthrough. Wampas eventually established a special committee "to handle all details of the annual baby star elections, when held, and projects affecting these baby stars and their WAMPAS activities."

Possibly by dint of great Wampas perspicacity—or more likely by sheer luck—the very first group of 13 actresses in 1922 indeed proved to be rife with potential. In that group of young women so willingly thrust into the spotlight were such luminaries-to-be as Colleen Moore, Patsy Ruth Miller, Bessie Love, Lois Wilson and Lila Lee. The original Wampas rules stated that actresses had to have credits in at least three films. (This was changed later on.)

Some of the first "class" had actually been on the screen for many years, but none of them had really yet enjoyed major stardom. Love, Wilson and beautiful blonde Claire Windsor were probably the most famous of the pioneer group at the time of their selection. Lightning was to strike almost at once for several others. As a whole, this first group was older when selected than future starlets were to be. Some had hit the ripe old age of 25, and even more.

Whether their designation as Wampas Baby Stars speeded the initial group of actresses toward fame, or their subsequent fame gave cachet to the designation, to be named a Baby Star soon became an extremely prestigious honor. It was to prove a major plum for the studios as well as for the young women. Theoretically, many actresses could be nominated in a given year, but until the 1930s no more than 13 ever were selected as winners. There were also two alternates in case any of the chosen stars dropped out—and that actually did occur.

The Wampas organization's counting of ballots was supposedly above reproach, and the publicity about the process obviously set the tone for the later Academy Award vote-counting excitement. In one year, for instance, votes were counted by the Wampas chaplain and a dignified, presumably neutral bank official. Because the publicists who made up the organization were fairly well divided among the studios, and there were also some freelancers, every major studio generally had at least one winner.

Another of the constitution's provisions stated: "It shall sponsor such social events from time to time as are decided by the membership." What better time to have such an event than the unveiling of that year's lucky 13? It soon became de rigueur to have a glittering ball every January to introduce that year's crop of Babies. The first festivities were held in 1922 in the modest-enough Alexandria Hotel, but the venues soon changed — a sign of the growing importance of the Baby Star promotion.

In later years the more prestigious and capacious Shrine Auditorium and Ambassador Hotel were utilized, and even the Olympic Stadium to coincide with Los Angeles Fiesta Days. The Ball and Frolic, as it soon came to called, attracted most of the major Hollywood stars, featured top entertainers as masters of ceremonies, and offered lavish entertainment. The newspapers all breathlessly speculated on who would appear.

Apparently it could be both a joyful and a stressful time. One young Baby Star–Elect fainted as she stepped on the stage to be introduced. Such was the ball's popularity that there were even instances of counterfeit tickets being sold. One year the ball was held in San Francisco, apparently because Los Angeles officialdom did not allow dancing after midnight.

Throughout the 1920s to be named a Wampas Baby Star remained a coveted prize, and the object of ongoing hype. The number of actresses who lived up to their promise continued to be fairly high throughout the decade, although only once was the achievement of the first "class" of selectees matched. The 1926 luminaries proved to be the most distinguished, among them Joan Crawford, Mary Astor, Dolores Del Rio, Janet Gaynor and Fay Wray.

There were of course a large number of Baby Stars who had entirely undistinguished careers, but many others were to become top celebrities — if not necessarily top actresses — with their share of Academy Award nominations. Joan Blondell, Clara Bow and Del Rio also were awarded special Wampas achievement trophies for the greatest advancement in their careers. There were also many who attained second-rank but nevertheless respectable stardom. In some ways the Wampas roster reads like a roll of the major leading ladies of the 1920s.

As that decade passed, the presidents of Wampas included such luminaries as Barrett Kiesling, publicity director for Cecil B. DeMille (who was his own best publicist), and Mark Larkin, the publicity maven for the king and queen of Hollywood royalty, Douglas Fairbanks and Mary Pickford. But Larkin resigned during the year of his presidency (1928), as did another president that year. There were signs of trouble brewing.

In 1929 the Frolic was canceled, supposedly because Wampas could not guarantee sufficient monies for the various charities that its activities supported. In 1930 Wampas merged with the Writers Club but still managed to retain its own identity. That year for the first time there was no Wampas Baby Star election. This was possibly because of the Depression, or there might have been dissension over whether the girls' vocal ability should be considered now that "talkers" were here to stay.

Worse travails were yet to come. As more publicists became part of the studios' apparatus rather than being freelancers, they felt their loyalty (and bread and butter) lay with their employers. There was, therefore, even less objectivity—if there ever was much to begin with (some Wampas members were married to some of the winners)—and they undoubtedly voted for their own studios' actresses.

Freelance performers had little chance of being selected (until 1934, when they were *all* freelancers). In 1931, the Fox studio did not have a winner. It thereupon denounced the proceedings and selected its own group of starlets which it dubbed the "Fox Debutantes." That studio's publicists, no doubt thoroughly abashed, resigned from Wampas.

Shortly thereafter, the studios still participating demanded that they, rather than Wampas, be able to decide which of their starlets would be eligible for election. In addition they refused to let their winners appear on the radio, by then considered a rival for audience attention to the cinema. Wampas managed to sidestep the demands for a change in the nomination process, and things limped along for a while longer.

In 1932 there was a triple tie for thirteenth place, and for the first and only time 15 girls were dubbed Baby Stars. One of the winners was also the first (and last) Asian-American selected. In that year there was no ball, probably because of the Depression. Instead a series of personal appearances was held at several Los Angeles theaters. In 1933 there was again no election for Baby Stars.

The following year Wampas defied the studio powers one final time. The organization decreed that only actresses *not* under contract to a studio were eligible for the Baby Star honor. Also screen tests were made of the nominees; that had never been done before. Paramount responded by dropping out of Wampas and, following Fox's lead, picked its own crop of actresses, dubbing them the "Paramount Protégées." One of these was Ida Lupino; another, Helen Mack, had previously been a "Fox Debutante."

Nineteen thirty-four proved to be the year the Baby Star promotion could not survive—and the end of the Wampas organization itself was not far behind. The Academy Awards were firmly established and were being broadcast and filmed for the entire nation, and they were for proven work, not just for potential. The crop of '34 Babies was generally an undistinguished group as well. In a last-ditch publicity effort, that year's winners were seen in two films: *Young and Beautiful* and *Kiss and Make-Up.*

Obviously, the idea of prognosticating future stars still had a bit of vitality left. In 1935 Warner Bros. began announcing which of their starlets would be groomed for the big time. Presciently selected as one of the "scintillating sextuplets," as one writer (who perhaps meant "sextet") dubbed them, was Olivia de Havilland.

In the years that followed, a few more attempts were made to present lists of nubile young performers who might break out into stardom. These included "The Flashlighters Starlets" (the term "starlet" now being au courant), "The Baby Stars of 1940" (of which Joan Leslie was one), and "The Star Ring of 1943." Eventually, though, the time for lists ran its course.

Surprisingly, in 1955 newspapers again carried publicity stories about the Wampas Baby Stars. There were 30 finalists who competed for the honor in front of a group of film directors and producers, with actress Merle Oberon serving as a kind of mistress of ceremonies. There was even a Wampas Ball scheduled for November of that year, perhaps not held.

None of the aspirants in that briefly resuscitated group was to make a name for herself, apart from the very minor careers enjoyed by "B" starlets Lita Milan and Fay Spain. That was, presumably, the final gasp for Wampas outside of an abortive attempt to sell something called the "Wampas Baby Star Reunion Show" to television in the mid–1960s. It was to feature personal appearances by some of the surviving actresses, together with clips from their films.

In spite of the Wampas concept's rather inglorious end, the reign of the Baby Stars coincided with — and may well have helped to create — one of the most glamorous eras in Hollywood history. The story of these lucky ladies is, after all, the story of the American cinema itself. Like other aspiring stars, a relative few succeeded wildly, some did respectably well, and, inevitably, the rest were destined for obscurity and rapidly disappeared from public consciousness. All were a mirror of the industry in which they strived.

The Baby Star Roster, Year by Year

1922

Many of the Babies of 1922 — Year One — were veterans. As a group, their average age was higher than any year's selectees would be again. Lois Wilson may have been the oldest of all at the time of her selection, at the ripe old age of 27 or so. Perhaps in this maiden year the Wampas judges were playing it safe. Although some of the actresses were relative newcomers, some had been in films since the mid-'teens. (At least two, Bessie Love and Pauline Starke, were in *Intolerance*.) It was also to prove one of the most successful groups. If they had not yet made their mark by 1922, all but one, Maryon Aye, would do so to some degree. Love and Wilson, for instance, had long, distinguished careers lasting into the 1970s.

The 1922 Babies were: Marion (Maryon) Aye, Helen Ferguson, Lila Lee, Jacqueline Logan, Louise Lorraine, Bessie Love, Kathryn McGuire, Patsy Ruth Miller, Colleen Moore, Mary Philbin, Pauline Starke, Lois Wilson and Claire Windsor.

1923

Year Two of the Wampas phenomenon saw more veterans selected, at least two of whom were definitely born in the 19th century; others certainly flirted with it. Evelyn Brent may have taken Wampas honors for having been in films the longest, perhaps all the way back to 1914 (and she was still active until the 1950s). Laura La Plante became the biggest female star at Universal in the 1920s. Except for one of the year's selectees, in fact, they all had careers that could be called at least respectable. Margaret Leahy, however, made only a single film.

The 1923 Babies were: Eleanor Boardman, Evelyn Brent, Dorothy Devore, Virginia Brown(e) Faire, Betty Francisco, Pauline Garon, Kathleen Key, Laura La Plante, Margaret Leahy, Helen(e) Lynch, Derelys Perdue, Jobyna Ralston and Ethel Shannon.

1924

Year Three delivered one superstar-to-be, Clara Bow, and two actresses who were to be dependable stars of the second rank well into the 1930s, Marion Nixon and Dorothy Mackaill. At least one may have hailed from the previous century; another, Lucille Ricksen, was shortly to die.

The 1924 Babies were: Clara Bow, Elinor Fair, Carmelita Geraghty, Gloria Grey, Ruth Hiatt, Julanne Johnston, Hazel Keener, Dorothy Mackaill, Blanche Mehaffey (aka Joan Alden and Janet Morgan), Margaret Morris, Marion (Marian) Nixon, Lucille Ricksen and Alberta Vaughn.

1925

Year Four continued the mixed track record of the previous year's Babies. Some remained in obscurity while a few, including June Marlowe, Dorothy Revier and Olive Borden, found minor stardom. Betty Arlen was perhaps unique in that she had no credited roles at all, while Madeline Hurlock restricted her career almost entirely to comedy shorts.

The 1925 Babies were: Betty Arlen, Violet Avon (La Plante), Olive Borden, Anne Cornwall, Ena Gregory (aka Marian Douglas), Madeline Hurlock, Natalie Joyce, June Marlowe, Joan Meredith, Evelyn Pierce, Dorothy Revier, Duane Thompson and Lola Todd.

1926

Year Five was the one that made the Wampas selectors look like they really did possess a crystal ball. No other year came close to matching it, except perhaps 1922. With such bright lights as Mary Astor, Joan Crawford, Dolores Del Rio and Janet Gaynor it was positively luminescent. Even some of those who did not reach the superstar ranks, like Joyce Compton and Fay Wray, could be justly proud of their achievements. Vera Reynolds was the "old-timer" of the crop, having been in films for almost ten years and possibly the last Wampas Baby to have been born before the 20th century.

The 1926 Babies were: Mary Astor, Mary Brian, Joyce Compton, Dolores Costello, Joan Crawford, Marceline Day, Dolores Del Rio, Janet Gaynor, Sally Long, Edna Marion, Sally O'Neil, Vera Reynolds and Fay Wray.

1927

Few actresses could have withstood comparison with the previous year's, but by any measure Year Six would have to be rated as a disappointment. Only a couple of Babies, Barbara Kent and Martha Sleeper, went into the 1930s as minor leading ladies. Helene Costello did have the distinction of starring in the first all-talkie and Sally Rand went on to much greater fame outside the movies, as an exotic dancer with her feathers and "bubbles." Sleeper also did better after she departed the screen to become a Broadway headliner. She was a replacement, having been named after French actress Jeanne Navelle opted out. The veteran of this group was Mary McAl(l)ister, who had begun as a child actress a dozen or so years before.

The 1927 Wampas Babies were: Patricia Avery, Rita Carewe, Helene Costello, Barbara Kent, Natalie Kingston, Frances Lee, Mary McAlister (McAllister), Gladys McConnell, Sally Phipps, Sally Rand, Martha Sleeper, Iris Stuart and Adamae Vaughn.

1928

Year Seven saw a slight recovery in the staying power of its Babies. It stands about squarely in the middle of the Wampas spectrum, not great but not bad either. Perhaps the most memorable of the year's actresses was Lupe Velez. Lina Basquette had been around the longest, having been onscreen sporadically since the mid-'teens. The private lives of both of these ladies made hot copy for the newspapers of the day. Among those having respectable careers as "B" leading ladies were Sally Eilers, Dorothy Gulliver, Sue Carol and June Collyer.

The Wampas phenomenon was at its height of popularity. Over 3,000 people attended the year's ball and thousands more waited outside — shades of the Academy Awards — to get a glimpse of the stars and entertainers.

The 1928 Wampas Babies were: Lina Basquette, Flora Bramley, Sue Carol, Ann Christy, June Collyer, Alice Day, Sally Eilers, Audrey Ferris, Dorothy Gulliver, Gwen Lee, Molly O'Day, Ruth Taylor and Lupe Velez.

1929

Year Eight featured two alumna who would break from the pack to become major stars. They were the first and last alphabetically of that year, Jean Arthur and Loretta Young. It was the only year in which sisters were selected at the same time: Young and her older sister Sally Blane. Only one other Baby was somewhat memorable, the interestingly named Helen Twelvetrees, a good actress who never really lived up to her potential. Caryl Lincoln apparently was a replacement for Sharon Lynn(e). MGM's Anita Page had her brief day in the sun, and at the time of writing — late 1998 — is still happy to talk about it.

It was probably the last year that the Baby Star selection was considered to be an important Filmtown event. The Academy Awards were in their ascendancy. It was to be downhill for Wampas from now on in terms of prestige, if not in the quality of some of the Baby Stars who would be named in the future.

The 1929 Baby Stars were: Jean Arthur, Sally Blane, Betty Boyd, Ethlyne Clair(e), Doris Dawson, Josephine Dunn, Helen Foster, Doris Hill, Caryl Lincoln, Anita Page, Mona Rico, Helen Twelvetrees and Loretta Young.

1930

No election.

1931

Year Nine was not one of which Wampas needed to be embarrassed. Several of the year's crop had distinguished careers. Of these, Joan Blondell came to symbolize the brassy but good-hearted blonde that seemed to be a fixture in De-

10 The Baby Star Roster, Year by Year

The 1928 Wampas Baby Stars. Bottom row, right to left: Flora Bramley, Lupe Velez, Ruth Taylor, Ann Christy, Dorothy Gulliver, Lina Basquette. *Top row, right to left:* Alice Day, Molly O'Day (kneeling), Audrey Ferris, June Collyer, Sally Eilers, Sue Carol, Gwen Lee.

pression-era movies. Constance Cummings and Karen Morley both metamorphosed into distinguished actresses. Others also displayed some staying power. All in all, it was the last really good year.

The 1931 Wampas Babies were: Joan Blondell, Constance Cummings, Frances Dade, Frances Dee, Sidney Fox, Rochelle Hudson, Anita Louise, Joan Marsh, Marian Marsh, Karen Morley, Marion Shilling, Barbara Weeks and Judith Wood.

1932

Among the hopefuls of Year Ten — the decade mark for Wampas — Ginger Rogers stands out as the last great Wampas star. Among the rest were some winning, and winsome, ladies, but none particularly destined for long-lasting fame except for two with a penchant for water. Eleanor Holm made a splash (pun intended!) as a swimmer, and Gloria Stuart came roaring back some 65 years later to gather honors in the mega-movie *Titanic*.

Toshia Mori, the only Asian-American selected by Wampas, was a replacement for Lillian Miles. Because of a three-way tie among the freelance actresses, it was the only time that 15 Babies made the big time. As a sign of its diminishing luster, this was the first year there was no

Six Wampas Baby Stars of 1932. Right to left: Mary Carlisle, Ginger Rogers, Toshia Mori (behind Rogers), Lillian Bond, Gloria Stuart, Eleanor Holm.

Wampas Ball. The Babies instead made appearances at various Los Angeles theaters. It wasn't quite the same.

The 1932 Wampas Babies were: Lona Andre, Lillian Bond, Mary Carlisle, June Clyde, Patricia Ellis, Ruth Hall, Eleanor Holm, Evalyn Knapp, Dorothy Layton, Patricia (Boots) Mallory, Toshia Mori, Ginger Rogers, Marian Shockley, Gloria Stuart and Dorothy Wilson.

1933

No election, although it is sometimes considered that the 1932 Babies were elected for 1932/33.

1934

In its Year Eleven — the final one — Wampas went out not with a bang, but with a whimper. Only Jacqueline Wells (later Julie Bishop) had anything approaching a stellar career. The rest are barely blips on the radar screens of even the most rabid film buffs. At the time of their selection none of the actresses were under contract to a studio. The official theory was that actresses already connected to a studio did not need the Wampas boost. As a publicity gimmick, most of them were cast en masse in two films, and a record was established when all 13 were given short-term featured player contracts for a single Mascot production.

The alternates that year were Jean Chapburn, Dorothy Granger, Neoma Judge, Lenore Keefe, Mary Kornman, and Irene Ware. Kornman was the best known of the also-rans, having been a veteran of the "Our Gang" comedies.

The Wampas Babies of 1934 were: Judith Arlen, Betty Bryson, Jean Carmen, Helen Cohan, Dorothy Drake, Jean Gale, Hazel Hayes, Ann Hovey, Lucille Lund, Lu Ann Meredith, Gigi Parrish, Jacqueline Wells (aka Julie Bishop) and Katherine Williams.

And so it ended.

The Wampas Baby Stars

Andre, Lona

(La Una Anderson); Nashville, Tennessee, 1915–1992; 5'3"; red or brown hair, blue eyes. *Wampas Baby Star:* 1932.

It was not unusual for Wampas Babies to have won beauty contests, but the one in which Lona Andre was a winner *was* a bit different. It was the "Panther Woman" contest that was held in several U. S. cities; she was the winner of her local contest. (The ultimate victor, Kathleen Burke, was cast as the Panther Woman in the horror classic *Island of Lost Souls*.) Andre did gain a Paramount contract in 1933 worth $75 a week initially (to increase to $750) and some leads in moderately-produced features and two-reelers with Buster Keaton and Leon Errol.

Though she was at one time rumored to be engaged to actor James Dunn, Andre's first husband was actor Edward Norris. Their marriage was a short one even by Hollywood standards; it was annulled after three or four days. She next wed Richard Patton and then James Boehling (sometimes reported as Bolling). She had a daughter.

Filmography

Shorts

1933–1940?

Hollywood on Parade, no. 9
One Run Elmer
The Timid Young Man
Three on a Limb
Ring Madness
Scrappily Married
Gobs of Trouble

Features

1933

The Mysterious Rider
The Woman Accused
College Humor
International House
Take a Chance

1934

Woman Unafraid
Let's Be Ritzy
Come On Marines!
Murder at the Vanities
Two Heads on a Pillow
Lost in the Stratosphere
The Merry Widow
By Your Leave

1935

School for Girls
Under the Pampas Moon

Border Brigands
Happiness C.O.D.
Skybound
*Broadway Melody of 1936

1936

Lucky Terror
Our Relations
Custer's Last Stand (serial)

1937

High Hat
The Plainsman
Death in the Air
The Great Hospital Mystery
Crusade Against Rackets

Trailin' Trouble
**Race Suicide
**Slaves in Bondage

1938

**The Sunset Strip Case (aka The Sunset Murder Case)

1940

Ghost Valley Raiders

1941

You're the One

1942

Pardon My Sarong

1943

Taxi, Mister
**Confessions of a Vice Baron

1947

The Case of the Baby Sitter

*Andre's participation in this film is uncertain.
**The release dates of these films are uncertain.

Arlen, Betty

Providence, Kentucky, 1904–1966; brown hair. *Wampas Baby Star:* 1925.

Ex-dancer Betty Arlen had the dubious distinction of having one of the least distinguished film careers of all the Wampas Baby Stars. She is the only one who apparently received no screen credit in features, but she may have done some uncredited bits. She is also probably the only one who did not show up for the gala installation ceremony.

It is possible that Arlen gave up her chance at stardom for something she considered more important — marriage. Her husbands were George Hartung and Louis Goldberg (or Golden), a theater manager. She may have returned to Hollywood in the early 1930s in an attempt to restart her career but by then she was "old news."

NOTE: *She is presumably not the Bette Arlen who made a couple of films in the 1940s.*

Arlen, Judith

(Laurette Rutherford); Hollywood, California, 1914–1968; brown hair. *Wampas Baby Star:* 1934.

Judith Arlen was the daughter of an opera singer known professionally as Gilbertini, and a silent film actress who had worked at the old Lubin studio. Little Laurette was on the stage in stock productions by the age of four. Later, she appeared in vaudeville, danced in the Fanchon and Marco troupe, and was heard on the radio.

Her stage name was similar to, and sometimes seems to be confused with, that of Judith *Allen,* who made numerous screen appearances from 1933 to the early '40s.

The sister of the more successful actress Ann Rutherford, whom she somewhat resembled, Arlen had a minimal film career. Signed to a short-term contract with Mascot at $125 a week, she appeared in the two films in which most of the 1934 Babies appeared. Except for some possible bit parts, that was the extent of her motion picture roles. In one of her films, *Young and Beautiful*, the other Judith — Allen — had the lead.

Judith Arlen was married to a film executive.

Filmography

1930
*Madam Satan

1934
Kiss and Make-Up
Young and Beautiful

*Arlen's participation in this film is uncertain.

Arthur, Jean

(Gladys Greene); New York, New York, 1898/1905–1991; 5'3"; brown hair (later blonde), blue eyes. *Wampas Baby Star:* 1929.

One of the few Wampas Baby Stars who went on to really major stardom, Jean Arthur reigned supreme as Columbia's top leading lady for almost ten years. She began humbly enough as a model and remained an undistinguished ingenue for several years in westerns and comedies, as well as generally unimportant "B" features and even a serial. Her early co-stars included comics Slim Summerville and Monty Banks and oater stars like Tom Tyler, Buffalo Bill, Jr., Buddy Roosevelt and Wally Wales.

After being signed by Paramount in 1928, her films did not improve much but the leading men were of the caliber of Emil Jannings, Richard Dix and William Powell. It was at that studio that she made her first fully sound picture in 1929, *The Canary Murder Case*. It should have been significant because of her unique voice but it went unremarked, and she continued to be cast as the bland (but not blonde) ingenue.

It became apparent to Jean Arthur that there would be no real future in the cinema unless she really learned how to act. Broadway was the place this was accomplished. In 1932 she left for New York and remained there intermittently for two-and-a-half years, making a few films as well. After appearing in plays with such veteran troupers as Dorothy Gish and Claude Rains she emerged a better actress and, to complete the image change, a blonde as well.

After signing with Columbia, Arthur finally became a respected leading lady with 1935's *The Whole Town's Talking*, co-starring Edward G. Robinson. Frank Capra's *Mr. Deeds Goes to Town*, with Gary Cooper, confirmed her stardom. She made some genuine classics, both serious dramas and all-out comedies, with many of the top leading men in pictures, among them Cary Grant, James Stewart, John Wayne and Charles Boyer.

In the mid–1940s Jean Arthur began suffering psychological problems related to performing, including serious stage fright, but returned to live theater, seemingly an odd choice for someone in her condition. She dropped out of *Born Yesterday* before it reached New York (enabling Judy Holliday to become a star) but did make a triumphant comeback in *Peter Pan*. None of her subsequent plays came to Broadway.

Arthur was a favorite of directors

and was highly praised by her leading men, but she could be very aloof off the set and rarely gave interviews. Her remarkable voice was both husky and high-pitched and was described by Frank Capra as "[breaking] into a thousand bells." The screen persona that brought her fame was that of a woman who could be both cynical and sweet, aggressive or even brassy, yet yielding to a lover. It was a potent combination that kept her (and still does) among the top pantheon of actresses.

Jean Arthur had script and director approval and she rejected all films after 1944 except *A Foreign Affair* and *Shane*. Both were successful. She turned to television in 1965 where she did not need to face a live audience and made her debut in an episode of *Gunsmoke*. *The Jean Arthur Show* followed the next year but did not last an entire season. During the 1970s she taught drama at Vassar College and then went into retirement.

Arthur was married twice, the first time only for a single *day*. She had the marriage annulled, claiming that her studio contract forbade her to marry. Her second one was to singer Frank Ross who later became a producer. As hard as she tried to remain out of the public eye (never giving autographs, etc.), she did make the news in 1973 when she was residing in North Carolina. She was arrested for trespassing and handcuffed when she went into a neighbor's yard to feed a chained German Shepherd.

Filmography

Shorts

1923–1927

Somebody Lied
Spring Fever
Case Dismissed
The Powerful Eye
The Mad Racer
Eight Cylinder Bull
Hello, Lafayette
Bigger and Better Blondes

Features

1923

Cameo Kirby

1924

*The Wine of Youth
The Temple of Venus
Fast and Fearless
Biff Bang Buddy
Bringin' Home the Bacon
Thundering Romance
Travelin' Fast

1925

*Galloping On
Drug Store Cowboy
Seven Chances
Tearin' Loose
The Fighting Smile
A Man of Nerve
Hurricane Horseman
Thundering Through

1926

Under Fire
Double Daring
*The Roaring Rider
*Riding Rivals
Lightning Bill
Born to Battle
The Fighting Cheat
The Cowboy Cop
Twisted Triggers
The College Boob
The Block Signal

1927

Husband Hunters
The Broken Gate
Horse Shoes
The Poor Nut
Flying Luck
The Masked Menace (serial)

1928

Wallflowers
Warming Up
Brotherly Love
Sins of the Fathers

1929

The Canary Murder Case
Stairs of Sand

The Mysterious Dr. Fu
   Manchu
The Greene Murder
   Case
The Saturday Night Kid
Half-Way to Heaven

1930

Street of Chance
Young Eagles
Paramount on Parade
The Return of Dr. Fu
   Manchu
Danger Lights
The Silver Horde

1931

The Gang Buster
The Virtuous Husband
The Lawyer's Secret
Ex-Bad Boy

1933

Get That Venus
The Past of Mary
   Holmes

1934

Whirlpool
The Defense Rests

The Most Precious
   Thing in Life

1935

The Whole Town's
   Talking
Public Hero No. 1
Party Wire
Diamond Jim
The Public Menace
If You Could Only Cook

1936

Mr. Deeds Goes to
   Town
The Ex–Mrs. Bradford
Adventure in
   Manhattan
More Than a Secretary

1937

The Plainsman
History Is Made at
   Night
Easy Living

1938

You Can't Take It with
   You

1939

Only Angels Have
   Wings
Mr. Smith Goes to
   Washington

1940

Too Many Husbands
Arizona

1941

The Devil and Miss
   Jones

1942

The Talk of the Town

1943

The More the Merrier
A Lady Takes a Chance

1944

The Impatient Years

1948

A Foreign Affair

1953

Shane

*Arthur's participation in these films is uncertain.

Astor, Mary

(Lucille Langhanke); Quincy, Illinois, 1906–1987; 5'6"; auburn hair, brown eyes (?). *Wampas Baby Star:* 1926.

Mary Astor was unfortunate enough to have had not only one stage parent but two. The actress who would become famous for such varied roles as those in *Dodsworth*, *The Maltese Falcon* and *Meet Me in St. Louis* was pushed into her career at a very young age. D. W. Griffith apparently considered using her but did not want to cope with her grasping father whom he termed a "walking cash register." This characterization was to be proven correct when her parents actually sued her in 1934 for non-support.

After modeling, movie bits, two-reelers for the Tri-Art studio, and a few features in the early 1920s, the serenely beautiful young Astor (called the "Cameo

Girl") was discovered by John Barrymore. He not only added her to his long list of amours but co-starred her in his *Beau Brummell* in 1924. They also appeared together in *Don Juan*, the first feature with accompanying Vitaphone sound. (He subsequently threw her over for fellow 1926 Wampas Baby Star Dolores Costello, who became his wife.)

Despite numerous roles it would be a while before Mary Astor showed the acting talent that would distinguish her best work. In the silent days she served as mere window dressing for various leading men including Lloyd Hughes, with whom she starred in several vehicles. There was an effort to make them a romantic teaming but the charisma was lacking. She later said of her silent picture days that she was on a "treadmill of trash" making "drivel."

Possessed of one of the best female voices in the cinema, Astor nonetheless did not make a talkie until 1930 (*Ladies Love Brutes*). This was supposedly because the studio moguls thought her voice was too low and masculine. After her appearance in a Los Angeles stage play they changed their minds and she remained busy throughout the 1930s and '40s. Among her major films, although rarely as the leading lady, were *Dodsworth*, *Red Dust*, *The Prisoner of Zenda*, *Midnight* and *The Palm Beach Story*. In the latter two films, both sophisticated comedies, she proved she could play in that genre with great skill. Her leading parts sometimes came in less rewarding films.

Mary Astor's career almost did not survive the mid–'30s. Married for a second time, to physician Franklyn Thorpe, and the mother of a little girl, she indiscreetly kept a diary that recounted in some detail her extra-marital affairs. The marriage was already in trouble when Thorpe discovered part of the diary and sued for divorce and child custody. The press had a field day, reprinting parts of her confessional and apparently exaggerating others. Given the public mores of the day, her career should have been ended by the scandal, but it was not. (The diary was burned by court order in 1951.)

Astor added to her laurels by winning the Best Supporting Actress Oscar for 1941's *The Great Lie* in which she played the "bad" woman opposite Bette Davis. That same year she appeared as another villainess, Brigid O'Shaughnessy, in the John Huston classic *The Maltese Falcon*. It seemed as if her long years in front of the camera were being rewarded when she signed with MGM in the early '40s, but in retrospect it was a misstep. Instead of getting star billing she was given a succession of mother roles beginning at the ripe age of 36 or so. There were occasional meatier roles such as the secondary one as a prostitute in *Act of Violence*.

Mary Astor never really attained the pinnacle to which her talents entitled her, perhaps because stardom was not something she chose to pursue. Her private life remained troubled, with alcohol problems and suicide attempts. Her first marriage to Kenneth Hawks, brother of director Howard Hawks, had ended when her young husband was killed in an airplane crash. After the disastrous marriage to Thorpe she wed twice more, to Manuel del Campo, with whom she had a son, and to Thomas Wheelock, a stockbroker.

Astor did quite a bit of stage work and made her Broadway debut in 1945. Her mellifluous voice also was much heard on the radio and later she was seen on television. She had other talents besides acting, authoring two frank autobiographies, *My Story* and *A Life on Film*, and several novels in the 1960s: *The Incredible Charlie Carewe*, *The Image of Kate*, *The O'Conners*, *Goodbye Darling, Be Happy* and *A Place Called Saturday*. To the end she remained an almost painfully open person who could talk about herself with no apparent star's ego. One could almost assume that Hollywood's honors—including her naming as a Baby Star—meant comparatively little to her.

Filmography

Shorts

1921–1930s

Brother of the Bear
My Lady o' the Pines
The Beggar Maid
Bashful Suitor
The Young Painter
Hope
The Scarecrow
The Angelus
The Hollywood Gad-About
*Prisoner of Swing

Features

1922

John Smith
The Man Who Played God
The Rapids (Canada)

1923

Second Fiddle
Success
Hollywood (cameo)
The Bright Shawl
The Marriage Maker
Puritan Passions
Woman-Proof

1924

Beau Brummell
The Fighting Coward
The Fighting American
Unguarded Women
The Price of a Party
Inez from Hollywood

1925

Enticement
Oh, Doctor!
Playing with Souls
Don Q, Son of Zorro
The Pace That Thrills
Scarlet Saint

1926

High Steppers
Wise Guy
Don Juan
Forever After

1927

The Sea Tiger
The Rough Riders
The Sunset Derby
Rose of the Golden West
No Place to Go
Two Arabian Nights

1928

Sailors' Wives
Dressed to Kill
Three-Ring Marriage
Heart to Heart
Dry Martini
Romance of the Underworld

1929

New Year's Eve
The Woman from Hell

1930

Ladies Love Brutes
The Runaway Bride
Holiday
The Lash

1931

The Royal Bed
Other Men's Women (aka Steel Highway)
Behind Office Doors
The Sin Ship
White Shoulders
Smart Woman

1932

Men of Chance
The Lost Squadron
Those We Love
A Successful Calamity
Red Dust

1933

The Little Giant
Jennie Gerhardt
The World Changes

The Kennel Murder Case
Convention City

1934
Easy to Love
Upperworld
Return of the Terror
The Man with Two Faces
The Case of the Howling Dog
I Am a Thief

1935
Straight from the Heart
Red Hot Tires
Dinky
Page Miss Glory
Man of Iron

1936
The Murder of Dr. Harrigan
And So They Were Married
Trapped by Television
Dodsworth
Lady from Nowhere

1937
The Prisoner of Zenda
The Hurricane

1938
No Time to Marry
Paradise for Three
There's Always a Woman
Woman Against Woman
Listen, Darling

1939
Midnight

1940
Turnabout
Brigham Young—Frontiersman

1941
The Great Lie
The Maltese Falcon

1942
Across the Pacific
In This Our Life (cameo)
The Palm Beach Story

1943
Young Ideas
Thousands Cheer

1944
Meet Me in St. Louis
Blonde Fever

1946
Claudia and David

1947
Desert Fury
Cynthia
Fiesta
Cass Timberlane

1948
Act of Violence

1949
Little Women
Any Number Can Play

1956
The Power and the Prize
A Kiss Before Dying

1957
The Devil's Hairpin

1958
This Happy Feeling

1959
Stranger in My Arms

1961
Return to Peyton Place

1964
Youngblood Hawke
Hush, Hush, Sweet Charlotte.

*Astor's appearance in this film is uncertain.

Avery, Patricia

Boston, Massachusetts, 1902–1973; brown hair. *Wampas Baby Star:* 1927.

Formerly a secretary at the MGM studio, Patricia Avery started out on a high note the year of her naming as a Baby Star. She appeared in *Annie Laurie*, an MGM film starring Lillian Gish, and then co-starred with fading legend Henry B. Walthall. After that her career seemed to just fizzle out, or perhaps she traded it for marriage to art director Merrill Pye. They were later divorced.

FILMOGRAPHY

1927
Annie Laurie
A Light in the Window
Night Life

1928
Alex the Great

Avon, Violet

(Violet La Plante or La Plant); St. Louis, Missouri, 1908–1984; blonde hair, blue eyes. *Wampas Baby Star:* 1925.

The younger sister of 1923 Wampas Baby Laura La Plante, Violet Avon went into extra work right from high school. While Laura went on to become the major Universal actress of the decade, Violet made some shorts and a few "B" features under her real name. She had changed it for the Wampas selection to avoid seeming to cash in on her sister's fame.

Avon co-starred with oater star Buddy Roosevelt in a handful of westerns and was otherwise a minor supporting player. In her final feature she was merely billed as "The Stenographer" and apparently made no appearances in talkies. After her screen career ended she worked as a receptionist.

FILMOGRAPHY

Shorts
The Haunted Homestead

Features

1924
Battling Buddy
The Clean Heart

Walloping Wallace
His Majesty the Outlaw

1925
The Hurricane Kid

1926
The Ramblin' Galoot

1928
My Home Town
How to Handle Women

Aye, Marion

(Sometimes Maryon); Chicago, Illinois, 1903–1951; 5'3"; brown hair, brown eyes. *Wampas Baby Star:* 1922.

Among the generally distinguished first class of Wampas Babies, vaudevillian Marion Aye perhaps made the least onscreen splash of any of her 1922 contemporaries. (She very probably came to the most unfortunate end as well.) Her naming to this group could have come about because she was married to press agent Harry Wilson, a member of Wampas.

Aye's first films had been made for Cactus Pictures a year prior to her selection, some 18 two-reel westerns with obscure oater hero Bob Reeves. She also did two-reel comedies and features, in which she sometimes had very small roles. In the prestige film *The Eternal Three*, for instance, she played a maid. She also was a stage performer in California in plays such as *White Collars* and *Kosher Kitty Kelly*. One claim to distinction was that she was said to have been the first to have a "purity" clause in her contract; i.e., that she was to behave in ways not detrimental to the industry.

In 1935 Marion Aye made her first suicide attempt, apparently over her inability to obtain acting roles. At the time she was quoted as saying that she was tired of living in the past. Although divorced from Wilson, he had guided her career and his death about that time was

Marion Aye

seen as a contributing cause of her depression. She succeeded in her fatal purpose in 1951 when she and current husband Ross For(r)ester were living in a motel. Unfortunately, the poison she took allowed her to linger for ten terrible days.

FILMOGRAPHY

Shorts

1921

The Western Whirlwind
One Glove Wilson
The Brand Blotters
His Brother's Blood
West Meets East
Fingers of Fate
Double Reward
Wanted
The Claim Jumper
Phantom of the Hills
The Western Way
No Man's Gold
The Streak of Yellow
A Weak-End Party

Features

1921

Montana Bill
The Vengeance Trail

1923

The Meanest Man in the World
The Eternal Three

1924

The Last Man on Earth
The Roughneck

1926

Irene

Basquette, Lina

(Lena Baskett or Baskette); San Mateo California, 1907–1994; 5'3½"; black hair, brown eyes. *Wampas Baby Star:* 1928.

At the time sultry Lina Basquette was dubbed a Baby Star she had already been in films sporadically for 12 years, beginning as a child dancer in a series of Universal "featurettes." Her public debut supposedly had come a year earlier as a dancer at the San Francisco World's Fair. It is necessary to qualify "facts" about her life because by her own account she had enough fateful encounters, triumphs and tragedies to have lived *three* people's lifetimes. Journalist Adela Rogers St. Johns dubbed her "The Screen Tragedy Girl"—and she was not referring to the plots of films.

Basquette was dancing in a Broadway revue called *Nifties of 1923* when impresario Florenz Ziegfeld signed her for his Follies. She became a premiere danseuse for the editions of 1923 to '25 and also gained the new spelling of her name. It was at this time, she claimed, that the world renowned ballerina Anna Pavlova decided to groom her as her successor.

Lina Basquette's dancing career came to an end when she wed the much older Sam, the Warner Brother who was most instrumental in bringing sound to the screen. The mother of a baby daughter, she was suddenly widowed in 1927 and as late as 1947 was still battling the Warner family in court to claim a share of her husband's fortune. She did not get it.

Basquette contended she had been blacklisted by the family but resumed on-camera appearances, soon co-starring with Richard Barthelmess in two films. One of them was her best silent film, *The Noose*. In the year of her Wampas selection she made her sound debut in the part-talkie *Show Folks*. Of her performance a review stated that she was surprisingly good and that her voice registered well. Later C. B. DeMille tapped her for the lead in his production of *The Godless Girl*. A typical perfervid melange of pseudo-religion and sex, it was released with a tacked-on talking sequence but was a failure anyway.

In the first years of the '30s Basquette continued to have leading roles in her motion pictures but invariably they were westerns or low-grade melodramas for such indies as Supreme, Tiffany, Sono-Art, Chesterfield, Majestic and Monogram. The decade was far more noteworthy for her stormy love life. Well-publicized affairs were interwoven with her numerous marriages. Jack Dempsey, whom she did not land in matrimony, seemed to be the great love of that time and she apparently tried suicide twice to win him.

Lina Basquette formed her own orchestra, The Hollywood Aristocrats, but the cinema was not quite through with her. She returned in 1936 to play "exotic" characters in several movies, generally in small roles. About this time she claimed to have caught the eye of no less than Adolf Hitler (who was reportedly much taken by her) and later it was a Japanese aristocrat. She also averred that she spied for the OSS during World War II.

Basquette was in the news again when she was raped in 1943 by a mentally disturbed soldier whom she had picked up hitchhiking. She eventually retreated into a more sedate life and apparently found fulfillment in raising champion dogs, particularly Great Danes.

She even wrote two books about dog training. In the 1950s she was a contestant on the quiz show *The $64,000 Question* and made it to the $16,000 plateau as an animal expert before being disqualified. According to her, she was one of the tainted contestants and had been coached beforehand.

About 1980 Basquette announced a proposed autobiography to be tellingly entitled *Virtue Is a Dirty Word*. It never appeared but *Lina, DeMille's Godless Girl* did, some ten years later. At the age of 84, almost 50 years after her previous picture, she was cast in the little-seen low-budget feature *Paradise Park*. In it she played an old woman who has a vision that God is coming to grant wishes to the inhabitants of a shabby trailer park.

In a 1989 *New Yorker* magazine story about Lina Basquette her half-sister, the dancer Marge Champion, said of her: "Lena has total recall. Of course it's *her* recall." Even if she did partly invent her life, what remained was *quite* a life and she lived it on her own terms. In a photo taken of the 1928 Wampas Baby Stars at a tea given by Hollywood doyenne Mary Pickford, she is the only one to be seen defying convention by sitting coatless and bareheaded among the other starlets with their modish hats and fur coats.

Basquette was married eight times to seven different men. Her second husband was cameraman Peverell Marley; she was widowed by the third, actor Ray Hallam. She next wed, divorced and re-wed fight trainer Teddy Hayes. Following him were actor Henry Mollison, Warren Gilmore and the artist Frank Mancuso. Besides her daughter she had a son.

FILMOGRAPHY

Shorts

1917 (as Lena Baskette)

The Juvenile Dancer Supreme
The Dance of Love
Shoes
The Black Mantilla
A Dream of Egypt
A Romany Rose
Little Mariana's Triumph
Amelita's Friend

1927 (as Lina Basquette)

Visions of Spain
*Gus Arnheim Orchestra

Features

1917 (as Lena Baskette)

The Gates of Doom
Polly Put the Kettle On

1919

The Weaker Vessel

1922

Penrod

1927 (as Lina Basquette)

Ranger of the North
Serenade

1928

The Noose
Wheel of Chance
Celebrity
Show Folks

1929

The Godless Girl
The Younger Generation
Come Across

1930

The Dude Wrangler

1931

Goldie
The Hard Hombre
Arizona Terror
Pleasure
Mounted Fury

1932

Arm of the Law
Midnight Lady

Hello Trouble
Phantom Express

1936
The Final Hour

1937
Souls at Sea
Ebb Tide

1938
The Buccaneer
Rose of the Rio Grande
Four Men and a Prayer

1942
A Night for Crime

1991
Paradise Park

*Basquette may not appear in the final version. Florenz Ziegfeld objected to inclusion of a number that may have involved her dance.

Blane, Sally

(Elizabeth Jane Jung, later Young); Salida, Colorado, 1910–1997; 5'4½"; brown hair, blue-green eyes. *Wampas Baby Star:* 1929.

Like her more famous younger sister Loretta Young, and their older sister Polly Ann, Sally Blane began to appear in films as a child extra. She later studied dancing and was supposedly spotted for pictures dancing professionally at a Hollywood night spot. About 1926 or so, her career began in earnest with the two-reel "Collegians" series; she graduated to features the following year. Like many a rising ingenue she did her share of "B" westerns with such heroes as Tom Mix and Hoot Gibson.

Sally and Loretta (born Gretchen) were look-alikes — their luminous large eyes being a mutually striking feature. Both were named Wampas Baby Stars in 1929, the only time sisters were so designated in the same year. They also were seen that year briefly dancing and singing together in the "Meet My Sister" number in Warner Bros.' *The Show of Shows*.

A Paramount contractee, in one of Blane's earliest talkies she was the leading lady of crooner and heart-throb Rudy Vallee in his first film *The Vagabond Lover*. The early sound period proved to be the highwater mark of her career. Although she made movies throughout the decade of the '30s (sometimes as many as a dozen in one year), they were often quickie melodramas for small companies like Artclass and Chesterfield. Sometimes she was starred, and even occasionally top-billed, but other roles were clearly in support. Reviews of her films and acting ability were often lukewarm.

Like many another fading American actress of the mid–1930s, Blane made

Sally Blane

a couple of pictures in England. Toward the end of her time in the limelight she and all her sisters, including half-sister Georgianna, appeared together as a novelty in *The Story of Alexander Graham Bell*. No doubt as a lark, she returned for a final screen role in a 1955 spy melodrama.

Blane was married to actor and director Norman Foster; a son and daughter completed their family.

Filmography

Shorts

1926–1932?

The Collegians series
The Leather Pushers (series)
The Circus Show-Up

Features

1917

Sirens of the Sea

1927

Casey at the Bat
*Rolled Stockings
Shootin' Irons

1928

Wife Savers
Dead Man's Curve
Her Summer Hero
A Horseman of the Plains
Fools for Luck
The Vanishing Pioneer
King Cowboy

1929

Outlawed
Wolves of the City
Eyes of the Underworld
The Very Idea
Half Marriage
Tanned Legs
The Vagabond Lover
The Show of Shows

1930

The Little Accident

1931

Once a Sinner
Ten Cents a Dance
Women Men Marry
Annabelle's Affairs
Star Witness
Shanghaied Love
A Dangerous Affair
The Spirit of Notre Dame
X Marks the Spot
Good Sport
Law of the Sea

1932

The Local Bad Man
The Reckoning
Escapade
Cross Examination
*Disorderly Conduct
Probation
Forbidden Company
The Phantom Express
Heritage of the Desert
The Pride of the Legion
I Am a Fugitive from a Chain Gang
Wild Horse Mesa

1933

Hello, Everybody!
Trick for Trick
Night of Terror

Advice to the Lovelorn
Mayfair Girl (U.K.)

1934

Stolen Sweets
No More Women
Half a Sinner
City Park
City Limits
She Had to Choose
Crime on the Hill (U.K.)
The Silver Streak
Against the Law

1935

**Crashin' Thru Danger (aka Crashing Through Danger, Crashing Thru Danger)
This Is the Life

1937

The Great Hospital Mystery
Angel's Holiday
One Mile from Heaven

1938

Numbered Women

1939

The Story of Alexander Graham Bell
Way Down South

Charlie Chan at Treasure Island
Fighting Mad

1955
A Bullet for Joey

*Blane's participation in these films is uncertain.
**This film may not have been released until 1938.

Blondell, Joan

(Rose Joan Blondell); New York, New York, 1906/09–1979; 5'2½"; green eyes, brown hair (later blonde). *Wampas Baby Star:* 1931.

Wampas showed good judgment in recognizing the potential of Joan Blondell so early, and they later awarded her with a special achievement trophy for the greatest advancement in her career. (Clara Bow and Dolores Del Rio were the only other Wampas Babies given this award.)

The daughter of roving vaudevillians, Blondell had been exposed to show business from infancy when she made her "official" debut onstage in Australia at the age of three. She left the family act at age 17 or so and took the well-worn path to stock and thence to Broadway. There she co-starred with another up-and-comer, Jimmy Cagney, in two plays. It was the latter of these, *Penny Arcade*, that sent them both to Hollywood in 1930. They ultimately appeared together seven times.

Joan Blondell and Warner Bros. were a good fit. Her persona was just right for that studio's product, although she had to resist its attempt to change her name to Inez Holmes. She worked in film after film, at first in support, almost without respite for the first half of the 1930s. Usually playing a brassy type with heart of gold or the best friend of the heroine, she was, on occasion, a "bad" girl. She rarely played against type; the audience would no doubt have found it difficult to accept her as a society woman. The script was the same in all her films, she said, "I just needed to change clothes."

Although not possessed with a memorable singing voice, Joan Blondell was a fixture in Busby Berkeley musicals and participated in one of the iconographic images of Depression cinema, the number "Remember My Forgotten Man" in *Gold Diggers of 1933*. Although she was one of the top ten box-office attractions through part of the 1930s, her film output diminished considerably in the following decade. It was then she played what she considered her best performance, as Aunt Cissy in 1945's *A Tree Grows in Brooklyn*.

Blondell's career as a character actress truly began with that film and she followed it with a praised role in *Nightmare Alley*. By then she had long departed from Warner Bros. and had been signed by MGM. Her sole Oscar nomination was for Supporting Actress in 1951's *The Blue Veil*; she received a Golden Globe nomination for John Cassavetes's *Opening Night*, one of her final pictures.

With time, Joan Blondell's appealingly cute features coarsened and her curvaceous figure became noticeably plump. She spent the last 20 years or so of her career playing blowsy, good-hearted roles in movies and television, including the series *Here Come the Brides* (on which she played a madam and for which she was Emmy-nominated), and *Banyon*. She also did many movies of the week between 1965 and '71. Previously, she had been much heard on the radio as well as continuing to appear sporadically in the theater, including a return to Broadway. In 1972 she penned an autobiographical novel called *Center Door Fancy*.

Blondell was first married to cameraman George Barnes, and then to crooner-turned-serious-actor Dick Powell. Her last spouse was the colorful impresario Mike Todd. Two children were born of her marriages.

FILMOGRAPHY

Shorts

1930

Broadway's Like That
The Devil's Parade

1937

A Day at Santa Anita

Features

1930

The Office Wife
Sinner's Holiday

1931

Other Men's Women (aka Steel Highway)
Illicit
Millie
My Past
Public Enemy
God's Gift to Women
Big Business Girl
Night Nurse
The Reckless Hour
Blonde Crazy

1932

Union Depot
The Greeks Had a Word for Them
The Crowd Roars
The Famous Ferguson Case
Make Me a Star
Miss Pinkerton
Big City Blues
Three on a Match
Central Park

1933

Lawyer Man
Broadway Bad
Blondie Johnson
Gold Diggers of 1933
Goodbye Again
Havana Widows
Footlight Parade
Convention City

1934

I've Got Your Number
Smarty
He Was Her Man
Dames
Kansas City Princess

1935

Traveling Saleslady
Broadway Gondolier
We're in the Money
Miss Pacific Fleet

1936

Colleen
Bullets or Ballots
Sons o' Guns
Stage Struck
Three Men on a Horse
Gold Diggers of 1937
Talent Scout (cameo)

1937

The King and the Chorus Girl
Back in Circulation
The Perfect Specimen
Stand-In

1938

There's Always a Woman

1939

Off the Record
East Side of Heaven
The Kid from Kokomo
Good Girls Go to Paris
The Amazing Mr. Williams

1940

I Want a Divorce
Two Girls on Broadway

1941

Topper Returns
Model Wife
Lady for a Night

1942

Three Girls About Town

1943

Cry Havoc

1945

A Tree Grows in Brooklyn

Don Juan Quilligan
Adventure

1947

Christmas Eve
The Corpse Came C.O.D.
Nightmare Alley

1950

For Heaven's Sake

1951

The Blue Veil

1956

The Opposite Sex

1957

Lizzie
This Could Be the Night
Desk Set
Will Success Spoil Rock Hunter?

1960

Angel Baby

1963

Advance to the Rear

1965

The Cincinnati Kid

1966

Ride Beyond Vengeance

1967

Waterhole No. 3

1968

Stay Away, Joe
Kona Coast

1969

Big Daddy (aka Paradise Road)

1970

The Phynx

1971

Support Your Local Gunfighter

1975

Won Ton Ton, the Dog Who Saved Hollywood

1977

Opening Night

1978

Grease
The Glove

1979

The Champ

1980

The Woman Inside

Boardman, Eleanor

Philadelphia, Pennsylvania, 1898/99–1991; 5'6"–5'7"; brown hair, gray-green eyes. *Wampas Baby Star:* 1923.

After some print modeling (she was known as "The Kodak Girl") and a bit of musical comedy and vaudeville, aristocratically beautiful Eleanor Boardman was signed for films in 1922 as the second lead in *The Stranger's Banquet*. Her potential was quickly spotted and the Wampas honor came a scarce year later. Most of her output at Metro and MGM was to be in romantic melodrama, and she was rarely anything but a leading lady, although usually mere window dressing. Only in the 1928 classic *The Crowd* did she show what she might be capable of, and that was a performance against type.

In a ceremony attended by Hollywood's highest society, Boardman married director King Vidor in 1926. He had directed her in some films. Interviewed for the television series *Hollywood* (and still looking coolly attractive at the age of 81 or so), she said that it might have been a double wedding if John Gilbert had succeeded in marrying Greta Garbo. However, the legendarily reclusive Swedish actress failed to show up.

Although their marriage resulted in two daughters, the Vidors had a stormy married life after the first few years and their troubles were added to by a charge of income tax evasion in 1929. Like many celebrities they blamed their accountant, but were still assessed a fine.

Eleanor Boardman divorced Vidor in 1933 but was still litigating over child custody as late as 1941. In 1929 she had made the first of her handful of talkies. Her low-pitched voice perfectly matched her patrician persona but sound films did not prove to be her medium. (Her best talkie is considered to be *The Great Meadow*, in which she once again played against her image.) Married to French director Harry d'Abbadie D'Arrast, she retired with him to Europe for many years. He directed her final film in Spain; it was unreleased in the United States.

Returning to Europe after World War II, Boardman became, for a brief time, a fashion commentator for the Paris bureau of *Harper's Bazaar*. In an adventure more spectacular than any of her films, when she and D'Arrast had left Europe at the start of the war their boat was intercepted in mid–Atlantic by the Germans and the passengers given a short time to evacuate.

According to reviews, Eleanor Boardman was a competent actress as well as a beautiful one. But she said that she preferred her bland heroine roles to the more memorable pictures in which she had been somewhat deglamorized. There is no question that she was a stunner in those period costumes!

FILMOGRAPHY

1922
The Stranger's Banquet

1923
Gimme
Souls for Sale
Vanity Fair
Three Wise Fools
The Day of Faith

1924
True as Steel
Wine of Youth
The Turmoil
Sinners in Silk
So This Is Marriage
The Silent Accuser
Wife of the Centaur

1925
The Way of a Girl
Proud Flesh
Exchange of Wives
The Only Thing
The Circle

1926
Memory Lane
The Auction Block
Bardelys the Magnificent
Tell It to the Marines

1928
The Crowd
Diamond Handcuffs

1929
She Goes to War

1930
Mamba
Redemption

1931
The Great Meadow
The Flood
Women Love Once
The Squaw Man

1933
*The Big Chance

1934
The Three-Cornered Hat (aka It Happened in Spain)

Boardman's participation in this film is uncertain.

Bond, Lillian

(sometimes Lilian); London, England, 1907/10–1991; 5'4½"; red hair (sometimes blonde), hazel eyes. *Wampas Baby Star:* 1932.

A dancer in England, as well as a player in pantomime and revue from the age of 14 and a beauty contest winner, Lillian Bond was signed for Earl Carroll's *Vanities* on Broadway. She also appeared in other New York and Los Angeles stage productions, including *Rio Rita*. Signed by MGM, for whom she made musical shorts, she had possibly been onscreen as early as 1927. Her feature career began with leading roles in "B" westerns and small supporting parts in other pictures. Among her early co-stars were the western actors Art Mix and Tom Tyler.

In the year of her Wampas selection, Lillian Bond made what is probably her best-known film today, the Gothic-esque thriller *The Old Dark House*. (Her small role as Lily Langtry in the often televised *The Westerner* (1940) may also be remembered.) Although she was cast in numerous films of the early 1930s, she was purported to be temperamental on the set and was probably fired by Warner Bros. She apparently departed MGM, Fox and Universal on less than friendly terms as well.

Although eventually shedding most of her British accent, Bond still retained the cool reserve that enabled her to play the "other woman" believably. In 1933 she reached co-starring status in *When Strangers Marry*, and then received top billing in *Her Splendid Folly*, but it was for the independent studio Progressive Pictures. The mid-'30s proved to be her high point; she was rarely to appear in more than a couple of pictures in any year thereafter. Her roles generally remained small and after 1940 she was on the screen only sporadically. She also appeared on television.

Perhaps temperamental in her private life as well, Lillian Bond was wed at least four times. After a brief teenage marriage, she wed socialite broker Sydney Smith. Her third spouse was Harry Shulman and she was widowed by Michael Fessier.

Filmography

Shorts

1927–1930s
Lost and Found
Putting It On
*No More Children
Hollywood on Parade, no. 9

Features

1930
Sagebrush Politics

1931
*The Great Lover
Rider of the Plains
Just a Gigolo
Stepping Out
God's Country and the Man
The Squaw Man

1932
Union Depot
Manhattan Parade
High Pressure
Fireman Save My Child
Beauty and the Boss
It's Tough to Be Famous
Man About Town
The Trial of Vivienne Ware
Hot Saturday
The Old Dark House
Air Mail

1933
Hot Pepper
Pick-Up

When Strangers Marry
The Big Brain
Double Harness
Take a Chance
Her Splendid Folly

1934

Affairs of a Gentleman
Hell Bent for Love
Dirty Work (U.K.)

1935

China Seas
The Bishop Misbehaves

1938

Blond Cheat

1939

The Women
The Housekeeper's Daughter
Sued for Libel

1940

The Westerner

1941

Scotland Yard

1942

A Desperate Chance for Ellery Queen
A Tragedy at Midnight

1945

The Picture of Dorian Gray

1946

The Jolson Story
Nocturne

1948

Fighter Squadron

1949

That Forsyte Woman

1950

Shadow on the Wall

1952

The Big Trees
The Sniper

1953

The Maze

1954

Man in the Attic

1955

Pirates of Tripoli

*Bond's appearance in these films is uncertain.

Borden, Olive

(Sybil Tinkle); Timpson, Texas or Richmond, Virginia, 1906/07–1947; 5' (or possibly taller); black hair, brown eyes. *Wampas Baby Star:* 1925.

The story of the rise and fall of vivacious Olive Borden is itself like some grim movie melodrama. She progressed from extra and bit player in 1923 to (possibly) one of Mack Sennett's Bathing Beauties and thence to Hal Roach, Pathé and Educational comedies. She had become one of Fox's most popular stars by the mid–1920s; among her early co-stars was Tom Mix. Her cousin was actress Natalie Joyce, who became a Wampas Baby the same year she did.

Borden's career as a major star was a short-lived one, perhaps two years, before her life spiraled out of control. She was making more than $1,500 a week at the height of her fame and lived up to and possibly beyond her means (e.g., five fur coats in one year). It was a lifestyle that required a high and steady income. The beginning of her decline came when she refused to take a salary cut from Fox in 1927 and her contract was terminated.

Known as "The Joy Girl" after one of her films, Olive Borden had a lushly curvaceous figure and was often seen in various states of undress. Tempestuous on and off the screen, she gained a public reputation for "temperament," a term often used in those days as a reason to drop highly paid stars. This was not an uncommon occurrence given Hollywood's panic about the future of these stars at the beginning of the sound era. Although the release from Fox did not end her career, it never regained its full momentum.

Borden had her last significant role in the 1930 movie *The Social Lion;* a few other roles followed, including at least one English film. There were some shorts in the 1930s as well. She was top-billed in her last picture, the melodramatic *Chloe: Love Is Calling You,* but the film, which was produced in Florida by an obscure company, was probably little seen and less noted.

Olive Borden's domestic life was sometimes messy. A great and good friend, and the possible fiancée, of frequent co-star George O'Brien (aka "The Torso"), she was twice married. The first time was to stockbroker Theodore Spector, who, it turned out, was already married. After what was left of her fortune had gone she wed railroad electrician John Moeller. She and her second husband lived in a small apartment outside of New York City before they divorced.

During World War II Borden joined the WACS but after her release she drifted and drank to excess. She occasionally found work at the Los Angeles Skid Row mission where her mother was employed and made her last "public" appearance in a Christmas pageant there. Her early death from the excesses of too much high living was almost a sadly inevitable end.

Filmography

Shorts
1923–25?, early 1930s
Gobs of Fun
The Mild West

Features
1923
*Ponjola

1925
*The Dressmaker from Paris
The Happy Warrior
The Overland Limited

1926
The Yankee Señor
My Own Pal
Yellow Fingers
Fig Leaves
Three Bad Men
The Country Beyond

1927
The Monkey Talks
The Secret Studio
The Joy Girl
Pajamas
Come to My House

1928
Virgin Lips
The Albany Night Boat
Gang War
Sinners in Love
Stool Pigeon

1929
The Eternal Woman
Love in the Desert
Half Marriage
Dance Hall
Wedding Rings

1930
The Social Lion
Hello Sister

1932
The Divorce Racket

1933
Hotel Variety
Leave It to Me (U.K.)

1934
Chloe: Love Is Calling You

Borden's participation in these films is uncertain.

Bow, Clara

Brooklyn; New York, 1904/05–1965; 5'2"–5'3"; auburn hair (later flaming red), brown eyes. *Wampas Baby Star:* 1924.

The actress who was to become the world-famous "It" girl began modestly enough as a teenager by winning a magazine "Fame and Fortune" contest that awarded her a role in one film. The picture was *Beyond the Rainbow* in 1922, but Clara Bow's part was cut in its initial release. She was noticed in a supporting role in her next picture, however, and it eventually led to a remarkable career as one of the major stars of the Jazz Age. She was one of three Baby Stars to be awarded a special achievement trophy by Wampas for the greatest advancement in their careers.

At the time Bow was designated a Wampas Baby, she had signed with B. P. (Bud) Schulberg for his Preferred Pictures and was appearing in numerous undistinguished films, mainly in support. Her real stardom was two or three years away, until Preferred merged with Paramount in 1926 and gave her the entree to a major studio.

Although untrained as an actress, liquid-eyed Clara Bow had the ability to show raw emotion on the screen. She no doubt tapped the experiences of an unfortunate childhood spent in poverty with a mentally unbalanced mother. Her persona developed into that of an archetypal flapper who seemed wild on the surface but who was actually highly moral, even virginal, underneath. In other words, her character was something of a sexual tease. She usually portrayed working class girls like manicurists, store clerks and waitresses. One of the manifestations of her characters' devil-may-care attitude was frequent appearances in various states of undress, often in lingerie and sometimes less.

Bow's first Paramount picture was *Dancing Mothers* and it helped to establish her as the symbol of the Roaring '20s. Fame arrived with *Mantrap* and her celebrity was absolutely cemented with *It*. The film was titled thus to publicize English author Elinor Glyn's designation of the actress as one of the few people who had "It," presumably a special kind of sex appeal.

Bow's private life was as tempestuous as that of her onscreen creations. She had numerous affairs (with Gary Cooper, Fredric March, Victor Fleming and Bela Lugosi to name a few) as well as a rocky engagement to cabaret singer Harry Richman. Legends have grown around her exploits that may or may not be completely true, but she certainly was not fully appreciated by her Hollywood peers, especially the "reigning" stars, or the studio. Despite making enormous sums of money for Paramount and getting 30,000–40,000 letters a year, she was comparatively low paid for a major star at $5,000 per week.

The fear that Clara Bow's Brooklyn accent would derail her talkie career was not realized, although reviews for her first sound film, *The Wild Party,* were mixed. She did speak with an accent, but it was not unpleasant to the ear and it did fit her persona. Her voice was contralto in tone and she could even sing a song when called upon. There were problems with remembering dialogue and adjusting to the stationary cameras of the early sound days, but they probably could have been overcome. It was her own demons that were to prove her undoing.

"Crisis-a-day Clara" was her nickname and Bow seemed to live up to it. She was sued for love piracy, a charge she denied but settled, and there was a minor gambling scandal. The major problem came when she accused her longtime secretary and companion, Daisy De Voe, of embezzling her money. The resultant publicity and trial, which laid bare the actress's supposedly lurid love life, dealt a serious blow to her popularity. Her always fragile emotional state began unraveling.

Clara Bow and Paramount came to a parting of the ways in 1931 and a period of breakdown and recuperation ensued, a pattern that was to repeat itself for the rest of her life. She signed with Fox to make the last films of her career. The first, *Call Her Savage* (1932), looked as if it might restore her to popularity, but the second one was not as well received. Although she was rumored to be under consideration for such films as *Red Headed Woman* (which was made with Jean Harlow), she was now truly done.

Bow married the "B" cowboy actor whose stage name was Rex Bell and she retired with him to the vastnesses of the Nevada desert. Later in the 1930s she opened a restaurant in Hollywood that did not succeed, and after the birth of two sons she was largely out of the public eye. In the mid–1940s she had one last small foray into show business as the voice of "Mrs. Hush" in a contest on the radio program "Truth or Consequences."

In and out of mental health facilities, Clara Bow succumbed to what she probably most feared, a mental breakdown like the one that her mother had suffered. She became a seldom-seen recluse, her last public appearance being at the 1962 funeral of Rex Bell, who had gone on to become Nevada's lieutenant-governor. They had lived apart for many years. At the time of her 1931 troubles she had been poignantly quoted as saying: "A sex symbol is always a heavy load to carry, especially when one is tired, hurt and bewildered."

FILMOGRAPHY

1922
Beyond the Rainbow

1923
Down to the Sea in Ships
The Enemies of Women
Maytime
The Daring Years

1924
Grit
Black Oxen
Poisoned Paradise — The Forbidden Story of Monte Carlo
Daughters of Pleasure
Wine
Empty Hearts
Helen's Babies
This Woman
Black Lightning

1925
Capital Punishment
The Adventurous Sex
My Lady's Lips
Parisian Love
Eve's Lover
Kiss Me Again
The Scarlet West
The Primrose Path
The Plastic Age
The Keeper of the Bees
Free to Love
The Best Bad Man
Lawful Cheaters
The Ancient Mariner
My Lady of Whims

1926
Dancing Mothers
Fascinating Youth (cameo)
The Shadow of the Law
Two Can Play

The Runaway
Mantrap
Kid Boots

1927

It
Children of Divorce
Rough House Rosie
Wings
Hula
Get Your Man

1928

Red Hair
Ladies of the Mob
The Fleet's In
Three Weekends

1929

The Wild Party
Dangerous Curves
The Saturday Night Kid

1930

Paramount on Parade
True to the Navy
Love Among the Millionaires
Her Wedding Night

1931

No Limit
Kick In

1932

Call Her Savage

1933

Hoop-la

1948

Gaslight Follies (a compilation of silent film clips)

Boyd, Betty

(Elizabeth Smith); Kansas City, Missouri, 1908–1971; 5'5"; auburn hair, brown eyes. *Wampas Baby Star:* 1929.

Betty Boyd, an alumna of regional theater, spent her feature film career in supporting roles except for a lead opposite Jack Hoxie in the 1933 "B" western *Gun Law*. She entered films about 1926, possibly as an extra, and appeared in about 15 Sennett and Educational comedy shorts with Andy Clyde and others.

On the domestic front Betty Boyd had her problems. Twice married, she went through a years-long divorce battle with her first husband, broker Charles Over, Jr. During the course of it, three supposedly final divorce decrees were set aside and one consequence was her citation for contempt of court. Her second marriage was to wealthy manufacturer Mason Olmsted. She had children.

FILMOGRAPHY

Shorts

Late 1920s?–1930s

Vacation Love
Pirates Beware
An Old Gypsy Custom

Features

1929

The Godless Girl

1930

Lilies of the Field
The Green Goddess
A Royal Romance
Under a Texas Moon
Paradise Island
Along Came Youth

1931

Maid to Order

1933

Gun Law

1934

A Modern Hero

An actress named Betty Boyd appeared in the following films, and it is presumed that it is the same person.

1945
Fallen Angel
*A Royal Scandal

1950
Samson and Delilah

*Boyd's appearance in this film is uncertain.

Bramley, Flora

London, England, 1909?–1993; blonde hair. *Wampas Baby Star:* 1928.

Flora Bramley came to New York as a cast member of the London musical *By the Way*, and it was while in that show that she was spotted for films. It also probably helped that she was related to a studio executive. She also appeared on the stage in Seattle and Los Angeles regional theaters.

Bramley's first feature, the "B" western *The Dude Cowboy*, was the only film in which she had co-starring credit. In her next she supported Buster Keaton and 1925 Wampas Star Anne Cornwall. Her few pictures, including a single talkie, left little imprint. She seemed to prefer the theater.

Filmography

1926
The Dude Cowboy

1927
College

1928
We Americans
*Sorrell and Son

1930
The Flirting Widow

*Bramley's participation in this film is uncertain.

Brent, Evelyn

(Mary Elizabeth Riggs); Tampa, Florida, 1899–1975; 5'4"; black hair, brown eyes. *Wampas Baby Star:* 1923

With her dark Italianate coloring and sharp features, Evelyn Brent could and did convincingly play shady ladies, if not outright villainesses, and "molls." For many years she was typecast in that persona. A cinema veteran, she began her career as an extra at the Fort Lee, New Jersey studios in the mid-teens; her credited films were made under the name of Betty Riggs until about 1916. Her career as a leading lady was really launched abroad. She spent some years making films in Spain, Great Britain and Holland and also did some stage work.

After her stint in Europe, Brent arrived in California in the early 1920s and worked at Fox, mainly in westerns, and then at FBO where she played outright criminals or rough and ready chorus girls. Such titles as *Silk Stocking Sal*, *Midnight Molly*, *Smooth as Satin* and *Lady Robinhood* give ample evidence of her type of role. Major stardom came at Paramount in the latter 1920s when she made an impact in Josef von Sternberg's *Underworld* as a mob lady known as Feathers. By then dubbed "Queen of the

Underworld," she was never thereafter to better her work with that director, although she was the top-billed actress in one of Paramount's earliest talkies, the popular all-star melodrama *Interference*.

During the most important part of Evelyn Brent's career she co-starred with such notables as Clive Brook, George Bancroft, Bert Lytell, Emil Jannings, Tommy Meighan and Adolphe Menjou, and was romantically linked to Gary Cooper. She did not prosper as well after being released by Paramount in 1930 and a few years later she attempted to win back an audience with a vaudeville tour. Two years before that she had even produced a film starring herself — *The Pagan Lady* — but it did not restore her luster.

Nevertheless, Brent continued on for almost two more decades in the movies, sometimes in leading roles and sometimes in support, often for very minor production companies like Liberty, Invincible, Ambassador and Monogram. There were also two serials along the way. One of her more memorable 1940s roles was that of the mysterious cult member Natalie Cortez in Val Lewton's *The Seventh Victim*.

Evelyn Brent did some television parts in the 1950s, her last known appearance being in an episode of the saga *Wagon Train* about 1959. She also tried her hand at being a talent agent. Three times she married men in show business: Brent's first husband, Bernard Fineman, was a producer, her second, Harry Edwards, a producer and director, and her third, Harry Fox, an actor turned entrepreneur.

Filmography

Shorts

1919–?

Into the River
The Border River

Features

1914

A Gentleman from Mississippi
The Pit

1915

The Shooting of Dan McGrew

1916

The Lure of Heart's Desire
The Soul Market
Playing with Fire
The Spell of the Yukon
The Weakness of Strength
The Iron Woman

1917

The Millionaire's Double
Who's Your Neighbor?
To the Death
Raffles, the Amateur Cracksman

1918

Daybreak

1919

Fool's Gold
Help! Help! Police
The Other Man's Wife
The Glorious Lady

1920

From this date to 1923, all U.K. unless otherwise specified.

The Shuttle of Life
The Law Divine

1921

The Door That Has No Key
Demos
Sybil
Laughter and Tears (Holland)
Sonia
Circus Jim (Holland)

1922

Trapped by the Mormons
Married to a Mormon
The Spanish Jade (Spain)
The Experiment
Pages of Life

1923

From this date, all U.S. unless otherwise specified.

Held to Answer

1924

Loving Lies
The Shadow of the East
The Arizona Express
The Plunderer
The Lone Chance
The Cyclone Rider
The Desert Outlaw
The Dangerous Flirt
My Husband's Wives
Silk Stocking Sal

1925

Midnight Molly
Forbidden Cargo
Smooth as Satin
Alias Mary Flynn
Lady Robinhood
Three Wise Crooks
Broadway Lady

1926

Queen o' Diamonds
Secret Orders
The Imposter
The Jade Cup
Flame of the Argentine
Love 'Em and Leave 'Em

1927

Love's Greatest Mistake
Blind Alleys
Underworld
Women's Wares

1928

Beau Sabreur
The Last Command
The Showdown
A Night of Mystery
The Dragnet
His Tiger Lady
The Mating Call

1929

Interference
Broadway
Fast Company
Woman Trap
Why Bring That Up?
Darkened Rooms

1930

Slightly Scarlet
Paramount on Parade
Framed
The Silver Horde
Madonna of the Streets

1931

Traveling Husbands
The Mad Parade
The Pagan Lady

1932

High Pressure
Attorney for the Defense
The Crusader

1933

The World Gone Mad

1934

Home on the Range

1935

Symphony of Living
Without Children (aka Penthouse Party)
The Nitwits
Speed Limited

1936

Song of the Trail
It Couldn't Have Happened
The President's Mystery
Hopalong Cassidy Returns

1937

Jungle Jim (serial)
King of Gamblers
The Last Train from Madrid
Night Club Scandal
Sudden Bill Dorn

1938

Daughter of Shanghai
Tip-Off Girls
Mr. Wong, Detective
The Law West of Tombstone

1939

Panama Lady
Daughter of the Tong
The Mad Empress

1941

Emergency Landing
Forced Landing
Wide Open Town
Dangerous Lady
Holt of the Secret Service (serial)

1942

Westward Ho
Wrecking Crew

1943

The Pay-Off
Silent Witness
Spy Train
The Seventh Victim

1944 Bowery Champs	Robin Hood of Monterey	(The Mystery of) the Golden Eye
1947 Raiders of the South	**1948** Stage Struck	**1950** Again, Pioneers

Brian, Mary

(Louise Dantzler); Corsicana, Texas, 1906/08–; 5'2"; brown hair, blue-gray or hazel eyes. *Wampas Baby Star:* 1926.

Winner of "Miss Personality" in a newspaper beauty contest, pretty Mary Brian came to prominence following her first major role as Wendy in 1924's *Peter Pan*. It led to a seven year contract as a Paramount leading lady, but she was frequently loaned out by the studio. On her home lot she was partnered with many of the top leading men, including Richard Dix, Gary Cooper and Richard Arlen. She also supported Ronald Colman, Cary Grant and even W.C. Fields. Almost always relegated to bland ingenue roles, a rare unsympathetic role in 1936's *Spendthrift* did little to reverse Hollywood's notion of her persona; i.e., as "The Sweetest Girl in Pictures."

Brian remained busy in the early days of sound, and even sang in one of her earliest talkies, but she generally followed prestigious films with mediocre ones. Paramount did not renew her contract in 1931 and she became a freelancer. When her U.S. career began declining in the mid–1930s she resorted to what many another fading actress did. She made films in the United Kingdom (which at that time had an insatiable desire for American stars) and also undertook vaudeville tours during which she showcased her skills as a dancer.

Eventually Mary Brian worked at most of the major studios, including Fox, Warner Bros., Universal and RKO, but also did stints at such indies as Monogram, Majestic, Allied and Remington. In the later 1930s she appeared in regional theater and during World War II was active in touring military bases as part of a USO troupe.

Brian had been romantically linked to Dick Powell and Buddy Rogers but her first marriage was to illustrator Jon Whitcomb. It was short-lived, effectively ending after a few weeks. Her second marriage was to the film editor George Tomasini, by whom she was widowed. In the 1950s she reappeared before the public with a recurring role as the title heroine's mother in the television series *Meet Corliss Archer*. She spent much of her later years painting and in the late 1990s, a white-haired 90 year old, she was interviewed on several television shows.

Filmography

Short

1938
Screen Snapshots

Features

1924
Peter Pan

1925
The Air Mail
The Little French Girl
The Street of Forgotten Men

A Regular Fellow

1926
The Enchanted Hill
Behind the Front
Brown of Harvard
Paris at Midnight
More Pay — Less Work
Beau Geste
The Prince of Tempters
Stepping Along

1927
Her Father Said No
High Hat
Knockout Reilly
Running Wild
Man Power
Shanghai Bound
Two Flaming Youths

1928
Under the Tonto Rim
Partners in Crime
Harold Teen
The Big Killing
Forgotten Faces
Varsity
Someone to Love

1929
The Man I Love
River of Romance
The Virginian
The Marriage Playground

1930
The Kibitzer
Burning Up
Only the Brave
The Light of Western Stars
Paramount on Parade
The Social Lion
Only Saps Work

1931
The Royal Family of Broadway
Captain Applejack
The Front Page
Gun Smoke
The Runaround
The Homicide Squad

1932
It's Tough to Be Famous
Blessed Event
The Unwritten Law
Manhattan Tower

1933
Hard to Handle
The World Gone Mad
Girl Missing
Song of the Eagle
Moonlight and Pretzels
One Year Later
Fog
Shadows of Sing Sing

1934
Ever Since Eve
Private Scandal
Monte Carlo Nights
College Rhythm

1935
Charlie Chan in Paris
The Man on the Flying Trapeze

1936
Spendthrift
Week End Millionaire (U.K.)
Three Married Men
Killer at Large
Two's Company (U.K.)

1937
Romance and Riches (U.K.)
Navy Blues
Affairs of Cappy Ricks

1941
The Captain of Koepenick

1943
Calaboose
I Escaped from the Gestapo
Danger! Women at Work

1947
Dragnet

Bryson, Betty

(Elizabeth [?] Meiklejohn); Los Angeles, California, 1911–1984; 5'1½"; red hair, sometimes blonde. *Wampas Baby Star*: 1934.

Like her fellow 1934 Wampas Baby Katherine Williams, Betty Bryson was related to a major Hollywood actor. In her case it was Warner Baxter, who was her uncle by marriage. Prior to her brief movie career, she had obtained some experience in regional theater and was a dancer with an opera company.

Bryson's "nom de film" came from her mother and aunt who were both actresses, the latter being the silent film star Winifred Bryson, Baxter's wife. One of her problems in establishing a screen presence was her presumed resemblance to another petite redhead, Fox's reigning star Janet Gaynor. She claimed that the similarity made studios reluctant to cast her.

In the late 1930s, Bryson was seriously injured in a head-on automobile collision, but her brief time in the sun had already passed. She did return for a few small roles several years after her last credited 1930s role, and might have had some uncredited bits.

Bryson was married to Albert Adams and then to dance director Le Roy Prinz. She had a son.

FILMOGRAPHY

1933
It's Great to Be Alive

1934
365 Nights in Hollywood
Kiss and Make-Up
Young and Beautiful

1935
Charlie Chan in Paris
The Great Hotel Murder

1941
Fiesta

1944
Hollywood Canteen
Shine On Harvest Moon

Carewe, Rita

(Violette Carewe); New York, New York or Ottawa, Ontario, 1908/09–1955; 5'4½"; brown hair (sometimes blonde), blue eyes. *Wampas Baby Star:* 1927.

The daughter of veteran director Edwin Carewe, not to be confused with actor Arthur Edmund Carew(e), Rita Carewe seems to have gotten a strong boost from that circumstance. Of her possibly six silent features, no fewer than five were directed by her father. Only in her one co-starring role, *The Stronger Will*, did she not work under his tutelage. Perhaps due to a 1928 throat operation that conceivably may have affected her voice, she seems to have appeared in no sound features. She did make at least one Mack Sennett sound short, however. Carewe was divorced from perennial "B" western villain LeRoy Mason (with whom she had appeared in *Revenge*), and she was known in later years as Rita Mason.

Filmography

Short

1930

Radio Kisses

Features

1925

Joanna

1926

High Steppers

1927

*Resurrection

1928

The Stronger Will

Ramona

Revenge

*Carewe's participation in this film is uncertain.

Carlisle, Mary

(sometimes Carlyle); Boston, Massachusetts, 1912–; 5'1"; blonde hair, blue eyes; *Wampas Baby Star:* 1932.

Round-faced Mary Carlisle is probably best remembered today for her three co-starring roles in the 1930s with Bing Crosby (*Doctor Rhythm, College Humor* and *Double or Nothing*). She had begun in the silent days with unremarkable bit roles and the two-reel "Collegians" series that ran until the sound era arrived. She also appeared in Christie comedies.

Carlisle was initially signed by MGM as a dancer. There, an early bit role was as the giggling bride in *Grand Hotel* who arrives just as the dead baron (played by John Barrymore) is carried out. The story of her signing by Paramount, where she spent much of the 1930s, is an amusing one if true. She was doing a Beverly Hills play and accidentally burped on the stage, making such an impression on a talent scout in the audience that he signed her up.

From 1932 she was the leading lady in numerous films and was occasionally top-billed in such pictures as *Girl o' My Dreams, Champagne for Breakfast* and *Tip-Off Girls*. By 1939, however, her career path seemed to be on the descendant, perhaps because of an ongoing weight problem, as evidenced by her roles in Bowery Boys and Gene Autry films. During the decade she also had gone to the United Kingdom to make a film.

Carlisle married actor James Blakely, later a 20th Century–Fox executive, and had one son. After her retirement from the screen she became the manager of an Elizabeth Arden salon in Beverly Hills where, no doubt, she could maintain a lively interest in her former profession.

Filmography

Shorts

Late 1920s–1930s

The Collegians (series)
The Devil's Cabaret
Hollywood on Parade, no. 9
*La Fiesta de Santa Barbara
*Popular Science #J-7-3

Features

1930

Children of Pleasure
Madam Satan

1932
This Reckless Age
Hotel Continental
Night Court
Down to Earth
Grand Hotel
Her Mad Night

1933
Men Must Fight
College Humor
Ladies Must Love
East of Fifth Avenue
Saturday's Millions
The Sweetheart of Sigma Chi
Should Ladies Behave

1934
Once to Every Woman
Palooka
This Side of Heaven
Hollywood Party
Murder in the Private Car
Handy Andy
Million Dollar Ransom
That's Gratitude
Kentucky Kernels
Girl o' My Dreams

1935
Grand Old Girl
The Great Hotel Murder
One Frightened Night
Champagne for Breakfast
The Old Homestead
Superspeed
It's in the Air
Kind Lady

1936
Lady Be Careful
Love in Exile (U.K.)

1937
Hotel Haywire
Double or Nothing
Hold 'Em Navy!

1938
Tip-Off Girls
Doctor Rhythm
Hunted Men
Touchdown Army
Illegal Traffic
Say It in French

1939
Fighting Thoroughbreds
Inside Information
Hawaiian Nights
Beware Spooks!
Call a Messenger
Rovin' Tumbleweeds

1940
Dance, Girl, Dance

1941
Rags to Riches

1942
Baby Face Morgan
Torpedo Boat

1943
Dead Men Walk

Carlisle's participation in these films is uncertain.

Carmen, Jean

(also known as Julia Thayer, Jeanne Carmen [?], and Jean Carmen Dillow); Portland, Oregon, 1913/14–1994; 5'2½"; blonde hair, blue eyes. *Wampas Baby Star:* 1934.

The daughter of a ballerina, Jean Carmen sang and danced in children's plays and folk dance festivals as "Baby Jean." Trained as well in swimming and other athletic pursuits, she broke into films as a riding and swimming double and played numerous bits. She then appeared in Hal Roach shorts before signing with Paramount. She also made comedy shorts later in the 1930s, including at least one with The Three Stooges.

It is undoubtedly for the Republic serial *The Painted Stallion* that current-day fans remember Carmen. As an Indian maid called the "Stallion Rider," she supposedly did her own stunts and generally outfought everyone else on the screen. The story goes that the studio had wanted an Englishwoman (!) for the role, so she temporarily changed her name to Julia Thayer.

Jean Carmen was also heard on the radio and appeared on Broadway in two successful plays, *Stage Door* and *The Man Who Came to Dinner*. Thereafter, she returned to make films in Europe and claimed to have appeared in the cinema of several countries, including England, Austria, Germany, Switzerland and Italy.

In the latter country Carmen starred in, produced, wrote and directed *The Pawn*, a film in which her young son also appeared. Among her other accomplishments was the oddly titled book *Western Bullets Are Blank, Mommy Angel*. Although it is not certain that it was the same person, an actress named *Jeanne Carmen* played supporting roles in several American "B" films of the latter 1950s.

Carmen first married Walter Lohman, who was some 30 years her senior. Her second husband was Barrett Dillow.

Filmography

Shorts

1930s
Healthy, Wealthy and Dumb
Yes, We Have No Bonanza

Features

(not including European films, with one exception)

1933
*Melody Cruise
Midshipman Jack

1934
*Strictly Dynamite
Kiss and Make-Up
Young and Beautiful

1935
Born to Battle

1937
The Arizona Gunfighter
Children of Loneliness
Wolves of the Sea

1938
Paroled from the Big House
*The Sunset Strip Case

1939
Four Girls in White
In Old Montana
Smoky Trails
Crashing Thru

1937 (as Julia Thayer)
Gunsmoke Ranch
The Painted Stallion (serial)

1957 (as Jeanne Carmen?)
Portland Expose
Untamed Youth
Guns Don't Argue!
War Drums

1958
The Monster of Piedras Blancas

1959
Born Reckless

1968 (as Jean Carmen Dillow)
The Pawn (Italy)

Carmen's participation in these films is uncertain.

Carol, Sue

(Evelyn Lederer); Chicago, Illinois, 1906–1982; 5'2"; brown hair, brown eyes. *Wampas Baby Star:* 1928.

Apple-cheeked Sue Carol was one of the legion of cute, bouncy actresses who were a fixture of the college stories that abounded on the screen for a few years before, and shortly after, sound arrived. Her frequent co-star in these slight pictures, and later her second husband, was the Romanian-born musician Nick Stuart.

Publicized as a socialite and heiress to a fortune, the non-professional Carol was discovered while on vacation in Hollywood and signed by Paramount as a "threat" to the restless 1924 Wampas Baby Clara Bow. From 1928 to 1930 she was always near the top of the cast list, and sometimes top-billed, but the types of films in which she sparkled were soon to be passé. Then, too, she was no great dramatic actress and her main claim to fame was that she had presumably been the inspiration for the song standard "Sweet Sue."

By 1931 Sue Carol was working at independent studios. She soon found her true métier as an agent whose major client was Alan Ladd and whom she took in marriage as her fourth husband. She was some seven years his senior. Two children were born of the marriage, including David Ladd, for a while a winning child actor. After her husband's death she became a Paramount producer. Her first husband had been home town boy Allan Keefer; her third was William Howard Wilson, a writer.

FILMOGRAPHY

Short

1927
[Title unknown]

Features

1927
Slaves of Beauty
Soft Cushions

1928
The Cohens and the Kellys in Paris
Skyscraper
Walking Back
The Air Circus
Win That Girl
Beau Broadway
Captain Swagger

1929
Girls Gone Wild
It Can Be Done
Fox Movietone Follies of 1929
The Exalted Flapper
Chasing Through Europe
Why Leave Home?

1930
The Lone Star Ranger
The Big Party
The Golden Calf
Dancing Sweeties
She's My Weakness
Check and Double Check

1931
Graft
In Line of Duty

1933
Secret Sinners
Straightaway

1937
A Doctor's Diary

Christy, Ann

(Gladys Cronin); Logansport, Indiana, 1905/09–1987; 5'; brown hair, blue eyes. *Wampas Baby Star:* 1928.

With the unmistakable features of an Irish colleen, Ann Christy may have taken her screen name from her days as a leading lady for three years (from about 1926) in Christie comedies. There the former bookkeeper co-starred with, among others, diminutive comic Bobby Vernon. In the late 1920s or 1930 she suffered a serious automobile accident and needed plastic surgery.

Christy's screen highlight came

when she briefly became Harold Lloyd's leading lady, replacing 1923 Wampas Baby Jobyna Ralston in *Speedy*, his last silent picture. (She was, in turn, replaced for Lloyd's first two talkies by 1927 Baby Barbara Kent.) She subsequently made comedy shorts at Sennett where she appeared with Bing Crosby in his first short and also worked with comic Andy Clyde. There was also at least one "Our Gang" comedy.

Christy married wealthy Texan Robert More, Jr., and went to live on a 500,000 (!) acre ranch. Their home was featured in an *Architectural Digest* article. Indulging her interest in historical buildings, she bought and restored the Tombstone, Arizona, home of Virgil Earp, brother of the (in)famous Wyatt.

Ann Christy had two sons.

FILMOGRAPHY

Shorts

1926?–early 1930s

Goodbye Legs
Hello Television
Big Ears
Dream House

Features

1927

The Kid Sister

1928

Speedy
The Water Hole

1929

Just Off Broadway
The Lariat Kid

1930

The Fourth Alarm

1932

Behind Stone Walls

Clair, Ethlyne

(sometimes Claire) (Ethlyne Williamson); Talladega, Alabama, 1904–1996; brown hair, brown eyes. *Wampas Baby Star:* 1929.

Probably best known in her own day for appearances in the serials *The Vanishing Rider* (1928) and *Queen of the Northwoods*, the year she was dubbed a Baby Star, Ethlyne Clair began the major part of her movie career in Universal comedy series. "The Newlyweds and Their Baby" had innumerable installments; another series in which she appeared for Universal was "Mike and Ike." In features she made three films with cowboy star Hoot Gibson.

Clair was never a major star and she openly regretted it. In a latter-day newspaper interview she said: "I wanted to do big things and become a big star... I just wanted to be a beautiful vamp." She certainly did manage to achieve the "beautiful" part of it. According to her she never achieved stardom because mogul Darryl F. Zanuck blacklisted her after she rejected his advances. In any event, her feature career was rarely in more than a minor key.

The thrice-wed Clair was briefly engaged to cowboy star Tom Tyler. She was first married to Lonsdale Hinshaw and then to famous make-up artist Ern(est) Westmore. The latter marriage began memorably when during the wedding ceremony Westmore's uninvited ex-wife and daughter appeared to beg him for the back alimony he owed. The marriage that endured was to car dealer Art Frost; they had five children.

FILMOGRAPHY

Shorts

1926–1929

Snookums' Tooth
Snookums' Buggy Ride
The Newlyweds Quarantined
The Newlyweds' Neighbor
Snookums' Outing
The Newlyweds Build
Snookums' Playmates
Snookums Disappears
Snookums' Merry Christmas
Snookums Cleans Up
The Newlyweds' Shopping Tour
Snookums Asleep
George Runs Wild
Dancing Fools
All for Uncle
The Newlyweds' Surprise
The Newlyweds' Trouble
The Newlyweds' Mistake
Dates for Two
There's a Will
What a Party!
The Newlyweds' Friends
No Blondes Allowed
The Newlyweds' Success
Taking the Count
The Newlyweds' Imagination
The Newlyweds' Christmas Party
Whose Wife?
The Newlyweds' Happy Day
The Newlyweds' Advice Broke Out
The Newlyweds' False Alarm
Cash Customers
Oh! Mabel
Newlyweds Unwelcome
The Newlyweds' Court Trouble
The Newlyweds Lose Snookums
The Newlyweds Need Help
The Newlyweds' Visit
The Newlyweds in Society
The Newlyweds' Anniversary
The Newlyweds' Hard Luck
The Newlyweds' Holiday
The Newlyweds' Excuse
This Way Please
Just the Type
The Newlyweds Camp Out
The Newlyweds' Pets
The Newlyweds' Angel Child

Features

1924

*Sandra

1925

*Chickie

1926

*Early to Wed

1927

A Hero on Horseback
Three Miles Up
Painted Ponies

1928

The Vanishing Rider (serial)
Riding for Fame
Guardians of the Wild
Hey Rube!

1929

Wild Blood
Gun Law
From Headquarters
Queen of the Northwoods (serial)
The Pride of Pawnee
The Show of Shows

1930

Second Choice

1931

God's Gift to Women

*Clair's appearances in these films is uncertain.

June Clyde

Clyde, June

St. Joseph, Missouri, 1909–1987; 5'1½"; blonde hair, brown eyes. *Wampas Baby Star: 1932.*

After singing in vaudeville as a child, where she was first known as the "Baby Tetrazzini" and then as "Little Missouri," June Clyde returned to show business as a dancer in Fanchon and Marco revues. She also toured in a *Topsy and Eva* company with the Duncan sisters. Besides some juvenile extra work, her first screen appearance may have come in a Vitaphone short. The year 1929 saw her first feature, *Side Street*, in which she danced in a specialty bit and was probably unbilled. On the other hand, she received top billing that year in the musical *Tanned Legs*.

At the beginning of Clyde's career she made the obligatory "B" westerns; her co-stars in them included John Wayne and Ken Maynard. The year she was named a Wampas Baby she made no fewer than ten films, with top billing in a few, among them *Strange Adventure*, *Thrill of Youth* and *Her Resale Value*. A Universal contractee, she also made films in England and appeared on the stage there. During the filming of one of her British pictures she sustained an injury falling from a trapeze.

June Clyde was one of the legion of Hollywood players who entertained the troops during the Second World War; she also returned to filmmaking during that period, mostly for independent studios like PRC. In the late 1940s she appeared in the theater in Australia; she had also been seen on Broadway in the '30s.

Clyde was married to director Thornton Freeland, whom she divorced and later remarried. They had a son.

FILMOGRAPHY

Shorts

Hal Coslow, the Broadway Minstrel

Features

1929

Side Street
Tanned Legs

1930

Hit the Deck
The Cuckoos
Midnight Mystery

1931
Arizona
The Mad Parade
Morals for Women
Branded Men
The Secret Witness
*Terror by Night

1932
File 113
Racing Youth
The Cohens and Kellys in Hollywood
Steady Company
Radio Patrol
Thrill of Youth
Back Street
The All American
Tess of the Storm Country
Strange Adventure

1933
Forgotten
Her Resale Value
Hold Me Tight
A Study in Scarlet
Only Yesterday

1934
Hollywood Hoodlum
I Hate Women
Hollywood Party

1941
Unfinished Business
Country Fair

1942
Sealed Lips

1943
Hi'Ya Chum

1944
Seven Doors to Death

1945
Hollywood and Vine

1946
Behind the Mask

1957
The Story of Esther Costello

*The release date of this film is not known with certainty.

Cohan, Helen

(sometimes billed as Helene); New York, New York, 1911/12–1996; 5'4½"; brown hair, blue/gray eyes. *Wampas Baby Star:* 1934.

The bearer of a famous name — she was the daughter of show business legend George M. Cohan — Helen Cohan made her theater debut with her father in the play *Billie*. They appeared together in other stage productions as well. She also did theater in Los Angeles, at which time she may have been discovered for the movies. In her most prominent role she played Will Rogers's daughter in *Lightnin'*.

Cohan's only lead came in *The Penal Code*, a 1932 quickie crime drama. Part of the reason she made so few films might have been poor health, although she ultimately lived to a ripe old age. There were occasional stories in the '30s that she had been hospitalized for various ailments.

Cohan was married to Colonel Ralph Isham.

FILMOGRAPHY

1930
Lightnin'

1932
The Penal Code

1934
Kiss and Make-Up

Collyer, June

(Dorothea Heermance); New York, New York, 1907–1968; 5'5"; brown hair (later blonde), hazel or brown eyes. *Wampas Baby Star:* 1928.

A daughter of New York high society, regally beautiful June Collyer was also a daughter of show business and she entered it straight out of finishing school. Her grandfather Dan Collyer had a stage career that lasted more than 50 years and her mother had appeared on Broadway as well. She obtained a Fox contract in the late 1920s and made her first film there. Later, she signed with Paramount.

Although Collyer was at times top-billed and usually prominent in the casts of her movies, her later career was spent mainly at small studios. Some believed she had been impeded by a supposed physical resemblance to 1926 Wampas Baby Mary Astor; that may be one reason she lightened her hair. Actually, their mellifluous voices at least were not dissimilar.

Collyer married comic-bumpkin actor Stuart Erwin and became the mother of two children. In the early days of television she co-starred with her husband on *The Trouble with Father* series and later on *The Stu Erwin Show*. Her brother Clayton (Bud) Collyer was also a popular radio and television personality who also had a Wampas connection. He was married to 1932 Baby Marion Shockley.

FILMOGRAPHY

1927
East Side, West Side

1928
Woman-Wise
Four Sons
Hangman's House
Me, Gangster
Red Wine

1929
Not Quite Decent
River of Romance
Illusion
The Love Doctor

1930
The 3 Sisters
A Man from Wyoming
Sweet Kitty Bellairs
Extravagance
Charley's Aunt
Damaged Love

1931
Kiss Me Again
Drums of Jeopardy
Dude Ranch
The Brat
Alexander Hamilton

1932
Honeymoon Lane

1933
Revenge at Monte Carlo
Before Midnight

1934
Cheaters
Lost in the Stratosphere
The Ghost Walks

1935
Murder by Television

1936
A Face in the Fog

Compton, Joyce

(Olivia Joyce Compton?) (some sources list her real name as Eleanor Hunt, but she has stated that her screen name is her real one); Oil City or Lexington, Kentucky, 1907–1997; 5'5"; red or brown hair (later blonde), blue eyes. *Wampas Baby Star*: 1926.

Joyce Compton became one of the earliest talkie exponents of the so-called "dumb blonde." Possessed of an enthusiastic stage mother, she won a newspaper beauty contest which resulted in her becoming a movie extra. This eventually led to work at First National and Fox. Of her selection as a Wampas Baby Star, she was quoted in an interview as saying that it "was perhaps the biggest boost [to my career] because of the worldwide publicity ... that put us on the map."

Most of Compton's silent days were spent doing publicity photos, together with a relative handful of featured roles. She entered talkies in 1929, supporting Clara Bow in her first two sound films, *The Wild Party* and *Dangerous Curves*. Having a choice of contracts at both Fox and Paramount, she chose Fox. In retrospect, she might have had a more fulfilling career had she accepted the latter.

Joyce Compton made a very successful crossover to the talkies but never quite lost the Southern drawl, which actually enhanced her usual screen characterizations. During the early 1930s some of her roles were quite small and there were comedy shorts for Mack Sennett, starring such character men as Walter Catlett and Franklin Pangborn. She claimed to have disliked this experience because of the long hours and low pay, as well as the fact that she was basically a straight woman.

Compton's later shorts with dapper Charley Chase were more fondly remembered by her. The mid–1930s to the early '40s proved to be her prime time in the cinema with notable roles in the screwball comedy *The Awful Truth*, the nursing drama *The White Parade* and the mystery *Sky Murder* (as Chris Cross, one of her favorite roles). In the '50s the demand for her screen services diminished and she closed out her career. Her last appearance was on the television show *Pete and Gladys*.

In the 1950s she began to work as a nurse for elderly people, a task she had done for her own aging parents. Her only marriage in 1956 ended after a very short time and she kept busy during her years of retirement by painting. It was a pastime for which she showed a distinct talent.

FILMOGRAPHY

Shorts

1930s

Caliente Love
Daddy Knows Best
Dream Stuff
Knockout Kisses
The Plumber and the Lady
Roadhouse Queen
Everything's Ducky
Manhattan Monkey Business
Public Ghost No. 1
Life Hesitates at 40
How to Watch Football

Features

1925

*The Golden Bed
*Sally
What Fools Men
Broadway Lady

1926
Syncopating Sue

1927
Ankles Preferred
The Border Cavalier

1928
Soft Living

1929
The Wild Party
Dangerous Curves
Salute
The Sky Hawk

1930
High Society Blues
The 3 Sisters
Wild Company
Lightnin'

1931
Not Exactly Gentlemen
Three Girls Lost
Women of All Nations
Up Pops the Devil
Annabelle's Affairs
Good Sport

1932
Under Eighteen
Lena Rivers
Westward Passage
Unholy Love
Lady and Gent
Hat Check Girl
A Parisian Romance
False Faces
Fighting for Justice
Beauty Parlor
Madison Square Garden
If I Had a Million

1933
Sing, Sinner, Sing
Only Yesterday

1934
The Trumpet Blows
Affairs of a Gentleman
Million Dollar Ransom
King Kelly of the U.S.A.
The White Parade
Imitation of Life

1935
Rustlers of Red Dog (serial)
Go Into Your Dance
Mr. Dynamite
Let 'Em Have It
College Scandal

1936
Magnificent Obsession
Valley of the Lawless
Love Before Breakfast
The Harvester
Trapped by Television
Star for a Night
Sitting on the Moon
Murder with Pictures
Ellis Island
Under Your Spell
Country Gentlemen

1937
China Passage
We Have Our Moments
Top of the Town
Pick a Star
Born Reckless
Wings Over Honolulu
Kid Galahad
Rhythm in the Clouds
The Toast of New York
She Asked for It

Sea Racketeers
Small Town Boy
The Awful Truth

1938
Love on a Budget
Women Are Like That
You and Me
Spring Madness
Artists and Models Abroad
Going Places
Trade Winds

1939
The Last Warning
The Flying Irishman
Rose of Washington Square
Elsa Maxwell's Hotel for Women
Reno
Balalaika
Escape to Paradise

1940
Honeymoon Deferred
I Take This Woman
Turnabout
I Take This Oath
They Drive By Night
City for Conquest
Sky Murder
The Villain Still Pursued Her
Who Killed Aunt Maggie?

1941
Let's Make Music
Manpower
Scattergood Meets Broadway
Moon Over Her Shoulder

Blues in the Night
Bedtime Story
Ziegfeld Girl

1942

Thunder Birds
Too Many Women

1943

*A Lady Takes a Chance
Silver Skates
A Gentle Gangster
Silver Spurs
Let's Face It

1944

Swing Out the Blues

1945

Hitch-Hike to Happiness

Pillow to Post
Roughly Speaking
Christmas in Connecticut
Mildred Pierce
Danger Signal

1946

Dark Alibi
Behind the Mask
Night and Day
Rendezvous with Annie
The Best Years of Our Lives

1947

Linda Be Good
Scared to Death
Exposed

1948

Sorry, Wrong Number
A Southern Yankee

1949

Incident
Grand Canyon
Mighty Joe Young

1957

Jet Pilot
The Persuader

1958

Girl in the Woods

Compton's participation in these films is uncertain.

Cornwall, Anne

Brooklyn, New York, 1897/99–1980; 4'11"; reddish-brown hair, brown eyes. *Wampas Baby Star:* 1925.

Anne Cornwall entered the movies in the later teens and honed her comedy skills in Christie comedies for about two-and-a-half years. She had previously performed in musical comedy on the New York stage. Her breakthrough came when she played the ingenue in Lionel Barrymore's *The Copperhead*; she had already appeared in some films with Alice Brady. Among the studios for which she appeared were Artcraft, Famous Players and Universal.

Into the early 1920s, Cornwall alternated between leads and supporting roles and in the middle of the decade her career blossomed for a couple of years when she was often top-billed or co-starred. Her best-known film today is undoubtedly *College*, one of Buster Keaton's lesser efforts, and apparently her last silent feature. Talkies put a virtual end to her career; they revealed her voice to be tonally flat. In her first sound feature she was relegated to a small part. By then she had already returned to the short subjects with which she had begun her career, one being a 1929 two-reeler with Laurel and Hardy. She continued to play bits and do extra work in films until the 1960s.

Among Cornwall's husbands were director Charles Maigne and architect Ellis Taylor. She had a son.

FILOGRAPHY

Shorts

1910s?–1930s
Two Tars
The Baby Bandit

Features

1918
The Knife

1919
The Indestructible Wife
The World to Live In
The Firing Line

1920
The Copperhead
Everything But the Truth
The Path She Chose
The Girl in the Rain
La La Lucille

1922
The Seventh Day
Her Gilded Cage
To Have and to Hold

1923
Only 38
Dulcy
The Gold Diggers

1924
The Arizona Express
40-Horse Hawkins
The Roughneck

1925
Introduce Me
The Rainbow Trail
Keep Smiling
The Wrongdoers

1926
The Splendid Crime
Under Western Skies
Racing Blood
The Flaming Frontier

1927
Eyes of the Totem
The Heart of the Yukon
College

1930
The Widow from Chicago

1937
True Confession

1939
Mr. Smith Goes to Washington

1940
Triple Justice

1944
*The Climax

1945
*The Southerner

1946
Below the Deadline
Don't Gamble with Strangers

1947
They Won't Believe Me

1948
Isn't It Romantic

1949
Knock on Any Door

1950
The Milkman

1955
Untamed

1960
Inherit the Wind

1962
Gypsy

Cornwall's participation in these films is uncertain.

Costello, Dolores

Pittsburgh, Pennsylvania, 1904/05–1979; 5'4"; blonde hair, blue eyes. *Wampas Baby Star:* 1926.

There is little question that Dolores Costello was one of the most beautiful leading ladies ever to grace the movie screen, a true Madonna. John Barrymore certainly thought so; he fell hard at first sight and became her husband in 1928. Her dazzling beauty had been apparent much earlier when she modeled for magazines as a child. The daughter of Vitagraph matinee idol Maurice Costello, she and her older sister Helen(e) appeared in many of her father's early films. They continued to be pushed by their ever-striving stage mother who shepherded them through vaudeville and the *George White's Scandals*.

Costello was to be dubbed "The Belle of the Box Office" by Warner Bros. in the later 1920s but she began modestly enough there in 1925 for the sum of $75 weekly. Prior to that she had done a couple of bits. Once Barrymore had lost his heart he provided a major boost, awarding her the leading role (originally intended for another actress) opposite him in *The Sea Beast*, an adaptation of the novel *Moby-Dick*. It was the same year she was named a Wampas Baby Star. They also were to appear together in *When a Man Loves*.

Dolores Costello's silent career was not particularly notable although she looked fetching in period costume. In talkies she continued to be lovely window dressing in such part-sound melodramas as *Glorious Betsy* and *Noah's Ark*. Her light speaking voice was unimpressive in the early sound days, being described as "gentle, inoffensive and monotonous." She and Helene appeared together again in *The Heart of Maryland* (1927), and for the only time in talkies doing an awkward song and dance in the "Meet My Sister" number in Warner Bros.' all-star *The Show of Shows*.

Costello gave the appearance of not being excessively interested in her career. She took several years off from acting to raise a son and daughter with Barrymore, returning only sporadically to the screen in the mid and late 1930s. Her best-remembered role from that period is as Little Lord Fauntleroy's mother in the film with Freddie Bartholomew. Her most notable screen performance is considered to be her penultimate one, as the ill-fated Isabel in Orson Welles's *The Magnificent Ambersons*. Still possessed of a mature beauty, she delivered a worthy performance as the mother of Tim Holt's character. He was in his mid–20s; she was but 37 or so herself. Her last appearance the following year was a mere cameo and her final show business foray came in a 1951 play.

The marriage of John and Dolores Costello Barrymore, as she often was billed, ended in divorce. She next wed Dr. John Vruwinck, who had been her gynecologist, but that too ended in the divorce courts. Other messy legal entanglements included a complex custody fight over Helene's daughter and a suit for support filed by her own father. There were also bouts of alcoholism. At one point in the early 1950s her daughter had to summon the police to calm her down.

Costello was interviewed for the late 1970s British television series *Hollywood*. It was not long before her death and she was thick of voice and ravaged of face. Her children were Dolores and John Drew, the latter a handsome and briefly popular leading man as John Barrymore, Jr. He sired the current crop of Barrymores, including the pouting and troubled nymphet, Drew, who began as a child actress herself.

Filmography

Shorts

1909
A Midsummer Night's Dream

1910
The Telephone

1911
A Geranium
The Child Crusoes
Her Sister's Children
A Thief in the Night
Some Good in All

1912
Meeting of the Ways
Captain Jack's Dilemma
Lulu's Doctor
The Troublesome Stepdaughters
The Money Kings
A Juvenile Love Affair
Wanted — A Grandmother
Vultures and Doves
Captain Barnacle's Legacy
The Toy Maker
A Reformed Santa Claus
Ida's Christmas
For the Honor of the Family

1913
The Birthday Gift
The Hindoo Charm
In the Shadow
Fellow Voyagers

1914
Some Steamer Scooping
Etta of the Footlights
Too Much Burglar

1915
The Evil Men Do
The Heart of Jim Brice

Features

1915
How Cissy Made Good

1923
The Glimpses of the Moon
Lawful Larceny

1925
*Bobbed Hair
Greater Than a Crown

1926
The Sea Beast
Mannequin
Bride of the Storm
The Little Irish Girl
The Third Degree

1927
When a Man Loves
A Million Bid
Old San Francisco
The Heart of Maryland
The College Widow

1928
Tenderloin
Glorious Betsy
Noah's Ark

1929
The Redeeming Sin
The Glad Rag Doll
The Madonna of Avenue A
Hearts in Exile
The Show of Shows

1930
Second Choice

1931
Expensive Women

1936
Little Lord Fauntleroy
Yours for the Asking

1938
The Beloved Brat
Breaking the Ice

1939
King of the Turf
Whispering Enemies
Outside These Walls

1942
The Magnificent Ambersons

1943
This Is the Army (cameo)

*Costello's participation in this film is uncertain.

Costello, Helene

(Helen Costello); New York, New York, 1902/04–1957; 5'2"; brown hair, blue eyes. *Wampas Baby Star:* 1927.

The Costello sisters' faces were like two sides of the same beautiful coin, except that Helene was a brunette and Dolores was fair. Helene was named a Wampas Baby Star a year after her sister, at the height of her brief fame with Warner Bros. In the following year what appeared to be a major career breakthrough—a role as leading lady in the first all-talking motion picture *Lights of New York*—turned out to be the virtual end of her career.

Costello came by her talents naturally enough from her father, Vitagraph matinee idol Maurice Costello. He and his small daughters appeared together, and separately as well, in many one- and two-reelers beginning in the first decade of the century and continuing until his popularity waned in the mid–teens. (The family was of Irish extraction rather than Italian, as the name might imply.)

The Costello sisters were also possessed of an archetypal stage mother who chaperoned her girls through vaudeville and the *George White's Scandals*. They were rediscovered by the cinema in the early 1920s and showcased primarily for their beauty; neither one was a great actress. They appeared together twice more onscreen, in *The Heart of Maryland* (1927) and the "Meet My Sister" number in Warner Bros.' all-star talkie melange *The Show of Shows*.

Although she made as much as $3,000 per week, Helene Costello's roles, mostly as a leading lady but occasionally

Helene Costello

in support, were generally in undistinguished melodramas.

She did not have the patronage of a major star like her brother-in-law John Barrymore to advance her career but she did marry one after her starring career had ended. Lowell Sherman, silent screen villain and sophisticated talkie comedian and director, was her second husband.

According to reviews, Costello's voice was not considered suitable for sound. Her contract with Warners ended in 1928, because, she claimed, she did not want to be the leading lady of dog star Rin-Tin-Tin. The next year marked her final starring one on the screen; her last films, including a serial, were silent except for the brief appearance in *The Show of Shows*.

The marriage to Sherman ended in a bitter and public divorce two years after it began. Her first husband had been school sweetheart John Regan and she was to marry twice more, to Cuban film producer Arturo del Barrio and George Le Blanc, a studio artist. The birth of a daughter in her final marriage eventually led to a stormy child custody hearing that also involved Dolores Costello, who had temporary custody of the child.

In the mid–1930s Costello had a small supporting part in the MGM film *Riffraff*, and there was some extra work, as well as a brief stint as a script reader for 20th Century–Fox. Mostly, her life was a struggle with illness (reputedly tuberculosis) and drug and alcohol addiction. She declared bankruptcy in 1942 (the same year her sister gave her best performance in the *Magnificent Ambersons*), and during the late '40s child custody battle she stated she was living in a single room.

Barely a dozen people attended Costello's funeral. She had died shortly after being committed to a California mental hospital for addiction. A friend's poignant eulogy was quoted in newspaper obituaries: "She was a talented, impulsive human being, wanting love and understanding more than anything else in life — but receiving very little of either. She wanted something better from the world than she ever got."

FILMOGRAPHY

Shorts

1909

The Galley Slave
A Midsummer Night's Dream

1911

Courage of Sorts
The Quaker Mother
A Geranium
Captain Barnacle's Baby
Her Crowning Glory
The Child Crusoes
Her Sister's Children
Regeneration
Auld Lang Syne
The Old Doll

1912

Captain Jack's Dilemma
Tom Tilling's Baby
Captain Barnacle's Messmate
The First Violin
She Never Knew
At Scrogginses' Corner
The Greatest Thing in the World
Lulu's Doctor
The Troublesome Stepdaughters
The Church Across the Way
The Black Sheep
Wanted — A Grandmother
Rip Van Winkle
In the Garden Fair
The Night Before Christmas
Two Women and Two Men
Meeting of the Ways

1913

Mr. Bolter's Niece
Buttercups
Grogan's Foundling
One Good Turn
Mystery of the Stolen Child
Fortunes Turn
The Hindoo Charm
The Other Woman
Heartbroken Shep
Matrimonial Maneuvers
The Doctor's Secret
Fellow Voyagers
A Christmas Story

1914

Some Steamer Scooping
Memories That Haunt
Etta of the Footlights
The Mysterious Lodger
The Barrel Organ
The Blood Ruby
Too Much Burglar
By the Governor's Order

1915

Lifting the Ban of Coventry
The Heart of Jim Brice

1916

Billy's Mother

Features

1915
How Cissy Made Good

1925
Ranger of the Big Pines
The Man on the Box

1926
The Love Toy
Wet Paint
Don Juan
The Honeymoon Express
Millionaires
While London Sleeps

1927
Finger Prints
The Broncho Twister
The Heart of Maryland
In Old Kentucky
Good Time Charley
The Fortune Hunter
Husbands for Rent

1928
Comrades
Burning Up Broadway
Phantom of the Turf
Lights of New York
The Midnight Taxi
The Circus Kid
Broken Barriers

1929
The Fatal Warning (serial)
When Dreams Come True
The Show of Shows

1935
Public Hero No. 1

1936
Riffraff

Crawford, Joan

(Lucille Le Sueur, also known as Billie Cassin); San Antonio, Texas, 1903/08–1977; 5'4"; brown hair, blue eyes. *Wampas Baby Star:* 1926.

After some years of dancing in clubs and the chorus of a Broadway show, the Wampas Baby who was to become the biggest of them all — and the embodiment of the STAR — began humbly in films as the uncredited back of Norma Shearer's head. That actress was playing twins, and in some scenes Joan Crawford played one twin as seen from the rear — or so the story goes. They were later to be the best of rivals at MGM, the studio at which Crawford was fortunate enough to make her start, albeit making only $75 a week at the beginning of her fabled reign.

Crawford got her screen name as the result of a magazine contest; originally she was to be Joan Arden. (Perhaps the studio thought her real name was *too* implausibly actressy.) Although there were some interesting films in her first years, like *The Unknown* with Lon Chaney, she had little to do with their success and there was scant indication that she would be anything but a conventional leading lady. No one reckoned on her iron will to establish herself at the top. From a chubby and untutored ingenue she metamorphosed into a glamorous and iconic legend.

Although Joan Crawford first achieved top billing in 1927 it was not until her role as the Charleston-mad Diana in 1928's *Our Dancing Daughters* that she became a legitimate star. The "jazz baby" phase of her career was short-lived and in 1930 her first reinvention came. Her "modern girl" roles occupied the next three years, with her first major dramatic role in *Paid*. The relative failure of *Rain* and its follow-up led to another image change, "the clothes-horse" period, which lasted the rest of the decade. She set fashion trends with her much-imitated padded shoulders and slash of bright red lipstick.

Crawford's major leading men in the late 1920s and '30s included Clark Gable (in eight films), James Stewart, Spencer Tracy, Franchot Tone and Douglas Fairbanks, Jr., who became her first husband. Tone was spouse number two. Despite the care lavished on her pictures, her popularity began slipping in the mid–'30s and in 1938 she and several other top actresses were dubbed "box office poison" by theater owners. Despite this, MGM gave her a new five-year contract and during that time her image changed once more. She became a more heavily dramatic actress. Her role in the ensemble film *The Women* in 1939 was actually a supporting one, but she got her expressed wish to play a "bitch."

One of Joan Crawford's best roles at MGM came in *A Woman's Face*, but it was to be her last big film at the studio and they did not renew her contract. An almost two-year hiatus ended with her signing by Warner Bros. They were rewarded by an Oscar-winning performance in *Mildred Pierce*, her first film there. The late 1940s marked a renaissance of her career; she received a second Oscar nomination for 1947's *Possessed*, considered by some her to be best performance.

It was to be a relatively brief revival of fortune for Crawford. The 1950s saw her increasingly cast in soap-opera-ish pictures and her output dwindled. There was a third Academy Award nomination for *Sudden Fear* but it did little to get her better roles. The smash hit *Whatever Happened to Baby Jane?*, costarring Bette Davis, launched her last career phase, the horror films, most of them being truly horrible.

Joan Crawford's third husband was actor Philip Terry. Sometime after this marriage ended she adopted three girls and a boy. The two younger girls were about the same age and she always referred to them as twins even though they were biologically unrelated. The eldest daughter, Christina, was to write the (in)famous 1978 book *Mommie Dearest* about the supposed horrors of their bringing-up. It was later made into a film starring an over-the-top Faye Dunaway.

Crawford's last marriage was to Pepsi-Cola chairman Alfred Steele. Although it was to be short-lived, she was made a director of the company. After his death she returned to make some television appearances but became increasingly reclusive in her New York apartment. Her death certainly did not end the fascination with her stardom. Christina's controversial book kept her name alive and in 1981 there was a song from the group Blue Oyster Cult called "Joan Crawford Has Risen from the Grave." (The song "Bette Davis Eyes," released about the same time, enjoyed a somewhat better reception.)

Rumors have always abounded about Crawford's beginnings, although she seemed very open about her modest origins. (They included working as a housekeeper in a girls' school.) The full truth will probably not be known because to stay on top she invented and reinvented herself often. Even her offscreen self was said to be a persona, the real person having disappeared somewhere along the way. One of her favorite directors, George Cukor, said

"The camera saw … a side of her that no flesh and blood lover ever saw." Even she admitted, "I was born in front of a camera. I don't know anything else."

FILMOGRAPHY

Short

1931
The Stolen Jools

Features

1925
Lady of the Night
Proud Flesh
Pretty Ladies
The Circle
Old Clothes
The Only Thing
Sally, Irene and Mary

1926
Tramp, Tramp, Tramp
The Boob
Paris

1927
Winners of the Wilderness
The Taxi Dancer
The Understanding Heart
The Unknown
Twelve Miles Out
Spring Fever

1928
West Point
The Law of the Range
Rose-Marie
Across to Singapore
Four Walls
Our Dancing Daughters
Dream of Love

1929
The Duke Steps Out
Our Modern Maidens
The Hollywood Revue of 1929
Untamed

1930
Montana Moon
Our Blushing Brides
Paid

1931
Dance, Fools, Dance
Laughing Sinners
This Modern Age
Possessed

1932
Grand Hotel
Letty Lynton
Rain

1933
Today We Live
Dancing Lady

1934
Sadie McKee
Chained
Forsaking All Others

1935
No More Ladies
I Live My Life

1936
The Gorgeous Hussy
Love on the Run

1937
The Last of Mrs. Cheyney
The Bride Wore Red

1938
Mannequin
The Shining Hour

1939
The Ice Follies of 1939
The Women

1940
Strange Cargo
Susan and God

1941
A Woman's Face
When Ladies Meet

1942
They All Kissed the Bride
Reunion in France

1943
Above Suspicion

1944
Hollywood Canteen (cameo)

1945
Mildred Pierce

1946
Humoresque

1947
Possessed
Daisy Kenyon

1949	1953	1962
Flamingo Road	Torch Song	Whatever Happened to Baby Jane?
It's a Great Feeling (cameo)	**1954**	
	Johnny Guitar	**1963**
1950	**1955**	The Caretakers
The Damned Don't Cry	Female on the Beach	Strait-Jacket
Harriet Craig	Queen Bee	**1965**
1951	**1956**	I Saw What You Did
Goodbye My Fancy	Autumn Leaves	**1967**
1952	**1957**	Berserk
This Woman Is Dangerous	The Story of Esther Costello	**1970**
Sudden Fear	The Best of Everything	Trog

Cummings, Constance

(Constance Halverstadt); Seattle, Washington, 1910–; 5'3"; auburn hair (sometimes blonde), blue eyes. *Wampas Baby Star:* 1931.

Constance Cummings had one of the longest continuously active careers of all the Baby Stars. A veteran of stock and a Broadway dancer by the age of 18, she signed with Columbia Pictures after being seen as an understudy in the play *June Moon*. Still relatively inexperienced as an actress, she was fired from her prospective first role in a Ronald Colman film but recouped to begin a promising screen career in *The Criminal Code* with Walter Huston.

Shortly, Cummings was top-billed (in *Lover Come Back*) and was never thereafter to be found far from the top of cast lists. One of her best remembered roles of the early 1930s was opposite Harold Lloyd in *Movie Crazy*, probably his best talkie. She was the fourth Baby to co-star with Lloyd, following Jobyna Ralston, Ann Christy and Barbara Kent. She eventually grew as an actress to the point where she became dissatisfied with her film roles and sued to break her contract.

Marriage to British playwright Benn Levy and a temporary sojourn in England gave Cummings the opportunity to appear in two English films. When her lawsuit against Columbia was settled she returned to Hollywood for a couple of years, but another stay in England proved to be a permanent one. She became a prominent member of the theatrical establishment in London and eventually a colleague of Sir Laurence Olivier. In 1974 she was presented with the Order of the British Empire.

Among Cummings's triumphant stage portrayals was that of the mother in Eugene O'Neill's *Long Day's Journey into Night*. She has also been seen in such classics as *Who's Afraid of Virginia Woolf?*, *The Cherry Orchard*, *Saint Joan* and various Shakespearean works. She returned to Broadway several times, in one instance to star in the highly praised drama *Wings*, for which she won a Tony award. She also has been seen on American television.

After Constance Cummings's relocation to England she made comparatively few films. Among those popular British films in which she starred were *Haunted Honeymoon*, *Blithe Spirit* and *The Battle of the Sexes*, with Peter Sellers. During her years in England she has, not unnaturally, acquired a kind of mid–Atlantic accent.

FILMOGRAPHY

1931
The Criminal Code
The Last Parade
Lover Come Back
Traveling Husbands
The Guilty Generation

1932
Behind the Mask
The Big Timer
Attorney for the Defense
American Madness
The Last Man
Movie Crazy
Night After Night
Washington Merry-Go-Round

1933
The Billion Dollar Scandal
The Mind Reader
Heads We Go (U.K.)
Channel Crossing (U.K.)
Broadway Through a Keyhole

1934
Looking for Trouble
Glamour
This Man Is Mine

1935
Remember Last Night?

The following films were made in the U.K. unless otherwise designated

1936
Seven Sinners
Strangers on a Honeymoon

1940
Haunted Honeymoon (aka Busman's Honeymoon)

1941
This England

1942
The Foreman Went to France

1945
Blithe Spirit

1951
Into the Blue

1953
Three's Company

1955
John and Julie

1956
The Intimate Stranger

1960
The Battle of the Sexes

1963
Sammy Going South (aka A Boy Ten Feet Tall)
In the Cool of the Day (U.S.)

1971
Jane Eyre

Dade, Frances

Philadelphia, Pennsylvania, 1908/10–1968; 5'5½"; blonde hair, blue eyes. *Wampas Baby Star:* 1931.

Daughter of a society family (her middle name was Pemberton), Frances Dade rather looked the part. Not conventionally pretty on the screen but possessing a certain hauteur, she is best

Frances Dade

known today for her role as Lucy Weston, the vampire victim, in 1931's *Dracula*. Indeed, the posed picture of Bela Lugosi gazing (blood)lustfully at her as she lies asleep is one of the best known images of 1930s cinema.

The year of her Wampas selection, 1931, was Dade's busiest year in movies. She had first come West with a touring company of *Gentlemen Prefer Blondes*, then later appeared in stock companies and finally on Broadway. Although she had signed a five-year contract with Sam Goldwyn in 1930, her reputation sprang as much from being one of the most elegantly dressed actresses in Hollywood as from any role she played. She was usually a second lead at best, her only co-starring roles coming in the Ken Maynard western *Range Law* and her sole 1932 outing *Big Town*, a minor studio production.

Dade married fellow socialite Brock Van Avery. Later she may have done some nursing.

FILMOGRAPHY

Short

1932
Love Thy Neighbor

Features

1930
He Knew Women
Raffles
Grumpy

1931
Dracula
Mother's Millions
Seed
Daughter of the Dragon
Pleasure
Range Law

1932
Big Town

1933
*Phantom Thunderbolt

*Dade's participation in this film is uncertain.

Dawson, Doris

Goldfield, Nevada, 1909–1986; 5'1"; brown or red hair, blue eyes. *Wampas Baby Star:* 1929.

Doris Dawson was seen in Christie comedies from about 1924. She made her feature debut in 1927 and had a very few leading roles; among them was one with Harry Langdon in his self-directed comedy *Heart Trouble*. Unfortunately, it came at a time when the once-admired comic was heading into decline. Her first sound film was the part-talkie *Little Wildcat* (1928); all her roles in talkies were in support.

In 1929, or perhaps the very early '30s, Dawson was hit by a car and received serious injuries. Whatever momentum her career may have had was stalled. For that reason, or because of her marriage to Pat Rooney III (son of the famous vaudevillian-dancer of the same name), she was out of films for several years.

Dawson, who at one time had been romantically linked to Spanish "Latin Lover" Antonio Moreno, returned after divorcing Rooney for one supporting role at RKO, but it marked finis to her career. She eventually married a businessman and raised dogs, a vocation shared with 1928 Wampas Star Lina Basquette.

FILMOGRAPHY

Shorts

1924?–1930?

The Royal Fourflusher

Features

1927

The Arizona Wildcat
Gold from Weepah

1928

The Little Shepherd of Kingdom Come
Heart Trouble
Do Your Duty
The Little Wildcat

1929

Naughty Baby

Children of the Ritz
His Captive Woman
Hot Stuff
Broadway Scandals

1934

The Silver Streak

Day, Alice

(Jacqueline?Alice Newlin); Boulder, Colorado, 1905/06–1995; 5'1½"; brown hair (sometimes blonde?), hazel eyes. *Wampas Baby Star:* 1928.

With her big eyes and demure manner, it was not difficult to depict little Alice Day as an old fashioned girl. This is just what Mack Sennett's publicity machine did after her brief time as a Sennett Bathing Beauty. She supposedly did not drink, smoke or wear makeup and really belonged — so the press releases said — back in the days of candles and spinning wheels.

Day (the surname was possibly her stepfather's) was a Los Angeles high school student and film extra — complete with an ambitious stage mother — when she was picked to play the small role of Norma Talmadge's daughter in *Secrets*. Prior to that she had gotten a second lead in a Fox picture but it was with Sennett that she spent the formative years of her career.

One of Harry Langdon's first leading ladies, Alice Day appeared in about eight two-reelers with him and then was awarded her own comedy series in late 1923, with a five-year contract beginning at $75.00 a week. When she departed Langdon's comedies her younger sister, 1926 Wampas Baby Marceline, took her place. Although there was two years difference in their ages, the early publicity about the sisters claimed they were twins.

Day made about 16 two-reelers of her own and was groomed as Mack Sennett's first important female star since his glory days of the teens. In 1925 she claimed that she had been underage when she signed her long-term contract and asked to be released from it. In her new one she received a higher salary, and continued making comedies with such co-stars as Ben Turpin and former matinee idol Ralph Graves. She supposedly departed Sennett when asked to wear an immodest costume.

From 1927 Alice Day at First National was sometimes a top-billed leading lady. She made the transition to sound with the part-talkie, *Hot Curves*, in January 1929 and all of her six remaining movies that year had at least some sound. It proved to be her busiest year before the cameras but it also was the last year she worked mainly for major studios. By the end of the decade she was beginning to appear in supporting roles. Also, she played her first unsympathetic role in the Richard Barthelmess starrer *Drag*.

The Day sisters made their only appearance together (dressed as German girls) briefly singing and dancing in the "Meet My Sister" ensemble number of *The Show of Shows*. In the 1930s Alice Day continued playing leads, but only for independent studios like Chesterfield and Tiffany. When she worked at major studios it was in supporting roles. In her final years on the screen she appeared mainly in second-rate melodramas and westerns, in which she supported Buck Jones and Jack Hoxie.

In the mid–'20s an engagement had been rumored between Day and Carl Laemmle, Jr., scion of the founder of Universal Pictures. She made the news one final time in the late 1930s when she sued her stockbroker husband Jack Cohn. She had previously been married to a man named Hawkins and was then the mother of two young sons.

FILMOGRAPHY

Shorts

1923–1926?

Should Husbands Marry?
His New Mama
Flickering Youth
The First Hundred Years
The Cats' Meow
The Plumber's Daughter
Kitty from Killarney
Shanghaied Lovers
Tee for Two
Love and Kisses
Cold Turkey
A Sweet Pickle
The Soap Suds Lady

Features

1923

The Temple of Venus

1924

Secrets

1926
His New York Wife

1927
See You in Jail
The Gorilla
Night Life

1928
The Smart Set
The Way of the Strong
Phyllis of the Follies

1929
Red Hot Speed
Drag
Skin Deep
Times Square
Is Everybody Happy?
Little Johnny Jones
The Show of Shows
The Love Racket

1930
In the Next Room

The Melody Man
Ladies in Love
Hot Curves
Viennese Nights

1931
The Lady from Nowhere

1932
Love Bound
Two Fisted Law
Gold

Day, Marceline

(Marceline Newlin); Colorado Springs, Colorado, 1907/08–; 5'3"; brown hair, blue-gray eyes. *Wampas Baby Star:* 1926.

The younger sister of 1928 Wampas Baby Alice Day, Marceline Day briefly took over as leading lady to Harry Langdon about 1924, when the elder Day got her own comedy series. She also appeared with Stan Laurel and Charley Chase. Supposedly spotted for films after accompanying her sister to the studio one day, her first job was probably as an extra. She became a somewhat bigger star than her sibling, co-starring with some of the major leading men of the day.

Day (the surname may have been her stepfather's) possibly had been a Sennett bathing beauty and bit player before moving up to better prospects, and also had modeled for a department store. For a time it seemed as if she were being groomed by Sennett as another Louise Fazenda, cast as a country girl in gingham dresses and corkscrew curls. This phase was short-lived, as was the early publicity which stated that she and Alice were twins instead of actually being two years apart.

Marceline Day did some westerns at the beginning of her feature career and would return to them on her way back down the ladder of stardom. She received top billing for the first time in 1926, the year of her naming as a Baby Star. She spent much of the silent era at MGM; among those with whom she co-starred there were Lon Chaney, Ramon Novarro, the popular comedy team of George K. Arthur and Karl Dane, and Buster Keaton (in *The Cameraman*). John Barrymore was her leading man at another studio in *The Beloved Rogue*.

Day made her first essay into sound with *The Jazz Age*, an early 1929 part-talkie, and seemed to make the transition to talkies without effort. In Warner Bros.' *The Show of Shows*, she and Alice, dressed as German girls, briefly appeared together for the only time in the "Meet My Sister" number. That year proved to be her last at MGM and thereafter she freelanced for independent studios like Tiffany, Darmour, Trojan, Invincible and Chesterfield, as well as being support in an occasional major studio film.

Among the 1930s pictures in which

Day appeared was *The Mad Parade*, a film that was billed as being the first with an all-female cast. Many of the others were cheapie melodramas and "B" westerns with such cowboy stars as Hoot Gibson, Ken Maynard and Tim McCoy. Among her last co-stars was the young John Wayne in *The Telegraph Trail*.

Marceline Day was married to a producer of movie shorts, Arthur Klein.

FILMOGRAPHY

Shorts

1924?
The Luck of the Foolish
The Hansom Cabman

Features

1925
Renegade Holmes, M.D.
The Taming of the West
The Wall Street Whiz
The White Outlaw
The Splendid Road

1926
Western Pluck
The Barrier
Hell's 400
Looking for Trouble
The Boy Friend
The Gay Deceiver
College Days
Fools of Fashion
That Model from Paris

1927
The Beloved Rogue
Red Clay
Rookies
Captain Salvation
The Road to Romance
London After Midnight

1928
The Big City
Under the Black Eagle
A Certain Young Man
Detectives
The Cameraman
Driftwood
Freedom of the Press
Restless Youth
Stolen Love

1929
A Single Man
The Jazz Age
Trent's Last Case
The Wild Party
The One Woman Idea
The Show of Shows

1930
Temple Tower
Sunny Skies
Paradise Island

1931
Sky Raiders
Mystery Train
The Mad Parade
The Pocatello Kid

1932
The Fighting Fool
Arm of the Law
From Broadway to Cheyenne
The King Murder
The Crusader

1933
Via Pony Express
The Telegraph Trail
Damaged Lives (Canada)
The Fighting Parson
By Appointment Only
The Flaming Signal

Dee, Frances

Los Angeles or Pasadena, California, 1907–; 5'3"–5'4½"; brown hair, blue-green or gray eyes. *Wampas Baby Star:* 1931.

Frances Dee appeared at the Pasadena Playhouse before making her first screen appearance as an extra in 1929's *Words and Music*. One of Hollywood's prettiest starlets in her (or perhaps any other) day, she remained a bit player until being personally selected by Maurice Chevalier as his co-star in *Playboy of*

Paris. Or so the publicity machine said upon her signing by Paramount.

In most of her early films just an attractive accessory (critic James Agee said she was one of the very few women in movies who *had* a face), Dee proved her acting mettle in *The Silver Cord*. Other of her major films in the '30s were *An American Tragedy* (her first big break in the year she was named a Wampas Baby Star), *Little Women* (as Meg) and *Of Human Bondage*, as the "nice" girl opposite Bette Davis. In some of her pictures she still was being seen in supporting roles.

Frances Dee departed Paramount in 1933 in a dispute over salary and signed with RKO. That was also the year she married handsome upcoming leading man Joel McCrea with whom she had appeared in *One Man's Journey*. (Other 1930s co-starring appearances with McCrea came in *The Silver Cord* and *Wells Fargo*.)

Most of Dee's films tended toward the pedestrian but in 1943, when her career was already winding down, she starred in the Val Lewton cult classic *I Walked with a Zombie*, a voodoo version of the novel *Jane Eyre*. In 1948 she and McCrea co-starred for a final time in the western *Four Faces West*. Later she appeared on television and was known for her interest in the Moral Disarmament movement.

Thanks to their real estate holdings the McCreas were one of the wealthiest couples in Hollywood, but their marriage was not without its vicissitudes. At one time he filed for divorce, but they later reconciled and at his death had been married 57 years. They had three sons, one of whom, Jody, acted in films as well.

Filmography

1930
Playboy of Paris
Along Came Youth

1931
June Moon
An American Tragedy
Caught
Rich Man's Folly
Nice Women
Working Girls

1932
This Reckless Age
Sky Bride
The Strange Case of Clara Deane
Love Is a Racket
The Night of June 13
If I Had a Million

1933
King of the Jungle
The Crime of the Century
The Silver Cord
One Man's Journey
Headline Shooter
Blood Money
Little Women

1934
Keep 'Em Rolling
Coming Out Party
Finishing School
Of Human Bondage

1935
Becky Sharp
The Gay Deception

1936
Half Angel

1937
Souls at Sea
Wells Fargo

1938
If I Were King

1939
Coast Guard

1941
So Ends Our Night
A Man Betrayed

1942
Meet the Stewarts

1943	1948	1953
I Walked with a Zombie	Four Faces West	Mr. Scoutmaster
Happy Land	**1951**	**1954**
1945	Payment on Demand	Gypsy Colt
Patrick the Great	Reunion in Reno	
1947	**1952**	
The Private Affairs of Bel Ami	Because of You	

Del Rio, Dolores

(Dolores Asunsolo Lopez Negrette); Durango, Mexico, 1905–1983; 5'3½"; black hair, brown eyes. *Wampas Baby Star:* 1926.

Well-bred Dolores del Rio, the young wife of Jaime del Rio, was living the life of a pampered socialite in Mexico City when she was spotted by director Edwin Carewe (father of 1927 Wampas Baby Star Rita Carewe). Her existence was perhaps stultifying as well as pampered because, against familial objections, she went to Hollywood.

Del Rio (now with the first letter of the surname capitalized) had mere bits in her first two films, but the crime drama *Pals First* proffered a better role (if not a better film) in the year of her Wampas Stardom. She was later one of three Babies to receive a special Wampas trophy for the greatest advancement in her career. Her breakthrough came as Charmaine in the popular World War I story *What Price Glory?*, a picture that had several sequels (without her) and a classic theme song named for her character.

The teary Native-American melodrama *Ramona* brought Dolores Del Rio to stardom and also completed her typecasting as the all-purpose movie "exotic." Beautiful but dark of complexion, it was almost inevitable that she would be viewed by the Hollywood moguls in that stereotypical way. No doubt having taken voice lessons to reduce her accent, she entered talkies tentatively, singing and speaking a few words as yet another foreign type in *Evangeline*.

There must have been some concern about Del Rio's future in sound because her first all-talkie did not come until 1930. It was the silly *The Bad One*, a melodrama set in a French brothel, in which her speaking voice turned out to be higher than audiences may have expected. It was, however, one with a pleasantly slight accent. She overcame the poor notices and a bout of ill health and signed with RKO. Co-starring Del Rio with the young and then popular Joel McCrea, her second picture there was *Bird of Paradise*. It was lushly photographed and very well received. This time she was a South Sea Islander and because bicultural love was frowned on in those days, she jumped into a volcano.

Dolores Del Rio's newfound popularity was temporarily cemented with *Flying Down to Rio* (1933), the first Fred

Astaire–Ginger Rogers teaming (although they were not the nominal stars). She was now considered a musical comedy star, but did not really have the personality to sustain such a role. She did dance a little and do a bit of warbling (but her voice was probably dubbed) in such follow-up musicals as *Wonder Bar* and *In Caliente*. By that time Warner Bros. had her under contract.

The remainder of Del Rio's American career was undistinguished and largely emphasized her beauty, not her acting talent. Like so many other fading leading ladies of the mid–'30s she made a picture in England. Her last U.S. film for many years was *Journey into Fear*, a muddled spy drama with her then-lover Orson Welles. Its reception probably helped to send her back to Mexico where her talents as an actress finally flowered. Her very first pictures there in 1943, *Flor Silvestre* and *Maria Candelaria*, rocketed her immediately into the top ranks of that country's stars.

During her Spanish-language acting career, which consisted mostly of tragedies, Dolores Del Rio was presented with four Mexican Arieles, the equivalent of Oscars, and a Quixote award from Spain where she also made films. She did a picture in Argentina too and continued to appear in an occasional English language picture, the first being the downbeat *The Fugitive*. Others included Elvis Presley's *Flaming Star* (she was his Native American mother) and *Cheyenne Autumn*.

Renowned for her mature beauty into old age (accentuated by her classic bone structure), Del Rio was now called the first lady of the Mexican theater. She appeared in numerous stage plays throughout Latin America, as well as continuing to make occasional movies and some American television programs. Assisting was her third husband, Lewis Riley, a theatrical producer specializing in Latin America. She had also been wed to the famous MGM art director Cedric Gibbons.

Filmography

1925
Joanna

1926
High Steppers
Pals First
The Whole Town's Talking

1927
What Price Glory?
Resurrection
The Loves of Carmen

1928
The Gateway of the Moon
Ramona
No Other Woman
The Red Dance
Revenge

1929
The Trail of '98
Evangeline

1930
The Bad One

1932
Girl of the Rio
Bird of Paradise

1933
Flying Down to Rio

1934
Wonder Bar
Madame Du Barry

1935
In Caliente
I Live for Love

1936
The Widow from Monte Carlo

1937
Accused (U.K.)
The Devil's Playground
Lancer Spy
Ali Baba Goes to Town (cameo)

1938
International Settlement

1940
The Man from Dakota

1942
Journey into Fear

All the following films are Mexican unless otherwise specified

1943
Flor Silvestre
Maria Candelaria

1944
Bugambilia
Las Abandonadas

1945
La Selva de Fuego

1946
La Otra

1947
The Fugitive (U.S.)

1948
Historia de una Mala Mujer

1949
La Malquerida
La Casa Chica

1950
Doña Perfecta

1951
Deseada

1953
Reportaje
El Nino y la Niebla

1954
Señora Ama (Spain)

1956
Torero! (cameo)

1958
La Cucaracha
A Donde Van Nuestros Hijos

1960
Flaming Star (U.S.)
El Pecado de una Madre

1964
Cheyenne Autumn (U.S.)

1966
La Dama del Alba (Spain)
Casa de Mujeres

1967
Once Upon a Time (aka More Than a Miracle) (Italy)
Rio Blanco

1969
Otra Día Veremos la Resurección de las Mariposas Disecadas

1977
The Children of Sanchez (U.S.)

Devore, Dorothy

(Alma Inez Williams); Fort Worth, Texas, 1899/1901–1976; 5'1"; brown hair, green or brown eyes. *Wampas Baby Star:* 1923.

Dorothy Devore arrived in Los Angeles as a child and eventually played in local stock companies and sang in vaudeville. She also had her own revue as a teenager. Her first films were made for Universal where she worked in one-reelers with the comedy team of Moran and Mack. About 1919 she signed with Christie, finding fame as a deft comedienne in some 75 one- and two-reelers. As a result of a salary dispute she went to Warner Bros. where her salary reached some $2,500 weekly and she could appear in features, both comedies and dramas.

Devore bought out her contract and

departed from that studio as well when she was asked to be one of Rin-Tin-Tin's leading ladies, usually a sign of falling fortunes for an actress. The Educational studio was her next home from 1927 to '29. There, with her two-reel "Dorothy Devore Comedies," she became one of the highest paid actresses of the 1920s, making $5,000 a week. These popular pictures featured romance as well as comedy and were carefully made, sometimes taking as much as three months apiece.

Dorothy Devore did not appear in a sound feature until early 1930 and that was only a part-talking film. It marked the end of her starring screen career and it can be speculated that her voice was not suitable to the new medium. Her only other known appearance was in a bit in a 1939 picture in which she was the "woman in the church." She may have done extra work.

The vivacious Devore lived up to her lofty income, being somewhat of an early "jet setter," and was famous for her lavish parties. After going through a messy divorce from A. Wiley Mather, a wealthy importer, in which they accused each other of infidelity, she married a theater owner and traveled with him extensively. They lived in various European countries as well as China. She had previously been briefly wed as a teenager.

Filmography

Shorts

Naughty Mary Brown
Fair Enough
Scrappily Married
Movie Mad
Nothing Like It
Saving Sister Susie
One Stormy Knight
Mile-a-Minute Mary
Let 'Er Run
Chop Suey
Hazel from Hollywood
The Restless Sex
Sneakers
Man vs. Woman
Kiddin' Katie
Kilties
Little Rube
Up in Arms
Rah, Rah, Rah!
Cutie
Companionate Service
Circus Blues
Auntie's Mistake
Babies Welcome
Winter Has Come

Features

1917

*The Law of the North

1919

*The Girl Dodger

1920

Forty-Five Minutes from Broadway

1921

The Magnificent Brute

1923

When Odds Are Even

1924

Hold Your Breath
The Narrow Street
The Tomboy

1925

A Broadway Butterfly
The Prairie Wife
Who Cares
Fighting the Flames
How Baxter Butted In
His Majesty Bunker Bean
The Midnight Flyer
Three Weeks in Paris

1926

The Man Upstairs
The Gilded Highway
The Social Highwayman
Señor Daredevil
Money to Burn
The Range Fighter

1927

The First Night

The Wrong Mr. Wright	**1928**	**1939**
Mountains of Manhattan	No Babies Wanted	Miracle on Main Street
Better Days	**1930**	**Devore's participation in these films is uncertain.*
	Take the Heir	

Drake, Dorothy

(also known as Mary Wallace); Santa Monica, California, 1910–; 5'3½"; blonde hair. *Wampas Baby Star:* 1934.

Dorothy Drake was on stage in Hollywood's annual *Pilgrimage Play* as a child. She began her film career under that name, but used it only for a brief period before adopting her mother's maiden name. After she signed with Mascot Pictures for $125 a week, two of the three features in which she appeared as Drake were those in which most of the 1934 class were seen as well, *Kiss and Make-Up* and *Young and Beautiful*.

Why Drake decided to change the name under which she had achieved Wampas Stardom is not known, but as Mary Wallace she really did not fare much better. Although she did make more films, her roles in them were usually bits. She also made some shorts.

Drake had been engaged to the much-engaged Carl Laemmle, Jr., scion of the founder of Universal Studios. She married screenwriter Cyril Hume and had three children.

FILMOGRAPHY

Shorts

Let's Have Adventure

Features
(as Dorothy Drake)

1933

*Little Women

1934

Eight Girls in a Boat
*Man of Two Worlds
*Success at Any Price
Kiss and Make-Up
Young and Beautiful

(as Mary Wallace)

1934

College Rhythm

1935

Mister Dynamite
Alias Mary Dow
The Raven
Lady Tubbs
Diamond Jim

1936

Riffraff
Neighborhood House

*Drake's participation in these films is uncertain.

NOTE: *Presumably not the actress of the same name who appeared in films from 1917 to 1920.*

Dunn, Josephine

(Mary Josephine Dunn); New York, New York, 1906–1983; 5'3½"; blonde hair, blue eyes. *Wampas Baby Star:* 1929.

A very pretty veteran of the Follies and almost 15 Broadway musicals, singer-dancer Josephine Dunn was supposedly discovered by chance for the movies when she accompanied someone else to the Paramount lot in Astoria, New York. Enrolled in the studio's School of Acting, she and other alumni (such as Charles "Buddy" Rogers) all appeared in *Fascinating Youth*. Although she was soon thereafter cast in a D. W. Griffith picture, *The Sorrows of Satan*, she had a minor role and he was past his prime.

Dunn was fired by Paramount in 1928. After a stint in Poverty Row productions, she was signed by MGM. Her claim to fame, such as it was, proved to be a mixed blessing. She had a leading role in the phenomenally successful Warner Bros. talkie *The Singing Fool*, Al Jolson's follow-up to *The Jazz Singer*, and one of the highest grossing pictures of the 1920s. She played Jolie's unfeeling wife and she did such a good job of portraying bitchiness that it largely typecast her thereafter in icy "other woman" roles.

This persona limited Josephine Dunn mainly to supporting parts, with only a few leading roles and occasional top billing, such as in 1929's *Black Magic*. The co-starring roles she did get were usually as a conventional heroine. She returned to her stage roots, where she seemed to be more successful. Her return for one film in the late 1930s was for an odd semi-documentary produced by the American Committee on Maternal Welfare.

Dunn was three times married, the first time to Clyde Greathouse. Attorney Eugene Lewis was her second husband; her last was Allen Case.

FILMOGRAPHY

1926
Fascinating Youth
It's the Old Army Game
The Sorrows of Satan

1927
Love's Greatest Mistake
Fireman Save My Child
Swim, Girl, Swim
She's a Sheik
Get Your Man

1928
A Million for Love
We Americans
Excess Baggage
The Singing Fool

1929
All at Sea
The Sin Sister
China Bound
A Man's Man
Black Magic
Melody Lane
Our Modern Maidens
A Most Immoral Lady
Big Time
Red Hot Rhythm

1930
Safety in Numbers
Second Honeymoon
Madonna of the Streets

1931
Air Police

1932
Two Kinds of Women
Murder at Dawn
One Hour with You
Forbidden Company
Big City Blues
Between Fighting Men
The Fighting Gentleman

1933
Mr. Broadway

1934
Playthings of Desire

1938
The Birth of a Baby

Eilers, Sally

(sometimes Sallye) (Dorothea Sallye Eilers); New York, New York, 1908–1978; 5'3½"; auburn hair, brown eyes. *Wampas Baby Star:* 1928.

After having been an extra and bit player, Sally Eilers broke into film leads in two-reelers at $75 a week with Mack Sennett about 1927. She was his last major female star, having replaced fellow 1928 Wampas Star Alice Day when Day went into features. Her first major lead came in the Sennett feature *The Goodbye Kiss* in mid–1928.

During the height of her career Eilers co-starred with the likes of Will Rogers, Spencer Tracy and Buster Keaton, but her best role is considered to have been in *Bad Girl* (1931), with leading man James Dunn in his film debut. They appeared together several times thereafter. The picture was nominated for a Best Picture Academy Award and the director, Frank Borzage, won an Oscar for Best Director.

Sally Eilers's films rarely reached this pinnacle again but she remained a Fox leading lady from about 1931 to 1934 and then appeared at RKO later in the decade. In between she freelanced at several other major studios and like many another star in decline made an English picture. Her output dropped drastically after 1939 and by the mid–1940s she was appearing in quickies. Her last two films were produced by her former husband Harry Joe Brown, the father of her only son.

Eilers was known for her salty language, irrepressible personality and occasional hell-raising as in 1965 when she was arrested for drunk driving. A four-time divorcée, Eilers's other husbands were the cowboy star Hoot Gibson, Navy Lt. Howard Barney, and the well-known television director Hollingsworth Morse.

FILMOGRAPHY

Shorts

1927–1928?

The Campus Vamp
The Campus Carmen
Matchmaking Mammas

Features

1927

*The Red Mill
*Paid to Love
Slightly Used
Sunrise

1928

*Cradle Snatchers
*The Crowd
Dry Martini
*Broadway Daddies
The Good-Bye Kiss

1929

Trial Marriage
Broadway Babies
The Show of Shows
The Long Long Trail
Sailor's Holiday

1930

She Couldn't Say No
Let Us Be Gay
Roaring Ranch
Trigger Tricks
Doughboys

1931

Reducing
Parlor, Bedroom and Bath
Clearing the Range
Quick Millions
The Black Camel
Bad Girl
A Holy Terror
Over the Hill

1932

Dance Team
Disorderly Conduct
Hat Check Girl

1933
State Fair
Second Hand Wife
Sailor's Luck
Made on Broadway
Central Airport
Hold Me Tight
Walls of Gold

1934
She Made Her Bed
3 on a Honeymoon

1935
Carnival
Alias Mary Dow
Pursuit
Remember Last Night?

1936
Don't Get Personal
Strike Me Pink
Florida Special
Without Orders

1937
We Have Our Moments
Talk of the Devil (U.K.)
Danger Patrol

1938
Lady Behave!
Nurse from Brooklyn
Everybody's Doing It
Condemned Women
Tarnished Angel

1939
They Made Her a Spy
Full Confession

1941
I Was a Prisoner on Devil's Island

1944
A Wave, a WAC and a Marine

1945
Strange Illusion

1948
Coroner Creek

1950
Stage to Tucson

Eilers's participation in these films is uncertain.

Ellis, Patricia

(Patricia O'Brien, later Leftwich); New York, New York, or Birmingham, Michigan, 1914/18–1970; 5'5"; brown hair (sometimes lightened?), violet-blue eyes. *Wampas Baby Star:* 1932.

The step-daughter of Broadway director and producer Alexander Leftwich, Patricia Ellis took full advantage of her connections, appearing in such plays as *The Royal Family of Broadway* and *Once in a Lifetime*, probably in stock companies. She had also studied dancing. After being spotted by a Warner Bros. scout, she made her debut the year she was dubbed a Baby Star.

Possessed of an innocent, plump-faced prettiness, Ellis was a fetching, if not charismatic, leading lady who occasionally had noticeable weight problems. Almost always cast in "B" films, especially after her early efforts, she nonetheless co-starred with several major leading men, among them Dick Powell, George Arliss, James Cagney, Paul Muni, Adolphe Menjou, Douglas Fairbanks, Jr., George Brent and Paul Lukas.

Patricia Ellis's most frequent onscreen partner was Warner's resident comic, the wide-mouthed, mugging Joe E. Brown. As the self-styled "Queen of Warner's B's," she was sometimes cast in as many as seven or eight films a year, often with top billing. But as a generic leading lady her star definitely began to wane by the later '30s.

Sometime in 1937 Ellis began freelancing, and in the final two years of her motion picture career she appeared at several studios. At Hal Roach, for instance, she stooged for Laurel and Hardy in 1938's *Block-Heads*, in the process getting herself waterlogged and locked in a trunk. It was a poor omen for continuing leading lady status, especially because her opposite number was the pseudo-German comic Billy Gilbert, best known for his sneezing act. He was a far cry from the leading men of but a few years earlier.

In the late '30s Patricia Ellis went to England to try to revive her career. After appearances in a handful of low-grade second features her onscreen career was over at the ripe age of 25 or so. Her last known professional appearance came in the 1941 stage musical *Louisiana Purchase*, after which she married fellow cast member George O'Maley and retired. They had a daughter.

Patricia Ellis

FILMOGRAPHY

Short

1933
Hollywood on Parade, no. 9

Features

1932
Three on a Match
Central Park

1933
*42nd Street
The King's Vacation
Picture Snatcher
Elmer the Great
The Narrow Corner
The World Changes
Convention City

1934
Easy to Love
Harold Teen
Let's Be Ritzy
Affairs of a Gentleman
Circus Clown
Here Comes the Groom
Big Hearted Herbert
The St. Louis Kid
Side Streets

1935
While the Patient Slept
Hold 'Em Yale
A Night at the Ritz
Stranded
Bright Lights
The Case of the Lucky Legs
The Payoff

1936
Freshman Love
Snowed Under
Boulder Dam
Love Begins at Twenty
Down the Stretch
Postal Inspector

1937
Sing Me a Love Song
Melody for Two
Step Lively, Jeeves!
Venus Makes Trouble
Rhythm in the Clouds

1938
The Gaiety Girls (U.K.)
Romance on the Run
Lady in the Morgue
Block-Heads

1939
Back Door to Heaven
Fugitive at Large

Ellis's participation in this film is uncertain.

Fair, Elinor

(Elinor Crowe); Richmond, Virginia, 1902/03–1957; 5'4"–5'5"; black hair, brown eyes. *Wampas Baby Star:* 1924.

Elinor Fair was reputed to have made her screen debut at the tender age of 13 after appearing on the musical comedy stage and in vaudeville. Her publicity claimed she was somewhat of a prodigy, having studied the violin in Germany prior to World War I. Her first film of note was 1919's *The Miracle Man*, a picture that greatly enhanced the careers of Lon Chaney, Betty Compson and Thomas Meighan. Although it did little for Fair's progress she was noticed in *Kismet*, and Clara Kimball Young's *The Road Through the Dark*, and was signed to a contract at Fox.

Fair's career fluctuated between leads and support, mostly for small studios. In the latter 1920s she appeared opposite William Boyd (later to be almost totally subsumed in his character of Hopalong Cassidy), and she married him in 1926 when both were appearing for Cecil B. DeMille. In a sense that director had rescued her career and her last several silent pictures were made for his company. Among her better-known films for him were *The Volga Boatman* and *The Yankee Clipper*. Although she was the leading lady in her first two talkies in 1932, they were both cheapie westerns. The male stars were Jack Perrin and Harry Carey. Her subsequent roles were bits.

Fair's second marriage to stockbroker, and former aviator, Thomas (or John) Daniels was annulled after a very brief time when he was caught passing a bad check. They were subsequently remarried.

FILMOGRAPHY

(as Elinor Crowe)

1916
The End of the Trail
The Fires of Conscience

1917
The Price of Her Soul
The Turn of a Card

(as Elinor Fair)

1918
The Road Through the Dark

1919
The End of the Game
Married in Haste
Words and Music By—
Be a Little Sport
Love Is Love

The Miracle Man
The Lost Princess
Vagabond Luck
Tin Pan Alley

1920
The Girl in Number 29
Wait for Me
Occasionally Yours
Kismet
Broadway and Home

1921
It Can Be Done
Cold Steel
Through the Back Door

1922
The Ableminded Lady
White Hands
Dangerous Pastime
Big Stakes

1923
Has the World Gone Mad!
One Million in Jewels
Driven
The Mysterious Witness
The Eagle's Feather

1924
The Law Forbids

1925
Gold and the Girl
Trapped
Timber Wolf
The Wife Who Wasn't Wanted
Flyin' Thru

1926
The Volga Boatman
Bachelor Brides

1927
Jim the Conqueror
The Yankee Clipper
My Friend from India

1928
Let 'Er Go Gallegher

1929
Sin Town

1932
*45 Calibre Echo
The Night Rider

1933
Midnight Club

1934
Whom the Gods Destroy
The Scarlet Empress
Broadway Bill

*The exact release date of this film is not known with certainty.

Faire, Virginia Brown

(also Browne) (Virginia La Buna); Brooklyn, New York, 1904–1980; 5'½"–5'1½"; black hair, brown eyes. *Wampas Baby Star:* 1923.

Darkly pretty Virginia Brown(e) Faire began as an extra in the New York area. In 1919 she was one of the winners of the *Fame and Fortune* magazine contest which awarded her a brief Universal contract. (A later winner of the same contest was 1924 Wampas Star Clara Bow.) She went to Hollywood to make a series of two-reelers in 1920 and became popular with the movie-going public.

Faire made her mark in the film *Without Benefit of Clergy* and assured herself of a respectable run as a leading lady throughout the decade. One of her roles was as Tinkerbell in Paramount's production of *Peter Pan*, and she was the second lead in Greta Garbo's early film *The Temptress*. She was frequently seen in westerns with such heroes of the genre as Hoot Gibson, Buck Jones, Tom Tyler and Ken Maynard, and was to finish her career in them as well, co-starring with the likes of John Wayne. Another co-star in the late 1920s was of the four-footed variety, the unfriendly German Shepherd Rin-Tin-Tin in *Tracked by the Police* and *A Race for Life*.

Although she appeared in the all-star early talkie *The Donovan Affair*, Virginia Brown Faire's sound movie career was undistinguished. After marrying her third husband, Chicago businessman William Bayer, she moved to that city and was heard on the radio there in the

1930s. She is also supposed to have appeared in some industrial films. Her first husband was Dick Durham; her second spouse was the director-producer Howard "Duke" Worne.

NOTE: Not to be confused with the actress Virginia Faire who lived circa 1899–1948.

FILMOGRAPHY

Shorts

1920–1934

Runnin' Straight
Masked
When the Devil Laughed
A Son of the North
The Girl and the Law
Big Stakes
The Forest Runners
The Timber Wolf
Rainbow Riders
Bud and Ben Featurettes

Features

1920

Under Northern Lights

1921

Without Benefit of Clergy
Fightin' Mad

1922

Monte Cristo
Omar the Tentmaker

1923

Stormswept
Vengeance of the Deep
The Cricket on the Hearth
Shadows of the North
Thundergate

1924

The Lightning Rider
Romance Ranch
Welcome Stranger
The Air Hawk
Peter Pan

1925

Friendly Enemies
Recompense
The Thoroughbred
His People
The Calgary Stampede

1926

Racing Romance
Chip of the Flying U
Broadway Billy
The Wolf Hunters
Frenzied Flames
The Temptress
Wings of the Storm
Desert Valley
The Mile-a-Minute Man

1927

White Flannels
Pleasure Before Business
The Devil's Masterpiece
Tracked by the Police
Hazardous Valley
Gun Gospel

1928

A Race for Life
Queen of the Chorus
The Chorus Kid
The Canyon of Adventure
Danger Patrol
Undressed
The House of Shame

1929

Untamed Justice
Burning the Wind
Devil's Chaplain
The Donovan Affair
The Body Punch
Handcuffed

1930

Murder on the Roof
The Lonesome Trail
Trails of Peril
Breed of the West
Sign of the Wolf (serial)

1931

Hell's Valley
Alias the Bad Man
Secret Menace
The Last Ride

1932

Lone Trail
Tex Takes a Holiday

1934

West of the Divide
*Tracy Rides

*The release date of this film is not known with certainty.

Ferguson, Helen

Decatur, Illinois, 1900/01–1977; 5'3"; black hair, brown eyes. *Wampas Baby Star: 1922.*

In terms of her experience, Helen Ferguson was one of the veterans of the first Wampas "class." She had been in films as a young teenager with the Essanay studio in Chicago and ultimately made perhaps 100 films, many of them one- and two-reelers, in New York as well as Hollywood. Among her eventual co-stars would be matinee idols like Taylor Holmes and Bryant Washburn, as well as action stars Buck Jones, Harry Carey and William Russell. For a time in the mid–1920s she also served a stint as a leading lady in serials.

Ferguson's career essentially ended with the coming of sound; she appeared in only two talkie features and two shorts. In the last of her features she played a small role as a secretary. In the late 1920s and early '30s she made stage appearances and about 1933 she began pursuing the profession in which she would find real lasting success, that of a press agent. Among her famous (and no doubt hard to please) clients were Loretta Young, Pat O'Brien, Jeannette MacDonald and Barbara Stanwyck. With Young she co-wrote the book *The Things I Had to Learn.*

Ferguson was widowed twice, the first time by rugged movie leading man William Russell, who died at the dawn of the talkies, and banker Richard Hargreaves.

FILMOGRAPHY

Shorts

1910s, 1929–1930

Sundaying in Fairview
Finders Keepers
Poor Aubrey
***Why Get Married?

Features

1917

Filling His Own Shoes
*The Golden Idiot
Fools for Luck
The Gift of Gab
The Small Town Guy

1919

Life's Greatest Problem
The Great Victory
Wilson or the Kaiser…
The Gamblers
The Lost Battalion

1920

Shod with Fire
Burning Daylight
Going Some
The Challenge of the Law
The Mutiny of the Elsinore
Just Pals
The Romance Promoters
**The Gray Brother

1921

The Right Way
The Freeze-Out
Straight from the Shoulder
To a Finish
Making the Grade
Desert Blossoms
Miss Lulu Bett
The Call of the North

1922

According to Hoyle
Rough Shod
The Crusader
Hungry Hearts
The Flaming Hour

1923

The Famous Mrs. Fair
Brass
Within the Law
Double Dealing
The Unknown Purple

1924

The Right of the Strongest
Racing Luck
The Valley of Hate
Never Say Die
Chalk Marks

1925
The Cloud Rider
My Neighbor's Wife
Spook Ranch
The Scarlet West
Nine and Three-Fifths Seconds
The Isle of Hope
Wild West (serial)

1926
Casey of the Coast Guard (serial)

1927
The Fire Fighters (serial)
Cheaters
Jaws of Steel

1929
In Old California

1930
Scarlet Pages

*Ferguson's participation in this film is uncertain.

**The release date of this film is uncertain.

***The exact nature of this film is not known with certainty.

Ferris, Audrey

(Audrey Kellar); Detroit, Michigan, 1909–1990; 5'2"; auburn hair, brown eyes. *Wampas Baby Star:* 1928.

A dancer and winner of several dance contests, as well as a singer and violinist, Audrey Ferris appeared in the movies from about 1926. For a few years at the end of the silent era she had a mildly flourishing career, and even top-lined some films. Although she did not long survive the coming of sound, she definitely was in at the beginning of the sound era. She played a chorus girl (with Myrna Loy) in the epoch-making first part-talkie *The Jazz Singer* (1927).

Perhaps Ferris's co-starring stint with dog hero Rin Tin Tin (in *Rinty of the Desert*), the year she was named to Wampas Stardom, was a sign of things to come. That ill-tempered canine's leading ladies usually were headed on their way down. After her film days were finished, she worked as a secretary in the office of the Los Angeles District Attorney.

In 1935 Audrey Ferris appeared in court to face the father she never knew when he was sued for back alimony by her mother. The publicity may well have won for her her final known film part the same year.

Audrey Ferris was married to Archer Huntington, scion of the famous mogul Collis P. Huntington, who was the builder of the Southern Pacific railroad.

FILMOGRAPHY

Shorts

The Question of Today

Features

1927
Woman's Law
Slightly Used

Sailor Izzy Murphy
The Jazz Singer
Ginsberg the Great
The Silver Slave

1928
Beware of Married Men
Powder My Back

Rinty of the Desert
Women They Talk About
Beware of Bachelors
The Little Wildcat

1929
Fancy Baggage

	1930	1935
The Glad Rag Doll		Within the Rock
Honky Tonk	Undertow	

Foster, Helen

Independence, Kansas, 1907–1982; 5'; brown hair (later blonde), gray eyes. *Wampas Baby Star*: 1929.

Helen Foster was the leading lady in many of her shorts and features, both silents and talkies, one of the latter being a remake of her silent film *Road to Ruin*. Most were for minor studios like Action, Trem Carr and Kent. She also played her share of supporting and small parts. Among her co-stars were western heroes Jack Perrin, Hoot Gibson, Rex Bell, Bob Steele and Fred Thomson, and a couple of dog performers. She became an extra after her starring days had ended.

In her private life Foster was married and subsequently widowed.

Filmography

Shorts

1924?
Irish Fantasy
Finders Keepers

Features

1925
On the Go
Reckless Courage
The Bandit's Baby

1926
Easy Going

1927
*The Courage of Collins
California or Bust
When a Dog Loves
Naughty Nanette
The Outlaw Dog
Hands Off

1928
13 Washington Square
The Road to Ruin
Haunted Island (serial)
Won in the Clouds
Hellship Bronson
The Mating Call
Sweet Sixteen
Should a Girl Marry?

1929
The Sky Skidder
Linda
Circumstantial Evidence
Hoofbeats of Vengeance
The Harvest of Hate
Gold Diggers of Broadway
So Long, Letty
Painted Faces

1931
The Primrose Path
Is There Justice?

1932
The Ghost City
The Saddle Buster
Temptation's Workshop
Boiling Point
Sinister Hands
Young Blood
Lucky Larrigan

1934
The Road to Ruin

1939
North of Shanghai

1940
The Westerner

1942
Parachute Nurse

1944
Swing Out the Blues

1947
Call Northside 777

1948
Good Sam
When My Baby Smiles at Me

*Foster's participation in this film is uncertain.

Fox, Sidney

(—Liefer), New York, New York, 1910–1942; 4'10"–5'; black hair, brown or hazel eyes. *Wampas Baby Star:* 1931.

In summer stock companies from about 1928, tiny Sidney Fox made her Broadway debut in 1929's *It Never Rains*, followed by *Lost Sheep*. Apparently seen then by Carl Laemmle, Jr., scion of Universal's founder, she left the stage to accept a contract at that studio. Her first film, *Bad Sister* (1931), is a picture that is more famous for also marking Bette Davis's screen debut. In some of her movies she was billed as "Miss Sidney Fox" because of her masculine first name.

Of Fox's relative handful of films, two were made in Europe with memorable co-stars Emil Jannings and the Russian basso Feodor Chaliapin. Another noted leading man was Bela Lugosi, who starred with a murderous ape in Fox's best-known film today, *The Murders in the Rue Morgue*. After her last film, made for a small independent studio, she returned to Broadway in 1937 and did a season of stock the following year.

Fox filed for divorce twice from, but remained married to, screen writer Charles Beahan. Her early death occurred under questionable circumstances and was considered a possible suicide.

FILMOGRAPHY

1931
Bad Sister
Six Cylinder Love
Strictly Dishonorable
Nice Women

1932
Murders in the Rue Morgue
The Mouthpiece
Once in a Lifetime
Afraid to Talk
The Cohens and Kellys in Hollywood (cameo)

1933
Le Roi Pausole (U.S. title The Merry Monarch)

1934
Midnight
Down to Their Last Yacht
Don Quixote (U.K.)

1935
School for Girls

Francisco, Betty

(Elizabeth Bartman); Little Rock, Arkansas, 1900–1950; 5'4½"; blonde hair, hazel eyes. *Wampas Baby Star:* 1923.

A Ziegfeld Follies showgirl in 1919, Betty Francisco also appeared in musicals and vaudeville before coming to the cinema in 1920. Her major career before the cameras, mostly in supporting parts, lasted about ten years. She played a few leads and was occasionally top-billed, as in 1926's *The Phantom of the Forest*. Among her popular co-stars were William Desmond, Buck Jones, Hoot Gibson, Wallace Reid and Lloyd Hughes.

Francisco was married to Fred Spradling.

Filmography

1920
A Broadway Cowboy
The Furnace
*Sic-Em (or Sic 'Em)

1921
Midsummer Madness
Straight from Paris
Greater Than Love
A Guilty Conscience
Riding with Death

1922
Across the Continent
Her Night of Nights

1923
Poor Men's Wives
Crinoline and Romance
A Noise in Newboro
Double Dealing
The Love Piker
Ashes of Vengeance
Flaming Youth
Maytime
The Darling of New York
The Old Fool

1924
Gambling Wives
How to Educate a Wife
Big Timber
Wife of the Centaur
East of Broadway
On Probation

1925
Fair Play
Jimmie's Millions
Fifth Avenue Models
Private Affairs
Wasted Lives
Faint Perfume
Seven Keys to Baldpate

1926
The Phantom of the Forest
Don Juan's Three Nights
The Lily
Man Bait

1927
Uneasy Payments
Too Many Crooks
The Gingham Girl
A Boy of the Streets
The Gay Retreat

1928
You Can't Beat the Law
Queen of the Chorus
Broadway Daddies

1929
The Spirit of Youth
Smiling Irish Eyes
Broadway

1930
Street of Chance
Madam Satan
Lotus Lady
The Widow from Chicago

1931
Charlie Chan Carries On
Good Sport

1932
Stowaway
Mystery Ranch

1933
Broadway Bad

1934
Whom the Gods Destroy
Romance in the Rain

*This film is believed to have been released in 1920 but its chronological order cannot be determined with certainty.

Gale, Jean

(also known as Jeanne Gail?); San Francisco, California, 1915–1984; 5'6"; brown hair, blue eyes. *Wampas Baby Star:* 1934.

One of the more interesting things about Jean Gale is that she was one of two sets of performing twin sisters who were just 14 months apart in age. As if that in itself were not noteworthy enough, the girls were publicized as quadruplets and apparently sustained that billing for some time. Joan Gale was her twin; Jane and June Gale were the other set. All were in pictures, but June had by far the most successful film career. (She then assumed the bumpy roller coaster ride inherent in being the wife of pianist, actor and world-class neurotic Oscar Levant.)

Jean and her sisters had worked together since early childhood in stock, vaudeville, the Fanchon and Marco dance troupe and Broadway's *George White's Scandals*. She may also have made some films under the name of Jeanne Gail, but this is uncertain. She did become an extra in the 1950s and had an occasional small role. This may have been due to the fact that her twin sister Joan's husband was an assistant to Darryl F. Zanuck at 20th Century–Fox.

In 1954 an engagement was announced between Gale and perennial bachelor George White; they apparently did not wed. She had previously been divorced from the theatrical agent Matty Rosen.

FILMOGRAPHY

(as Jean Gale)

Short

1932
Poor Little Rich Boy

Features

1934
Bottoms Up
Kiss and Make-Up
Young and Beautiful

1935
The Miracle Rider (serial)

1937
A Star Is Born

1940
The Girl from Avenue A

1954
The Egyptian

(as Jeanne Gail?)

1945
The Woman Who Came Back

1947
It's a Wonderful Life
Road to Rio

1948
The Tender Years
Arthur Takes Over

1950
My Blue Heaven

Garon, Pauline

(Marie Pauline Garon); Montreal, Canada, 1900/04–1965; 5'–5'1"; blonde hair, hazel eyes. *Wampas Baby Star:* 1923.

Previously a performer on the New York stage, pert Pauline Garon reputedly made her screen debut doubling for Dorothy Gish and was thereafter a protégée of Lillian Gish. Her initial pictures were made in New York. The role that brought her to prominence early in her career was the one opposite Richard Barthelmess in the teary melodrama *Sonny*. She also became a favorite of Cecil B. DeMille, for whom she appeared in *Adam's Rib*, the year she became a Wampas Baby Star. After that film she apparently refused the proffered Paramount contract, claiming she wished the freedom of freelancing.

Although freelancing generally resulted in reduced career possibilities, Garon did find a measure of fame throughout the silent years, mainly in comedies. She became associated in the public's mind as a typical saucy flapper in vehicles like *The Painted Flapper*, *Eager Lips*, *Passionate Youth* and *Temptations of a Shop Girl*. At some point she also made at least one Canadian film.

The changing mores brought on by the Depression era and the sound revolution brought Garon's starring career to a virtual halt. Like many other actors whose first language was not English, she appeared in foreign-language remakes of Hollywood films. In her case they were French-language versions that were shot in MGM's Paris studios.

By the mid–1930s Pauline Garon's roles were becoming little more than bits. In the 1935 French language version of *Folies Bergeres de Paris* her role was a small one, whereas in previous foreign language films she had either starred or had been near the top of the cast list. In 1935's *Dangerous* (for which Bette Davis won an Academy Award), Garon played a French maid, the kind of role in which she was increasingly to be seen.

The 11th child of an obviously large French-Canadian family, Pauline Garon was three times married, the first time being to actor-director Lowell Sherman, later the husband of 1927 Baby Helene Costello. Her second husband, John Alban, was also an actor. Her third was Ross For(r)ester, who was also married to 1922 Wampas Baby Marion Aye.

Filmography

Short

Letters

Features

1920

A Manhattan Knight

1921

The Power Within

1922

Reported Missing
Sonny

1923

Adam's Rib
The Man from Glengarry
You Can't Fool Your Wife
Children of Dust
Forgive and Forget
The Marriage Market

1924

The Average Woman
Pal o' Mine
The Spitfire
Wine of Youth
The Turmoil
The Painted Flapper

1925

Speed
Passionate Youth
Fighting Youth
Compromise
The Love Gamble
The Great Sensation
Rose of the World
Satan in Sables
Where Was I?
The Splendid Road
Flaming Waters

1926

Christine of the Big Tops

1927

Driven from Home
The Love of Sunya
The Princess on Broadway
Eager Lips

Ladies at Ease
Naughty
The College Hero
Temptations of a Shop
    Girl

1928

The Heart of Broadway
Dugan of the Dugouts
The Girl He Didn't Buy
The Devil's Cage
Riley of the Rainbow
    Division
Must We Marry?
*The Candy Kid

1929

The Gamblers
In the Headlines
The Show of Shows

1930

Le Spectre Vert (the
    French version of The
    Unholy Night)
The Thoroughbred

1931

The Royal Bed (French
    version)
The Woman Between
    (French version)

1933

The Phantom Broadcast
Easy Millions
By Appointment Only
One Year Later

1934

Wonder Bar
The Merry Widow
    (French version)
Lost in the Stratosphere

1935

The White Cockatoo
Going Highbrow
Folies Bergeres de Paris
    (French version)
Becky Sharp
Dangerous

1936

It Had to Happen
Song of the Saddle
Colleen
King of Hockey

1937

Shall We Dance

1938

Bluebeard's Eighth Wife

1941

The Cowboy and the
    Blonde

1950

Bunco Squad

This film is presumed to have been released in 1928 but its chronological place is not known with certainty.

Gaynor, Janet

(Laura Gainer); Philadelphia, Pennsylvania, 1906–1984; 5'; red hair, brown eyes. *Wampas Baby Star:* 1926.

Although it may be difficult for some modern audiences to understand why, Janet Gaynor was one of the most popular stars of the late silent and early talkie eras. Her elfin appearance and mannerisms, later complemented by a piping little voice, endeared her to moviegoers and her teaming with Charles Farrell made them the top romantic duo of the cinema for several years. She also had the honor of winning the very first Academy Award for Best Actress.

The Wampas selectors had again been prescient; they chose Gaynor a year before she made her first major successes in *Seventh Heaven* and *Sunrise*. A mere two years had gone by since she had broken in as an extra and then appeared in Hal Roach two-reel comedies. A supporting role in 1926's *The Johnstown Flood* was an important entree into features. In making that film, as the story goes, she did not know how to swim and had to be saved from drowning. With the Fox studio she found fame for the next ten years and for a time was touted as the "next" Mary Pickford.

In 1928 Janet Gaynor appeared in the first of several part-talkies and the next year made her all-sound debut with Farrell in the very popular *Sunny Side Up*, supposedly the first musical to be written directly for the screen. Both stars sang and she danced. Neither revealed outstanding musical comedy skills but they were close enough to their personas so that the public accepted them. The romantic team made more than a dozen films together, both dramatic and musical, but she was clearly the dominant member.

After the relative failure of her next musical pictures, Gaynor said she was not suited to musicals and she threatened to walk out on her contract if Fox continued to cast her in that genre. Despite her demure onscreen demeanor, she was outspoken in defending what she considered to be in her best interest. She staged a seven month walkout and Fox acquiesced. In 1931/32 she was voted the top box office star behind Marie Dressler, and for a couple of more years remained near the top. However, poor vehicles in mid-decade headed her career on a downward slope, and when Darryl F. Zanuck assumed leadership of the combined 20th Century–Fox studio he announced that she would no longer be individually starred.

Janet Gaynor made an almost legendary return, albeit brief, to top stardom in the successful David O. Selznick production of *A Star Is Born*, and it resulted in another Oscar nomination for her. Only a few more movies followed, including one some 20 years later. She also did some radio broadcasts (including a recreation of *Seventh Heaven* with Charles Farrell), 1950s television, regional theater and debuted on Broadway in the musical version of the cult film *Harold and Maude*. In private life she had become a talented painter.

Gaynor was three times married, the first time being to attorney, later scenarist and Paramount associate producer Lydell Peck. The famed MGM designer Gilbert Adrian, widely known only by his surname, was her second husband. This marriage produced a son and for many years they lived on a Brazil coffee plantation. Her last was Broadway producer Paul Gregory, who survived her when she died from the lingering results of a severe automobile accident in which she had been critically injured two years earlier.

Filmography

Shorts
1924–26?

Features

1926
The Johnstown Flood
The Shamrock Handicap
The Midnight Kiss
The Blue Eagle
The Return of Peter Grimm

1927
Seventh Heaven
Sunrise
2 Girls Wanted

1928
Street Angel
Four Devils

1929
Christina
Lucky Star
Sunny Side Up

1930
Happy Days (cameo)
High Society Blues

1931
The Man Who Came Back
Daddy Long Legs
Merely Mary Ann
Delicious

1932
The First Year
Tess of the Storm Country

1933
State Fair
Adorable
Paddy, the Next Best Thing

1934
Carolina
Change of Heart
Servants Entrance
La Ciudad de Carton (cameo)

1935
One More Spring

The Farmer Takes a Wife

1936
Small Town Girl
Ladies in Love

1937
A Star Is Born

1938
Three Loves Has Nancy
The Young in Heart

1957
Bernardine

Geraghty, Carmelita

Rushville, Indiana, 1901–1966; 5'4½"; black hair, brown eyes. *Wampas Baby Star:* 1924.

Dark and vivacious in keeping with her Spanish-sounding first name, Carmelita Geraghty appeared with a Los Angeles stock company and did a stint as a script girl for Mack Sennett and others. She was promoted by director George Fitzmaurice into an on-camera career, in the early part of which she performed Spanish dances and played exotic characters in a series of all-star Sennett comedies. Perhaps it did not hurt that her father Thomas Geraghty was a well-known Hollywood scenario writer.

Leaving Sennett a year or so later, Geraghty began playing small roles, then second leads and leading ladies in westerns and melodramas. She had one of her best silent roles as Mary Pickford's sister in Pickford's final silent, *My Best Girl*. She also co-starred with such leading men as Tom Mix and Warner Baxter. Her talkie work was almost entirely in supporting roles and she appeared in two serials.

Carmelita Geraghty married MGM writer-producer Carey Wilson, and they remained wed until his death. She was a well-respected painter whose works were exhibited in galleries.

Filmography

Shorts

The Campus Carmen
Button My Back
Fight and Win (series)

Features

1922
*To Have and to Hold

1923
*Rosita
*The Eternal Three
Jealous Husbands
Bag and Baggage

1924
Through the Dark
Discontented Husbands
High Speed
Geared to Go
Black Oxen

1925
Brand of Cowardice
Passionate Youth
The Mysterious Stranger
Cyclone Cavalier
Under the Rouge
My Lady of Whims
The Pleasure Garden
   (U.K.—directed by
   Alfred Hitchcock)

1926
The Flying Mail
The Lily
The Great Gatsby
Josselyn's Wife
The Canyon of Light

1927
The Last Trail
What Every Girl Should
   Know
Venus of Venice
My Best Girl
The Small Bachelor
The Slaver

1928
The Good-Bye Kiss
South of Panama
Object—Alimony

1929
Paris Bound
The Mississippi Gambler
This Thing Called Love
After the Fog

1930
What Men Want
Men Without Law
Rogue of the Rio Grande
Fighting Thru

1931
Millie
Fifty Million Frenchmen
Texas Ranger
Graft
Night Life in Reno
Forgotten Women
The Devil Pays

1932
Prestige
Escapade
The Jungle Mystery
   (serial)

1933
Malay Nights
Broadway Bad

1934
**The Flaming Signal

1935
Manhattan Butterfly

1936
The Phantom of Santa
   Fe

Geraghty probably had bit roles in these films.

**The release date of this film is not known with certainty.*

Gregory, Ena

(also known as Marian Douglas); Sydney, Australia, 1905/1908–1993; 5'2"–5'3"; blonde hair, blue/green eyes. *Wampas Baby Star:* 1925.

After stage experience in Australia, Ena Gregory was supposed to have appeared in about 200 American comedy shorts. In features her co-stars in westerns included Art Acord, Tim McCoy and Jack Hoxie.

Gregory apparently was a Wampas replacement for the already announced Virginia Lee Corbin. In spite of the fact that she became a Wampas Star under her real name, from 1928 she made films as Marian Douglas. She said it was done as an homage to her favorite stars Mary Pickford and Douglas Fairbanks after a mystic told her that her real name was a hindrance to achieving stardom.

Gregory was three times wed, her first husband being "B" film director Albert Rogell. In a well-publicized lawsuit, he sued the man accused of being her lover for alienation of affection. When a suit was served on the presumed rival, the actress was found attempting to hide in his home. Her second spouse was Dr. Frank Nolan and her third James Talbot. After her screen career ended, she became a real estate agent.

FILMOGRAPHY

(as Ena Gregory)

Shorts

1919–?

Features

1920
Up in Mary's Attic

1921
Short Skirts

1922
Defying the Law

1923
The Devil's Dooryard
The Law Rustlers
In the Palace of the King
Prepared to Die

1924
The Folly of Vanity

1925
Cold Nerve
The Desert Flower
The Calgary Stampede

1926
Sporting Life
The Better Man
Doubling with Danger
One Man Trail
Red Hot Leather

1927
Rough and Ready
Blazing Days
Down the Stretch
Grinning Guns
Men of Daring
The Western Rover
Romantic Rogue
The Rose of Kildare

1932
*What Price Hollywood?

1937
Live, Love and Learn

(as Marian Douglas)

1928
The Shepherd of the Hills
The Wagon Show
The Devil's Trademark
The Upland Rider
The Power of Silence
The Bushranger

1929
Sioux Blood

1931
Aloha

*The actress in this film was billed as Edna Gregory — possibly the same person?

Grey, Gloria

(sometimes Gray); Stockton, California, 1909–1947; 5'2"; blonde hair, blue eyes. *Wampas Baby Star:* 1924.

Before Gloria Grey entered films she was in vaudeville as a member of Gus Edwards's troupe (like 1922 Baby Lila Lee) and on the New York stage. She made her movie debut as a teenager, and at a presumed 15 years of age was one of the youngest Wampas Baby Stars at the time of her naming. From 1927 to 1929 she made a series of western two-reelers under the name Gloria Gray. In her only two pictures with sound in 1929 she had small roles.

Grey was married to Ramon Romero, a fan magazine writer. They had one daughter.

NOTE: *Not to be confused with the later nightclub and TV singer of the same name.*

FILMOGRAPHY

(as Gloria Gray)

Shorts

1927–1929

On Special Duty
The Red Warning
Winged Hoofs
A Tenderfoot Hero
Days of Daring
Dodging Danger

(as Gloria Grey)

Features

1922

The Great Alone

1923

The Supreme Test
Bag and Baggage

1924

The Spirit of the U.S.A.
Dante's Inferno
A Girl of the Limberlost
The No-Gun Man
The Millionaire Cowboy
Little Robinson Crusoe
The House of Youth

1925

The Snob Buster
Heartless Husbands

1926

Unknown Dangers
Thrilling Youth
The Ghetto Shamrock
Officer Jim
The Night Watch

The Hidden Way
The Boaster

1927

The Thrill Seekers
Range Courage
The Broncho Buster
Blake of Scotland Yard
 (serial)

1928

Put 'Em Up
The Hound of Silver
 Creek
The Cloud Dodger

1929

Married in Hollywood
Lucky Star

Gulliver, Dorothy

Salt Lake City, Utah, 1908–1997; 5'–5'2"; brown hair, brown or hazel eyes. *Wampas Baby Star: 1928.*

Dorothy Gulliver won a beauty contest sponsored by Universal in her home town which led to a contract with that studio. Beginning as an extra, she was featured in at least 50 of the two-reel Collegians series, beginning about 1926, which remained popular to the end of the silent days.

Gulliver also played in numerous westerns, both two-reelers and features, with the likes of Hoot Gibson and Jack Hoxie, and was yet another leading lady of dog star Rin Tin Tin in *A Dog of the Regiment*. (Some filmographies list her as appearing, some 50 years later, in the 1970s spoof *Won Ton Ton, the Dog Who Saved Hollywood* but she claims not to have been in the picture.)

In the mid–'30s Dorothy Gulliver was involved in an accident that kept her off the screen for a lengthy time, to the detriment of her career. Nevertheless, she continued to be a decorative leading lady in westerns and serials of the 1930s and in smaller roles until the early 1940s. She had been off the screen for almost 25 years when she suddenly materialized in director John Cassavetes's *Faces* playing a blowsy, middle-aged harridan.

There was some speculation Gulliver might be nominated for a Best Supporting Actress Oscar, but that, as well as subsequent film opportunities, came to naught. She did also make appearances in television and regional theater.

Dorothy Gulliver was married to Chester De Vito, an assistant director at Universal, and then to Jack Proctor, a publicist.

Filmography

Shorts

1926

One Wild Time
The Shoot 'Em Up Kid
Benson at Calford
Fighting to Win
Making Good
The Last Lap
Around the Bases
Fighting Spirit
The Relay

1927

The Dude Desperado
Cinder Path
Flashing Oars
Breaking Records
Crimson Colors
The Winning Five
The Dazzling Coeds
The Fighting Finish
Samson at Calford
The Winning Punch
Running Wild
Splashing Through
The Winning Goal
Sliding Home

1928

The Junior Year
Calford vs. Redskins
Kicking Through
Calford in the Movies
Paddling Coeds
Fighting for Victory
Dear Old Calford
Calford on Horseback
The Bookworm Hero
Speeding Youth
The Winning Point
Farewell

1929

King of the Campus
The Rivals
On Guard
Junior Luck
The Cross Country Run
Sporting Courage
The Varsity Drag
Flying High
On the Side Lines
Use Your Feet
Splash Mates
Graduation Daze

1930

Voice of Hollywood
Big Hearted

Features

1926

The Winking Idol (serial)
Strings of Steel (serial)

1927

The Rambling Ranger
A Dog of the Regiment
One Glorious Scrap
The Shield of Honor

1928

Good Morning, Judge
Honeymoon Flats
The Wild West Show
Clearing the Trail

1929

College Love
Night Parade
Painted Faces

1930

Troopers Three
Under Montana Skies

1931

The Phantom of the West (serial)
In Old Cheyenne
The Galloping Ghost (serial)
The Fighting Marshal

1932

The Shadow of the Eagle (serial)
Honor of the Press
The Last Frontier (serial)

Outlaw Justice

1933

Revenge at Monte Carlo
King Kong
Cheating Blondes

1934

Stand Up and Cheer!

1935

Fighting Caballero
*The Pecos Dandy

1936

Custer's Last Stand (serial)

1938

In Early Arizona

1939

North of Shanghai
Lone Star Pioneers

1941

Borrowed Hero
Appointment for Love

1942

A Tragedy at Midnight

1944

Sweethearts of the U.S.A.

1968

Faces

*This film may have been released in 1934.

Hall, Ruth

(Ruth Ybanez); Jacksonville, Florida, 1912–; 5'3"; brown hair, brown eyes. *Wampas Baby Star:* 1932.

Supposedly a great-niece of Spanish novelist Vicente Blanco Ibanez, author of *The Four Horsemen of the Apocalypse*, Ruth Hall began her screen career with an uncredited bit in *Hell's Harbor* in 1930. She essentially remained an extra until being cast in her first major role in the Marx Brothers' *Monkey Business*, in which she played the girlfriend of hapless Zeppo Marx. Besides that chaotic comedy, her best-known films are probably *The Kid from Spain* and *One Way Passage*.

Although Hall appeared in 13 films in 1932, the year she was named to Wampas Baby Stardom, her career proved to be a brief one. Among her co-stars were Eddie Cantor and western heroes John Wayne and Ken Maynard. By the mid–1930s she had gone to live in London with her husband, the famed cinematographer Lee Garmes, to whom she was married for some 45 years and with whom she had two daughters. (He filmed *Gone with the Wind*, among many other pictures.)

NOTE: She is presumably not the actress of the same name who made films in the 1950s.

FILMOGRAPHY

Short

Hollywood on Parade, no. 9

Features

1930

Hell's Harbor

1931

*Drums of Jeopardy
Monkey Business
Local Boy Makes Good
Her Majesty Love

1932

Union Depot
A Fool's Advice
Manhattan Parade
The Heart of New York
Miss Pinkerton
Blessed Event
Ride Him Cowboy
Dynamite Ranch
Between Fighting Men
Gambling Sex
The Kid from Spain
Flaming Guns
One Way Passage

1933

The Three Musketeers (serial)
The Return of Casey Jones
Laughing at Life
Man from Monterey
Strawberry Roan
Murder on the Campus

1934

Beloved
Badge of Honor

*Hall's participation in this film is uncertain.

Hayes, Hazel

La Crosse, Kansas, 1913–; 5'7"; brown hair, blue eyes. *Wampas Baby Star:* 1934.

The year that Hazel Hayes attained Wampas Stardom was also the last year of her screen career. She had been a featured singer in her first picture, the maiden Ginger Rogers–Fred Astaire teaming *Flying Down to Rio*. In two other films she was joined by almost all the other Baby Stars of 1934.

Hayes had enjoyed a respectable career as a Broadway dancer prior to her Hollywood sojourn, and she went on to a more auspicious career thereafter. She was lauded as one of America's most promising dramatic sopranos by no less a personage than world-famed Irish tenor John McCormack.

Trained as an opera singer, Hayes appeared in opera productions as well as in vaudeville and on the radio, and she also concertized in the late 1930s. She had been the winner of a voice contest sponsored by the International Federated Music Clubs.

FILMOGRAPHY

1933

Flying Down to Rio

1934

Journal of a Crime
Kiss and Make-Up
Young and Beautiful

Hiatt, Ruth

(Ruth Redfern); Cripple Creek, Colorado, 1906/08–1994; 5'2"–5'3"; blonde hair, blue eyes. *Wampas Baby Star:* 1924.

Beauty contest winner Ruth Hiatt may have appeared in films as early as 1915 for the Lubin studio, and by 1922 she was doing extra and bit parts. The following year she co-starred at Educational pictures with funnyman Lloyd

Hamilton before becoming the leading lady to Mack Sennett comics Jack White and later Harry Langdon. In 1925 she received a long-term contract from Sennett and played the wife in the "Smith" series with Raymond McKee.

Hiatt made very few features, and in many of the later ones her parts were very small. Released from her Sennett contract in 1928, she re-signed for talking shorts about three years later. Among those made at Columbia was *Men in Black*, the only Three Stooges Oscar-nominated short. She also co-starred in a couple of 1930s "B" westerns.

Hiatt divorced her rancher husband Pierre Masciotra because he called her a "dribblepuss" for her reluctance to drink with him. She also averred that he wanted her to work in the fields with a plow. He counter-claimed that she was a heavy imbiber. She was married and divorced three times, her other spouses being Harry Liberman and a Mr. French. After her final film work in the early 1940s she owned a professional make-up business.

FILMOGRAPHY

Shorts

1910s–1930s

Smith's Baby
Smith's Vacation
Smith's Landlord
Smith's Visitor
Smith's Uncle
Smith's Picnic
Smith's Pets
Smith's Customer
Smith's New Home
Smith's Surprise
Smith's Kindergarten
Smith's Pony
Smith's Fishing Trip
Smith's Cousin
Smith's Cook
Smith's Modiste Shop
Smith's Candy Shop
Smith's Army Life
Smith's Holiday
Smith's Farm Days
Smith's Restaurant
Smith's Catalina Rowboat Race
Smith Baby's Happy Birthday
Men in Black
Forgotten Babies
Beginner's Luck
Little Papa
Fifty Million Husbands
The Big Flash
Taxi Troubles
Just Speeding
Oh, My Nerves
Carnival Revue
The Rodeo
Wandering Willies
Saturday Afternoon

Features

1918

The Vigilantes

1927

His First Flame
The Missing Link

1928

The Chinatown Mystery (serial)

1929

Shanghai Rose

1930

Her Man
Night Work

1932

Sunset Trail

1934

Good Dame
Ridin' Thru
Broadway Bill

1935

*The Drunkard

1936

The Broken Coin

1941

Double Trouble

The actress in this film is billed as Ruth Hyatt, but it is believed to be the same person.

Hill, Doris

Roswell, New Mexico, 1905?–1976; 5'2½"; red hair, blue eyes. *Wampas Baby Star:* 1929.

Trained as a vaudeville dancer, Doris Hill had performed in Los Angeles theater before her first role of note opposite Sydney Chaplin in his popular World War I comedy *The Better 'Ole*. (It was the second feature to have an accompaniment of music and sound effects by the Vitaphone process.) Her first few films were made for FBO and she was then signed by Paramount, which announced they were going to groom her for stardom.

Prior to her first talkie appearance, Hill took voice training and made a successful enough transition to the talkies, one of the first being the unfortunate John Gilbert starrer *His Glorious Night*. (She played Hedda Hopper's daughter.) From about 1930 her appearances were mainly at Poverty Row studios and were almost entirely in westerns. She appeared with most of the major oater stars, among them Buck Jones, Hoot Gibson, Ken Maynard, Tim McCoy and Bob Steele. Her last films may have been comedy shorts.

Hill was married three times; her first two spouses were actor George Derrick and Monte Brice.

Doris Hill

Filmography

Shorts

1930s?
Hotel Anchovy
Girl Trouble
Ridin' Gents

Features

1926
Tom and His Pals
The Better 'Ole
Is That Nice?
The Timid Terror

1927
Casey at the Bat
Beauty Shoppers
Rough House Rosie
Tell It to Sweeney
Figures Don't Lie

1928
Tillie's Punctured Romance
A Thief in the Dark
Court-Martial
Take Me Home
Avalanche

1929
The Studio Murder Mystery
His Glorious Night
Darkened Rooms

1930
Men Are Like That
Song of the Caballero
Sons of the Saddle
Code of Honor

1931
The Montana Kid
The One Way Trail

1932
The Spirit of the West
South of the Rio Grande
Tangled Destinies

1933
Via Pony Express
Trailing North
Crashing Broadway
Galloping Romeo
Ranger's Code

1934
*Texas Tornado
*The Battling Buckaroo

Both these films may have been released as early as 1932.

Holm, Eleanor

Brooklyn, New York, 1913/14–; 5'1"; brown hair, blue eyes. *Wampas Baby Star:* 1932.

Eleanor Holm became a Wampas Baby Star in a most unusual way, by being a championship swimmer and subsequently winning a medal in the Olympics. She had a major role in only a single picture, and that came six years after being named a Baby Star and being signed by Warner Bros. for $500 a week. She may possibly have had some uncredited movie bits in the early '30s in order to give her "seasoning."

A pretty young teenager when she won third place as a swimmer in the 1928 Olympics, Holm also was the national women's backstroke champion that year. Her promise was fulfilled when she took the Olympic gold medal in the 50-yard race and set a new world's record in that event in 1932. She was to earn over 70 medals as a swimmer. In the meantime she had already flirted with a show business career, debuting as a showgirl at the age of 16.

Holm married singer and bandleader Arthur Jarrett in the early 1930s and launched a singing career with his band in nightclubs and on the radio.

Swimming was always apparently first in her heart, though, and she qualified for the 1936 Olympics to be held in Berlin. Ever unmindful of public opinion, the feisty athlete was quoted by newspapermen as saying "I train on champagne and cigarettes."

Eleanor Holm was not joking. She was seen drinking on the ship going to Europe and was disqualified from participating in the Olympics. (The Hearst International News Service made her a Berlin correspondent but her column was ghosted by someone else.) It was not long before another contretemps erupted. She fell in love with pint-sized showman Billy Rose, who was also married at the time to the legendary Fannie Brice. They divorced their spouses in the full glare of unsympathetic publicity.

It probably was just this publicity that got Holm her chance at movie stardom at last. She was cast as a kind of Jane substitute (called Eleanor in the film) in *Tarzan's Revenge*, with 1936 Olympian Glenn Morris in the title role. It was a rival production to the MGM series with Johnny Weissmuller and was not successful. Although Holm was given plenty of opportunity to display her swimming prowess, her acting prowess was notably lacking and her Brooklyn accent was also much in evidence.

This was not the end of Eleanor Holm's career. She next became the star of Billy Rose's "Aquacade," a water extravaganza that toured the country. Always irrepressible, she managed to stay in the news. A bitter divorce battle with Rose in the early 1950s received reams of publicity and was wittily dubbed "The War of the Roses." They were known for their high living and *Life* magazine quoted him as saying that she "would not be satisfied with anything less than the Taj Mahal on ball bearings."

Holm was married for a third time to professional soccer player Thomas Whelan and settled into a career as an interior decorator in Miami Beach, but she was not to remain out of the news. In 1960 she almost died from an overdose of sleeping pills, which, she claimed, was an accident, and two years later was arrested for drunk driving. Outspoken as ever now in her eighties, she still occasionally manages to get her colorful opinions in print.

Filmography

Shorts

early 1930s

Hollywood on Parade, no. 9

Ted Husing's Sports Thrills, no. 1

Feature

1938

Tarzan's Revenge

Hovey, Ann

Mount Vernon, Indiana, 1912/14–; 5'3"; black hair, brown eyes. *Wampas Baby Star:* 1934.

Little is known about Ann Hovey's early life except that she was blind in one eye when she was a teenager, but recovered full sight. Her roles onscreen rarely rose above small parts and sometimes they were bits. Prior to her film work she had been in New York musical comedy.

Hovey was married to press agent Robert Husey.

FILMOGRAPHY

1933
**Gold Diggers of 1933
**42nd Street
The Little Giant
Private Detective 62
Mary Stevens M.D.
Wild Boys of the Road

1934
Journal of a Crime
Kiss and Make-Up
Young and Beautiful

1935
*Circus Shadows
**The Calling of Dan Matthews

1936
The Glory Trail

1937
**On Again — Off Again
Annapolis Salute
Danger Patrol

1938
Flirting with Fate

*The release date of this film is not known with certainty.

**Hovey's participation in these films is uncertain.

Hudson, Rochelle

Oklahoma City, Oklahoma, 1914/16–1972; 5'3"; brown hair, blue-gray eyes. *Wampas Baby Star:* 1931.

Rochelle Hudson was a sweet-faced ingenue whose innocent face often kept her from getting really meaty roles, although she had a respectable enough career in the early and mid–1930s. Later on, after the inevitable aging process had set in, she sometimes was cast as a "bad" girl. She had originally trained as a dancer with Ernest Belcher, stepfather of 1928 Wampas Baby Lina Basquette. Her first contract was at Fox but the studio dropped her option without ever putting her in a picture. At the time she was no more than 16 years old.

Hudson's chance came at RKO in 1931 when she won a small role in *Laugh and Get Rich*, the year she was named a Baby Star. Fox re-signed her in 1933, possibly as a "threat" to their ever-demanding star Janet Gaynor. Among the male stars with whom she appeared was Will Rogers, who took a great interest in her career, and they made four films together, beginning with *Doctor Bull*. (Studio publicity said that they were both born in Claremore, Oklahoma. Neither was, although they were both Sooners.) She also played Shirley Temple's older sister in *Curly Top*.

Probably Rochelle Hudson's most memorable role was that of W. C. Fields's daughter in the sound remake of *Poppy*. For a while Darryl F. Zanuck was said to be interested in promoting her career; apparently he saw more potential in Loretta Young (a 1929 Baby Star). In 1939 Hudson was signed by Columbia but was rarely cast in anything but "B" films. For most of the 1940s she was to be seen in the product of independent studios like PRC and Monogram.

Hudson went on to appear in over

Rochelle Hudson

60 films and was still onscreen as late as the mid–1960s, when she appeared with Joan Crawford in *Strait-Jacket*. She had made a brief "comeback" as James Dean's mother in one of the most-talked about pictures of the 1950s, *Rebel Without a Cause*. After the major part of her film career ended, she toured with mugging comic Bert Lahr in the play *Burlesque* and in the mid–'50s had a recurring role on the television series *That's My Boy*.

When Rochelle Hudson made her final films, her face had hardened and bore little resemblance to that of the delicately pretty leading lady of 30 years before. Four times divorced, she supposedly accompanied one of her spouses to Mexico during World War II and while there engaged in spying for the United States against Nazi interests in that country. Her husbands were Disney story editor Harold Thompson, sports writer Dick Hyland, C. K. Brust, Jr., a manufacturer and, last, Robert Mindell.

Hudson went into the real estate business after her show business career ended. To prove that no screen personality is ever *really* forgotten, she was "honored" with a song that was featured in an off–Broadway revue. It was called "The Rochelle Hudson Tango."

Filmography

1931
Laugh and Get Rich
Public Defender
Are These Our Children?
Fanny Foley Herself

1932
Penguin Pool Murder
Beyond the Rockies
Hell's Highway
Secrets of the French Police
The Savage Girl

1933
The Past of Mary Holmes
She Done Him Wrong
Lucky Devils
Scarlet River
Love Is Like That
Notorious but Nice
Wild Boys of the Road
Doctor Bull
Walls of Gold
Mr. Skitch

1934
Harold Teen
Such Women Are Dangerous
Bachelor Bait
Judge Priest
Imitation of Life
The Mighty Barnum
I've Been Around

1935
Life Begins at 40
Les Miserables
Curly Top
Way Down East
Show Them No Mercy!

1936
The Music Goes Round

Everybody's Old Man
The Country Beyond
Poppy
Reunion

1937

Woman-Wise
That I May Live
Born Reckless
She Had to Eat

1938

Rascals
Mr. Moto Takes a Chance
Storm Over Bengal

1939

Pride of the Navy
Pirates of the Skies
Smuggled Cargo
Missing Daughters
A Woman Is the Judge
Konga, the Wild Stallion

1940

Convicted Woman
Men Without Souls
Babies for Sale
Island of Doomed Men
Girls Under 21

1941

Meet Boston Blackie
The Officer and the Lady
The Stork Pays Off

1942

Rubber Racketeers

1943

Queen of Broadway

1947

Bush Pilot

1948

The Devil's Cargo

1949

Sky Liner

1955

Rebel Without a Cause

1964

Strait-Jacket
The Night Walker

1967

Dr. Terror's House of Horrors (U.K.)
*Broken Sabre

*This film cannot be identified with certainty and is perhaps a British production.

Hurlock, Madeline

Federalsburg, Maryland, 1899?–1989; 5'3½"; dark hair, brown eyes. *Wampas Baby Star: 1925.*

One of the most famous of the Mack Sennett bathing beauties, Madeline Hurlock began to work for him about 1923 and, unique among the Wampas Stars, remained for her entire career playing leads in one- and two-reelers. She claimed to have chosen to work at Sennett because it had been the training ground for many important stars, among them Gloria Swanson. Hurlock was credited with only a single feature and in that played a minor role. Possessed of large and liquid eyes, she became known for her "vamp" portrayals, especially those opposite the cross-eyed Ben Turpin. Previously she had appeared in stock and musical comedy.

Hurlock's film career ended in the late 1920s, apparently without a foray into talkies, but she obviously had more to offer than a pretty face. She married two of Broadway's premier playwrights of the 1920s and '30s, both Pulitzer Prize winners, Marc Connelly and then Robert E. Sherwood.

Filmography

Shorts

1923–1928?

When a Man's a Prince
The Prodigal Bridegroom
A Harem Knight
Flirty Four Flushers
A Small Town Princess
Duck Soup
Cured in the Excitement
The College Kiddo
For Sale a Bungalow
The Bull Fighter
Love in a Police Station
The Beach Club
Where Is My Wandering Boy This Evening?
Pitfalls of a Big City
Asleep at the Switch
The Dare-Devil
In Bad the Sailor
The Half-Back of Notre Dame
His New Mama
The First Hundred Years
The Luck of the Foolish
Three Foolish Weeks
Wandering Waistlines
Bull and Sand
The Cannon Ball Express
The Wild Goose Chaser
Water Wagons
Lions' Whiskers
The Marriage Circus
Raspberry Romance
Butter Fingers
Sneezing Beezers
From Rags to Britches
Whispering Whiskers
Trimmed in Gold
Circus Today
A Sea Dog's Tale

Feature

1926

Don Juan's Three Nights

Johnston, Julanne

(sometimes Julianne); Indianapolis, Indiana, 1900/06–1988; 5'6"; brown hair, gray eyes. *Wampas Baby Star:* 1924.

After performing as a dancer with the famous Ruth St. Denis and appearing in vaudeville and local theater, Julanne Johnston entered films in dancing bits. Her debut possibly came as an extra in Cecil DeMille's *Joan the Woman* in 1916. She eventually graduated to Fox comedies but was still primarily being seen as a dancer in movies until the early 1920s.

Johnston made a picturesque leading lady as the Princess in 1924's *The Thief of Bagdad,* starring Douglas Fairbanks. It was her breakout film and biggest success. Although she occasionally was starred thereafter (e.g., in 1926's *Dame Chance*), her career remained in a distinctly minor key. She is also reputed to have made some films in Europe in the 1920s.

By the end of the decade, Johnston's career had foundered. Her close friendship with Colleen Moore perhaps got her some later roles; in the late 1920s she supported that popular star in a few pictures. Although she was seen in a couple of prestigious talkies her roles were essentially bits. It was only in 1930's *Strictly Modern* that she had a substantial part in talkies.

Julanne Johnston married David Rust, an executive in an automobile accessory company, and retired to the life of a socialite in posh Grosse Pointe, Michigan. Two daughters and a son (who preceded her in death) were born of the marriage.

FILMOGRAPHY

(not including European films)

1919
Better Times

1920
Seeing It Through
Miss Hobbs
Fickle Women

1923
The Brass Bottle
Madness of Youth
Tea — With a Kick

1924
The Thief of Bagdad

1925
Big Pal

1926
Pleasures of the Rich
Aloma of the South Seas
Dame Chance
Twinkletoes

1927
Venus of Venice
Good Time Charley
Her Wild Oat

1928
The Whip Woman
Name the Woman
The Olympic Hero
Oh, Kay!

1929
Synthetic Sin
The Younger Generation
Prisoners

Smiling Irish Eyes
The Show of Shows
General Crack

1930
Strictly Modern
Golden Dawn
Madam Satan

1932
Stepping Sisters

1933
Midnight Club
Morning Glory

1934
The Scarlet Empress
Cleopatra

Joyce, Natalie

New York, New York or Virginia, 1902?–1992; 5'5"; black hair, brown eyes. *Wampas Baby Star:* 1925.

Natalie Joyce had performed in musical comedy prior to her screen appearances. Her feature career was brief — less than five years — and she also made two-reel comedies for Educational and Christie, where she supported comic Neal Burns. Her only starring films were "B" westerns with the likes of Tom Mix, Tom Tyler, Buck Jones and Bob Steele. In her other films she was usually down in the cast list, sometimes as a Spanish senorita, a portrayal no doubt aided by her brunette good looks. In this she resembled her cousin and fellow 1925 Wampas Baby, Olive Borden.

Although 1929 was her busiest year in features, seven of Joyce's nine films were silent. This may give a clue to the suitability of her voice or perhaps it was because many were quickie westerns, the last genre to find its "voice." In her two 1930 sound pictures her roles were negligible.

Natalie Joyce had a son.

Filmography

Shorts

1920s

Features

1927
Whispering Sage
The Circus Ace

1928
Daredevil's Reward
A Girl in Every Port
Through the Breakers

1929
Naughty Baby
Laughing at Death
Pals of the Prairie

Law of the Plains
The Man from Nevada
Sailor's Holiday
Times Square

1930
Cock o' the Walk
Midnight Daddies

Keener, Hazel

(She may also have performed under the name of Barbara Worth, although this is uncertain); Fairbury, Illinois, 1904–1979; 5'6"; brown hair, hazel eyes. *Wampas Baby Star:* 1924.

Hazel Keener started out in Midwestern stock companies and in 1921 won a beauty contest sponsored by the *Chicago Tribune*. At that time she was given the title of "Iowa's Most Beautiful Girl." She won another prize in 1923 when she was awarded the "Miss Hollywood" honors in Atlantic City. She also was dubbed "The Most Photographed Girl in the World," presumably because of the modeling career she pursued before briefly becoming Harry Langdon's co-star.

A former player in the Los Angeles theater, Keener's best known film was undoubtedly Harold Lloyd's 1925 classic *The Freshman*, in which she had a supporting role, but her most frequent co-star was popular cowboy Fred Thomson. Among their films together were *The Silent Stranger*, *Galloping Gallagher* and *The Dangerous Coward*. She also worked with Buck Jones.

Sporadically during the 1920s, and then in all of her pictures from 1929 to the mid–'30s, Hazel Keener may have used the name of Barbara Worth. If so, under that name she co-starred mainly in "B" westerns, often appearing with dog and horse "stars." Later, there were some small talkie roles under her real name up to the beginning of the 1950s. In later years she was reported to have become a minister in the Church of Religious Science.

Filmography

(as Hazel Keener)

Shorts

1920s

Features

1922
The Married Flapper

1923
The Brass Bottle
Tea — with a Kick

1924
The Mask of Lopez
North of Nevada

Galloping Gallagher
The Silent Stranger
His Forgotten Wife
The Dangerous Coward
The Fighting Sap
Empty Hands
Hard Hittin' Hamilton

1925
Ports of Call
Ten Days
Parisian Love
The Freshman

1926
Vanishing Hoofs

1927
The First Night
One Hour of Love
Whispering Sage
The Gingham Girl

1928
The Scarlet Arrow (serial)

1937
Wells Fargo

1938
Gateway

1940
I Love You Again
Untamed
That Gang of Mine

1941
Murder by Invitation

1943
So Proudly We Hail

1944
And Now Tomorrow
The Story of Dr. Wassell

1946
Undercurrent

1947
Killer at Large
The Farmer's Daughter

1948
A Double Life
Joan of Arc

1950
Caged
The Great Jewel Robber
The Milkman

1951
The Racket
*The Blue Veil

(as Barbara Worth?)

1923
An Old Sweetheart of Mine

1926
Broken Hearts of Hollywood

1927
The Prairie King
Fast and Furious
On Your Toes

1928
The Fearless Rider

1929
Bachelor's Club
Below the Deadline
Fury of the Wild
Plunging Hoofs
The Prince of Hearts

1931
Lightnin' Smith's Return

1934
The Fighting Trooper

1935
*Reckless
Men of Action
I Live My Life
Racing Luck

*Keener's participation in these films is uncertain.

Kent, Barbara

(Barbara Clowtman, Klowtman, Cloutman and other versions of the name); Gadsby, Alberta, 1906/07–; 4'11"–5'1½"; brown hair, blue eyes. *Wampas Baby Star:* 1927.

The round-faced and pretty Canadian girl who was to become Barbara Kent graduated from Hollywood High School and won the "Miss Hollywood" contest in 1925. She signed a five year contract with Universal later that year. The most prominent of her silent films were probably *The Drop Kick*, with Richard Barthelmess, and *Flesh and the Devil*, the sizzling melodrama co-starring John Gilbert and Greta Garbo. Her first sound appearance came in the 1928 part-talkie *Lonesome*, a poignant film that is now considered almost on a par with the silent classic *The Crowd*.

Kent soon was signed as Harold Lloyd's leading lady in his first two talkies, *Welcome Danger* (initially made as a silent, then partially reshot and released as a sound film) and *Feet First* the following year. As Lloyd's co-star she succeeded Wampas Baby Stars Jobyna Ralston (1923) and Ann Christy (1928). She was in turn succeeded by 1931 Baby Constance Cummings. Her busiest time in sound pictures was the first part of the 1930s, when she was occasionally top-billed. After 1935 she was seen only three more times onscreen in supporting roles.

Kent's first husband was Harry Edington, an agent, business manager and MGM associate producer.

NOTE: Kent is not to be confused with the English actress or the American scenario writer of the same name.

FILMOGRAPHY

1926
Prowlers of the Night
Flesh and the Devil

1927
No Man's Law
The Drop Kick
The Lone Eagle
The Small Bachelor

1928
That's My Daddy
Stop That Man
Modern Mothers
Lonesome

1929
The Shakedown
Welcome Danger

1930
Night Ride
Dumbbells in Ermine
What Men Want
Feet First

1931
Indiscreet
Chinatown After Dark
Freighters of Destiny
Grief Street

1932
Emma
Vanity Fair
Beauty Parlor
No Living Witness
Exposed
The Pride of the Legion
Self-Defense

1933
Oliver Twist
Her Forgotten Past
Marriage on Approval

1935
Swell-Head
Old Man Rhythm
Guard That Girl

1939
Blondie Meets the Boss

1941
Under Age

1942
The Fleet's In

Key, Kathleen

(Kathleen [?] "Kitty" Lanahan); Buffalo, New York, 1903–1954; 5'3"; brown hair, brown eyes. *Wampas Baby Star: 1923.*

Best remembered as Tirzah, the sister of Ben-Hur in the 1925 MGM epic of the same name, Kathleen Key was in such other major films as *The Four Horsemen of the Apocalypse* (a bit) and the 1924 version of *The Sea Hawk* with Milton Sills. Supposedly a descendant of Francis Scott Key, she was a stalwart in westerns, co-starring with such oater stars as Buck Jones, Tom Mix and Hoot Gibson. Earlier, after a few roles in American movies, she was reported to have made

Kathleen Key

New York in the later 1920s.

Whatever kind of career Key might have had in the talkies was ended after a well-publicized, and apparently physical, fight with Buster Keaton in his MGM dressing room. It may well have been a lover's spat, because rumor had it that she and the famous comic actor were more than just good friends. Keaton's version of the tiff was that she attacked him viciously after he refused her request for a loan of some $25,000.

Whatever the actual reason, its effects were final. She was in the cast of at least two talking pictures but in them she had the merest bits. In Mae West's *Klondike Annie*, for instance, she was a dance hall girl. In 1941 she was arrested for drunk driving and claimed she could not pay the fine because she was destitute and living on the handouts of friends and movie extra work.

about eight Australian pictures as well. Generally, her roles in American films were in support but she played a few leads in modest programmers. She also appeared on the stage in Los Angeles and

FILMOGRAPHY

American films

1921
The Rookie's Return
The Four Horsemen of the Apocalypse

1922
Where Is My Wandering Boy Tonight?
West of Chicago
Bells of San Juan
The Beautiful and Damned

1923
Hell's Hole
North of Hudson Bay
The Rendezvous
The Man from Brodney's
Reno

1924

The Trouble Shooter
The Sea Hawk
Revelation

1925

A Lover's Oath
Ben-Hur

1926

Under Western Skies
Money Talks
The Flaming Frontier
College Days
The Desert's Toll

1927

Hey! Hey! Cowboy
Irish Hearts

1928

Golf Widows

1929

The Phantom of the North

1930

*Sweeping Against the Winds

1935

Thunder in the Night

1936

Klondike Annie

*Key's appearance in this film is uncertain.

Kingston, Natalie

Vallejo or Sonoma, California, 1904/05–1991; 5'6"; brown hair, brown eyes. *Wampas Baby Star:* 1927.

A player in regional theater and a dancer with the Fanchon and Marco troupe and on the New York stage, Natalie Kingston claimed to be the great-granddaughter of General Vallejo, the first governor of Mexican California. She also claimed kinship with Count Herazthy, who introduced the wine grape to California.

Kingston's onscreen career began about 1924 with small roles in two-reelers at the Mack Sennett studio for $85 a week. She then advanced to leads with Harry Langdon, Ben Turpin and other stalwarts of the Sennett lot. Her stay at Sennett lasted for about a year and a half; during that time she may have been one of the famous Bathing Beauties.

In the later 1920s Kingston appeared in what may be her best-remembered role, as Jane in two serials based on the Tarzan character, *Tarzan the Mighty* and *Tarzan the Tiger*.

Kingston was married to a stock broker.

FILMOGRAPHY

Shorts

1923–26? 1930s?

The Daredevil
Yukon Jake
All Night Long
The Reel Virginian
Feet of Mud
Romeo and Juliet
His Marriage Wow
Remember When?
Lucky Stars
Boobs in the Woods
Soldier Man
*Plain Clothes
*Doctor's Orders

Features

1926

Wet Paint
Lost at Sea
Don Juan's Three Nights
Kid Boots
The Silent Lover

1927
The Night of Love
Love Makes 'Em Wild
His First Flame
Lost at the Front
Framed
Figures Don't Lie
The Harvester

1928
A Girl in Every Port
The Port of Missing Girls
Street Angel
Painted Post
Tarzan the Mighty (serial)

1929
River of Romance
Pirate of Panama (serial)
Tarzan the Tiger (serial)

1930
The Swellhead
Her Wedding Night

Under Texas Skies

1933
Forgotten
His Private Secretary
Only Yesterday

*The nature of these films and Kingston's appearance in them are uncertain.

Knapp, Evalyn

(Evelyn Knapp); Kansas City, Missouri, 1908–1981; 5'3"–5'4"; blonde hair, blue/gray eyes. *Wampas Baby Star*: 1932.

Starting out as a schoolteacher, Evalyn Knapp made it to Broadway after working in stock companies and tent shows. She was signed to make two-reelers, of which she made about two dozen, before attaining feature status with Warner Bros. In the early years her roles ranged from leading lady to support, and her leading men ran the gamut from supremely dignified George Arliss, "gangsters" Edward G. Robinson and James Cagney to anything but dignified Joe E. Brown. One of her claims to fame was that she was supposed to have possessed the smallest waist in show business — 21 inches.

Knapp's personal life did not always run as smoothly as her professional one. In 1931 she fell from a cliff while hiking and fractured her spine. For a while the injury was believed to have impaired her ability to walk and she was encased in a cast for several weeks. She was released by Warners in 1932.

Evalyn Knapp made only one serial, but it was one which bore the famous title *The Perils of Pauline*, Pearl White's famous chapterplay. It was reported that she won the part over 50 other actresses. During it she was once again injured

Evalyn Knapp

when her horse collided with another rider's. By this time she was freelancing. In some of her movies she did receive top billing but eventually her career petered out into westerns and melodramas for indies like Monogram, Chesterfield and Principal, and then into bit parts.

An announcement was made in the early '30s about Knapp's engagement to actor Donald Cook, but she married physician George Snyder, who may have attended her after her serious accident.

FILMOGRAPHY

Shorts

late 1920s?–1930s

Gentlemen of the Evening
Hard Boiled Hampton
Big Time Charlie
The Smooth Guy
Beach Babies
Haunted
The Master Sweeper
The Pet Shop
Taxi Talks
System
Wednesday at the Ritz
Chills and Fever
Keeping Company
The Tight Squeeze
All Stuck Up
Hollywood on Parade

Features

1930

Sinner's Holiday
River's End
Mother's Cry

1931

Smart Money
The Millionaire
Fifty Million Frenchmen
The Bargain
Side Show

1932

The Night Mayor
This Sporting Age
High Pressure
Fireman Save My Child
The Vanishing Frontier
The Strange Love of Molly Louvain
A Successful Calamity
Slightly Married
Big City Blues
Madame Racketeer

1933

Bachelor Mother
State Trooper
Air Hostess
Corruption
His Private Secretary
Police Car 17
Dance, Girl, Dance

1934

The Perils of Pauline (serial)
In Old Santa Fe
Speed Wings
A Man's Game

1935

One Frightened Night
Confidential
Ladies Crave Excitement

1936

Laughing Irish Eyes
Three of a Kind
Bulldog Edition

1937

*The Fire Trap

1938

Hawaiian Buckaroo
Rawhide
Wanted by the Police

1939

Mr. Smith Goes to Washington

1940

Girl in 313

1941

The Lone Wolf Takes a Chance
Roar of the Press

1943

Two Weeks to Live

*This film was probably made in 1935 but not in general release until 1937.

La Plante, Laura

(Laura La Plant?); St. Louis, Missouri, 1903/04–1996; 5'2"; brown hair (later blonde), blue-gray eyes. *Wampas Baby Star:* 1923.

Although she initially worked at Fox, Laura La Plante was Universal's biggest female star throughout much of the 1920s. Previously she had been an extra from the late teens and a player in one- and two-reel Christie comedies. Among the latter were some based on the "Bringing Up Father" ("Maggie and Jiggs") comic strip. She also appeared in serials. Her feature work remained mostly in comedy, although some of her roles called for little more than looking decorative or, in some cases, frightened. She did sometimes show dramatic acting ability in films such as the romantic drama *Smouldering Fires*.

La Plante's break came in the 1921 Charles Ray picture *The Old Swimmin' Hole*, when she still had her brunette locks. She did her share of "B" westerns with such heroes as Tom Mix and Hoot Gibson, and appeared in the popular Leather Pushers series with the English actor Reginald Denny, who was to be a frequent costar. Her trademark became her distinctively short, shingled now-blonde hair; latter-day film historians refer to her as the silents' Doris Day.

Sporting Youth, co-starring Denny, proved to be popular in 1924 and Universal elevated La Plante to stardom with *Excitement* in that same year. Her best-known film nowadays is probably the 1927 thriller *The Cat and the Canary*, directed by German Paul Leni, which set the tone for the numerous "dark old house" melodramas to come. (Another of their well-regarded horror films together was *The Last Warning*.) She also donned a dark wig to appear as Magnolia in the first version of the musical *Show Boat*, made mostly as a silent but with talking and singing sequences. It has been said that she was the first woman to be heard singing from the screen in a feature film, but this is uncertain.

At the height of her career La Plante was making some $3,500 weekly, but the coming of sound put an end to the major phase of her stardom. Her first all-talkie, *Hold Your Man*, came after a few part-talkies and it revealed that her voice was satisfactory, albeit not more than that. It is probable that Universal, like so many other studios, wanted to divest itself of high-priced stars and they released her in 1930. Before that she was the top billed actress in the musical melange *The King of Jazz*, but actually had almost nothing to do. In that year's *Captain of the Guard* the critics thought she was miscast.

After a handful of mostly mediocre sound efforts, Laura La Plante and her husband Irving Asher went to England where he was employed by Warner Bros. While there she did some theater, made an occasional film, and was in the news in 1935 by having to be rescued from a burning house. She returned to the screen for one film each in the 1940s and '50s, and made regional theater appearances as well as doing occasional stints on television. One of her co-stars in both silents and talkies, Edward Everett Horton, was onstage with her in the 1950s.

Later, La Plante lost her voice due to a condition called spastic dysphonia, but an operation restored it. She had been married first to director William Seiter, whom she divorced in a single day in Riga, Latvia. (He was later the spouse of 1924 Wampas Star Marian Nixon.) She and Asher had a daughter and son together.

Laura La Plante was one of several pairs of sisters to be named Wampas Baby Stars. Her sister Violet, using the stage name Violet Avon, attained Wampas status a year after she did but never came close to the fame of her sibling.

FILMOGRAPHY

Shorts

1919–1922?, 1930s

Four Fathers
Back from the Front
Jiggs in Society
Father's Close Shave
Jiggs and the Social Lion
Should Husbands Do Housework?
Old Dynamite
Brand of Courage
The Alarm
The Deputy's Double Cross
A Bottle Baby
Fighting Back
Matching Wits
The Trail of the Wolf
Desperation
The Call of Courage
A Treacherous Rival
Society Sailors
Taking Things Easy
The Big Ranger
Easy to Cop
Stout Hearts and Willing Hands
Lost in Limehouse

Features

1919

The Great Gamble (serial)

1920

"813" (serial)

1921

The Old Swimmin' Hole
Big Town Ideas
Big Town Round-Up
Play Square

1922

The Wall Flower
Perils of the Yukon (serial)
Around the World in 18 Days (serial)

1923

Dead Game
Burning Words
Shootin' for Love
Out of Luck
The Ramblin' Kid
Crooked Alley
The Thrill Chaser

1924

Sporting Youth
Ride for Your Life
Excitement
The Dangerous Blonde
Young Ideas
The Fast Worker
Butterfly
The Fatal Plunge (feature version of The Great Gamble)

1925

Smouldering Fires
Dangerous Innocence
The Teaser

1926

The Beautiful Cheat
Skinner's Dress Suit
The Midnight Sun
Poker Faces
Her Big Night
Butterflies in the Rain

1927

The Love Thrill
Beware of Widows
The Cat and the Canary
Silk Stockings

1928

Thanks for the Buggy Ride
Finders Keepers
Home James

1929

The Last Warning
Scandal
Show Boat
The Love Trap
Hold Your Man

1930

Captain of the Guard
The King of Jazz

1931

Lonely Wives
Meet the Wife
God's Gift to Women
Arizona
Men Are Like That
Sea Ghost

1933

Her Imaginary Lover (U.K.)

1934

The Girl in Possession (U.K.)
The Church Mouse (U.K.)

1935

Widow's Might (U.K.)
Man of the Moment (U.K.)

1946 or '47

Little Mister Jim

1957

Spring Reunion

Layton, Dorothy

(Dorothy Wannenwetsch); Virginia Beach, Virginia, or Cincinnati, Ohio, 1912–; 5'2"; blonde hair, blue eyes. *Wampas Baby Star:* 1932.

After regional stage experience, Dorothy Layton made some Hal Roach shorts as a member of his "stock" company. Her feature career was extremely brief, with apparently only two to her credit, one of which starred Laurel and Hardy. In both of them she had small roles. Afterward, she worked as a recreation director.

Layton was married to Howard Taylor, Jr.

FILMOGRAPHY

Shorts

early 1930s

Hollywood on Parade, no. 9
County Hospital
The Chimp
Chickens Come Home

Features

1932

Pack Up Your Troubles

1933

Pick-Up

Leahy, Margaret

England, 1902–1967; blonde hair, blue eyes. *Wampas Baby Star:* 1923.

Margaret Leahy came to notice after winning the Miss England beauty contest, in which she was said to have bested 80,000 (!) other entrants. She was one of only two Wampas Babies to have a credited role in but a single feature film (Eleanor Holm was the other). Her only known film appearance was as Buster Keaton's co-star in *Three Ages*.

Dubbed "The Girl with the Perfect Film Face," she was taken under the wing of the famous star Norma Talmadge, who apparently met Leahy while in England and made her a protégée. At the time Talmadge was Buster Keaton's sister-in-law, which no doubt explains Leahy's casting. Even with that powerful backing, however, she did not prosper in the cinema and eventually became an interior decorator.

Leahy is believed to have been married several times. Her death was a possible suicide.

FILMOGRAPHY

1923
Three Ages

Lee, Frances

(Merna Tibbetts); Eagle Grove, Iowa, 1908–; 5'; brown hair, blue eyes. *Wampas Baby Star:* 1927.

Starting out as a dancer in vaudeville, Frances Lee signed with the Christie studio in 1925 to work with diminutive comic Bobby Vernon. Among her pictures was the *Confessions of a Chorus Girl* series. Her roles in features were mostly in support, but she did co-star in a handful of films, the last being *These Thirty Years*, a 1934 semi-documentary film distributed by the Ford Motor Company.

Lee was married to Alex Bennett, the brother of Australian film actresses Enid and Marjorie Bennett.

FILMOGRAPHY

Shorts

1925–1930s
The Stronger Sex
Adam's Eve
Marching to Georgie
Down with Husbands
**The Tabasco Kid

Features

1927
Good as Gold

1928
The Little Snob
Chicken a la King

1929
The Carnation Kid
Divorce Made Easy
The Show of Shows

1933
Phantom Thunderbolt
Her Splendid Folly

1934
*These Thirty Years
Babbitt
Flirtation Walk

1935
Traveling Saleslady

*The exact release date of this film is not known with certainty.

**The exact nature of this film is uncertain, as is Lee's participation in it.

Lee, Gwen

(Gwendolyn Le Pinski or Lepinski); Hastings, Nebraska, 1904/05–1961; 5'7" (or possibly taller); blonde hair, blue eyes. *Wampas Baby Star:* 1928.

After modeling in an Omaha department store, doing regional musical theater and possibly movie extra work, Gwen Lee wound up at MGM where she would play the wisecracking best friend, golddigger or bad girl for the remainder of the silent years and beyond. The breakthrough role that led to her being signed by the studio was in *Lady of the Night*. Top supporting roles were perhaps the best that an actress of her stature (she was possibly the tallest of the Wampas Babies) and sharp features could hope for, although she did possess striking pale blue eyes.

Comparable to a "silent" Eve Arden in her characterizations, and having a persona similar to that of silent actress Lilyan Tashman, Lee's characters frequently had working-class names like Maizie, Dora, Mabel and Daisy. There were plans to star her in a series of comedies but they did not materialize. By the time talkies came her persona was well established, and she made an easy transition to sound, but after MGM released her in 1930 her career was never the same as a freelancer. She had appeared with all of MGM's leading ladies, including Joan Crawford, Greta Garbo and Norma Shearer.

In the early '30s Gwen Lee's mother filed a guardianship petition stating that the actress was unable to handle her own business affairs. In another negative bit of publicity she was sued for failure to pay for some clothing she had purchased. She continued to appear in movies, sometimes in very small roles in quickie productions, throughout most of the decade and in comedy shorts. By 1936 she was virtually a bit player in features but she did have a fair-sized role in her last known film in 1938.

Little is known about Lee's private life, although in 1929 she was rumored to be engaged to Paramount comic Jack Oakie.

FILMOGRAPHY

Shorts

Late 1930s

Boy, Oh Boy
Candid Cameramaniacs
A Night at the Movies

Features

1925

The Plastic Age
Lady of the Night
Pretty Ladies
His Secretary

1926

The Boy Friend
The Lone Wolf Returns
There You Are!
Upstage

1927

Women Love Diamonds
Heaven on Earth
Orchids and Ermine
Twelve Miles Out
Adam and Evil
After Midnight
Her Wild Oat

1928

Sharp Shooters
The Actress
Laugh, Clown, Laugh
Diamond Handcuffs
A Thief in the Dark
The Baby Cyclone
Show Girl
A Lady of Chance

1929

Lucky Boy

The Hollywood Revue of
   1929
The Man and the
   Moment
Fast Company
Untamed

1930

Chasing Rainbows
Lord Byron of Broadway
Free and Easy
Caught Short
Our Blushing Brides
Extravagance
Paid

1931

Inspiration
The Lawless Woman
Traveling Husbands
The Pagan Lady
West of Broadway
The Galloping Ghost
   (serial)

1932

Alias Mary Smith
From Broadway to
   Cheyenne
Midnight Morals
The Intruder

1933

The Warrior's Husband
Corruption
*Meet the Baron

1934

City Park
One in a Million

1935

$20 a Week

1936

Fury

1937

My Dear Miss Aldrich
Double Wedding

1938

Man-Proof
Mannequin
Paroled from the Big
   House

Lee's participation in this film is uncertain.

Lee, Lila

(Augusta Appel); New York, New York, 1901/1905 (at least one 1920s source gives 1895 as a birthdate)–1973; 5'5"–5'6"; black hair, brown eyes. *Wampas Baby Star: 1922.*

Pretty, apple-cheeked Lila Lee was named a Wampas Baby Star the same year she played her most famous role as the young and innocent wife of bullfighter Rudolph Valentino in *Blood and Sand*. Other of her prominent leading men were Wallace Reid, Roscoe "Fatty" Arbuckle, James Kirkwood and Thomas Meighan. She had made her first real mark playing a servant girl in Cecil B. DeMille's popular *Male and Female* in 1919. By that time she was already a veteran of the stage and the vaudeville circuit, where she was one of Gus Edwards's discoveries, known as "Cuddles."

Lee alternated between major and quickie films in the '20s and her career path accordingly went up and down, resulting in several announced "comebacks." Potential opportunities were also lost through bouts of frequently poor health, sometimes ascribed to tuberculosis but also possibly to alcoholism or other addiction. By the end of the decade she had reestablished her reputation, helped by her smooth speaking voice that eased the move into sound films.

For a year or two it seemed Lila Lee might be a major leading lady in talkies, but continuing poor health and indifferent roles doomed her to leads in quickies and supporting roles, sometimes small ones, in more important films. Her best sound role was in the remake of Lon Chaney's *The Unholy Three*; her announced lead in *Little Caesar* shortly thereafter was lost due to illness.

In 1936 a scandal in which Lee did not seem to be involved may have hastened the end of her career. She was a guest at the home of a wealthy socialite when another guest was murdered there. The killing was ascribed by the tabloid press to mob vengeance. The end of her Hollywood days did not finish her show business career; she appeared on the stage both on Broadway and in stock for many years thereafter.

In 1957 Lila Lee again came to the notice of film fans when she was the surprised guest on the popular *This Is Your Life* television program. She made news again the following year when she fell into a tub of scalding hot water and was seriously injured.

Lee's son was writer and actor James Kirkwood, Jr., from one of her three failed marriages, this one to matinee idol James Kirkwood, who was considerably older than she. "Junior"'s novel *There Must Be a Pony* has an actress character that is generally believed to be unflatteringly based on his mother. Her other marriages were to stockbrokers Jack Peine and John Murphy.

FILMOGRAPHY

1918
The Cruise of the Make-Believes
Such a Little Pirate

1919
Puppy Love
The Secret Garden
Rustling a Bride
Rose o' the River
A Daughter of the Wolf
The Heart of Youth
Male and Female
Hawthorne of the U.S.A.

1920
Terror Island
The Prince Chap
The Soul of Youth

1921
Midsummer Madness
The Charm School
The Easy Road
The-Dollar-a-Year Man
*If Women Only Knew

Crazy to Marry
Gasoline Gus
After the Show

1922
Rent Free
One Glorious Day
Is Matrimony a Failure?
The Dictator
Blood and Sand
The Ghost Breaker
Ebb Tide
Back Home and Broke

1923
The Ne'er-Do-Well
Homeward Bound
Hollywood (cameo)
Woman-Proof

1924
Love's Whirlpool
Wandering Husbands
Another Man's Wife

1925
Coming Through
The Midnight Girl
Old Home Week

1926
Broken Hearts
The New Klondike
Fascinating Youth (cameo)

1927
One Increasing Purpose
Million Dollar Mystery

1928
Top Sergeant Mulligan
The Man in Hobbles
You Can't Beat the Law
A Bit of Heaven
Thundergod
United States Smith
The Adorable Cheat
Black Butterflies
Just Married

The Little Wild Girl
The Black Pearl

1929

Queen of the Night Clubs
Honky Tonk
The Argyle Case
Drag
Flight
Dark Streets
The Sacred Flame
Love, Laugh and Live
The Show of Shows

1930

Second Wife
Double Crossroads
Murder Will Out
The Unholy Three
Those Who Dance
The Gorilla

1931

Misbehaving Ladies
Woman Hungry

1932

War Correspondent
Radio Patrol
Exposure
**The Unfortunate Bride
Unholy Love
The Night of June 13
False Faces
Iron Master
Officer 13
The Intruder

1933

Face in the Sky
Lone Cowboy

1934

Whirlpool
In Love with Life
I Can't Escape
Stand Up and Cheer

1935

Within the Rock (aka The Marriage Bargain)
The People's Enemy
Champagne for Breakfast

1936

The Ex-Mrs. Bradford
Country Gentleman

1937

Two Wise Maids
Nation Aflame

Lee's participation in this film is uncertain.

**A rerelease of the 1926 Broken Hearts *with added scenes and narration.*

Lincoln, Caryl

Oakland, California, 1908–1983; 5'4½"; red hair, brown eyes. *Wampas Baby Star:* 1929.

Caryl Lincoln apparently was a last-minute substitution as a Wampas Baby Star for actress Sharon Lynn(e), who had already been announced in the newspapers. In her first feature film, *Wolf Fangs*, she was the "co-star" to Thunder, a dog. She had previously appeared in about 15 shorts for Christie, Fox and Roach.

Lincoln's career did not much exceed that modest beginning. She appeared with another dog (named Ranger) the following year in *Tracked*. Among her human partners were Tom Mix, Tom Tyler, Tim McCoy and Buck Jones.

Although Caryl Lincoln had some leads in modest programmers, they were mostly quickie westerns. Her appearances in higher-grade material were limited to small roles and in her last talkies she played only bits. After her credited movie roles ended, she may have done extra work into the 1950s.

It can be speculated that Lincoln's nomination as a Wampas Baby was helped by the fact that she was married to George Brown, director of publicity for Columbia Studios. She was also wed at one time to Byron Stevens, and thus the sister-in-law of Barbara Stanwyck (née Stevens). She had a son.

FILMOGRAPHY

Shorts

1926–?
*At the Ridge

Features

1927
Wolf Fangs

1928
A Girl in Every Port
Hello Cheyenne
Wild West Romance
Tracked

1930
The Land of Missing Men

1931
The Spider
The Cyclone Kid
Quick Trigger Lee

1932
Tangled Fortunes
*Dancers in the Dark
Man from New Mexico
Thrill of Youth
Okay America
Back Street
The Lost Special (serial)

1933
Man of Action
War of the Range
Only Yesterday

1934
3 on a Honeymoon

*The Life of Vergie Winters
Charlie Chan's Courage
Elinor Norton
The Merry Widow

1944
Cover Girl
None Shall Escape

1947
Body and Soul

Caryl Lincoln

Golden Earrings

1949

That Wonderful Urge

1950

Cheaper by the Dozen
Mother Didn't Tell Me
The Jackpot

1951

Love Nest

*Lincoln's participation in these films is not known with certainty.

Logan, Jacqueline

San Antonio, Texas, 1901/02–1983; 5'5"; auburn hair, gray eyes. *Wampas Baby Star: 1922.*

Jacqueline Logan was supposedly a newspaper reporter and editor in Colorado prior to going into show business. One of the most beautiful of the silent actresses, she had also been a model and a dancer in the Ziegfeld Follies and other Broadway shows. Her screen career started innocuously enough in a Johnny Hines comedy short and progressed to leading roles in numerous films. She began to get top billing about 1923; her most famous role was undoubtedly that of Mary Magdalene in Cecil DeMille's *The King of Kings*.

Logan was a popular second-level star and counted among her leading men such silent picture luminaries as Milton Sills, Thomas Meighan, Ricardo Cortez, Richard Dix, William Powell, Lionel and John Barrymore and Lon Chaney. Her voice was apparently unsuitable for sound and she made few talkies. Her first part-talkie was 1928's *The River Woman*, and she starred in a couple in 1929, including one of the very earliest part-sound serials, *King of the Kongo*. That appearance in a serial was itself an ominous sign and her roles later in that year were little more than cameos.

After the failure of her talkie career, Logan journeyed to England where she appeared in one film and co-directed another, the short *Strictly Business* (1932). While there she made stage appearances; there were also New York theater performances slightly later.

Jacqueline Logan was three times married, one of her husbands having been William Winston. In later life she became known as an outspoken crusader for conservative political causes.

FILMOGRAPHY

Short

1921?

Features

1921

A Perfect Crime
White and Unmarried
The Fighting Lover
Molly O'
Fool's Paradise

1922

Gay and Devilish
Saved By Radio
A Tailor Made Man
Burning Sands
Ebb Tide
A Blind Bargain

1923

Java Head
Mr. Billings Spends His Dime
Sixty Cents an Hour
Salomy Jane
Hollywood

The Light That Failed

1924

Flaming Barriers
The Dawn of a Tomorrow
Code of the Sea
Dynamite Smith
The House of Youth
Manhattan

1925

A Man Must Live
The Sky Raider
Playing with Souls
If Marriage Fails
Peacock Feathers
Thank You
Wages for Wives
When the Door Opened

1926

The Outsider
White Mice
Out of the Storm
Tony Runs Wild
Footloose Widows

1927

One Hour of Love
The King of Kings
The Blood Ship
For Ladies Only
The Wise Wife

1928

The Leopard Lady
Midnight Madness
Broadway Daddies
The Cop

Power
Stocks and Blondes
The Charge of the Gauchos
The Look Out Girl
Nothing to Wear
Ships of the Night
The River Woman

1929

The Faker
Stark Mad
King of the Kongo (serial)
The Bachelor Girl
The Show of Shows
General Crack

1930

The Middle Watch (U.K.)

Long, Sally

(Sarah); Kansas City, Missouri, 1901–1987; 5'5"; black hair, hazel eyes. *Wampas Baby Star:* 1926.

Sally Long may not have been among the prominent Babies of her year, but she was certainly their equal in beauty. A featured performer in the Ziegfeld Follies and Broadway, she had been publicized as the "Love Insurance Girl." This was supposedly because Ziegfeld had insured her for $100,000 against falling in love and leaving his shows. It was a nice story anyhow.

Long also was dubbed the "Most Photographed Girl in the World," a dubiously-proven title that others were also to claim. Her very first film was a Lloyd Hamilton comedy and the rest of her oeuvre consisted largely of westerns, with such oater heroes as Buck Jones and Hoot Gibson. There was also a serial with screen Tarzan Elmo Lincoln. In her non-westerns she usually had supporting roles.

Most of Sally Long's movie activity came in the year she was named a Baby Star and by the next year it had already begun petering out. She returned in 1930 for her sole talkie, in which she was far down the cast list. Her first husband was Leo Tuhey (or Tuey) with whom she had two children. The composer Jean Schwartz, best known for his song standard "Chinatown, My Chinatown," was her second; after his death she remarried.

Filmography

1924
His Darker Self

1926
Fifth Avenue
The Fighting Buckaroo
The Man in the Saddle
Going the Limit
The Border Whirlwind

1927
King of the Jungle (serial)
The Kid Sister
The Thrill Seekers
When Danger Calls

1930
Cock o' the Walk

Sally Long

Lorraine, Louise

(also known as Louise Fortune) (Louise Escovar); San Francisco, California, 1901–1981; 5'1"–5'2"; auburn or brown hair, brown eyes. *Wampas Baby Star:* 1922.

Louise Lorraine was probably Universal's major female serial queen of the early 1920s. Starting out as an extra, she graduated to two-reel Century comedies in which she co-starred with one of the more unusual Charlie Chaplin imitators, the Chinese comic actor Chai Hong. It was in those days that she was called Louise Fortune.

Lorraine appeared in a series of two-reel westerns at Universal; in her serials a sometime leading man was screen Tarzan Elmo Lincoln. She was to play Jane to his Tarzan in *The Adventures of Tarzan*. Her chapterplays were interspersed with features, in some of which she was top billed.

Among Louise Lorraine's other costars were cowboy actors Hoot Gibson and Art Acord, with whom she appeared several times and who was her husband for three years in the '20s. She worked at MGM as a supporting player during the later 1920s, while remaining a leading lady with other studios.

Lorraine also remained a heroine in some of the earliest sound serials. Otherwise, her crossover into the talkies was brief, consisting of a few "B" westerns, and her last appearance was in a short. After her departure from motion pictures, she married businessman Chester Hubbard and had two children.

Filmography

Shorts

1910s–1920s, 1932

*Sea Shore Shapes
*Get-Rich-Quick Peggy
*Sweetie
*Little Red Riding Hood
The Trigger Trail
The Midnight Raiders
The Knockout Man
The Outlaw
Double Crossed
The Valley of the Rogues
True Blue
Moonlight and Cactus

Features

1920

Elmo the Fearless (serial)
The Flaming Disc (serial)

1921

The Adventures of Tarzan (serial)
The Fire Eater

1922

With Stanley in Africa (serial)
Headin' West
Up in the Air About Mary
The Radio King (serial)
The Altar Stairs

1923

The Gentleman from America
The Oregon Trail (serial)
McGuire of the Mounted

1925

The Great Circus Mystery (serial)
The Verdict
The Wild Girl
Three in Exile
Borrowed Finery
Pals

1926

The Blue Streak
The Silent Guardian
Exit Smiling
The Silent Flyer (serial)
The Stolen Ranch

1927

Winners of the Wilderness
Hard Fists
Rookies
The Frontiersman
Legionnaires in Paris

1928

Baby Mine
Circus Rookies
Chinatown Charlie
The Wright Idea
Shadows of the Night

1929

The Diamond Master (serial)
A Final Reckoning (serial)

1930

The Mounted Stranger
The Jade Box (serial)
The Lightning Express (serial)
Near the Rainbow's End
Beyond the Law

The nature of these films and Lorraine's participation in them is uncertain.

Louise, Anita

(Anita Louise Fremault); New York, New York, 1915/17–1970; 5'3½"; blonde hair, blue eyes. *Wampas Baby Star:* 1931.

Well known in the years before her death as a Hollywood hostess and indefatigable party-giver, Anita Louise literally grew up in show business. As Anita Fremault, the swanlike delicate blonde beauty appeared on Broadway as a child (about 1923) and began playing small roles in New York City-made movies the next year. Before her days as an actress she had posed for commercial artists and was known as the "Post Toasties Girl." She was also an accomplished pianist who won several prizes for her playing.

Louise dropped her real surname professionally in 1929 and began the major part of her career, sometimes playing the leading woman as a girl. (One of her last silent roles was that of Greta Garbo's character as a child in *A Woman of Affairs*.) Sometimes top-billed, she alternated at first between leading and supporting parts.

One of the youngest starlets to be named a Wampas Baby, Anita Louise worked primarily at Warner Bros. and then Columbia. She became an important enough star to be considered for leads in major pictures like *A Bill of Divorcement, Little Women, Gone with the Wind* and *The Adventures of Robin Hood*. (The latter two went to Olivia De Havilland.) Many of the parts she did get were also in top "A" productions.

Louise's most prestigious motion pictures came in the mid–1930s and were often costume dramas. Especially remembered is her portrayal of Titania in the all-star version of *A Midsummer Night's Dream*. Because of her physical appearance, which seemed fragile, she was rarely given meaty dramatic roles and she said that she never played against her looks. "Ethereal" was a word often used to describe her.

By the time of Anita Louise's first marriage, to 20th Century–Fox head Buddy Adler, her star was beginning to wane somewhat. With Adler she had a son and a daughter and was widowed some 20 years later. She later married wealthy entrepreneur Henry Berger and it was with him that her reputation as a hostess flourished.

A veteran of radio and stock, in the 1950s Louise turned to television, winning a recurring role on *My Friend Flicka*, as well as leads in live television. Later she was seen on such detective shows as *Mannix*. When she and Berger resided in New York during the 1960s much was made of their friendship with Richard and Pat Nixon. The president-to-be shared her birthday.

FILMOGRAPHY

1924
The Sixth Commandment
Lend Me Your Husband

1925
The Street of Forgotten Men

1926
The Untamed Lady

1927
The Music Master

1928
A Woman of Affairs

1929
The Spirit of Youth
Square Shoulders
Wonder of Women
Four Devils
The Marriage Playground

1930
What a Man
The Florodora Girl
Just Like Heaven
The Third Alarm

1931
The Great Meadow
Millie
Everything's Rosie
The Woman Between
Heaven on Earth

1932
The Phantom of Crestwood

1933
Our Betters

1934
Cross Streets
Are We Civilized?
I Give My Love
Most Precious Thing in Life
Judge Priest
Madame Du Barry

The Firebird
Bachelor of Arts

1935
Lady Tubbs
Here's to Romance
A Midsummer Night's Dream
Personal Maid's Secret

1936
The Story of Louis Pasteur
Brides Are Like That
Anthony Adverse
Stage Struck

1937
Green Light
Call It a Day
The Go Getter
That Certain Woman
First Lady
Tovarich

1938
My Bill
Marie Antoinette
The Sisters
Going Places

1939
The Little Princess
The Gorilla
These Glamour Girls
Main Street Lawyer
Reno
Hero for a Day

1940
Wagons Westward
Glamour for Sale
The Villain Still Pursued Her

1941
Two in a Taxi
Harmon of Michigan

1943
Dangerous Blondes

1944
Nine Girls
Casanova Brown

1945
Love Letters
The Fighting Guardsman

1946
Shadowed
The Bandit of Sherwood Forest
The Devil's Mask
Personality Kid

1947
Blondie's Big Moment
Bulldog Drummond at Bay

1952
Retreat, Hell!

Love, Bessie

(Juanita Horton); Midland, Texas, 1898–1986; 5'; brown hair (later blonde), brown eyes. *Wampas Baby Star:* 1922.

Bessie Love resided in Los Angeles as a teenager and was supposedly discovered by D. W. Griffith himself. After extra work her first role of note was that of the Bride of Cana in the Jesus storyline of *Intolerance*. By the time she was dubbed a Baby Star she already had a solid career behind her, but it was one that was filled with numerous peaks and valleys. However, her overall 65 years in show business certainly awarded her one of the longest sustained careers of any of the Babies.

During the teens Love made many pictures for Triangle, where her penchant was playing waiflike heroines in romantic drama. Like Mary Pickford, her diminutive size and youthful face made it easy for her to play child parts well into her teen years and beyond. Early co-stars included such disparate actors as William S. Hart, Douglas Fairbanks and Sessue Hayakawa. *A Sister of Six* was one of her earliest starring efforts. Late in the 1910s she was signed by Vitagraph but for much of the time she freelanced, one of the factors in the rise and fall of her career.

Love always earned praise for her naturalistic acting style; a French critic said as early as 1919: "The way Bessie Love expressed gaiety, innocence and sensitivity was sheer poetry." She was versatile in various genres, e.g., tear-jerkers like *Soul-Fire* (with Richard Barthelmess) and *Forget-Me-Not*, *The Lost World*, a science fiction thriller, the drug melodrama *Human Wreckage*, the homespun comedy-drama *Lovey Mary* and the sophisticated comedy *The King on Main Street*. Many other of her pictures were cheaply made and distinctly unmemorable.

"The Little Brown Wren," as Love was fondly nicknamed, worked steadily throughout the silent era and was supposedly the first actress to perform the Charleston (silently) onscreen. In 1928 she even toured with a dance troupe and made her stage debut, possibly in a road company of *Burlesque*. It was as a blonde that she staged her biggest comeback of all in the wildly successful 1929 MGM musical *The Broadway Melody*. Thus, she perhaps could be termed the first female musical comedy star. The film won the Academy Award as the best picture of the year, and Love was nominated for Best Actress. As one of two sisters in love with the same man (the other was top-billed 1929 Wampas Baby Anita Page) she showed her all-around versatility. Her enhanced status at MGM was clear when she was assigned several song and dance numbers in *The Hollywood Revue of 1929*.

The advent of the talkies was the means of reviving Bessie Love's career; one review called her "the best femme principal in talkers." As had happened in her silent career, she could not sustain her newly found popularity. Poor musicals, of which the public was tiring, and cheesy melodramas sent her career in a downward spin again. In 1935 she went to England, presumably on a holiday, and stayed for most of the remainder of her life, eventually becoming a British subject. She starred in occasional films there beginning in the mid-'30s, but mainly was seen on the stage (*Death of a Salesman*, *The Glass Menagerie*, a musical version of *Gone with the Wind*) and on television. She also wrote a play based on her own experiences as an expatriate.

As an appealingly cute old lady, Love played cameo and character roles in British and American pictures and was still performing in them as late as 1983. She tried her hand at many things, even working as a studio technician in England during World War II. She also produced an autobiography, *To Holly-*

wood — With Love, that was published by an English firm. She had been married to William Hawks, brother of director Howard Hawks, and had one daughter.

FILMOGRAPHY

Shorts
1910s–1920s, 1940s
The Mystery of the Leaping Fish
The Adventures of Prince Courageous (a series among which were The Little Knight, The Little Defender and The Little Reformer)
*The American
Amateur Night
The Swell(ed) Head
*Screen Snapshots no. 8
London Scrapbook

Features
1915
The Birth of a Nation

1916
The Flying Torpedo
Intolerance
The Aryan
Acquitted
Reggie Mixes In
The Good Bad Man
Stranded
Hell-to-Pay Austin
A Sister of Six

1917
Cheerful Givers
Nina, the Flower Girl
A Daughter of the Poor
The Sawdust Ring
Polly Ann
The Heiress at Coffee Dan's
Wee Lady Betty

1918
Her Great Adventure
How Could You, Caroline?
A Little Sister of Everybody
The Dawn of Understanding

1919
The Enchanted Barn
The Wishing Ring Man
Carolyn of the Corners
A Yankee Princess
Cupid Forecloses
The Little Boss
Over the Garden Wall
A Fighting Colleen

1920
Pegeen
The Midlanders
Bonny May

1921
Penny of Top Hill Trail
The Swamp
The Sea Lion

1922
The Vermilion Pencil
Forget-Me-Not
Bulldog Courage
Night Life in Hollywood
The Village Blacksmith
Deserted at the Altar

1923
Three Who Paid
Souls for Sale (cameo)
Purple Dawn
Mary of the Movies
The Ghost Patrol
St. Elmo
Human Wreckage
The Eternal Three
Slave of Desire
Gentle Julia

1924
Torment
Those Who Dance
The Woman on the Jury
Dynamite Smith
The Silent Watcher
Sundown
Tongues of Flame

1925
The Lost World
The King on Main Street
Soul-Fire
A Son of His Father
New Brooms

1926
The Song and Dance Man
Lovey Mary
Meet the Prince
Young April
Going Crooked

1927
Rubber Tires
Dress Parade
A Harp in Hock

1928
The Matinee Idol

Sally of the Scandals
Has Anybody Here Seen Kelly?

1929
The Broadway Melody
The Idle Rich
The Girl in the Show
The Hollywood Revue of 1929

1930
Chasing Rainbows
Conspiracy
They Learned About Women
Good News
See America Thirst

1931
Morals for Women

1936
I Live Again (U.K.)

1941
Atlantic Ferry (U.K.)

1945
Journey Together (U.K.)

1950
The Magic Box (U.K.)

1951
No Highway in the Sky

1953
The Weak and the Wicked (U.K.)

1954
Beau Brummell
The Barefoot Contessa

1955
Touch and Go (U.K.)

1957
The Story of Esther Costello

1958
Next to No Time (U.K.)
Nowhere to Go (U.K.)

1959
Too Young to Love (U.K.)

1961
Loss of Innocence (U.K.)
The Roman Spring of Mrs. Stone

1963
Children of the Damned (U.K.)
The Wild Affair (U.K.)

1964
I Think They Call Him John (U.K.)

1965
Promise Her Anything

1967
I'll Never Forget What's 'Is Name (U.K.)
Battle Beneath the Earth (U.K.)

1968
Isadora

1969
On Her Majesty's Secret Service

1971
Sunday, Bloody Sunday (U.K.)
Catlow

1973
*Pollyanna (TV)

1974
Mousey (U.K.)
Vampyres (U.K.)

1975
Gulliver's Travels (U.K.)

1976
The Ritz

1980
Edward and Mrs. Simpson (TV)

1981
Lady Chatterley's Lover (U.K.)
Ragtime
Reds

1983
The Hunger

*Love's participation in these films is uncertain.

Lund, Lucille

Buckley, Washington, 1913–; 5'4½"; blonde hair, blue eyes. *Wampas Baby Star:* 1934.

Lucille Lund appeared with some regional stock companies and was the winner of an All-American Girl contest in which she supposedly competed against 1,200 of her fellow college co-eds. Her victory brought her to Hollywood, and in her first film she was actually billed as "Lucille Lund the All-American Girl." She went on to a modest career in which she alternated leads in "B" westerns (*Fighting Through, Range Warfare, Timber War*) and melodramas (*Prison Shadows*) with smaller, sometimes minuscule, roles.

In several of her later films Lund had such bits as a "cigarette girl," "show girl," "bridesmaid," "receptionist," and "girl in the bar." She also appeared in a Canadian production and comedy shorts with Charley Chase, The Three Stooges and others toward the end of her career.

Lund was married to radio producer Kenneth Higgins.

Filmography

Shorts
1937–1939?
Calling All Doctors
The Big Squirt
Three Dumb Clucks
The Awful Goof
Healthy, Wealthy and Dumb

Features
1933
Saturday's Millions
Horseplay

1934
Pirate Treasure (serial)
The Black Cat
*Fighting Through
Kiss and Make-Up
Young and Beautiful

1935
Folies Bergeres de Paris
*Range Warfare
Broadway Melody of 1936
Timber War

1936
Don't Get Personal
Rio Grande Romance
Panic on the Air
Prison Shadows
The Cowboy Star

1937
*Blake of Scotland Yard (serial and feature version)
Criminals of the Air
The Devil Is Driving
A Fight to the Finish
Girls Can Play
What Price Vengeance (aka Vengeance) (Canada)
It Happened in Hollywood

1938
Start Cheering
There's That Woman Again

The exact release dates of these films are uncertain.

Lynch, Helen

(also Helene); Billings, Montana, 1900/04–1965; 5'3½"; blonde hair, blue/green eyes. *Wampas Baby Star:* 1924

Helen Lynch was the winner of a beauty contest sponsored by a Billings newspaper and it helped her enter the cinema about 1917 as an extra. She remained before the camera until 1940. For most of her career she was mired in secondary parts but occasionally starred in such "B" efforts as *Avenging Fangs* (as sidekick to the dog Sandow), *Bustin' Through* and *The Arizona Sweepstakes*. She also appeared in Jimmy Aubrey comedy shorts for Vitagraph.

In the later '20s Lynch made the transition from small independent studios to the majors but her roles in prestigious pictures like *Underworld*, *The Singing Fool* (her first talkie) and *In Old Arizona* remained secondary ones. Talkies rather firmly put an end to anything but bit roles; in her first known sound film she played a telephone operator. She also did theater work in Los Angeles.

Lynch was married to actor Caroll Nye, who died the same year as his wife.

FILMOGRAPHY

Shorts
19–?

Features

1920
Honor Bound

1921
What's a Wife Worth?
The House That Jazz Built
Live and Let Live
My Lady Friends

1922
Midnight
Glass Houses
Fools First
The Dangerous Age
The Other Side
Minnie

1923
Cause for Divorce
The Eternal Three
The Meanest Man in the World

1924
The Valley of Hate
In High Gear
American Manners
On Probation
The Tomboy

1925
Smouldering Fires
Oh, Doctor!
Fifth Avenue Models
Bustin' Through
After Marriage
Smilin' at Trouble
Three Weeks in Paris

1926
The Arizona Sweepstakes
My Own Pal
General Custer at Little Big Horn
Speeding Through
Tom and His Pals

1927
Cheaters
Avenging Fangs
Underworld
Husbands for Rent

1928
Love and Learn
The Showdown
Thundergod
Ladies of the Mob
The Singing Fool
Romance of the Underworld
Stolen Love

1929
In Old Arizona
Speakeasy
Why Bring That Up?

1930
City Girl (silent version)

1933
Emergency Call

1934
Elmer and Elsie

1936	1940
Hell-Ship Morgan	Women Without Names

McAlister, Mary

(also McAllister); Salt Lake City, Utah, or Los Angeles, California, 1909/12–1991; 5'1"–5'2"; blonde hair, brown eyes. *Wampas Baby Star:* 1927.

After playing a little boy in her initial film appearance, Mary McAlister became one of the very first popular child stars of the cinema. She had already been onscreen at least ten years when dubbed a Baby Star and was also a veteran of the stage. She may have made her first movie as early as 1915, perhaps at New York's Biograph studios, and later was an Essanay player sometimes billed as "Little Mary."

McAlister, familiarly known as Billie, made the transition to adult film roles with seeming ease, and from 1925 to the end of the silent career often received co-star billing. In the late 1920s she was named on at least one list as being among the best ten film stars of the year. Talkies were a different matter; her two roles were negligible. She went back on the stage in the early 1930s.

McAlister was married to businessman Robert Brigham.

FILMOGRAPHY

Shorts

1910s

Borrowed Sunshine
The Little Missionary
Where Is My Mother?
The Uneven Road
The Little White Girl
The Bride of Fancy
Whosoever Shall Offend
Do Children Count?

Features

1917

Little Shoes
On Trial
Pants
Young Mother Hubbard
The Kill-Joy
Sadie Goes to Heaven

1920

Half a Chance

1923

Ashes of Vengeance

1924

The Measure of a Man

1925

A Roaring Adventure
The Boomerang
The Red Rider
The Ace of Spades (serial)

1926

The Sap
One Minute to Play
The Waning Sex
The Man in the Shadow

1927

The Midnight Watch
Fire and Steel
Singed

1928

Wickedness Preferred
The Devil's Skipper
Into No Man's Land
Loves of an Actress

1930

On the Level
Madam Satan

McConnell, Gladys

Oklahoma City, Oklahoma, 1907–1979; 5'5½"; blonde hair, blue eyes. *Wampas Baby Star:* 1927.

Although she made some features, Gladys McConnell's fame, such as it was, came as a serial heroine in the last days of the silents. She also had co-star billing in two of Harry Langdon's final starring comedies, *Three's a Crowd* (in the year of her Wampas selection) and *The Chaser*. By that time, however, Langdon had passed his prime. Among her other leading men were Buck Jones and Ken Maynard, with whom she made her sole talkie.

McConnell was married twice, the first time to Arthur Hagerman, an official of the Wampas organization. It could be assumed that this did not hinder her naming as a Baby Star.

Filmography

Shorts

His Big Minute

Features

1926
A Trip to Chinatown
The Flying Horseman
The Midnight Kiss

1927
Marriage
Riding to Fame
Three's a Crowd

1928
The Chaser
The Bullet Mark
The Code of the Scarlet
The Perfect Crime
The Glorious Trail
The Tiger's Shadow (serial)

1929
Cheyenne
The Fire Detective (serial)

1930
The Woman Who Was Forgotten
Parade of the West

McGuire, Kathryn

(sometimes Maguire); Peoria, Illinois, 1897/1904–1978; 5'4"; brown hair (sometimes blonde), green eyes. *Wampas Baby Star:* 1922.

Although Kathryn McGuire perhaps did not make quite the success that most of her "class" did *during* her career, she may well be seen on modern-day screens longer than any of them. Her roles as the unhelpful heroine in two of Buster Keaton's best-remembered comedies, *The Navigator* and *Sherlock, Jr.*, have assured her of a secure place in cinema history. The rising appreciation of Keaton's genius has given her lasting visibility as well.

A former dancer, McGuire had an unmistakable "map of Ireland" on her face and she was reputedly called the prettiest blonde in Hollywood by famous poster artist James Montgomery Flagg. Supposedly discovered by director Thomas Ince while dancing in a Hollywood High School program, she began her screen career working with Mack Sennett in comedy shorts at $45 a week in 1920. She also was the foil of Lupino Lane, the diminutive, acrobatic English star of Educational two-reelers.

Kathryn McGuire's feature career

Kathryn McGuire

started in 1921 in supporting roles with comedians such as Charlie Murray, Ben Turpin and James Finlayson. She also played in many melodramas and had the dubious distinction of appearing with one of the first canine stars, Strongheart, in 1921's *The Silent Call*.

As a co-star in Clara Kimball Young's *Woman of Bronze*, McGuire played a model who posed for a sculpture of "Victory." This gave rise to the story that she was the model for Columbia Pictures' logo, the lady holding a torch, but this is probably untrue. By 1925 she was increasingly seen in action melodramas and westerns. In the latter she played the leading lady to such oater stars as Hoot Gibson, Jack Hoxie and Roy Stewart. Among her non-comic, non-western and non-canine co-stars were Rod La Rocque, Richard Talmadge, Cullen Landis and William Haines.

The prestige of Kathryn McGuire's films took a decided step up with appearances in the Colleen Moore starrers, *Naughty but Nice* and *Lilac Time*, the second a popular World War I melodrama. But the size of her roles had diminished and the casting of McGuire may have been due to friendship with Moore, who was known to be generous in casting her friends. There was to be one more film with Moore, *Synthetic Sin*, in 1929.

In that transitional year McGuire went back to such silent westerns as *The Big Diamond Robbery* with Tom Mix. It was in another '29 shoot-em-up, *The Long, Long Trail*, that she made her talkie debut. In her only other talkie and final film, *The Lost Zeppelin*, she had but a brief scene, although receiving important billing. A contemporary review said "she had but one speech but got a laugh on it."

Besides her status as a pioneer Baby, Kathryn McGuire had yet another Wampas connection. She was the widow of George Landy, public relations man and literary agent, who also happened to be last president of Wampas. The couple had one daughter.

Filmography

Shorts

1920

Features

1921

Home Talent
Bucking the Line
The Silent Call
Playing with Fire

1922

The Crossroads of New York

1923

The Flame of Life

The Woman of Bronze
The Shriek of Araby
The Printer's Devil
The Love Pirate

1924

Phantom Justice
Sherlock, Jr.
The Navigator

1925

Tearing Through
Dashing Thru
Easy Going Gordon
The Gold Hunters
Two-Fisted Jones

1926

The Thrill Hunter
Buffalo Bill on the U.P. Trail
Midnight Faces
Somebody's Mother
Stacked Cards
Davy Crockett at the Fall of the Alamo
Mystery Pilot (serial)

1927

Naughty but Nice
The Girl in the Pullman

1928

Lilac Time

1929

Synthetic Sin
Children of the Ritz
The Big Diamond Robbery
The Border Wildcat
The Long, Long Trail
The Lost Zeppelin

Mackaill, Dorothy

Hull, England, 1903–1990; 5'4½"; blonde hair, green eyes. *Wampas Baby Star:* 1924.

A veteran of Flo Ziegfeld's "Midnight Follies" and trained as a dancer on the London stage, Dorothy Mackaill became a popular silent star with First National. Among her co-stars were Richard Barthelmess, who appeared with her several times, notably in *Shore Leave,* and Jack Mulhall, with whom she was seen in a dozen pictures, mainly romantic comedies. Before that she had been noticed as Johnny Hines's leading lady in that comic actor's popular Torchy series.

Stardom came for Mackaill in *Chickie,* and she alternated between comedy and drama for the rest of the silent era, usually playing aggressive, even hard-boiled characters. Among her other hits in the 1920s were *Joanna* (which introduced 1926 Wampas Baby Dolores Del Rio to the cinema), and the part-talkie *The Barker.* When sound arrived it was revealed that she had lost almost all of her Yorkshire accent. Now working at Warner Bros., which had absorbed First National, she was unhappy with her roles and she sued the studio.

The success of the film *Office Wife* made them realize her ongoing popularity and Mackaill was signed to a new contract. Although she ultimately was not able to contend with the new crop of talkie stars she did appear with two actors who were to be among the biggest, Clark Gable (in *No Man of Her Own*) and Humphrey Bogart (in *Love Affair*). (The former film also marked the only onscreen pairing of Gable with his future wife Carole Lombard.)

By 1934, Dot Mackaill was making pictures for indie studios like PDC/Majestic, First Division and Liberty. After her Hollywood career ended, she made her final appearance in a British film and in 1955 retired to Hawaii where the Royal Hawaiian Hotel became her permanent residence. While there she did some guest shots on the television program *Hawaii Five-O.*

Mackaill was married three times, the first time being to European director Lothar Mendes and then to Neil Miller, a singer of Hawaiian melodies with whom she had done a vaudeville tour. She was last wed to orchid grower Harold Patterson.

FILMOGRAPHY

Shorts

early 1920s

Eclair Comedies (France)
Torchy's Millions
Torchy Mixes In
Torchy's Promotion

Features

1921

The Face at the Window (U.K.)
French film (title unknown)
Bits of Life

1922

Isle of Doubt
A Woman's Woman
The Streets of New York
The Inner Man

1923

Mighty Lak' a Rose
The Broken Violin
The Fighting Blade
The Fair Cheat
His Children's Children
Twenty-One

1924

The Next Corner
What Shall I Do?
The Man Who Came Back
The Painted Lady
The Mine with the Iron Door

1925

The Bridge of Sighs
One Year to Live
Chickie
The Making of O'Malley
Shore Leave
Joanna

1926

The Dancer of Paris
Ranson's Folly
Subway Sadie
Just Another Blonde

1927

The Lunatic at Large
Convoy
Smile, Brother, Smile
The Crystal Cup
Man Crazy

1928

Ladies Night in a Turkish Bath
Lady Be Good
Waterfront
The Whip
The Barker

1929

Children of the Ritz
His Captive Woman
Two Weeks Off
Hard to Get
The Great Divide
The Love Racket

1930

Strictly Modern
The Flirting Widow
The Office Wife
Man Trouble
Bright Lights

1931

Once a Sinner
Kept Husbands
Party Husband
Their Mad Moment
The Reckless Hour
Safe in Hell

1932

Love Affair
No Man of Her Own

1933

Curtain at Eight
Neighbor's Wives
The Chief
Picture Brides

1934

Cheaters

1937

Bulldog Drummond at Bay (U.K.)

Mallory, Patricia

("Boots"); New Orleans, Louisiana, 1913?–1958; 5'6"–5'7"; blonde hair, blue-gray eyes. *Wampas Baby Star:* 1932.

A versatile performer who was playing in a girl's band at the age of 12, Patricia Mallory, better known as "Boots," advanced to vaudeville and thence to Broadway in the George White Scandals and the Ziegfeld Follies. She signed with Fox in 1932, the year of her Wampas designation. The following year was her busiest, perhaps an example of a Wampas Baby career boost. She asked to be released from her contract in a dispute over casting; Monogram and RKO were among the studios for which she later worked.

Mallory's major screen opportunity came when she was selected by Erich von Stroheim to star in what he hoped would be his talkie comeback as a director. The finished product — and his final American directorial work — was originally called *Walking Down Broadway*. The production was plagued by the same problems that had marred most of von Stroheim's silent pictures and the studio partially reshot and reedited it. The truncated result, now called *Hello, Sister!*, suffered a quick death at the box office.

Mallory, who made occasional news for transgressions such as drunk driving, was first wed to William Cagney (brother of screen tough guy James), the father of her twins. Actor Charles Bennett had previously been her common-law husband; she garnered some publicity when she sought to shed him via divorce proceedings. Her last spouse, who survived her, was British movie star Herbert Marshall.

Filmography

Short

1933
Hollywood on Parade, no. 9

Features

1932
Handle with Care

1933
Humanity
Hello, Sister!
The Wolf Dog (serial)
*My Weakness
The Big Race
Carnival Lady

1934
Sing Sing Nights

1935
Powdersmoke Range

1937
Here's Flash Casey

1938
Swiss Miss

*Mallory's participation in this film is uncertain.

Marion, Edna

(Edna Hannam); Chicago, Illinois, 1906/08–1957; 5'1"; blonde hair, gray eyes. *Wampas Baby Star:* 1926.

A vaudeville veteran, from about 1925 Edna Marion was an established comedienne in Stern Brothers comedies and then rose a notch to appear at Christie and Educational studios. She was one of Charley Chase's leading ladies, and Laurel and Hardy were also to be co-stars. She had her own comedy series as well.

Marion's feature career was fairly minimal and the coming of sound effectively ended it. In her first talkie in 1929 she was billed merely as the "Neighbor's wife." Her sole lead in talking pictures came in the 1930 "B" oater *Romance of the West*, which starred Jack Perrin.

Marion was wed to a stockbroker named Paxon and later married a Mr. Naisbett.

Filmography

Shorts

1925?–

A Haunted Heiress
The Sting of Stings
Assistant Wives
The Lighter That Failed
Aching Youths
Busy Lizzie
Giddy Gobblers
Her Daily Dozen
My Baby Doll
Powdered Chickens
Putting on Airs
Puzzled by Crosswords
Dangerous Peach
Flying Elephants
Sugar Daddies
From Soup to Nuts
Should Married Men Go Home?
Limousine Love

Features

1925

The Desert's Price

1926

The Still Alarm
The Call of the Wilderness
Readin', 'Ritin, 'Rithmetic

1927

For Ladies Only

1928

Sinner's Parade

1929

Skinner Steps Out

1930

Romance of the West
Today

1931

*Murders in the Rue Morgue

*Marion's participation in this film is uncertain.

Marlowe, June

(Gisela Goetten); St. Cloud, Minnesota, 1903/07–1984; 5'1½"; brown hair, brown eyes. *Wampas Baby Star:* 1925.

Pert June Marlowe got her start working in a Lloyd Hamilton comedy and had bits in the "Fighting Blood" series in the mid–1920s. She also appeared in two-reelers with comics Harry Langdon and Charley Chase. Her major studio during the decade was Warner Bros., and like some other Wampas Babies she furnished the feminine appeal in Rin-Tin-Tin movies. In fact she probably was his most frequent female "co-star," always dangerous work with the ill-tempered German Shepherd. Among their films together were *The Night Cry*, *Below the Line* and *Clash of the Wolves*.

Marlowe seemed to specialize in such roles. Not only did she appear with Rinty, but also in two pictures with the dog Silverstreak. In addition, she worked with the top-billed horse Black King in *Riddle Ranch*, her last '30s feature. Occasionally top-billed herself, toward the end of the silent era she signed on with Universal. Probably because of her German heritage, the studio sent her to Germany where she appeared in films and on the radio. When she returned to America the sound revolution was in full effect and her voice was unimpressive.

In June Marlowe's first full-length talking picture, *Pardon Me*, she appeared in but a single scene with only a few lines. Her greatest recognition in the talkies came for her role as Miss Crabtree, the ever-patient teacher, in several "Our Gang" comedy shorts. She is also reputed to have made films in Argentina.

Marlowe was married to businessman Rodney Sprigg.

June Marlowe

FILMOGRAPHY

Shorts

1920s–1930s

Teacher's Pet
School's Out
Love Business
Little Daddy
Shiver My Timbers
Readin' and Writin'
Fast Work

Features

1924

When a Man's a Man
The Tenth Woman
Find Your Man
A Lost Lady

1925

The Man Without a Conscience
Tracked in the Snow Country
The Wife Who Wasn't Wanted
Below the Line
Clash of the Wolves
The Pleasure Buyers

1926

The Night Cry
Don Juan
The Old Soak
Fangs of Justice

1927

The Fourth Commandment
The Life of Riley
On the Stroke of Twelve
Wild Beauty

1928

Alias the Deacon
Their Hour
Branded Man
The Foreign Legion
The Grip of the Yukon
Free Lips
Code of the Air

1929?

Die Dame Jewellen Hast (Germany)
Fallen Angels (Germany)
The House of Glass (Germany)

1930

The Lone Defender (serial)

1931

Pardon Us
Bote en Bote (Spanish version of Pardon Us)

1932

The Devil on Deck

1934

The Lone Defender (feature version of the 1930 serial)

1935

Riddle Ranch

1947

Slave Girl

Marsh, Joan

(also known as Dorothy Rosher) (Nancy Rosher); Porterville, California, 1914–2000; 5'1½"; blonde hair, blue eyes.

The daughter of Mary Pickford's longtime cameraman Charles Rosher, Joan Marsh may have made some bit appearances as a nine-month-old baby. She also reportedly made movies with Harry Houdini and Charlie Chaplin. Her juvenile career was ended by about the age of seven but she was back as a teenager (if her birth year is accurate) with a contract from Universal. One of her studios was MGM, where she supported Greta Garbo in two films.

Marsh — no relation to fellow 1931 Wampas Baby Marian Marsh — was top-billed in a very few films like *Rainbow Over Broadway* and *What Becomes of the Children?*, made for minor studios. In most of her pictures she had substantial roles, but also was seen in supporting roles in prestigious films. She made some comedy shorts for Mack Sennett, and with her three-octave voice also sang on the radio in the mid–1930s. She usually played somewhat brassy characters, like reporters, on the screen.

Joan Marsh's last "A" picture was the Bob Hope–Bing Crosby starrer *Road to Zanzibar* in 1941. She went to Monogram thereafter where she co-starred in a couple of Bowery Boys quickies. It was in one of their knockabout comedies that she ended her screen career.

Reputedly a great-granddaughter of President Rutherford B. Hayes, Marsh was married at least twice, the first time to screenwriter Charles Belden. Her second husband was Captain John Morrill. After her film days were over, she became a businesswoman.

FILMOGRAPHY

Shorts

1930s

The Leather Pushers (series)

Features

(as Dorothy Rosher)

1917

How Could You, Jean?
Women's Weapons

1920

Young Mrs. Winthrop
Thou Art the Man

(as Joan Marsh)

1930

All Quiet on the Western Front
The Little Accident

1931

Inspiration
Dance, Fools, Dance
A Tailor Made Man
Three Girls Lost
Meet the Wife
Shipmates
Politics
Maker of Men

1932

Are You Listening?
The Wet Parade
Bachelor's Affairs

1933

Daring Daughters
High Gear
It's Great to Be Alive
The Man Who Dared: An Imaginative Biography
Three Cornered Moon
*Take a Chance
Speed Demon
Rainbow Over Broadway

1934

You're Telling Me!
Many Happy Returns
We're Rich Again

1935

Champagne for Breakfast
Anna Karenina

1936

Dancing Feet
Brilliant Marriage

What Becomes of the Children?

1937

Hot Water
Life Begins in College
Charlie Chan on Broadway

1938

The Lady Objects

1939

Idiot's Delight
Fast and Loose

1941

Road to Zanzibar

1942

The Man in the Trunk
Police Bullets

1943

Keep 'Em Slugging
Mr. Muggs Steps Out
Secret Service in Darkest Africa (serial)

1944

Follow the Leader

Marsh's appearance in this film is uncertain.

Marsh, Marian

(also known as Marilyn Morgan) (Violet Krauth); Trinidad, West Indies, 1913–; 5'2"; blonde hair, gray or hazel eyes. *Wampas Baby Star:* 1931.

The sister of film actress Jean(ne) Morgan — but no relation to fellow 1931 Wampas Baby Joan Marsh — former Hollywood High Schooler Marian Marsh had lightning strike the year she was dubbed a Baby Star. The would-be dancer was selected by John Barrymore to play the leading role of Trilby in *Svengali*, in which he played the title character. Almost totally inexperienced before the camera except for a couple of bits under the name of Marilyn Morgan, she scored a success as the singer in thrall to the mesmerist.

The speculation was that Marsh's selection may have been due to Barrymore's (or Jack Warner's) feeling that she resembled Dolores Costello, Barrymore's wife at the time. The perfervid melodrama (and semi-horror film) was a success for several reasons, perhaps one being the brief flash of nudity shown by Marsh as an artist's model. She later revealed (no pun intended) that it was a body double. The picture's box-office grosses led to her re-teaming with Barrymore in *The Mad Genius*.

It was also reported that Marsh had caught the eye of none other than Charlie Chaplin and was considered, if not actually tested, for the lead in his 1931 classic *City Lights*. (He had grown disenchanted with the performance of Virginia Cherrill but she is in the completed film.)

Marian Marsh made a long string of comedy shorts with character actor James Gleason, and appeared with distinguished co-stars like Edward G. Robinson, Richard Barthelmess, James Cagney, William Powell and Boris Karloff. Her career rarely lived up to its propitious beginnings, however, and when she was on her way downhill she worked for the Poverty Row studio Monogram. In the mid–'30s she made two films in England and one in Switzerland. She may have made some films as late as the 1950s, including a short that was her final picture appearance.

Marsh was known for her melodious voice, which she used to advantage on the stage in Los Angeles stock companies and perhaps elsewhere. She also supposedly was the first Honorary Mayor of Hollywood. Divorced at least twice previously, once from mining promoter Albert Scott, and the mother of two daughters, she was widowed by aviation pioneer Clifford Henderson.

Filmography

Shorts

1933?, 1959?

Features

(as Marilyn Morgan)

1930

Hells Angels
Whoopee!

(as Marian Marsh)

1931

Svengali
Five Star Final
The Road to Singapore
The Mad Genius

1932

Under 18
Alias the Doctor
Beauty and the Boss
Strange Justice
The Sport Parade

1933

Daring Daughters
The Eleventh Commandment
Over a Garden Wall (U.K.)
Love at Second Sight (U.K.)
The Lost Son (aka The Prodigal Son) (Switzerland)
Notorious but Nice
A Man of Sentiment

1934

I Like It That Way
A Girl of the Limberlost

1935

In Spite of Danger
The Black Room
Unknown Woman

Crime and Punishment

1936

Lady of Secrets
Counterfeit
The Man Who Lived Twice
*Theodora Goes Wild
Come Closer, Folks

1937

When's Your Birthday?
The Great Gambini
Saturday's Heroes
Youth on Parole

1938

Prison Nurse
A Desperate Adventure

1939

Missing Daughters

1940

Prison Camp (aka Fugitive from a Prison Camp)

1941

Gentleman from Dixie
Murder by Invitation

1942

House of Errors

1950s

?

*Marsh's appearance in this film is uncertain.

Mehaffey, Blanche

(also known as Joan Alden and Janet Morgan); Cincinnati, Ohio, 1906/07–1968; 5'2"–5'3"; red hair, gray-blue eyes. *Wampas Baby Star:* 1924.

With the delicate coloring and features of an Irish colleen, Blanche Mehaffey was a Ziegfeld Follies girl in 1923. She began making films the next year, when she was named a Baby Star, and remained a leading lady well into the 1930s. Presumably, when her career flagged she briefly appeared under the names of Joan Alden and Janet Morgan.

Emerging from obscurity in 1948 about ten years after she had made her last movies, Mehaffey sued to prevent her films from being shown on television. She did not prevail and the case may well have set a precedent for what could be televised in those early days of the new medium.

Blanche Mehaffey was married to George Hansen (or Hanson), a big game hunter, and then to producer Ralph Like.

FILMOGRAPHY

(as Blanche Mehaffey)

Shorts

1924–1930s

The Haunted Honeymoon
Pirate Party on Catalina Island
Powder and Smoke

Features

1924

The Battling Orioles
The White Sheep

1925

His People
A Woman of the World

1926

The Texas Streak
The Runaway Express
Take It from Me

1927

The Silent Rider
The Denver Dude
The Princess from Hoboken
The Tired Business Man
Finnegan's Ball

1928
The Air Mail Pilot
Marlie the Killer

1929
Smilin' Guns

1931
Sunrise Trail
Riders of the North
Dugan of the Badlands
Is There Justice?
Dancing Dynamite
The White Renegade
Mounted Fury
The Mystery Trooper (serial)
The Sky Spider
Soul of the Slums

1932
Sally of the Subway
Dynamite Denny
Alias Mary Smith
Passport to Paradise

1935
*Border Guns
The Silent Code
*Devil Monster
*North of Arizona
*Wildcat Saunders

1938
Held for Ransom
*The Wages of Sin

(as Joan Alden)

1928
Call of the Heart

(as Janet Morgan)

1935
The Cowboy and the Bandit
The Outlaw Tamer

*The release dates of these films are not known with certainty.

Meredith, Joan

(Catherine Jelks); Hot Springs, Arkansas, 1905/07–1980; 5'. *Wampas Baby Star:* 1925.

Joan Meredith's entrée into films was a Los Angeles beauty contest. She had but a single co-starring role, in the 1926 western *King of the Saddle* opposite Bill Cody. Her entire career lasted but a scant year or so after her Wampas designation.

The niece of a former governor of Alabama, Meredith was married to Harry Kiener.

Filmography

1925
Blue Blood
The Perfect Clown

1926
The Count of Luxembourg
The Fighting Boob
King of the Saddle
The Truthful Sex

Meredith, Lu Ann

(also Lu-Anne); Dallas, Texas, 1914/15–; 5'3"; blonde hair, blue eyes. *Wampas Baby Star:* 1934.

Dancing was a strong influence in Lu Ann Meredith's background as a member of the Fanchon and Marco troupe and the Fannie Brice Revue, the latter supposedly when she was 13. She also appeared in the 1931 version of the Ziegfeld Follies and was a cast member of the Broadway musical *Fifty Million Frenchmen*. It is no surprise that her first picture appearance was as a dancer in *George White's Scandals*.

Although she was selected as a potential star by no less a personage than Harold Lloyd and signed to a Mascot contract at $125 per week, Meredith had small parts in only a handful of American motion pictures. Two were those in which most of the 1934 Babies appeared, *Kiss and Make-Up* and *Young and Beautiful*. In her final U.S. film she was merely the "girl in the swimming pool." She went to England and appeared in some films there, one co-starring with comic Stanley Lupino. In the mid–1930s she danced in Paris.

Meredith was married to John Fitz-Gerald and was the mother of two daughters.

FILMOGRAPHY

1934
George White's Scandals
Whirlpool
Kiss and Make-Up
Young and Beautiful

1935
Night Life of the Gods

1936
Ball at Savoy (U.K.)
Sporting Love (U.K.)

1937
Sing as You Swing (U.K.)

Miller, Patsy Ruth

(Patricia Miller); St. Louis, Missouri, 1904–1995; 5'1½"; brown hair (sometimes auburn?), brown eyes. *Wampas Baby Star:* 1922.

Patsy Ruth Miller had the brunette looks which enabled her to convincingly play Esmeralda, the Gypsy girl, in her best-remembered film, *The Hunchback of Notre Dame*, starring Lon Chaney. She supposedly got her start when the famous Russian actress Alla Nazimova met her and arranged a screen test. They became fast friends and the result was a small role in that actress's eccentric version of *Camille*. She was named a Baby Star a year prior to her first success, as the object of Charles Ray's ardor in *The Girl I Loved*.

Miller had a certain flair for comedy and went on to a busy and respectable if not major career in the silents, alternating light and dramatic roles, and co-starring with such contemporaries as Richard Barthelmess, Warner Baxter, William S. Hart, Tom Mix, Glenn Tryon, Hoot Gibson and Monte Blue. She was often top-billed after signing with Warner Bros. about 1925 and soon appeared in one of her best films, Ernst Lubitsch's sophisticated comedy *So This Is Paris*. Her first talkie, *The Fall of Eve*, was also a comedy; it had been preceded by another of her popular films, *Marriage by Contract*.

After a handful of talkies into the very early 1930s, including several with comedy actor Edward Everett Horton, she left the screen. She later claimed it was voluntary, but by then her output was much reduced and her career had seemed to be waning. She returned 20 years later, as a lark, for a bit in 1951's *Quebec*, and was even rumored to be considering a comeback in the late 1970s. In 1982 the feisty ex-Baby filed a $2,000,000 suit against the publishing firm of Knopf and other defendants, contending that a book had stated she was an alcoholic.

Patsy Ruth Miller appeared in regional theater in the late 1920s and '30s and displayed yet another talent, writing. She published some short stories in the 1930s as well as the novel *That Flannigan Girl*. A later play, *The Windy Hill*, was produced and she wrote the book for a Broadway musical. In the 1980s her autobiography, *My Hollywood*, appeared in combination with the shooting script of *The Hunchback of Notre Dame*.

In her personal life Miller had an adventurous bent, and learned how to fly. She also lived abroad for several years in the 1930s. In later years, she was generous in sharing her memories with interviewers but expressed some regret that she was remembered largely for her role in *Hunchback*. Dubbed "The Most Engaged Girl in Hollywood" in the 1920s, she married three times: director Tay Garnett, screenwriter John Lee Mahin, and finally businessman Effingham S. Deans. She had one adopted son.

FILMOGRAPHY

1921
Camille
The Sheik

1922
Handle with Care
Where Is My Wandering Boy Tonight?
Watch Your Step
The Fighting Streak
For Big Stakes
Trimmed
Fortune's Mask
Remembrance
Omar the Tentmaker

1923
The Girl I Loved
Souls for Sale (cameo)
The Hunchback of Notre Dame
The Drivin' Fool

1924
Name the Man
The Yankee Consul
Singer Jim McKee
My Man
Daughters of Today
The Breaking Point
Fools in the Dark
A Self-Made Failure
Girls Men Forget
The Wise Virgin
The Breath of Scandal
The Girl on the Stairs
Those Who Judge

1925
Back to Life
Her Husband's Secret
Head Winds
Lorraine of the Lions
Red Hot Tires
Rose of the World
Hogan's Alley

1926
The Fighting Edge
The King of the Turf
Hell-Bent fer Heaven
Oh, What a Nurse!
So This Is Paris
Why Girls Go Back Home
Broken Hearts of Hollywood
Private Izzy Murphy
The White Black Sheep

1927
Wolf's Clothing
What Every Girl Should Know
The First Auto
Painting the Town
Shanghaied
Once and Forever
A Hero for a Night
South Sea Love

1928	**1929**	**1930**
Red Riders of Canada	The Fall of Eve	Wide Open
The Tragedy of Youth	The Hottentot	Last of the Lone Wolf
We Americans	Twin Beds	
Hot Heels	Whispering Winds	**1931**
Beautiful but Dumb	The Sap	Lonely Wives
Marriage by Contract	So Long, Letty	Night Beat
The Gate Crasher	The Aviator	
Tropical Nights	The Show of Shows	**1951**
		Quebec

Moore, Colleen

(Kathleen Morrison); Port Huron, Michigan, 1900/03–1988; 5'3"–5'4"; auburn hair, one brown eye, one blue (they both photographed dark on film). *Wampas Baby Star:* 1922.

Little in Colleen Moore's early film career indicated that she would be the very symbol of the "Jazz Age" in the 1920s, dubbed that by no less a personage than novelist F. Scott Fitzgerald. Legend has it that she was discovered by D. W. Griffith but this is apparently untrue, although her first picture may have starred Griffith leading man Robert Harron. Helpful connections had gotten Moore her first chance in the movies; uncle Walter Howey was the influential editor of the *Chicago Examiner*. She received a six-month contract, possibly at the Fine Arts studio, and was a minor lead from 1917 with such stars as Tom Mix, Charles Ray, Sessue Hayakawa and John Barrymore. She also did two-reel comedies for Christie.

When Moore was selected as a Wampas Baby Star, she was still a relative unknown although she already had been making movies for some five years. That was to change the following year with her second First National picture *Flaming Youth*. Suddenly, she was the very symbol of the archetypal flapper. According to Fitzgerald: "I was the spark that lit up flaming youth, Colleen Moore was the torch." In the flapper films her persona was that of a girl who may have seemed to be wild but was really an innocent underneath her paint.

The studio's natural inclination was to keep providing Colleen Moore with similar roles, but she feared stereotyping and occasionally held out for dramas like *So Big*, in which she proved herself a sensitive actress. She also seemed to specialize in silent versions of popular Broadway musicals. With her distinctive Dutch boy bobbed hair, she remained a major star at First National for the remainder of the decade, even though she broke her back on one location.

Moore was the number one box office star in 1926 and '27, thanks to such films as *Irene* and *Ella Cinders*. Although she was earning $12,500 per week at her prime she staged a walkout from the studio over dissatisfaction with her films. She was wooed back with the promise of better vehicles, the World War I drama *Lilac Time* (co-starring Gary Cooper) being one. A popular song, "Jeannine,

I Dream of You in Lilac Time," based on her character, came from the picture.

As an important star, Colleen Moore took voice lessons from two of the top voice teachers, the character actresses Constance Collier and Laura Hope Crews. She made two talkies in 1929, the first of which, the plodding *Smiling Irish Eyes*, was not particularly successful. She essayed an Irish brogue throughout. Her follow-up picture *Footlights and Fools* was somewhat better but did little to establish her as a sound star. She again used an accent, French this time, ostensibly to show her versatility with dialogue.

There then ensued a long hiatus for reasons both personal (a disintegrating marriage) and professional (lack of success of her first two vehicles). During this time a new crop of stars replaced Moore in the public's heart. She was not professionally inactive, however, performing in regional theater and a play which was Broadway bound but did not arrive there. One Los Angeles play did result in renewed interest by the studios and she was signed by MGM.

The studio loaned Colleen Moore out almost immediately, but it was fortunately for what turned out to be her best talkie — and possibly best picture part — *The Power and the Glory*, costarring Spencer Tracy. Although the film did not find its audience, possibly due to a narrative device called "narratage" that scrambled the story's chronology and confused the public, it has become somewhat of a respected classic. Her ensuing sound films, while competent, did not reestablish her and some critics sniped at her playing characters that were too young for her.

In the mid–1930s Moore undertook the construction of a fabulous doll house in the form of a castle and furnished it accordingly. When completed it weighed all of a ton and cost more than $400,000, an enormous sum in those Depression days. She toured the country with it to raise money for children's charities and also wrote a book about it. An extremely wealthy woman, she wrote another book entitled *How Women Can Make Money in the Stock Market*; a popular autobiography, *Silent Star*, appeared in 1968.

Colleen Moore had a rocky first marriage to press agent John McCormick, later head of production at her studio. Her second marriage was to New York stockbroker Albert Scott and her third to another broker, wealthy Chicagoan Homer Hargrave, with whom she resided in the Windy City for many years. After his death she was wed a fourth time, to Paul Maginot, the man who had built her central California ranch home. Over the years she had also maintained a romantic relationship with director King Vidor.

Filmography

Shorts

1920s

A Roman Scandal
Her Bridal Nightmare

Features

1917

Bad Boy
An Old Fashioned Young Man
Hands Up!
The Savage

1918

A Hoosier Romance

Little Orphant [sic] Annie

1919
The Busher
The Wilderness Trail
The Man in the Moonlight
The Egg Crate Wallop
Common Property

1920
The Cyclone
The Devil's Claim
So Long, Letty
When Dawn Came
Dinty

1921
The Sky Pilot
The Lotus Eater
His Nibs
Broken Hearts of Broadway

1922
Come On Over
The Wall Flower
Affinities
Forsaking All Others
Broken Chains
The Ninety and Nine

1923
Look Your Best
Slippy McGee
The Nth Commandment
April Showers
Broken Hearts of Hollywood
The Huntress
Flaming Youth

1924
Through the Dark
Painted People
The Perfect Flapper
Flirting with Love
So Big

1925
Sally
The Desert Flower
We Moderns

1926
Irene
Ella Cinders
It Must Be Love
Twinkletoes

1927
Orchids and Ermine
Naughty but Nice
Her Wild Oat

1928
Happiness Ahead
Oh, Kay!
Lilac Time

1929
Synthetic Sin
Why Be Good?
Smiling Irish Eyes
Footlights and Fools

1933
The Power and the Glory

1934
Success at Any Price
Social Register
The Scarlet Letter

Mori, Toshia

(also known as Toshiye Mori, Toshia Mori Jung, Shia Jung and possibly Toni Mori) (Toshia Ichioka); Kyoto, Japan, 1913–1995; 5'; black hair, brown eyes. *Wampas Baby Star:* 1932.

Coming to America from Japan at the age of ten, Toshia Mori studied dancing and joined a Los Angeles ballet troupe. She basically had been an extra in American films when she returned to her native country in 1931 to appear in a couple of Japanese movies in which she danced as a featured player. Supposedly a protégée of Mary Pickford, and the only ethnic Asian actress to be selected for Wampas Stardom, she was not the first choice of her studio the year she was nominated. She moved up from an alternate position when one of the original starlets, Lillian Miles, declined the honor.

Supposedly discovered by director Frank Capra while working in a curio shop or as a hotel cigarette girl (the stories vary), Mori was a pretty, round-faced actress who wore her hair in distinctive bangs. Like most "oriental" actors of the time, her (type)casting was mainly in pictures that had an ambiance of the forbidden East, however ersatz. Her best role was in *The Bitter Tea of General Yen*, an improbable but interesting Capra melodrama. (The title character, a Chinese warlord, was played by the Swedish actor Nils Asther.)

A couple of times, Toshia Mori played the obligatory girlfriend of Charlie Chan's "number one son" (Keye Luke). Although her career ultimately proved to be an undistinguished one, she had more visibility than most Asian-American actresses, perhaps a credit to her Wampas designation. At the conclusion of her movie career, she worked as an editorial assistant with Robert Ripley of *Believe It or Not* fame. She was married.

FILMOGRAPHY

(as Toshiye Ichioka)

1927

Streets of Shanghai

(as Toshia Mori)

1931

*Reaching for the Moon

1932

The Hatchet Man
Roar of the Dragon
The Secrets of Wu Sin

1933

The Bitter Tea of General Yen

Blondie Johnson

1935

George White's 1935 Scandals
Chinatown Squad
East of Java

1937

Charlie Chan on Broadway

(as Shia Jung)

1936

Charlie Chan at the Circus

1939

Port of Hate

(as Toni Mori)

1933

Fury of the Jungle

(as Toshia Mori Jung)

1934

The Painted Veil

*Mori's participation in this film is uncertain.

Morley, Karen

(Mildred Linton); Ottumwa, Iowa, 1910–; 5'4"; brown hair (sometimes blonde), hazel eyes. *Wampas Baby Star:* 1931.

Undeniably one of the more talented actresses to come out of the Wampas Baby Star selection, Karen Morley was previously a Los Angeles theater player. An extra from about 1929, she began as a featured player at MGM, appearing in her first role with Greta Garbo. Legend has it that she was discovered when she spoke unwittingly into a live microphone during a break in the shooting of *Inspiration*.

Morley claimed not to have been awed by the imperious Garbo and that seemed to be in keeping with her temperament. The most outstanding trait she evinced throughout her acting career was a natural dignity and aura of calm. Although not as conventionally pretty as many Hollywood starlets, she had a beautifully modulated husky voice and was a convincingly romantic leading lady, more than holding her own with co-stars such as John Barrymore. She remained at MGM until 1934. There is some speculation that the studio believed she considered herself *too* good an actress and was, therefore, too independent. Her release resulted in a freelance career that did little to sustain stardom.

Offscreen, Morley was a left-wing activist among whose activities was the founding of the Screen Actors Guild. This did not endear her to the conservative Republican studio heads, but she remained undeterred. As time went on, her movie career was irretrievably damaged by her political activism and the unadmitted blacklist that existed in the late 1940s and much of the '50s. However she did appear on the stage, playing her last Broadway role in 1952.

Whether or not she was actually a member of the Communist Party, Karen Morley refused to answer questions in 1951 before the House Un-American Activities Committee. (It did not help her cause when she averred that the Soviet Union was not a dictatorship.) She refused to name names but former movie colleagues of hers had no such scruples and she *was* named, and accused of having Party meetings in her home.

Although Morley's film career ended, her political involvement did not. She ran for the Lieutenant Governorship of New York State in 1954 on the American Labor Party ticket and, not unexpectedly, lost. She was married at least twice. Her first husband was European director Charles Vidor; another was the actor Lloyd Gough, himself a victim of the blacklist. She had one son.

FILMOGRAPHY

1931

Inspiration
Strangers May Marry
Never the Twain Shall Meet
Daybreak
High Stakes
Politics
The Cuban Love Song
The Sin of Madelon Claudet
Mata Hari

1932

Arsene Lupin
Are You Listening?
Scarface
Man About Town
The Washington Masquerade
Downstairs
The Phantom of Crestwood
The Mask of Fu Manchu
Flesh

1933

Gabriel Over the White House
Dinner at Eight

1934

Crime Doctor
Straight Is the Way
Our Daily Bread
Wednesday's Child

1935

Black Fury
$10 Raise
The Healer
Thunder in the Night
The Littlest Rebel

1936

Devil's Squadron
Beloved Enemy

1937

Outcast
The Girl from Scotland Yard
The Last Train from Madrid
On Such a Night

1938	1946	1949
Kentucky	The Unknown Betty Co-Ed	Samson and Delilah
1940		**1951**
Pride and Prejudice	**1947**	M
1945	The Thirteenth Hour	**1953**
Jealousy	Framed	Born to the Saddle

Morris, Margaret

Minneapolis, Minnesota, 1898/1903–1968; 5'5½"; red hair, brown eyes. *Wampas Baby Star:* 1924.

Margaret Morris came to the movies from stock companies. With four serials to her credit she could be considered one of the Wampas serial "queens."

Throughout most of the silent days she remained a leading lady in features and shorts, and she was top-billed in her final silent. Talkies put an end to her starring career; she had the lead only in two 1930s "B" westerns. Otherwise, her roles in talking pictures were bits.

Morris, a widow, became a businesswoman in later years.

FILMOGRAPHY

Shorts

1923–1927?

Rustlin'
Face to Face
Twilight Trail
The Doctor
The Angelus
The Mother
Sin
The Lady of Lyons
The Fight That Failed
Where's There's a Bill
The Last of His Face
When a Man's a Fan
The Midnight Son
Bruisers and Losers
Little Miss Bluffit
Ladies Prefer Brunettes
Assorted Nuts
Blisters Under the Skin
The Knight Before Christmas

Features

1920

Her First Elopement

1921

Hickville to Broadway

1923

The Town Scandal
Ghost City (serial)
Beasts of Paradise (serial)

1924

The Galloping Ace
The Iron Man (serial)
Horseshoe Luck

1925

Welcome Home
Youth's Gamble
Wild Horse Mesa
The Best People
Womanhandled

1926

That's My Baby
Born to the West

1927

The Magic Garden
Moulders of Men

1928

Mark of the Frog (serial)
The Avenging Shadow

1929

The Woman I Love

1932

Single-Handed Saunders

1934

The Personality Kid

1935

Alice Adams

1936

Magnificent Obsession
Desert Guns
The Bride Walks Out
Wanted: Jane Turner

1937

*There Goes My Girl
The Toast of New York

*Morris's participation in this film is uncertain.

Margaret Morris

Nixon, Marion

(sometimes Marian); Superior, Wisconsin, 1904/05–1983; 5'1½"; brown hair, brown eyes. *Wampas Baby Star:* 1924.

Elfin Marion Nixon came to Hollywood about 1922 via vaudeville. At first an extra, the ex-dancer advanced to bits in comedy shorts and then found her way into low-budget westerns in which she was appearing when she was recognized by Wampas. Among her leading men were the likes of Tom Mix, Buck Jones and Hoot Gibson. In the next few years she worked her way up to leading lady status (sometimes top billed) in the types of programmers that were the meat of the theater bills in the silent era. Few of them could be considered in any way important.

During her career Nixon worked at major studios which included Universal, Warner Bros. and Fox. Making her sound debut in the part-talkie *Geraldine* in early 1929, she continued to prosper mildly for several more years, alternating between major and minor studios and leading and supporting roles. During her time at Fox, where she made what she termed her favorite picture, *Rebecca of Sunnybrook Farm* (1932), the studio used her as a threat to keep in line their major but rebellious star Janet Gaynor, to whom she bore a strong physical resemblance.

A piquantly pretty but uncharismatic actress with a rather high-pitched voice that made her seem younger than she was, Marion Nixon played competently enough in many genres of film and went on to make about as many talkies as silents. Her final films were for independent studios. Although she did not make much news for her motion pictures, she did make the papers in 1932 when she was robbed at gunpoint aboard a Santa Fe train.

Nixon was first married to boxer Joe Benjamin, and then to Edward Hillman, scion of a wealthy merchant family. Her marriage to director William Seiter, the former husband of 1923 Wampas Baby Laura La Plante, lasted to his death. So did the late-in-life marriage to former leading man Ben Lyon, widower of actress Bebe Daniels. She died after open-heart surgery, leaving two daughters and a son.

Marion (Marian) Nixon

Filmography

Shorts

The City of Stars

Features

1923

Rosita
Big Dan
Cupid's Fireman
The Courtship of Miles Standish

1924

Just Off Broadway
The Vagabond Trail
The Circus Cowboy
The Last of the Duanes

1925

The Hurricane Kid
The Saddle Hawk
Riders of the Purple Sage
Let 'Er Buck
I'll Show You the Town
Durand of the Bad Lands
Where Was I?
Sporting Life

1926

Hands Up!
What Happened to Jones
Rolling Home

Devil's Island
Spangles

1927

Heroes of the Night
The Auctioneer
Taxi! Taxi!
Down the Stretch
Out All Night
The Chinese Parrot

1928

The Fourflusher
Out of the Ruins
How to Handle Women
Jazz Mad
Red Lips

1929

Man, Woman and Wife
Silks and Saddles
Geraldine
The Red Sword
The Rainbow Man
Say It with Songs
In the Headlines
Young Nowheres
The Show of Shows
General Crack

1930

Courage
Scarlet Pages
College Lovers
The Pay Off
The Lash
Ex-Flame

1931

Sweepstakes
Women Go on Forever
A Private Scandal

1932

Charlie Chan's Chance
After Tomorrow
Amateur Daddy
Winner Take All
Rebecca of Sunnybrook Farm
Madison Square Garden
Too Busy to Work

1933

Face in the Sky
Best of Enemies
Pilgrimage
Doctor Bull
Chance at Heaven

1934

The Lineup
Strictly Dynamite
We're Rich Again
Embarrassing Moments
By Your Leave
Once to Every Bachelor

1935

Sweepstake Annie

1936

Tango
The Drag-Net
The Reckless Way
Captain Calamity

O'Day, Molly

(sometimes Mollie) (also known as Sue O'Neil) (Suzanne Noonan); Bayonne, New Jersey, 1909/12–1998; 5'2½"; brown hair, blue-green eyes. *Wampas Baby Star:* 1928.

The sister of 1926 Wampas Star Sally O'Neil, and the youngest of about 11 Noonan siblings, Molly O'Day was a pretty colleen who bore the "map of Ireland" on her face. She got her start in Hal Roach comedies, in which she appeared for almost two years as a teenager. She was signed by First National and seemed to have a promising career in features after her first one, *The Patent Leather Kid*, co-starring Richard Barthelmess. Only a handful more followed before she began showing signs of a weight problem against which she was to struggle for years.

The studio gave O'Day an ultimatum that she was to lose the excess poundage in a period of time variously reported between one and three months. She did not make the deadline. One consequence was that the studio gave her promised role in the part-talkie *The Barker* to 1924 Wampas Baby Dorothy Mackaill. The picture was a big hit and could have helped her career considerably.

First National dropped Molly O'Day and that basically ended her budding career; she never regained the chance at real stardom. In her continuing, perhaps even desperate, effort to become thinner she underwent a well-publicized operation to remove several pounds of fat from her lower body. It was not notably successful. About the same time, her sister Sally was having career problems too and they signed up to tour in a Fanchon and Marco revue. It provided a temporary boost to O'Neil's career but did little for her sister. Another vaudeville tour followed.

The only screen appearances O'Day made in the two years following her release by First National were with Sally. In 1929 she had a mere minute or two of screen time singing and dancing with her in the "Meet My Sister" number of *The Show of Shows*. (They, not unexpectedly, were dressed as Irish girls.) The other picture was Columbia's *Sisters*; they had previously co-starred together in the silent *The Lovelorn*. (Another sister, perhaps having the stage name Isabel(le) O'Neil, was also supposed to have appeared in the cinema.)

The major offscreen news Molly O'Day made in the early 1930s occurred when the car she and Sally were riding in was shot at. The suspicion was that it had something to do with the trial of their brother, a convicted criminal and jailbreaker. She also was sued a few times for various unpaid bills. Impecuniousness seemed to be a Noonan family problem; both Sally and her mother were sued more than once for the same thing.

O'Day did finally manage to lose weight, and continued to get sporadic supporting roles until 1935, with help from a sympathetic producer of her acquaintance. She played brassy roles, but could also be quietly effective in a film like *The Life of Vergie Winters*. In her last "B" movies she was the leading lady.

Although her name had been romantically linked to actors George Raft and James Dunn, Molly O'Day was first married to nightclub entertainer Jack Durant, a match that resulted in three daughters and a son. In the 1940s it was reported that she had saved her son from death after a sand trench collapsed on him.

After her divorce from Durant, O'Day married James Kenaston and thus became the sister-in-law of actress Billie Dove, who was married to Kenaston's brother. This turned out to be the so-called "slapstick" marriage. In her suit for divorce O'Day accused him of, among other things, breaking a raw egg over her head, throwing drinks in her face, spraying shaving cream in her hair, and literally kicking her into an oven when she was bent over basting a turkey! Needless to say, the marriage did not prosper.

FILMOGRAPHY

Shorts
1925–1926?

Features

1927
Hard-Boiled Haggerty
The Patent Leather Kid
The Lovelorn

1928
The Shepherd of the Hills
The Little Shepherd of Kingdom Come

1929
The Show of Shows

1930
Sisters

1931
Sea Devils
Sob Sister

1932
Devil on Deck

1933	Chloe: Love Is Calling You	Lawless Border
Gigolettes of Paris	The Life of Vergie Winters	Bars of Hate
1934		The Law of 45s
Hired Wife	**1935**	
Playthings of Desire	*Skull and Crown	*The release date of this film is uncertain.

O'Neil, Sally

(sometimes O'Neill), (Virginia Noonan); Bayonne, New Jersey, 1908/11–1968; 5'1"–5'2"; brown hair, blue eyes. *Wampas Baby Star:* 1926.

Sally O'Neil was one of a large clan of Irish-American stock; her face bore the unmistakable lineaments of her ancestry as did that of her sister, 1928 Wampas Baby Star Molly O'Day. (A third sister, Isabel(le), apparently also made some films.) Sally had a major success with her first released picture, *Sally, Irene and Mary*, produced by MGM. (She played the role of Mary; the other ladies of the title were two major stars-to-be, fellow 1926 Wampas Baby Joan Crawford and Constance Bennett.) Another early picture was *Battling Butler* with Buster Keaton; popular William Haines was also a co-star.

MGM typecast O'Neil in the persona of a spunky gamine and tomboy, and there seemed to be an effort to market her as yet another "new" Mary Pickford. Perhaps because of her dislike of the persona — she later referred to her early roles as "sickening kid stuff" — she became rebellious. She also began filming on two pictures which were not completed. In 1927 MGM released her for "temperament," a commonly used reason in those days for termination of a contract. Although she was to remain in films off and on for another eight years she never recaptured the promise of those early years.

As freelancers, and no doubt concerned about the advent of sound movies, Sally O'Neil and sister Molly (who had been released by First National) undertook a tour with the Fanchon and Marco troupe in 1929. It apparently succeeded in its purpose because O'Neil appeared in eight films that year and was considered to have made a successful transition to sound. One was the musical melange *The Show of Shows*, in which the sisters performed in the "Meet My Sister" number. They had previously appeared together in the silent *The Lovelorn* and were to make *Sisters* in 1930.

To today's audiences O'Neil's voice sounds high-pitched, even grating, and is very redolent of the accents of her suburban New York birthplace. But many of her roles called for brassiness, and audiences of that time may have been more attuned to that kind of characterization. By the early 1930s it seemed that each time she made a new film newspaper accounts spoke of a "comeback." She had signed with Fox for the John Ford-directed film version of her Broadway play *The Brat*, but made no other films for that studio.

Sally O'Neil was quoted as being bitter toward Hollywood for the ups and downs she was experiencing. Perhaps events in her personal life contributed to those feelings as well. She was sued several times for unpaid back taxes, unpaid-for automobiles, furniture, groceries and even books from a lending library. She and Molly were shot at as they rode in an automobile. (They suspected the incident might have had something to do with their appearance at the trial of their brother, a convicted felon and prison escapee.) In 1930 both sisters had declared bankruptcy.

Some of O'Neil's later pictures were for small studios like Monogram, Invincible and Screencraft. She made her last American film in 1935 and then a final one in Ireland where, she claimed, the Irish Republic cast did not accept her until they found out that her real name was Noonan. After her picture career ended she played in stock and on Broadway again.

A sufferer since childhood from a rheumatic heart, Sally O'Neil lived in Costa Rica in the late 1940s or early '50s in an effort to regain her health. While there she apparently had a brief marriage to a Costa Rican national. The marriage that "took" was her second to businessman Stewart Battles, with whom she retired to a small city in Illinois.

Sally O'Neil

Filmography

1925

Don't
Sally, Irene and Mary

1926

The Auction Block
Mike
Battling Butler

1927

Slide, Kelly, Slide
Frisco Sally Levy
The Callahans and the Murphys
Becky
The Lovelorn

1928

Mad Hour
Bachelor's Paradise
The Battle of the Sexes
The Floating College

1929

Broadway Fever
The Girl on the Barge
Hardboiled
On with the Show
The Sophomore
Broadway Scandals
Jazz Heaven
The Show of Shows

1930

Girl of the Port
Hold Everything
Sisters
Kathleen Mavourneen

1931
Salvation Nell
Murder by the Clock
The Brat

1933
By Appointment Only
Ladies Must Love

1934
Sixteen Fathoms Deep
The Moth
Beggar's Holiday
Convention Girl

1935
Too Tough to Kill

1938
Kathleen (Ireland)

Page, Anita

(Anita Pomares); Flushing, New York, 1910–. 5'4"; red-blonde (possibly later lightened) hair, blue eyes. *Wampas Baby Star:* 1929.

Beauteous Anita Page was dubbed a Baby Star the year she scored her biggest success, top-billed in the Academy Award winning MGM musical picture *The Broadway Melody*. (It was to her that the classic standard "You Were Meant for Me" was sung.) In the film she played one of two show business sisters in love with the same man; her sibling was portrayed by 1922 Wampas Star Bessie Love. In the previous year, her first in featured roles, she had made quite a splash (or at least a *splat*) by plunging headlong down a flight of stairs in the Joan Crawford starrer *Our Dancing Daughters*.

Having gone from extra to star at one of the major studios in less than two years, Page's future seemed assured. For a time, she supposedly received more fan mail at MGM than any other actress except Greta Garbo. However, her future was to be in increasingly less prestigious vehicles. Among the high-powered stars at MGM her acting seemed colorless and she lacked a charismatic personality. She soon drifted into ingenue roles, in which she was rendered invisible by the likes of Marie Dressler and Polly Moran, and then to supporting status.

Released by MGM about 1932, Anita Page thereafter made films for such independents as Chesterfield and Monogram where she was top-billed for the last time in the title role of *Jungle Bride*. She had gone from such prestigious leading men as Lon Chaney, Ramon Novarro, William Haines (several times) and Buster Keaton to the likes of animal trainer Clyde Beatty and Regis Toomey.

Page has occasionally made the news in recent years. In 1988 she was scheduled to appear at the Academy Award ceremonies, as were many Hollywood old-timers, but a traffic jam caused many attendees to walk some distance to the theater. In the 90 degree heat she fainted and had to be taken to a hospital by paramedics, thus missing the festivities. She remains an enthusiastic booster of the "old" Hollywood and frequently is seen at film retrospectives.

Page, briefly married to songwriter Nacio Herb Brown (of "Singin' in the Rain" fame) later wed Herschel House, a U.S. Naval officer who later became an admiral. She has two daughters.

Filmography

1928

Telling the World
Our Dancing Daughters
While the City Sleeps

1929

The Flying Fleet
The Broadway Melody
The Hollywood Revue of 1929
Our Modern Maidens
Speedway
Navy Blues

1930

Free and Easy
Caught Short
Our Blushing Brides
The Little Accident
War Nurse

1931

Reducing
The Easiest Way
Gentleman's Fate
Sidewalks of New York

1932

Under 18
Are You Listening?
Night Court
Skyscraper Souls
Prosperity

1933

Jungle Bride
The Big Cage
Soldiers of the Storm
I Have Lived

1936

Hitch Hike to Heaven

Parrish, Gigi

(also Gi-Gi); Cambridge, Massachusetts, 1912/13–; 5'4"; brown hair, brown eyes. *Wampas Baby Star:* 1934.

After appearing in local theater, Gigi Parrish was signed by Samuel Goldwyn as one of his "Goldwyn Girls" in the Eddie Cantor musical romp *Roman Scandals*. The year she was named to Wampas Baby Stardom was her busiest, with roles in six movies. One of them, *Kiss and Make-Up*, was a film in which most of the Wampas Stars had cameo roles.

Parrish was married to writer, newspaper publisher and documentary filmmaker John Weld. She had previously been wed to Dillwyn Parrish, from whom she took her stage name.

Filmography

1933

Roman Scandals

1934

Twentieth Century
The Love Captive
Kiss and Make-Up
Down to Their Last Yacht
A Girl of the Limberlost
Girl o' My Dreams

1935

Symphony of Living

1936

August Week-end

Perdue, Derelys

Kansas City, Missouri, 1902–1989; 5'5½"; brown hair, brown eyes. *Wampas Baby Star:* 1923.

The interestingly-named Derelys Perdue made about a dozen mostly forgettable pictures. She had begun as a dancer with the Marion Morgan troupe and possibly entered pictures as a supervisor of dance numbers. She may have also danced in three Olive Thomas starrers before 1920. Her big break came the year she was named a Baby Star, with her role in *The Bishop of the Ozarks*.

Perdue was chosen from among 40 actresses to pose for a statue placed at the entrance to the Studio City Film Center. The sculptor reportedly said that she had a perfect profile. Her pictures encompassed several genres, including comedy, drama and westerns with popular silent leading men like Warner Baxter, Lloyd Hughes and Earle Foxe. It is possible that she made some two-reelers as well.

It was in "B" oaters that the rather regal-looking Derelys Perdue ended her career at the dawn of sound, never having made a talking picture. The FBO studio may have planned to change her first name and she possibly brought a legal suit to prevent it.

Perdue had temporarily left films in the mid–1920s for marriage to L. W. Feldman, whom she later divorced. She remarried.

Derelys Perdue

Filmography

Short

1929

The Range of Fear

1922

A Dangerous Adventure (serial, and also a feature version)

1923

The Bishop of the Ozarks

Daytime Wives
Blow Your Own Horn

1924

Untamed Youth
The Last Man on Earth

1925

Paint and Powder
Where the Worst Begins

1927

The Gingham Girl

1928

Quick Triggers
The Mystery Rider (serial)

1929

The Smiling Terror

Philbin, Mary

Chicago, Illinois, 1903/04–1993; 5'2"; brown hair (occasionally blonde), blue/gray eyes. *Wampas Baby Star*: 1922.

Few Wampas winners could boast of being part of one of the cinema's iconographic images as Mary Philbin could. That claim to screen immortality was the unmasking scene in Lon Chaney's 1925 version of *The Phantom of the Opera*. It was the shrinking Philbin who, pulling the benign mask off the Phantom's face, discovers the skull-like horror beneath.

The runner-up in a Chicago newspaper beauty contest, Philbin got noticed by Hollywood, as did the contest winner, popular '20s actress Gertrude Olmsted (Olmstead), and she went to Universal. Her first big break came with Erich von Stroheim's *Merry-Go-Round* in 1923 and she began receiving top billing the next year. Of fragile appearance — although her long life suggests otherwise — she tended to play tragic innocent roles in which she suffered considerably. She was known to her coworkers as a genuinely sweet and shy lady.

Mary Philbin seems to have been a casualty of the talkies. She was in but four sound pictures, one of which, *The Last Performance*, appears to have been originally made as a silent and had sound added later. The rest were all produced in 1929. Her last screen appearance technically came in 1930 in the rereleased version of *Phantom* with added footage and sound effects.

Philbin never married, although she was engaged to Paul Kohner (later the father of actress Susan Kohner), the casting director and head of foreign language production at Universal. Although she spent most of the long years of her retirement in the heart of Hollywood she rarely showed up at revivals or festivals of silent films. Perhaps the reason was that she had grown tired of being associated with, and questioned about, only one film. She could sometimes be glimpsed at the grave site of Rudolph Valentino paying her respects on the anniversary of his death.

FILMOGRAPHY

1921
The Blazing Trail
Danger Ahead
Red Courage
False Kisses

1922
The Trouper
Human Hearts

1923
Penrod and Sam
Merry-Go-Round
The Age of Desire
Where Is This West?
The Temple of Venus
The Thrill Chaser

1924
Fools' Highway
The Gaiety Girl
The Rose of Paris

1925
Fifth Avenue Models
The Phantom of the Opera
Stella Maris

1927
The Man Who Laughs
The Last Performance
Surrender

1928
Drums of Love
Love Me and the World Is Mine

1929
Girl Overboard
After the Fog
The Shannons of Broadway

1930
The Phantom of the Opera (rerelease with added sequences)

Phipps, Sally

(Byrnece Beutler); San Francisco, California, 1909/11–1978; 5'2"; brown eyes, auburn hair. *Wampas Baby Star*: 1927.

Supposedly having appeared in a "Broncho Billy" film at the age of five or so, Sally Phipps began her screen career seriously in 1926. Her contract had a clause stipulating that she must maintain her weight below 130 pounds for the contract's five year duration, but her career did not last for five years. Except for her co-starring features the year she was named a Wampas Baby, she was usually to be found down in the cast list. In her final film she was merely one of the "lady passengers on the boat."

In the year Phipps made her final films she filed suit against her mother and stepfather to be freed from their financial control and to get an accounting of her finances. She subsequently went to Broadway as one of the cast of the successful Kaufman-Hart comedy *Once in a Lifetime*. It was a spoof on the talkies in which she herself had not appeared. She was in at least one other stage production as well in the mid–'30s; interestingly, it also spoofed Hollywood.

Sally Phipps was divorced from Benedict Gimbel, Jr., an heir to the Gimbel department store fortune, before a more successful marriage to musician Alfred Harned. She had one son.

FILMOGRAPHY

Short

1927
Girls

Features

1915
Broncho Billy and the Baby

1926
Bertha, the Sewing Machine Girl

1927
Love Makes 'Em Wild
High School Hero

1928
Why Sailors Go Wrong
The News Parade
None But the Brave

1929
Joy Street
The One Woman Idea

Pierce, Evelyn

Del Rio, Texas, 1908–1960; 5'4"; blonde hair, gray eyes. *Wampas Baby Star*: 1925.

Supposedly called the prettiest girl in the world by no less a connoisseur than Florenz Ziegfeld, Evelyn Pierce had a small handful of co-starring roles in the silents. The first was in a "B" western opposite Fred Humes. She made her sound film debut in the part-talkie *Tenderloin*.

Like several other Wampas Baby Stars, Pierce appeared with dog hero Rin Tin Tin (in *The Million Dollar Collar*). That proved to be her last major role. She supposedly got the part after being "rediscovered" by Warner Bros. in her bit part in *Tenderloin*. She thereafter reverted to bits, with at least one comedy short to her credit.

Pierce entered the real estate game after her show business days came to an end. She was married to the singing movie cowboy actor Robert (Bob) "Tex" Allen (born Theodore or Irving Baehr). They had a son and a daughter.

FILMOGRAPHY

Shorts

1930s?
I'm a Father

Features

1925
Don't

1927
The Border Cavalier

1928
Tenderloin
Sonia

1929
The Million Dollar Collar

1930
Once a Gentleman

1931
An American Tragedy
Monkey Business

1934
Broadway Bill

1935
Carnival
Death Flies East
Men of the Hour
Love Me Forever
The Girl Friend

Ralston, Jobyna

(Jobyna Raulston); South Pittsburg, Tennessee, 1899/1904–1967; 5'3"; brown hair, gray eyes. *Wampas Baby Star:* 1923.

After studying dancing, demurely pretty Jobyna Ralston came from vaudeville and a role in Broadway's *Two Little Girls in Blue* to work as an extra in one- and two-reelers in the late teens. She went on to hone her comic talents in some 60 Hal Roach comedies and then appeared with French comic actor Max Linder in one of his few American features, the Fairbanks burlesque *Three-Must-Get-Theres* in 1922.

The training in knockabout comedies no doubt proved very valuable for Ralston, who by all accounts had a lively and likable personality. She became best known as leading lady to the enormously popular Harold Lloyd when he wed his previous co-star Mildred Davis. That was in 1923, the year she was tapped for Wampas stardom.

Why Worry? was Jobyna Ralston's first effort with Lloyd and she also was seen in his *Hot Water*, *Girl Shy* and *The Kid Brother*. Most memorably she played his sympathetic college sweetheart in his biggest success, *The Freshman* (1925). She remained with the comedian until 1926 and was replaced by 1928 Baby Ann Christy. She is considered to have been his finest leading lady, one who could credibly be involved in some of his comedy situations rather than being a passive observer of them. Of her role in *Girl Shy* a critic said she "Proves herself considerable of an actress, in addition to being decidedly pretty."

Jobyna Ralston

Besides her Lloyd pictures, none came close to matching the classic status of the 1927 William Wellman epic *Wings*. In it she had the small role of the archetypal girl-next-door waiting for her beaux to return from the Great War. One of the male stars was Richard Arlen, whom she wed that same year. It also proved to be the year that Jobyna Ralston was first top billed in films like *Lightning* and *Pretty Clothes*. It was also her busiest in the cinema with eight pictures to her credit, mostly action melodramas and society dramas. Among her very varied costars were Eddie Cantor, Rod La Rocque, the football hero Harold (Red) Grange, Buck Jones and Douglas Fairbanks, Jr.

Despite her increased activity, *Wings* was Ralston's last significant film. Her talkie debut came in 1929's *College Coquette*, in which she played somewhat of a "bad girl" role. Reviews differed about the quality of her voice. One stated that it was "curiously childish" and "indistinct," but to others it was acceptable. None alluded to a strong Southern accent, which, if she had one, may by then have been smoothed out by voice training.

Whether it was good or not, Jobyna Ralston's voice was heard in only two further sound films. She had the thankless task of portraying Rin-Tin-Tin's female stooge in 1930's *Rough Waters*, and the next year made her swan song. One reviewer termed her last film "a sheer waste" and dubbed it "one of the most nonsensical films around." A short subject made the following year showed the Arlens at home.

Prior to making her last pictures Ralston had returned to the stage in Los Angeles to appear in the play *Bad Babies*. It proved an ill-starred adventure; the play was raided for being indecent and the entire cast was arrested. She was convicted in 1930 and paid a fine.

In 1933 Jobyna Ralston and Arlen had their only child, a son. As in her first marriage to hometown beau John Campbell, marital bliss was not lasting. In her 1945 suit for divorce she said that her husband had left in 1938 and never returned. The last 20 years of her life were spent in increasingly poor health from rheumatism and a series of strokes.

Filmography

Shorts

1919–1921?, 1932

The Property Man
Me and My Pal
Dogs of War (cameo)
Hollywood on Parade

Features

1922

The Call of Home
Three-Must-Get-
 Theres

1923

Why Worry?

1924

Girl Shy
Hot Water

1925

The Freshman

1926

For Heaven's Sake
Sweet Daddies
Gigolo

1927

The Kid Brother
Special Delivery
Wings
A Racing Romeo
Pretty Clothes
Special Delivery
Little Mickey Grogan

1928

The Night Flyer
The Count of Ten
The Big Hop
Black Butterflies
The Power of the Press
The Toilers

1929

Some Mother's Boy
The College Coquette

1930

Rough Waters

1931

Sheer Luck

Rand, Sally

(Helen Beck), Winchester, Kentucky or Elkton, Missouri, 1902/04–1979; 5', blonde hair, gray eyes. *Wampas Baby Star:* 1927.

Supposedly working in a Kansas City cafe as a cigarette girl by the age of 13, Sally Rand went into stock and vaudeville with Gus Edwards shortly thereafter. She may have also appeared in carnivals and the Barnum and Bailey Circus. Her Hollywood appearances began in one- and two-reel Sennett, Christie and Roach comedies. Bigger things seemed in store for her when Cecil B. DeMille made her a member of his stock company. (He supposedly chose her name from a Rand-McNally atlas.) Her first film for him was probably the reincarnation melodrama *The Road to Yesterday*, in which she had a minuscule role.

Sally Rand's first sizable feature role was in the "B" western *The Texas Bearcat* (1925) starring Bob Custer. DeMille had supposedly dubbed her the most beautiful girl in pictures but he continued to cast her in films like *His Dog*. She left Hollywood in 1928, just one year after being named a Wampas Baby Star.

Rand returned to dancing and vaudeville. She discovered her place in the limelight at the Chicago World's Fair of 1932/33 in the Streets of Paris exhibition. There she became one of the most controversial of all the Wampas Babies. With some huge ostrich plumes—and little else — she popularized the fan dance and became the hit of the Fair.

Despite the great notoriety that had come with Rand's presumed nude dancing, she saved herself from another career lull by devising the bubble dance, featuring specially designed five-foot transparent balloons ("bubbles") designed by an Akron rubber company. It was said of this dance that it competed with the Empire State Building as one of the sights of New York.

Rand's publicity brought new offers from Hollywood but she was not destined to succeed in the talkies. Her notoriety made her readily identifiable to audiences but the studio moguls were nervous about a backlash and censors had their knives out. Also, her voice was not particularly good, being described as low but nasal with an Ozark twang.

In *Hotel Variety*, Sally Rand's initial talkie, she did not have a large role but she was third-billed in her next, *Bolero*, with George Raft and Carole Lombard. The film's publicity referred to her as the sensation of the Chicago Fair; in it she recreated part of her fan dance. It was partially cut by some state and city censors, although she reportedly was wearing a bathing suit.

For her stage debut, Rand chose the character of Sadie Thompson in a 1935 summer theater production of Somerset Maugham's *Rain*. (Among her co-stars was Humphrey Bogart.) In her final film she was top-billed in the slyly-titled *The Sunset Strip Case*. It had very limited if indeed any distribution. Not straying too far from type casting, she played a woman who goes undercover in a nightclub to try to identify her father's killer.

By the late 1930s Sally Rand was still one of the top drawing cards in vaudeville, but her future lay in increasingly dingy nightclubs. Well into her sixties, and ever a whiz at self-publicity, she still did her titillating fan dance to the strains of "Clair de Lune" and Chopin's "Waltz in C-Sharp Minor." She had always claimed that she was not really a stripper and what audiences thought they saw was not necessarily what they got. "The Rand is quicker than the eye," was her oft-repeated tagline. The law, however, frequently accused her of actually being nude and she spent many nights in jail for going beyond the bounds of propriety.

In the mid–1950s Rand played Las Vegas and had a television show there. She also appeared on a network program called *Carny* in which she explained how carnival games really worked. In addition, she was the narrator of the revue *This Was Burlesque* in 1965. Months before her death the inimitable and still shapely blonde was still making "brief" appearances.

Sally Rand was wed three times. Her first husband was her manager Harry Finkelstein. The second was rodeo performer Thurkel "Turk" Greenough, and her last the plastering contractor Fred Lalla. She had an adopted son.

FILMOGRAPHY

Shorts

Features

1925

The Texas Bearcat
The Road to Yesterday
Braveheart

1926

Bachelor Brides
Sunny Side Up
Gigolo
El Relicario (with Spanish intertitles)
Man Bait

1927

The Night of Love
Getting Gertie's Garter
The King of Kings
His Dog
The Fighting Eagle
Galloping Fury
Heroes in Blue

1928

A Woman Against the World
Nameless Men
Crashing Through
A Girl in Every Port

Black Feather
Golf Widows

1933

Hotel Variety

1934

Bolero

1938

*The Sunset Strip Case (aka Sunset Murder Case)

*This film may have not been released until the early 1940s.

Revier, Dorothy

(Doris, Dorothy or Dorethea Velegra or Velagra, and other variations of the name); San Francisco, California, 1904–1993; 5'4½"; brown hair (later blonde), gray eyes. *Wampas Baby Star:* 1925.

The strikingly pretty Baby Star who was to become "The Queen of Poverty Row" really wanted to be a dancer. Dorothy Revier was discovered dancing at one of San Francisco's well-known cafes, but after her entree into films that talent was not much utilized. Instead, she became known as one of the premier villainesses of the silent screen. One her best-remembered "bad" performances was as Milady de Winter in Douglas Fairbanks's part-talkie *The Iron Mask* in 1929. Among her other prominent leading men were Jack Holt, Richard Barthelmess and Cullen Landis. A star with whom she did not get to appear was Rudolph Valentino. They were set to co-star in *The Hooded Falcon* but it never got produced.

In 1925, the year of her Baby Stardom, Revier began a long professional association with Columbia Pictures, which was indeed a "Poverty Row" studio until the 1930s. She was frequently loaned out to other small independent studios like Chesterfield, Action and Monogram, thus truly becoming the Poverty Row's "queen." There was a long-term personal relationship with the autocratic Harry Cohn, head of the Columbia studio.

Although she played varying kinds of roles, Dorothy Revier's usual silent movie "vamp" persona could be inferred from the titles of such films as *Dangerous Pleasure*, *Fate of a Flirt*, *When the Wife's Away* and *The Other Kind of Love*. Her popularity extended to a line of skin preparations marketed under her name in department stores.

As is evident from her large number

of sound movies, Revier made the transition to talkies with no problem, her first being the all-star *The Donovan Affair*. However, by the early 1930s she had shed the "bad girl" persona that had been her trademark to become a conventional leading lady. She was thus little different from hundreds of other pretty ingenues. Worse yet from her point of view, she began appearing in "B" westerns.

After departing, or being dropped by, Columbia in 1934, about the time it began its rise to being a major studio, Revier's fortunes declined permanently into low-budget films and low-rent studios. She ended her career, although she claimed that she subsequently was offered the part of Belle Watling in *Gone with the Wind* (played by Ona Munson in the film).

Dorothy Revier's first husband was director Harry Revier, whose name she retained throughout her career. She later was wed to Charles Johnson and then to artist William Pelayo. Afterward, she remarried Johnson.

FILMOGRAPHY

Short

1928

Cleopatra

Features

1921

Life's Greatest Question

1922

The Broadway Madonna

1923

The Wild Party
The Supreme Test

1924

The Other Kind of Love
Do It Now
Marry in Haste
The Martyr Sex
The Sword of Valor
Call of the Mate
The Cowboy and the Flapper
The Virgin
Border Women
The Rose of Paris
That Wild West
Man from God's Country
Down by the Rio Grande

1925

Dangerous Pleasure
Just a Woman
An Enemy of Man
The Danger Signal
Sealed Lips
Steppin' Out
When Husbands Flirt
The Fate of a Flirt

1926

The Far Cry
Poker Faces
The False Alarm
When the Wife's Away
The Better Way

1927

Wandering Girls
Stolen Pleasures
The Price of Honor
Poor Girls
The Clown
The Drop Kick
The Tigress
The Warning
The Siren

1928

The Red Dance
Beware of Blondes
Sinner's Parade
Submarine

1929

The Iron Mask
The Donovan Affair
Father and Son
The Quitter
Light Fingers
The Dance of Life
Tanned Legs
The Mighty

1930

Murder on the Roof
Vengeance
Hold Everything
Call of the West
The Way of All Men
The Squealer

The Bad Man

1931

The Avenger
The Black Camel
Graft
Leftover Ladies
Anybody's Blonde
The Last Ride

1932

Sally of the Subway
Sin's Pay Day
Arm of the Law
Night World
The Widow in Scarlet
No Living Witness
Beauty Parlor
The King Murder
A Scarlet Weekend
The Secrets of Wu Sin

1933

Love Is Like That
Thrill Hunter
Above the Clouds
By Candlelight

1934

The Fighting Ranger
Unknown Blonde
Green Eyes
The Curtain Falls
When a Man Sees Red

1935

Circumstantial Evidence
$20 a Week
The Eagle's Brood
The Lady in Scarlet
Circus Shadows
Frisco Waterfront

1936

The Cowboy and the Kid

Reynolds, Vera

(Norma?); Richmond, Virginia, 1899/1905–1962; 5'–5'1"; brown hair (sometimes blonde), blue/green eyes. *Wampas Baby Star:* 1926.

Trained as a dancer, Vera Reynolds was an extra and then a veteran of one- and two-reel comedies at such studios as Christie, Gayety and Sennett, with whom she signed for $20 a week in 1917 as a chubby youngster. She rose to the level of comic ingenue. Her career blossomed as a Paramount leading lady when Cecil B. DeMille signed her. She was featured and then starred in some of his 1920s pictures including *Feet of Clay*, in which she received top billing, *The Golden Bed* and *The Road to Yesterday*. Her first major feature role had come as Gloria Swanson's sister in 1923's *Prodigal Daughters*.

For the remainder of the silent era Reynolds stayed at the top as a minor leading woman, but with the advent of talkies she did not have major studio backing. Although remaining a leading lady, it was in quickie films for independent studios. Such later pictures as *Gorilla Ship* and *The Monster Walks* (both featuring gorillas) are ample evidence of her descent.

Vera Reynolds

Reynolds was married to Earl Montgomery but, she later claimed, not finally divorced from him when she wed screenwriter Robert Reel Ellis (not the actor Robert Ellis with whom he is sometimes confused). This was a mistake she did not discover for ten years, or at least this is what she said when divorcing Ellis.

FILMOGRAPHY

Shorts

1910s–1920s?

Bedlam
A Saphead's Sacrifice
Dry and Thirsty
Parked in the Park
Hearts of Oak
*His Hidden Talent
*Caught in the End

Features

1923

Prodigal Daughters
Woman-Proof

1924

Flapper Wives
Shadows of Paris
Icebound
For Sale
Broken Barriers
Feet of Clay
Cheap Kisses

1925

The Golden Bed
The Million Dollar Handicap
The Night Club
The Limited Mail
Without Mercy
The Road to Yesterday

1926

Steel Preferred
Silence
Sunny Side Up
Risky Business
Corporal Kate

1927

The Little Adventuress
The Main Event
Almost Human

1928

Golf Widows
Divine Sinners
Jazzland

1929

Back from Shanghai
Tonight at Twelve

1930

The Last Dance
The Lone Rider
Borrowed Wives

1931

The Lawless Woman
Hell Bent for Frisco
Neck and Neck
Dragnet Patrol

1932

The Monster Walks
Gorilla Ship
Tangled Destinies

The exact nature of these films is unknown.

Ricksen, Lucille

(also Rickson) (Lucille Ericksen); Chicago, Illinois, 1909–1925; 5'2½"; blonde hair, brown eyes. *Wampas Baby Star:* 1924.

Lucille Ricksen acted on the stage as a child and appeared in Essanay pictures while still in Chicago. About 1920, she was signed by Samuel Goldwyn to appear in two series, the "Edgar" and "Penrod" shorts, both based on Booth Tarkington stories. Although still in her early teens, she segued rapidly into "adult" roles in which she primarily played flappers.

Ricksen was said to be the youngest leading lady in films at the time and she certainly was one of the youngest Wampas Babies at the time of her selection.

Among the studios for which she worked were Universal and First National, before receiving a Metro contract. She made only a single film there before succumbing to the ravages of the illness from which she died. Stricken with what the newspapers called a "wasting" disease (probably tuberculosis), her malady was no doubt exacerbated by overwork. She had made nine films in the year before she died.

The story told about Lucille Ricksen's final days is, if true, more shockingly melodramatic than any film could possibly have been. She was being tended to by her mother when the older woman — no doubt worn out by months of nursing — suddenly fell across her daughter's bed, dead of a heart attack. The devastated young actress followed short weeks later. Her supposed last words, poignant if accurate, were quoted by contemporary papers: "I think Mother is waiting. Goodbye everybody."

FILMOGRAPHY

Shorts
1920–1921?
The Adventures and Emotions of Edgar Pomeroy series including:
Edgar and the Teacher's Pet
Edgar Camps Out
Edgar's Jonah Day
Edgar's Little Saw
Edgar Takes the Cake

Features
1921
The Old Nest

1922
The Social Buccaneer (serial)
The Married Flapper
The Girl Who Ran Wild
Remembrance
The Stranger's Banquet
Forsaking All Others

1923
Trimmed in Scarlet
Human Wreckage
The Rendezvous

1924
Judgment of the Storm
The Hill Billy
Galloping Fish
Those Who Dance
Behind the Curtain
Young Ideas
Vanity's Price
The Painted Lady
Idle Tongues

1925
The Denial

Rico, Mona

(Maria Enriqueta Valenzuela); Mexico City, Mexico, 1906/09–1994; 5'2"; brown hair, brown eyes. *Wampas Baby Star:* 1929.

After doing extra work, Mona Rico signed a five-year contract with United Artists in 1928. She was supposedly selected for her role in John Barrymore's *Eternal Love* by director Ernst Lubitsch because of her pretty hands. Her few film roles tended to be small ones, except for three Hollywood-produced Spanish language films. In the serial *Zorro Rides Again*, for instance, she was billed only as a "singer."

Nothing she did onscreen matched the drama of Rico's private life. In 1931, she was flying to her honeymoon in a private plane when it crashed and killed the pilot. She required plastic surgery to remove a facial scar caused by the accident. In a messy and well-publicized divorce case a couple of years later, she shed James Crofton, the husband who had survived the airplane crack-up with her.

FILMOGRAPHY

Shorts
Hearts and Hoofs
La Señorita de Chicago

Features

1929
Eternal Love
Shanghai Lady
Sombras de Gloria

1930
Alma de Gaucho
*A Devil with Women
Just Imagine

1932
Thunder Below

1935
Goin' to Town

1937
Zorro Rides Again (serial)

1941
My Life with Caroline

*Rico's appearance in this film is uncertain.

Rogers, Ginger

(Virginia McMath); Independence, Missouri, 1911–1995; 5'5"; brown-red hair (later blonde), blue eyes. *Wampas Baby Star*: 1932.

Memorable as the sylph-like partner of dancer Fred Astaire in their fabled RKO musicals of the 1930s, Ginger Rogers was the last important star to be favored by the Wampas organization. Her dancing skills matured early, enabling her to win a Charleston contest and a booking in vaudeville. Her act incorporated the use of baby talk, a gimmick that she also occasionally used in the cinema.

By 1929, Rogers (the name was her stepfather's) was in New York as a band singer and had signed on for her first Broadway role in *Top Speed*. The more famous *Girl Crazy* soon followed, in which she introduced the standards "But Not for Me" and "Embraceable You." She could certainly put over a song, and her voice was pleasant enough, but she did warble through her nose at times.

Ginger Rogers's first essays into movies were shorts made in New York. The oft-quoted line "Cigarette me, big boy" from her first full-length picture *Young Man of Manhattan* was an early example of her knack for a sassy wisecrack. Her roles at Paramount and Pathé developed her persona as a brassy gold digger, a common enough movie character in the early 1930s. In that kind of role she was seen to advantage in Warner Bros.' popular *Gold Diggers of 1933* and *42nd Street*.

Rogers no doubt recognized the need to broaden her range in order to have a significant career, and this she did when she was signed by RKO. Her first film there was *Flying Down to Rio*, in which she and Astaire were the second leads to stars Gene Raymond and Dolores Del Rio. In it they performed a snippet of a dance called the Carioca. Six Rogers films later they reteamed for *The*

Gay Divorcee, the dance called the Continental and fame.

Most of the famous songwriters of the day, including George Gershwin, Cole Porter and Irving Berlin, wrote for the duo who were now sensationally popular. Although neither could boast of being a great actor or singer, their dancing was a different matter. Together, they made magic on the screen, aided by such melodies as "Night and Day," "Smoke Gets in Your Eyes," "Lovely to Look At," "Cheek to Cheek," "The Way You Look Tonight" and numerous others.

During much of the 1930s the films that Ginger Rogers made apart from the "team" were of little significance. She sought more important roles as a solo performer and by the latter part of the decade had the clout to get them. Such films as *Stage Door* and *Bachelor Mother* established her as a deft comedienne in her own right, and she also found a solid drama in the soap opera-ish *Kitty Foyle*. This Academy Award–winning role for Best Actress was to mark the height of her fame, although such early '40s comedies as *Tom, Dick and Harry* and *The Major and the Minor* proved popular too.

Inevitably, as she aged Rogers's career began to wane. Her last attempt at a major musical, *Lady in the Dark*, was not very successful. By the late '40s she was receiving poor vehicles with co-stars less important than those with whom she had previously appeared, although she could occasionally land the likes of Cary Grant. Earlier leading men had included Henry Fonda, James Stewart and William Powell. Astaire and she made one last appearance together in their first color film, *The Barkleys of Broadway* in 1949, but she was actually a substitute for another actress. It is perhaps possible that the strident anti–Communist activities during this time of her notorious mother, Lela Rogers, eventually hurt her career.

Ginger Rogers was heard on the radio and she made some television appearances as well. She also turned increasingly back to the theater, one of her popular shows being *Hello, Dolly!* which she performed on Broadway and on tour for over three years. Other star vehicles included the title roles in *Mame* and *Coco*.

Rogers was always a plain-spoken lady and she made good copy in her interviews. Her husbands were one frequent topic of conversation. They were Edward Culpepper (known in vaudeville as Jack Pepper), actor Lew Ayres, Jack Buggs, a marine, French actor Jacques Bergerac (more than 15 years her junior) and finally William Marshall.

Although she resided on an Oregon ranch much of the time, Ginger Rogers remained visible in one arena or another nearly to the time of her death. Her latter-day appearances were increasingly made in a wheelchair and it was only too obvious that her once ultra-slender body had become noticeably bloated.

Filmography

Shorts

1930
A Night in a Dormitory
Office Blues
Campus Sweethearts

Features

1930
Young Man of Manhattan
Queen High
The Sap from Syracuse
Follow the Leader

1931
Honor Among Lovers
The Tip-Off
Suicide Fleet

1932
Carnival Boat
The Tenderfoot
The Thirteenth Guest
Hat Check Girl
You Said a Mouthful

1933
42nd Street
Broadway Bad
Gold Diggers of 1933
Professional Sweetheart
A Shriek in the Night
Don't Bet on Love
Rafter Romance
Sitting Pretty
Flying Down to Rio
Chance at Heaven

1934
Finishing School
Twenty Million Sweethearts
Change of Heart
Upper World
The Gay Divorcee

1935
Romance in Manhattan
Roberta
Star of Midnight
Top Hat
In Person

1936
Follow the Fleet
Swing Time

1937
Shall We Dance
Stage Door

1938
Having Wonderful Time
Vivacious Lady
Carefree

1939
The Story of Vernon and Irene Castle
Bachelor Mother
Fifth Avenue Girl

1940
The Primrose Path
Lucky Partners
Kitty Foyle

1941
Tom, Dick and Harry

1942
Roxie Hart
Tales of Manhattan
The Major and the Minor
Once Upon a Honeymoon

1943
Tender Comrade

1944
Lady in the Dark
I'll Be Seeing You

1945
Weekend at the Waldorf

1946
Heartbeat
The Magnificent Doll

1947
It Had to Be You

1949
The Barkleys of Broadway

1950
Perfect Strangers
Storm Warning

1951
The Groom Wore Spurs

1952
We're Not Married
Monkey Business
Dreamboat

1953
Forever Female

1954
Black Widow
Twist of Fate

1955
Tight Spot

1956
The First Traveling
 Saleslady
Teenage Rebel

1957
Oh, Men! Oh, Women!

1964
The Confession (aka Seven Different Ways and Quick Let's Get Married)

1965
Harlow

Shannon, Ethel

(also known as Ethel Shannon Jackson); Denver, Colorado, 1898/1900–1951; red hair, blue eyes. *Wampas Baby Star:* 1923.

Dubbed the perfect type of Irish beauty, Ethel Shannon began in films as an extra and from 1919 was a leading lady to such stars as William S. Hart and Charles Ray, and even Babe Ruth. She had previously been in stage productions with such theater greats as Maude Adams and E. H. Sothern.

Most of Shannon's films were produced for small "indies" but in them she was usually starred or was to be found near the top of the cast list. After an eight-year absence from the screen she returned to make her first talkie in 1935 under a long-term contract from Warner Bros. After one very minor role she basically served out her time as an extra.

Ethel Shannon possibly may have left the cinema in the late 1920s for family life. She was married to screenwriter Joseph Jackson, with whom she had a son. Jackson, who died in an accidental drowning, had been the president of Wampas the year of her selection, probably no small factor in her designation. She later married Cuban diplomat Jose Medinille y Grau.

FILMOGRAPHY

Shorts

1924
Fight and Win (series)

1919
Easy to Make Money
John Petticoats

1920
A Master Stroke
The Breath of the Gods
Beware of the Bride
An Old Fashioned Boy

1921
The Hope Diamond Mystery (serial)

1922
Man's Law and God's
Watch Him Step
The Top o' the Morning

1923
The Hero
The Girl Who Came Back
Daughters of the Rich

Maytime

1924
Riders Up
Lightning Romance

1925
Charley's Aunt
Stop Flirting
Speed Wild
High and Handsome
The Texas Trail
The Phantom Express

1926	The High Flyer	Through Thick and
Danger Quest	The Silent Power	Thin
The Speed Limit	The Buckaroo Kid	**1935**
The Sign of the Claw	**1927**	Stars Over Broadway
Oh, Baby!	Babe Comes Home	

Shilling, Marion

(Marion Schilling); Denver, Colorado, 1910–; 5'4"; brown hair, brown eyes. *Wampas Baby Star:* 1931.

Pretty, round-faced Marion Shilling's previous show business experience in stock companies as a child did not seem to be much training for the cinema, but she began at the top with MGM. Her first film, *Wise Girls,* was the first MGM talkie that was not also made in a silent version. She did not long remain at the studio, being released from her contract after the failure of the 1930 musical *Lord Byron of Broadway,* in which she co-starred.

Shilling next worked at Paramount and RKO, with such solid (and sometimes stolid) leading men as Richard Dix, Joel McCrea and Dick Powell. Another Powell—William—was also an early co-star. Her time at Paramount was spent mostly on loan-outs and her career had begun trending downward by the early 1930s. She became affiliated with independent studios like Monogram, Burr, Diversion and Kent. Somewhat of a western "queen," she appeared with most of the oater heroes, among them Hoot Gibson, Buck Jones, Tim McCoy, Tom Tyler and Rex Bell.

Marion Shilling later claimed that her career decline was due to the incapacitating illness of her agent in late 1931, the year of her Wampas Baby Stardom. Because of her ease in public speaking, she had been designated spokesperson for her year's crop of Babies. Beginning in 1933, she appeared in on-screen commercials, often in Technicolor, which promoted various products like cigarettes. In mid-decade she also returned to the stage.

Shilling married financier Edward Cook and had a son and a daughter. Rediscovered by western film buffs in the early 1970s, she has made several appearances at film festivals. She has been cheerfully interviewed about her days in the sun, remarking how nice it was to make the transition from grandmother to ex-movie star.

FILMOGRAPHY

Shorts

1932

Talking Screen Snapshots
Niagara Falls
Rule 'Em and Weep

Features

1929

Wise Girls

1930

Lord Byron of Broadway
Shadow of the Law
The Swellhead

On Your Back

1931

Beyond Victory
Young Donovan's Kid
The Common Law
Sundown Trail
Forgotten Women

1932

The County Fair
Shop Angel
A Man's Land
A Parisian Romance
Heart Punch

1933

The Red Rider (serial)
Curtain at Eight

1934

Fighting to Live
Thunder Over Texas
Elinor Norton
Inside Information
The Westerner
Blazing Guns

1935

Stone of Silver Creek
A Shot in the Dark
The Keeper of the Bees
Gun Play

Society Fever
Captured in Chinatown
Rio Rattler

1936

Romance Rides the Range
Cavalcade of the West
Idaho Kid
The Clutching Hand (serial) (Feature version: The Amazing Exploits of the Clutching Hand)
Gun Smoke
I'll Name the Murderer

Shockley, Marian

(sometimes Marion); Kansas City, Missouri, 1911–1981; 5'1"; blonde hair. *Wampas Baby Star*: 1932.

A leading lady of the Vanity Talking Comedies made by the Educational studio, Marian Shockley apparently was first seen in features in 1930's *Sweethearts on Parade*. It may have been a minuscule role or possibly an extra turn. Her brief day in the sun came prior to her naming as a Wampas Baby in her one feature co-starring part in the Bob Steele western *Near the Trail's End*.

After her 1930s film days ended, Shockley made her Broadway debut in George M. Cohan's *Dear Old Darling* and was heard frequently on the radio, including in her role as Nikki, the secretary of detective Ellery Queen, on the popular mystery show. Her brief turn in 1943's *Stage Door Canteen* was lost among the numerous big and little names of show business.

Previously divorced from Colin Craig, she became the wife of Clayton (Bud) Collyer, and therefore the sister-in-law of 1928 Wampas Baby Star June Collyer. With her husband she appeared in radio soap operas like *The Guiding Light* and *The Road of Life*. Shockley had three children.

FILMOGRAPHY

Shorts

1930s

The Freshman's Goat
College Cuties
Torchy Turns Turtle
Torchy's Kidd Coup
Torchy's Loud Spooker
Jimmy's Two Toots
Torchy Raises the Auntie
Torchy Rolls His Own
Torchy Turns the Trick
Torchy's Busy Day
Torchy's Night Cap

Features

1930
Sweethearts on Parade

1931
Heroes of the Flames (serial)
Near the Trail's End

1932
*Western Limited

1934
Elinor Norton

1943
Stage Door Canteen (cameo)

Shockley's appearance in this film is uncertain.

Sleeper, Martha

Lake Bluff, Illinois, 1907/1911–1983; 5'4"; brown hair, later blonde. *Wampas Baby Star:* 1927.

Martha Sleeper had one of the more memorable Wampas Baby surnames. Despite it, she had a solid career on Broadway where she had gone after abandoning her less than fulfilling film roles. It was there she gained her real fame. Her New York stage debut came in 1934's *Good Men and True*; she had earlier appeared in Los Angeles theater.

Sleeper, the niece of a studio head, was a young girl when she appeared in her first film, *The Mailman*, and was the top-billed actress in that picture. She returned to features five years later, after appearing in several two-reel comedies. It was about that time that Wampas selected her as a replacement for ailing French actress Jeanne Navelle. Her roles were generally in support until she began working for smaller studios in whose pictures she sometimes starred.

Martha Sleeper returned for one film in the 1940s and soon thereafter left acting entirely. For about 20 years she resided in Puerto Rico where she operated a dress shop. She was three times married, her first husband being the actor Hardie Albright. She then became the wife of an engineer named Deutschbein, and, finally, was wed to former Colonel Howard Stelling.

FILMOGRAPHY

Shorts

192?–, 193?
There Goes the Bride
The Chimp
Better Movies
Long Fliv the King
Crazy Like a Fox
Jewish Prudence
Flaming Fathers
Fluttering Hearts
Pass the Gravy

Features

1923
The Mailman

1928
The Little Yellow House
Skinner's Big Idea
Danger Street
Taxi 13

1929
The Air Legion
The Voice of the Storm

1930
Our Blushing Brides
Madam Satan
War Nurse

1931
Girls Demand Excitement

A Tailor Made Man
Ten Cents a Dance
Confessions of a Co-ed

1932

*Rasputin and the Empress
Huddle

1933

Midnight Mary
Penthouse
Broken Dreams
*Bombshell

1934

Spitfire
*Hollywood Party
Tomorrow's Youth

1935

West of the Pecos
Great God Gold
The Scoundrel
Two Sinners

1936

Rhythm on the Range

1937

Four Days' Wonder

1945

The Bells of St. Mary's

Martha Sleeper

*Sleeper's participation in these films is uncertain.

Starke, Pauline

Joplin, Missouri, 1900/01–1977; 5'3"–5'4"; brown hair, blue/gray eyes. *Wampas Baby Star:* 1922.

A veteran of Triangle films, freckle-faced Pauline Starke, with her strikingly wide-spaced eyes, had been in Hollywood as early as 1915. She purportedly was an extra in D. W. Griffith's *The Birth of a Nation* and then one of hundreds of dancing girls in *Intolerance*. It took several years of playing small roles before she emerged into stardom at Fine Arts. When she did it was generally as a beset

Pauline Starke

heroine in weepy melodramas. In magazine articles of the early 1920s she was characterized as being solemn in person, and "Poor Pauline" onscreen. She was known as the "Glad-Sad Girl."

Starke was named a Wampas Baby Star one year after her breakout films *A Connecticut Yankee in King Arthur's Court* and *Salvation Nell*. Initially cast in a country girl persona, in the 1920s she assumed a more glamorous aura at MGM. As a result it was later said that she was an ugly duckling who became a great beauty. One of her most successful roles was in 1927's *Women Love Diamonds*, a part that Mae Murray had turned down. Other major motion pictures were *Sun-Up* and *Man Without a Country*.

When the talkies came Pauline Starke was no longer in demand. According to her version this happened because director James Cruze wanted to cast his wife Betty Compson in the 1929 talkie *The Great Gabbo*, for which Starke had already been signed. The director claimed that Starke could not remember her lines and she was indeed replaced by Compson. She brought suit against the director for damaging her career. She also claimed to have been blacklisted by Louis B. Mayer when under contract to MGM, forcing her to work in Poverty Row productions.

Starke did not have any sound pictures in release until 1930, and they did little to boost her to talkie stardom. In 1933 one of her silent films, *Missing Daughters*, was rereleased by an independent studio with added talking sequences, music and sound effects. Her final starring film, a small studio production, came five years after she had last faced a camera but she was, at least, top-billed. She afterward appeared in some small bits.

In 1933 Pauline Starke appeared on Broadway in the play *Zombie*, which had a respectable run, and she may also have done other stage work. Much was made of her "rediscovery" as an elderly woman by movie buffs when she was living quietly in the heart of moviedom in Santa Monica. She was purported to have been very surprised that anyone still cared.

Pauline Starke was married to stage producer George Sherwood and had previously been married to film producer Jack White. She and her husband resided in Europe from the mid–1930s to 1940 and later lived aboard a sailboat which they took around the world several times. In 1948 she reappeared in the news when she apparently attempted suicide by drug overdose and was in very serious condition. It was noted at that time that she had suffered from declining health during the previous ten years.

FILMOGRAPHY

1916

Intolerance
The Rummy
The Wharf Rat

1917

Cheerful Givers
Madame Bo-Peep
The Regenerates
Until they Get Me

1918

The Argument
Innocent's Progress
The Shoes That Danced
The Man Who Woke Up
Alias Mary Brown
Daughter Angele
The Atom
Irish Eyes

1919

Whom the Gods Would Destroy
The Fall of Babylon (a rerelease of the Babylon segment of Intolerance with added footage)
Eyes of Youth
The Life Line
The Broken Butterfly
Soldiers of Fortune

1920

The Little Shepherd of Kingdom Come
Dangerous Days
The Courage of Marge O'Doone
Seeds of Vengeance
The Untamed
A Connecticut Yankee at King Arthur's Court
*The Forgotten Woman

1921

Snowblind
Salvation Nell
Wife Against Wife
Flower of the North

1922

My Wild Irish Rose
If You Believe It, It's So
The Kingdom Within

1923

Lost and Found on a South Sea Island
The Little Church Around the Corner
The Little Girl Next Door
His Last Race
In the Palace of the King
Eyes of the Forest

1924

The Arizona Express
Missing Daughters
Dante's Inferno
Hearts of Oak
Forbidden Paradise

1925

The Man Without a Country
The Devil's Cargo
Adventure
Sun-Up
Bright Lights

1926

Honesty — The Best Policy
War Paint
Love's Blindness

1927

Women Love Diamonds
Captain Salvation
Dance Magic
Streets of Shanghai

1929

Man, Woman and Wife
The Viking

1930

A Royal Romance
What Men Want

1933

Missing Daughters (rerelease of 1924 film)

1935

$20 a Week

1941

She Knew All the Answers

1944

Lost Angel

NOTE: *Some sources report that Starke appeared in two films shot much later in India:* Nine Hours to Rama *and* The Big Hunt.

*The release date of this film is not known with certainty.

Stuart, Gloria

(Gloria Finch); Santa Monica, California, 1909/10–; 5'5"; blonde hair, blue/green eyes. *Wampas Baby Star:* 1932.

An alumna of regional theater, including the Pasadena Playhouse, liquid-eyed and regally beautiful Gloria Stuart was sought by both Universal and Paramount for the movies. She signed with Universal, much to her expressed regret later on. Although she was no "scream queen" she lent her presence to a few horror films such as *The Invisible Man* and *The Old Dark House*. There were also prestigious pictures like *The Prisoner of Shark Island* and *Gold Diggers of 1935* (in which "Lullaby of Broadway" was featured). Nevertheless, she continually denigrated her roles and, at least once, threatened to walk out on her contract.

As early as 1934 Stuart had been unusually candid in an interview for the fan magazine *Motion Picture*: "I've only had two really good roles... The rest of the time I've just been there in front of the camera... It isn't big roles I want. Just good ones." She later said her parts had been "stupid and cliched." She was not to change her mind in the five years left in her starring career, even after she signed with 20th Century–Fox. While busy at her home studio and in many loan-outs, she also turned her considerable energy to projects like the establishment of the Screen Actors Guild, in which she was a board member.

Gloria Stuart did have the opportunity to co-star with such luminaries as Claude Rains, Charles Laughton, James Cagney, Melvyn Douglas and Dick Powell. And of course there was Shirley Temple. In a television interview as part of a biography of that child phenomenon, she spoke about what it was like playing opposite little Shirley in a couple of films.

Although she had achieved a career many other Wampas Baby Stars might have envied, after her Fox contract expired in 1939 Stuart mainly devoted herself to private interests such as perfecting her painting skills. There were a few more scattered movie roles in the 1940s. She became a proficient enough artist to have shows in prominent galleries; she lived in New York and Europe for a time.

Show business was not yet through with the feisty Stuart. She appeared on television, including several made-for-television movies and series like *Murder, She Wrote*. No longer possessing the beauty of her youth, but with a face full of impishly intelligent character — and considered quite a character in the eccentric sense — she still freely purveyed her strong opinions whenever a forum presented itself.

In 1997, Gloria Stuart returned to the screen to portray a 101-year-old woman in the highest earning film of all time, the $200 million extravaganza *Titanic*. Although the publicity surrounding the film stated that she had not appeared in the movies for 50 years, she actually had done small/bit roles in the 1980s. For her role of the heroine as an old woman in the modern-day framing story of *Titanic*, she received both the Golden Globe and Academy Award nominations for Best Supporting Actress. In a tie with another actress, she won an award from the Screen Actors Guild as Best Supporting Actress. She is, to date, the oldest person ever to be nominated for an Oscar. She subsequently penned an autobiography.

After her divorce from artist Blair

Newell, Gloria Stuart married comedy writer Arthur Sheekman, a frequent collaborator of the Marx Brothers. They had a daughter.

FILMOGRAPHY

Short

1933
Hollywood on Parade, no. 9

Features

1932
The Cohens and Kellys in Hollywood
Street of Women
The Old Dark House
The All American
Air Mail

1933
Laughter in Hell
Roman Scandals
The Kiss Before the Mirror
Private Jones
The Girl in 419
It's Great to Be Alive
The Invisible Man
Secret of the Blue Room
Sweepings

1934
Beloved
I Like It That Way
I'll Tell the World
Here Comes the Navy
The Love Captive
Gift of Gab

1935
Maybe It's Love
Gold Diggers of 1935
Laddie

1936
The Prisoner of Shark Island
Professional Soldier
Poor Little Rich Girl
36 Hours to Kill
The Girl on the Front Page
Wanted: Jane Turner
The Crime of Doctor Forbes

1937
The Lady Escapes
Girl Overboard
Life Begins in College

1938
Rebecca of Sunnybrook Farm
Change of Heart
Island in the Sky
Keep Smiling
Time Out for Murder
The Lady Objects

1939
The Three Musketeers
It Could Happen to You
Winner Take All

1943
Here Comes Elmer

1944
The Whistler
Enemy of Women

1946
She Wrote the Book

1975
The Legend of Lizzie Borden (TV)
Adventures of the Queen (TV)

1976
The Flood (TV)

1977
In the Glitter Palace (TV)

1979
The Best Place to Be (TV)
The Incredible Journey of Doctor Meg Laurel (TV)
The Two Worlds of Jennie Logan (TV)

1980
Fun and Games (TV)

1981
The Violation of Sarah McDavid (TV)

1982
My Favorite Year

1984
Mass Appeal

1986
Wildcats

1988	1999	*Stuart's participation in this is uncertain.
*Shootdown (TV)	The Love Letter	
1997	The Million Dollar Hotel	
Titanic		

Stuart, Iris

(Frances McCann); Brooklyn, New York, 1903–1936; 5'7"; brown hair, brown eyes. *Wampas Baby Star:* 1927.

As a renowned hands-and-face model, Iris Stuart was known as the "Girl with a Million Faces" because of her appearances in numerous magazine advertisements. From modest beginnings as a secretary, she became one of the highest-priced models in the world at the time. Her film career, however, was very brief. Given her short life, its brevity may well have been due to illness.

In 1927, the year of her Wampas selection, there already were news reports that she was ill. She made but a single feature before being selected as a Wampas Baby. In it she played a supporting role, as she would in the three Paramount pictures that followed. In a film with Clara Bow she played a character named Mousie, although the statuesque actress was anything but.

Stuart was married to publisher Bert McKinnon.

Filmography

1926	1927	Children of Divorce
Stranded in Paris	Casey at the Bat	Wedding Bill$

Taylor, Ruth

Grand Rapids, Michigan, 1907–1969; 5'2½"; blonde hair, blue eyes. *Wampas Baby Star:* 1928.

After extra work, Ruth Taylor may have had a very minor part in a Warner Bros. feature and then was put under five-year contract, starting at $60 weekly, to Mack Sennett in 1925. Before being signed she underwent plastic surgery on her nose, one of the rare times such a procedure was publicized in those days. Taylor had come from Broadway where she appeared in musicals including the Ziegfeld Follies. She also appeared on the stage in Los Angeles. Her first two-reel comedy co-lead may have come in a Slim Summerville film, and she eventually worked with such Sennett notables as Raymond McKee, Billy Bevan, Harry Langdon, Ralph Graves and Ben Turpin. She was said to have been the only Sennett leading lady never to have been seen in a bathing suit.

Bigger things were in store for Ruth Taylor in 1928, the first year she starred in full-length films. The first was her selection as a Wampas Baby Star. Then she was signed to play what must have been one of the most sought-after roles of that year, Lorelei Lee in Anita Loos's *Gentlemen Prefer Blondes*.

Despite the success of the film, Taylor made only three more features, including two talkies in 1929. Perhaps she left it all for marriage, but perhaps the handwriting was on the wall. In her first sound film she was top billed; in the next one she was far down the cast list. For whatever reason, she did depart films after marrying stockbroker Paul Zuckerman and became the mother of writer-humorist Buck Henry.

Filmography

Shorts

1925–1927?
A Hint to Brides

Features

1928
Gentlemen Prefer Blondes

Just Married

1929

College Coquette
This Thing Called Love

NOTE: She is not to be confused with the actress of the same name who made films in the late 1910s.

Thompson, Duane

(Duane Maloney); Red Oak, Iowa, 1903/05–1970; 5'1½"; brown hair (later blonde), blue eyes. *Wampas Baby Star:* 1925.

Although former dancer Duane Thompson made a fair number of films following her Wampas designation, they were of little consequence. She may have been in pictures as early as 1922 in Christie comedies, where she served as Walter Hiers's leading lady. Among her other co-stars were Richard Talmadge, Charles Ray and cowboy heroes Tom Tyler, Bill Cody and Buzz Barton. Oater star Ted Wells, also known as Pawnee Bill, Jr., was her most frequent leading man.

In 1928 Thompson signed a five-year contract with Universal but apparently did not receive billing in any talking pictures until ten years later. In her one credited sound film role her character was that of a telephone operator. She also made stage and radio appearances.

Duane Thompson was married to actor Buddy Wattles.

FILMOGRAPHY

Shorts

1922?
Up and at 'Em

Features

1925
Some Pun'kins
The Mysterious Stranger

1926
April Fool
College Days
The Lodge in the Wilderness

1927
The Silent Avenger
One Hour of Love
Husband Hunters
False Morals
The Desert Pirate

1928
Beauty and Bullets
The Fightin' Redhead
The Flying Buckaroo
Her Summer Hero
Phyllis of the Follies
Phantom of the Range
The Price of Fear
Wizard of the Saddle

1929
Frozen River
Slim Fingers
Born to the Saddle
The Tip-Off
Voice of the City

1938
Hollywood Hotel

Todd, Lola

(also known as Carol Mason); New York or Spuyten Duyval, New York, 1904–1995; 5'4½"; brown hair, brown eyes. *Wampas Baby Star*: 1925.

Supposedly in films from the age of 15, Lola Todd had a few co-starring roles. Most of them were in quickie westerns and serials with such leading men as Buck Jones, William Desmond, Jack Hoxie and Fred Thomson. She had been "discovered" by a friend of the family, none other than "Uncle" Carl Laemmle, founder of Universal Studio. She had another influential connection as well, supposedly related on her mother's side to playwright Eugene O'Neill.

In the late 1920s Todd announced her intention of assuming the stage name of Carol Mason. This was ostensibly to avoid comparisons with blonde comedienne Thelma Todd, although she did not physically resemble her. There is no evidence that she made any films under that name and her motion picture career ended about the same time.

FILMOGRAPHY

Shorts

1924–1925
Flying Eagle
The King's Command
The Border Cafe
The Best Man

Features

1923
Ghost City (serial)

1924
Dark Stairways
The Iron Man (serial)

1926
The Scarlet Streak (serial)
The Demon
The Count of Luxembourg
The Tough Guy

	1927	1928
The Fighting Peacemaker	The War Horse	Wallflowers
The Bells	Red Clay	Taking a Chance
Remember	The Return of the Riddle Rider (serial)	
	The Harvester	

Twelvetrees, Helen

(Helen Jurgens); Brooklyn, New York, 1908–1958; 5'2"–5'3"; blonde hair, blue eyes. *Wampas Baby Star:* 1929.

Surely the most intriguingly surnamed of all the Wampas Baby Stars (with Martha Sleeper perhaps a close second), Helen Twelvetrees came by her unusual name legitimately. Her first husband was stage actor Clark (or Clarke) Twelvetrees who apparently was unhappy about her competing career. When she signed her movie contract he jumped out of a sixth floor window, but amazingly survived. She too had been a stage actor before she entered the cinema, having appeared in many plays in stock and regional theater. Before that she modeled for magazine covers.

Later to be dubbed "The Perfect Ingenue," Twelvetrees was signed by Fox in 1928 and made her debut top-billed in that studio's second all-talking film *The Ghost Talks*. Although she was later to prove herself a fine screen actress, the studio dropped her option after six months and three pictures. Pathé (later absorbed by RKO) picked her up and it was there she began to establish her reputation with soapy but successful melodramas such as *Millie*, which gave her a big boost toward stardom, and *Her Man*.

Among Helen Twelvetrees's co-stars were some of the biggest names in Hollywood, but they were mostly at the start or toward the end of their major careers. Clark Gable was among them in one of his earliest leads, as a villain in *The Painted Desert*. Others included John Barrymore, Spencer Tracy and Maurice Chevalier. She almost never got the big pictures but was rumored to be going to star in George Cukor's *What Price Hollywood?*, a potential career-maker. (Constance Bennett played the part instead.)

Although Twelvetrees had occasionally been compared to Lillian Gish in the soulfulness of her performances, after her release by RKO any chance at major stardom seemed at an end. Many of her roles were as a hardboiled but vulnerable lady who suffered at length, a persona that may have palled on filmgoers. She did go on to make films at Columbia, Paramount, MGM, Fox and Republic, and also made an Australian film. She was supposedly the first American talkie actress to appear in their cinema.

Afterwards, Helen Twelvetrees made only three more pictures. In one she had only a scene with a couple of lines, but in her last she was again top-billed. In it she looked like she had actually been suffering; her face was puffy and she seemed older than her years.

Although the movies were through with her, she was not quite through with them. She sued RKO over the 1940 film *I'm Still Alive*, claiming it was based on her life with her ex-husband Frank Woody. The case was settled for a minor amount.

Twelvetrees returned to the stage and made her Broadway debut in 1941. Later she played Blanche Du Bois in *A Streetcar Named Desire* to some acclaim. On the domestic front, she married her third husband Conrad Payne, an Air Force officer. Her second marriage, to Woody, had given her a son. She developed health problems and her death from an overdose of barbiturates was deemed a suicide. Although she was born on Christmas Day, later life for the actress had proven to be no great gift.

FILMOGRAPHY

1929
The Ghost Talks
Blue Skies
Words and Music

1930
The Grand Parade
Swing High
Her Man
The Cat Creeps

1931
The Painted Desert
Millie
A Woman of Experience
Bad Company

1932
Panama Flo
Young Bride
State's Attorney
Is My Face Red?
Unashamed

1933
A Bedtime Story
Disgraced
My Woman
King for a Night

1934
All Men Are Enemies
Now I'll Tell
She Was a Lady
One Hour Late

1935
Times Square Lady
She Gets Her Man
The Spanish Cape Mystery
Frisco Waterfront

1936
Thoroughbred (Australia)

1937
Hollywood Round-up

1939
Persons in Hiding
Unmarried

Vaughn, Adamae

(sometimes Ada Mae); Ashland, Kentucky, 1907–1943; brown hair (later blonde). *Wampas Baby Star:* 1927.

The sister of 1924 Baby Star Alberta Vaughn, Adamae Vaughn was the unfortunate lady who fainted at her year's Wampas ceremonies. Of course, a cynic might say it garnered her a bit more publicity than her career might merit. She may also be the only Baby who married royalty; in 1929 her betrothal to a French viscount was announced.

Vaughn's full-length film roles were few, although it is possible she also appeared in two-reelers. Her first feature role came a couple of years prior to her Wampas designation in a small role as a stenographer. In 1926 she reached co-starring status for the only time with cowboy star Tom Tyler in the "B" western *Arizona Streak*. Later that year she was back in support — to the top billed dog, Ranger, in *Flashing Fangs*.

Adamae Vaughn did not emerge again in full-length films until she and Alberta danced and sang briefly together in the "Meet My Sister" number from the all-star farrago *The Show of Shows*. It was noticeable that the pert Alberta carried out her part with some flair while Adamae was stiff and ungainly. It also seemed that the latter had a pronounced lisp. After a supporting part in a 1930 musical, the only pictures in which Vaughn is known to have appeared, virtually as an extra, were two in mid-decade. It is possible that she performed as an extra in others.

Adamae Vaughn was first wed to Albert Hindman. Her long-delayed marriage to the viscount (known as Joseph D'Auvray, though his full blue-blooded name was much longer) finally took place in 1934.

Filmography

1925
The Last Edition

1926
The Arizona Streak
Flashing Fangs

1929
The Show of Shows

1930
Dancing Sweeties

1934
The Notorious Sophie Lang

1936
Love Before Breakfast

Vaughn, Alberta

Ashland, Kentucky, 1904/06–1992; 5'2"–5'3"; brown or auburn hair, brown eyes. *Wampas Baby Star:* 1924.

There are various stories about how Alberta Vaughn came into films. One of them says that other chorines in a Broadway show disliked her and, as a cruel joke, entered her in a "Funny Face" contest. She won it. In truth, she would have to be deemed cute rather than really pretty, although she supposedly had been dubbed the "prettiest girl in Kentucky."

Vaughn may have been a Sennett Bathing Beauty after she signed with him in 1923 for $100 a week. She also played in two-reel Pathé comedies with such gagsters as Billy Bevan, Clyde Cook, Lee Moran and Harry Gribbon. A versatile performer, she also appeared in dramas, and several series of shorts including The Go Getters, The Adventures of Mazie, The Telephone Girl, The Pacemakers, Racing Blood and perhaps even some of the popular Leather Pushers.

Among other studios for which Vaughn worked were Fox, Universal, Vitagraph and Joseph P. Kennedy's FBO, where she was top-billed in several features. She and her sister Adamae (or Ada Mae), a 1927 Wampas Baby (who fainted on her way up to accepting her award), appeared together in a brief segment of song and dance in the "Meet My Sister" number of the 1929 all-star extravaganza *The Show of Shows*.

Vaughn's somewhat high-pitched voice matched her elfin features and she went on to appear in the talkies for several years. Her pictures were minor ones but she did have several co-starring roles, particularly in westerns with the likes of Hoot Gibson and a very youthful John Wayne. Another leading man was the "original" Harrison Ford, a popular silent screen light comedian, in his only sound feature, *Love in High Gear*.

In 1934 Alberta Vaughn eloped with casting director Joe Egli. It was an unlikely development because, oddly enough, she had sued him the previous year when she was a passenger in his car and was injured in a crash. Her second husband was roofer John Thomas and it is possible she was married subsequently.

Vaughn's later life was not a happy one; she suffered from alcoholism and was arrested for drunk driving numerous times, sometimes in bizarre circumstances. In the mid–1940s she was picked up while dancing alongside a highway clad in GI long johns. She claimed she was entertaining troops from a nearby Army camp so they would furnish her with some cigarettes. In 1948 she was sentenced to a year in jail for repeated drunkenness and failure to pay restitution for a 1945 auto accident. She served six months of it.

FILMOGRAPHY

Shorts

1923–1925?, 1930–?

Picking Peaches
Smile Please
For the Love of Mike
King Leary
Sherlock's Home
Flip Flops
Nip and Tuck
The Go-Getters
A Miss in the Dark
The Sleeping Cutie
Who's Hooligan?
In the Knicker Time
Speed
He Who Gets Rapped
Welcome Granger
The Fast Male
What Price Gloria?
Don Coo Coo
Amazing Mazie
Adventures of Mazie
So's Your Old Man
Tea for Toomey
Mazie's Married
Fighting Hearts
The Lightning Slider
The Big Charade
When Sally's Irish Rose
The Pirate
The Orphan
The Artist
The Cyclist
A Small Town Romeo
The Son of Wallingford
Shipwrecked Among the Animals

Features

1923

A Friendly Husband

1926

Collegiate
The Adorable Deceiver

1927

Uneasy Payments
Ain't Love Funny?
Sinews of Steel
Backstage
The Romantic Age
The Drop Kick

1928

Skyscraper
Old Age Handicap
Forbidden Hours

1929

Noisy Neighbors
Molly and Me
Points West
The Show of Shows

1931	1933	*The release date of this film is not known with certainty.
Spell of the Circus (serial)	Alimony Madness	
Wild Horse	Emergency Call	NOTE: Also listed among Vaughn's credits is the (presumably silent) serial Flying Fate, but its release date and existence were not determined.
Working Girls	Dance Hall Hostess	
1932	**1934**	
Dancers in the Dark	Randy Rides Alone	
Love in High Gear	**1935**	
Daring Danger	The Laramie Kid	
Midnight Morals	*The Live Wire	

Velez, Lupe

(Guadalupe Velez Villalobos); San Luis de Potosi, Mexico, 1908/09–1944; 5'1½"; black hair (later red), brown eyes. *Wampas Baby Star:* 1928.

The leap from Hal Roach two-reelers directly into a dramatic Douglas Fairbanks, Sr., film mirrored the subsequent career of Lupe Velez, which seesawed between comedy and heavy drama. The intense and tempestuous actress could be equally effective in both but it is for the 1940s "Mexican Spitfire" series that she is largely remembered and unfortunately stereotyped.

Although Velez was partly educated in San Antonio, Texas, she never lost the accent which established her as the screen's major "hot pepper" (at least until English-mangling Carmen Miranda came along). It was an accent that condemned her to all-purpose "exotic" roles, including Indians and French-Canadians, as well as Latin types. She may have had some theater experience as a young girl and she did do some minor Hollywood stage work about 1927, the year she debuted in comedies with Charley Chase and Laurel and Hardy.

Doug Fairbanks saw in the minor comedy player the qualities he was looking for to play the Mountain Girl in his film *The Gaucho*. It was a part that had been rejected by Hollywood's most prominent Mexican actress, 1926 Wampas Star Dolores Del Rio. After Lupe Velez claimed that she had been underage when signed by Roach, United Artists was quick to sign her to a five-year contract. She was a dramatic actress in such pictures as D. W. Griffith's part-talkie *Lady of the Pavements* (in which she sang three songs) and *Where East Is East* (with Lon Chaney). She also made Spanish-language films, most of them versions of her English-language pictures, a common practice in the early 1930s.

It was not very long before the movie-going public became more entranced by Velez's flamboyant offscreen life than by her screen performances. Her lengthy and open affair with Gary Cooper (with whom she had co-starred in *Wolf Song*) stirred up gossip for years. So did her subsequent amours with John

Gilbert, Charles Chaplin, Tom Mix, Jack Dempsey and Randolph Scott. Known as "Whoopee Lupe," she finally "settled down" to very *un*domestic bliss with screen Tarzan Johnny Weissmuller. Public quarreling marked their five-year marriage, which was to be her only one. A much-quoted statement attributed to her was: "Always peoples say I am a wild girl, but I am not wild, I am Lupe."

In the '30s Lupe Velez began alternating motion pictures with occasional Broadway musicals such as Ziegfeld's *Hot Cha* and *Strike Me Pink*. In films she returned to comedy with Gregory La Cava's well-received *The Half-Naked Truth*. After the failure of the melodrama *Laughing Boy*, in which she played an Indian maiden, she appeared almost exclusively in comedies with then-popular Jimmy Durante and Wheeler and Woolsey, among others.

In mid-decade Velez traveled to the United Kingdom to star in a revue. While there she made three pictures before returning to America for some vaudeville appearances. Her first Mexican-made film came in 1937 and proved to be popular in her native country. Her first Hollywood-made film after an absence of two years set the pattern for the rest of her picture career. It was *The Girl from Mexico*, which gave rise to the "Spitfire" series co-starring rubber-legged Leon Errol.

Lupe Velez spent the next several years in "B" films where her much-imitated fractured English typed her as a flamboyant señorita in cheapies like *Playmates*, the last lamentable film of John Barrymore. Finally, she took a leaf from Dolores Del Rio's book and returned to Mexico to try to resuscitate a serious career—*Nana* being the result—but her troubled personal life intervened. She was a deeply religious woman in spite of her public image. When, as an unmarried woman, she became pregnant, she apparently saw suicide as the only alternative. Her death has been the source of speculation in several books.

FILMOGRAPHY

Shorts

1927
What Women Did for Me
Sailors Beware

1928
The Gaucho
Stand and Deliver

1929
Lady of the Pavements
Wolf Song
Where East Is East
Tiger Rose

1930
Hell Harbor
The Storm
East Is West
Oriente y Occidente (Spanish version of East Is West)

1931
Resurrection
Resurreción (Spanish version of Resurrection)
The Squaw Man
The Cuban Love Song

1932
Hombres in Mi Vida (Spanish version of Men in Her Life; she did not appear in the English version)
The Broken Wing
Kongo
The Half-Naked Truth

1933
Hot Pepper
Mr. Broadway (cameo)

1934
Laughing Boy
Palooka
Hollywood Party
Strictly Dynamite

1935
The Morals of Marcus (U.K.)

1936
Gypsy Melody (U.K.)
Stardust (U.K.)

1937
High Flyers
La Zandunga (Mexico)

1939
The Girl from Mexico

1940
Mexican Spitfire
Mexican Spitfire Out West

1941
Six Lessons from Madame La Zonga
Mexican Spitfire's Baby
Playmates
Honolulu Lu

1942
Mexican Spitfire at Sea

Mexican Spitfire Sees a Ghost
Mexican Spitfire's Elephant

1943
Ladies Day
Mexican Spitfire's Blessed Event
Redhead from Manhattan

1944
Nana (Mexico)

Weeks, Barbara

(also known as Sue Kingsley); Boston, Massachusetts or Binghampton, New York, 1913– ; 5'5"; brown hair (sometimes blonde), blue eyes. *Wampas Baby Star:* 1931.

A Broadway theater and Ziegfeld Follies performer, Barbara Weeks appeared with comic Eddie Cantor in the stage version of the musical *Whoopee!* and may have made her film debut in the screen version. Signed to a long-term contract with Warner Bros., she played many supporting parts but also had some leads in "B" westerns and other second features.

Among Weeks's oater co-stars were Buck Jones, Charles Starrett and Tim McCoy. She made news when she was clawed by a leopard during the filming of one quickie. In the later 1930s she was heard on the radio, one of her roles being in a soap opera, and appeared in more Broadway shows.

Weeks was divorced from test pilot Lewis Parker. She also had been married to the character actor Guinn ("Big Boy") Williams, whose screen specialty was playing dumb.

NOTE: Not the actress of the same name who made a few films in the 1950s.

FILMOGRAPHY

Short

1931
Revenge Is Sweet

Features

1930
*Whoopee!
Man to Man

1931
*The Guilty Generation
Party Husband
Men in Her Life

*My Past
*Illicit
*Fifty Million Frenchmen
*Men of the Sky
Palmy Days
Two Fisted Justice

1932

Discarded Lovers
Stepping Sisters
Cheaters at Play
Devil's Lottery
Hell's Headquarters
By Whose Hand?
The Night Mayor
White Eagle
Deception
Forbidden Trail
Sundown Rider

1933

State Trooper
Soldiers of the Storm
Rusty Rides Alone
My Weakness
Olsen's Big Moment

1934

Woman Unafraid
The Quitter
The Crosby Case
Now I'll Tell
She Was a Lady
When Strangers Meet

1935

School for Girls

1937

Pick a Star
Two Fisted Sheriff
One Man Justice
The Old Wyoming Trail

1938

Dramatic School

1939

Paris Honeymoon

1940

Dad Rudd, MP (Australia)

*Weeks's appearances in these films are not known with certainty.

Wells, Jacqueline

(also known as Julie Bishop and Diane Duval) (Jacqueline Brown); Denver, Colorado, 1914–; 5'4"; red hair, hazel eyes. *Wampas Baby Star*: 1934.

Having studied dancing and ballet, Jacqueline Wells was already appearing in films before she reached her teens. Later she had regional theater experience at the famed Pasadena Playhouse and other venues. Said to have an almost perfect shoulder line (something they apparently found important in those days), she initially signed with Paramount. After her first marriage ended, she left Hollywood temporarily to join a Midwestern stock company and upon returning became a Warner Bros. contract player.

Given the large number of pictures she made, Wells would have to be credited with a successful career, but it was one in which she generally had large parts in "B" films and smaller ones in major productions. She changed her name in an attempt to get away from unfulfilling ingenue roles and in the mid–1940s she did appear in some prestige films, if not necessarily in major roles (e.g., Mrs. Ira Gershwin in the biopic *Rhapsody in Blue*). During the 1950s she worked on television, including in Robert Cummings's *My Hero*.

Wells was married to Walter Brooks, General Clarence Shoop and William Bergin.

FILMOGRAPHY

(as Jacqueline Wells)

Shorts

193?
Skip the Maloo!
In Walked Charley

Features

1923
*Maytime
*Children of Jazz
*Bluebeard's Eighth Wife

1924
*Captain Blood
*Dorothy Vernon of Haddon Hall
*The Good Bad Boy

1925
The Home Maker
Classified
The Golden Bed

1926
The Bar-C Mystery (serial)
The Family Upstairs

1931
Scareheads

1933
Tillie and Gus
Alice in Wonderland
Clancy of the Mounted (serial)
Tarzan the Fearless (serial)

1934
Happy Landing
The Black Cat
Kiss and Make-Up
The Loudspeaker

1935
Square Shooter
Night Cargo
Coronado

1936
The Bohemian Girl

1937
Counsel for Crime
She Married an Artist
Paid to Dance
The Frame-Up
Girls Can Play

1938
Little Miss Roughneck
When G-Men Step In
Spring Madness
Flight into Nowhere
Flight to Fame
The Little Adventuress
The Main Event
Highway Patrol

1939
My Son Is a Criminal
Behind Prison Gates
The Kansas Terrors
Torture Ship
My Son Is Guilty

1940
Girl in 313
Young Bill Hickok
The Ranger and the Lady
Her First Romance

1941
Back in the Saddle

(as Diane Duval)

1932
Heroes of the West (serial)

(as Julie Bishop)

1941
International Squadron
The Nurse's Secret
Steel Against the Sky
Wild Bill Hickok Rides

1942
Lady Gangster
Busses Roar
The Hidden Hand
Escape from Crime
I Was Framed

1943
The Hard Way
Princess O'Rourke
Action in the North Atlantic
Northern Pursuit

1944
Hollywood Canteen

1945
Rhapsody in Blue
You Came Along

1946
Cinderella Jones
Idea Girl
Strange Conquest
Murder in the Music Hall

1947
High Tide
Last of the Redmen

1949
Deputy Marshal
The Threat
Sands of Iwo Jima

1951
Westward the Women

1953
Sabre Jet

1954
The High and the Mighty

1955
Headline Hunters

1957
The Big Land

*Wells's participation in these films is uncertain.

Williams, Katherine

Seattle, Washington, 1914?–1982; 5'5½"; blonde hair, brown eyes. *Wampas Baby Star:* 1934.

Katherine Williams had some regional theater experience going for her, including time at the Pasadena Playhouse. Perhaps a bigger asset was her relationship — that of second cousin — to longtime MGM character star Lewis Stone. (Fellow 1934 Wampas Star Betty Bryson also had well-known cinema relatives; she was a niece of leading man Warner Baxter and silent actress Winifred Bryson.)

Notwithstanding that connection, Williams's career apparently consisted of but four features. Two of those were *Kiss and Make-Up* and *Young and Beautiful*, in which many of the 1934 Wampas Baby Stars appeared, largely as a publicity stunt.

Williams was married to college professor Daniel Vandraegen.

FILMOGRAPHY

1933
The Big Race

1934
Where Sinners Meet
Kiss and Make-Up
Young and Beautiful

Wilson, Dorothy

Minneapolis, Minnesota, 1909–1998; 5'1¼"; brown hair, blue eyes. *Wampas Baby Star:* 1932.

According to her publicity Dorothy Wilson was a Hollywood stereotype come true, causing her to be dubbed the "Cinderella of Hollywood." She supposedly was discovered by the director Gregory La Cava while toiling at RKO as a stenographer. Whether or not the director then followed the hackneyed Hollywood script by shouting "I must have that girl!" is not known, but she did receive a Paramount contract and had top billing in her first film. She received the Wampas honor that same year.

Among Wilson's major films, in

which she sometimes had leading roles, were *Craig's Wife*, *The White Parade*, *The Last Days of Pompeii* and *The Milky Way*, starring Harold Lloyd. She became the fifth and last Wampas Baby to co-star with Lloyd following Jobyna Ralston, Ann Christy, Barbara Kent and Constance Cummings. She also appeared with Will Rogers in his final film. Other leading men were Victor McLaglen, James Dunn, Richard Dix and the western heroes Ken Maynard, George O'Brien and Buck Jones. Her last known fling at show business was a test for the role of Melanie in *Gone with the Wind*.

Wilson was married to screenwriter Lewis Foster, later the winner of an Academy Award for the screenplay of *Mr. Smith Goes to Washington*. They had two sons.

Filmography

Short

1933

Hollywood on Parade, no. 9

Features

1932

The Age of Consent
Men of America

1933

Lucky Devils
Scarlet River
*Professional Sweetheart
Before Dawn
Above the Clouds

1934

Eight Girls in a Boat
One in a Million
His Greatest Gamble
The Merry Widow
The White Parade

1935

When a Man's a Man
**Circus Shadows
Bad Boy
The Last Days of Pompeii
In Old Kentucky

1936

The Milky Way
*Hollywood Boulevard
Craig's Wife

1937

Speed to Spare

Wilson's participation in these films is uncertain.

**The release date of this film is uncertain.*

Wilson, Lois

Pittsburgh, Pennsylvania, 1894/98–1988; 5'5½"; brown hair (sometimes blonde), brown or hazel eyes. *Wampas Baby Star: 1922.*

Lois Wilson had a greatly varied career in films, theater, radio and television. She was arguably one of the most respected and talented actresses of all the Baby Stars. Her beginnings were like many another Baby; she won a beauty contest as Miss Alabama. She had previously, but briefly, been a rural school teacher. Her looks, especially those wonderfully expressive eyes, proved to be the entree to her first major studio, Universal, where she was a frequent co-star of popular J. Warren Kerrigan.

Other of Wilson's early studios were Paralta and California, but it was as a Paramount star from the late 'teens to 1927 that she shone. Her first film, as an extra, had come about 1915 and small parts soon followed. Although she was most often a conventional leading lady playing the "good" girl, she also had an affinity for character leads and was willing to conceal her natural prettiness when it was required. One of her best roles, and her favorite, came in 1921 with *Miss Lulu Bett*. In it she portrayed a shy and distinctly plain spinster much older than her real age.

Lois Wilson's best remembered role today is undoubtedly that of Molly in the western epic *The Covered Wagon*, but she had other memorable roles in the 1920s. One was in the comedy-drama *Only 38*, again playing a part older than her age. Another was in the first version of *The Great Gatsby* in which she varied from type by playing a semi-bad girl. Although Paramount had a sizable number of important female stars, they sent her to represent the motion picture industry at the British Empire Exposition in 1924.

A frequent Paramount co-star of Wilson's was rugged Richard Dix, one of the silent screen's most popular heroes, to whom she was engaged at one time. Her other leading men included Rudolph Valentino, Wallace Reid and Thomas Meighan, all huge stars of the silents. She also worked with comedian Edward Everett Horton, with whom she appeared in her first sound vehicle, the Vitaphone short *Miss Information*. Like most other stars at the studio she made some pictures for C. B. DeMille and appeared in a few of the Zane Grey westerns in which Paramount specialized.

All was not always rosy between Lois Wilson and Paramount. In 1927 she refused to co-star with a young newcomer and suffered a lengthy suspension. He was Gary Cooper, so in retrospect she probably regretted her action. She joined Warner Bros. after leaving Paramount, but by then talkies had established themselves and the careers of many old-line Hollywood stars were on the decline. Hers was to prove no exception, especially after she began freelancing in 1930.

Wilson made numerous films through 1936, and sporadically into the next decade as well, but for the most part she was finished as a major Hollywood name and inevitably slipped into supporting roles. One of her best sound films was *Seed* (with Bette Davis who was just starting her film career). She had made her first stage appearance in the late 1920s and it was to the theater that she increasingly turned as the films grew less important. Among the plays in which she appeared were *Junior Miss*, *Chicken Every Sunday* and, much later, *I Never Sang for My Father* in the 1970s. Often she replaced such stars as Dorothy and Lillian Gish but she also created some of her roles.

Lois Wilson had a good speaking voice and she made many radio broadcasts as well as appearing on television, including in soap opera. She also kept busy with such avocations as polo. Although two of her sisters acted in movies under the names of Connie Lewis and Diana Kane, their careers were not comparable to hers. It was a worthy one indeed, covering as it did some 60 years. She never married.

Filmography

Shorts

1910s, late 1920s, 1930s

The New Adventures of Terrance O'Rourke
Married on the Wing
Hulda the Silent
He Wrote a Book
Arthur's Deep Resolve
Her Chance
The Whispered Name
Black Evidence
Flames of Treachery
The Road to Paradise
When a Queen Loved O'Rourk
Miss Information
A Bird in the Hand
Temptation
Her Husband's Women
For Love or Money
Screen Snapshots

Features

1916

*The Decoy
*The Pool of Flame
The Gay Lord Waring
A Son of the Immortals
The Silent Battle
The Dumb Girl of Portici
Langdon's Legacy
The Beckoning Trail
The Morals of Hilda

1917

Treason
Alimony

1918

A Man's Man (reedited and reissued in 1923)
The Turn of a Card
His Robe of Honor
One Dollar Bid
The Bells
Maid o' the Storm
A Burglar for a Night
Prisoners of the Pines
Three X Gordon

1919

The Drifters
Come Again Smith
The End of the Game
The Best Man
Gates of Brass
Love Insurance
A Man's Fight
The Price Woman Pays
Why Smith Left Home
It Pays to Advertise

1920

Too Much Johnson
Thou Art the Man
A Full House
Burglar Proof
The City of Masks
What's Your Hurry?
Who's Your Servant?

1921

Midsummer Madness
What Every Woman Knows
The City of Silent Men
The Lost Romance
The Hell Diggers
Miss Lulu Bett

1922

The World's Champion
Is Matrimony a Failure?
Our Leading Citizen
Manslaughter
Broad Daylight
Without Compromise

1923

The Covered Wagon
Bella Donna
Only 38
A Man's Man
Hollywood (cameo)
Ruggles of Red Gap
To the Last Man
The Call of the Canyon

1924

Pied Piper Malone
Another Scandal
Icebound
Monsieur Beaucaire
The Man Who Fights Alone
North of 36

1925

Contraband
The Thundering Herd
Welcome Home
Rugged Water
The Vanishing American
Irish Luck

1926

Bluebeard's Seven Wives
Let's Get Married
Fascinating Youth (cameo)
The Show Off
The Great Gatsby

1927
New York
Broadway Nights
The Gingham Girl
Alias the Lone Wolf
French Dressing

1928
Ransom
Coney Island
Sally's Shoulders
On Trial
Object — Alimony
Conquest

1929
Kid Gloves
The Show of Shows
The Gamblers
Wedding Rings

1930
The Furies
Lovin' the Ladies
Once a Gentleman

1931
Seed
The Age for Love

1932
The Expert
The Crash

Rider of Death Valley
The Secrets of Wu Sin
Divorce in the Family
Drifting Souls
The Devil Is Driving

1933
Obey the Law
Laughing at Life
Deluge
Female
In the Money

1934
The Show Off
No Greater Glory
There's Always Tomorrow
School for Girls
Ticket to a Crime
Bright Eyes

1935
Public Opinion
Born to Gamble
Cappy Ricks Returns
Society Fever
Your Uncle Dudley

1936
The Return of Jimmy Valentine

Wedding Present
Laughing at Trouble

1938
*Life Returns

1939
Bad Little Angel
For Love or Money

1940
Nobody's Children

1941
For Beauty's Sake

1949
The Girl from Jones Beach

*The production date of this film is uncertain. It may have been made as early as 1934 but the earliest known release date is 1938.

**Wilson's participation in this film is uncertain.

Windsor, Claire

(Clara Cronk); Cawker City, Kansas, 1897/98–1972; 5'6½"; auburn hair (later blonde), blue/gray eyes. *Wampas Baby Star:* 1922.

Rarely was a story written in the 1920s about Claire Windsor that did not refer to her as the screen's greatest beauty. She claimed to have been given the name Windsor because she looked patrician and she certainly was that, having been dubbed "The Perfect American Beauty." A former Seattle Queen of the Carnival, she had studied voice and piano and worked her way up from an extra and bit player starting about 1918. Although her films were generally no more than ordinary melodramas, she had a penchant for getting publicity.

One of the first times Windsor made the news was for her ostensible disappearance in 1921 for a day-and-a-half. Charlie Chaplin even put up a reward for her safe return. (The whole affair was presumably "put up" as well.) She was found "semi-conscious," supposedly from a fall. Another bit of publicity sprang from the fact that she spoke openly about her son from a dissolved marriage to Mr. Boweston (or Bowes). In those days it was considered death to a leading actress's career to talk about—or even *have*—children. (Her son adopted her stage name as his own and was known as William Windsor.)

In 1921 Claire Windsor was taken under the wing of Lois Weber, probably the most famous woman director of her day, and cast in a series of romantic dramas. She went on to become one of the most popular leading ladies of the silents, working at such studios as Tiffany-Stahl, Goldwyn, Fox, First National, Paramount, Universal and MGM.

Windsor's typical films in the '20s were slickly produced melodramas and she also could occasionally (but perhaps unintentionally) spoof her heavily dramatic image in a picture like *Nellie, the Beautiful Cloak Model*. She eventually began to freelance and with the advent of talkies her fortunes declined. She made her sound debut in 1929's *Midstream* and was then off the screen for three years in spite of her announced "voice culture" lessons.

The reason for the renewed interest in Windsor in the 1930s undoubtedly came from yet another burst of publicity. In 1932 she was sued for $100,000 for alienation of affection for supposedly stealing away a woman's husband. The so-called "heart balm" suit dragged on in court until 1933. During that time she returned to the screen in a Monogram cheapie that could not unintentionally have been titled *Self-Defense*.

The publicity surrounding the trial lasted long enough for Claire Windsor to make a few more pictures for small independent studios like Mayfair and Invincible the next year. In a couple she received top billing. A judgment ultimately was brought against her for $75,000, but she appealed and eventually settled out of court for a mere $1,200. When the trial ended so did her leading film roles and she appeared only sporadically thereafter. A "B" comedy in the 1940s was her final traceable on-screen effort, but she later worked in the theater and on television.

Windsor was in the public eye again in 1937 when she claimed she had been swindled in an oil stock deal, but the most bizarre occurrence came in 1966. Silent screen beauty Corinne Griffith, who was being sued for divorce, claimed the real Griffith was dead and that she was her much younger sister or stand-in (her accounts varied). Windsor testified that the woman in the courtroom was indeed the actress she had known in the 1920s.

Windsor was married, for the second time, to stage and screen matinee idol Bert Lytell. She did not thereafter remarry but always had her share of beaux. In Lita Grey Chaplin's autobiography, for instance, she is named as one of Charlie Chaplin's great and good friends. In her retirement she devoted herself to painting, an avocation at which she was skilled enough to be exhibited in galleries.

FILMOGRAPHY

1920
The Luck of the Irish
To Please One Woman

1921
What's Worth While?
The Raiders
Too Wise Wives
The Blot
Dr. Jim
What Do Men Want?

1922
Grand Larceny
Fools First
One Clear Call
Rich Men's Wives
Brothers Under the Skin
Broken Chains
The Stranger's Banquet

1923
Souls for Sale
Little Church Around the Corner
Rupert of Hentzau
The Eternal Three
The Acquittal

1924
Nellie, the Beautiful Cloak Model
A Son of the Sahara
For Sale
Born Rich

1925
The Dixie Handicap
The Denial
The White Desert
Just a Woman
Souls for Sables

1926
Dance Madness
Money Talks
Tin Hats

1927
A Little Journey
The Claw
The Frontiersman
The Bugle Call
Foreign Devils
Blondes by Choice
The Opening Night

1928
Satan and the Woman
Nameless Men
The Grain of Dust
Domestic Meddlers
Fashion Madness

1929
Captain Lash
Midstream

1932
Self-Defense

1933
Sister to Judas
The Constant Woman
Kiss of Araby

1934
Cross Streets

1937
*Topper

1938
Barefoot Boy

1945
How Do You Do?

Windsor's participation in this film is uncertain.

NOTE: *Windsor claimed her last film was 1952's* The Last Act. *No film by that name has been identified and, if made, was perhaps unreleased.*

Wood, Judith

(Helen Johnson); New York, New York, 1906–; 5'5"; blonde hair. *Wampas Baby Star:* 1931.

After studying painting in Paris and playing in vaudeville, Judith Wood made her first few films in 1930 and '31 under her real name of Helen Johnson. In the middle of 1931, when she was named a Wampas Baby, she assumed her new one. It was also the year she received her only top billing, in *Working Girls*.

Having been under contract to

MGM and Paramount, Wood found her career temporarily derailed in the early '30s by an automobile accident in which her nose was shattered. This had a certain amount of irony about it because her character in 1930's *The Divorcée* suffered the same fate.

Upon her recuperation, Wood, who somewhat resembled then-star Ann Harding, did a stint on the Broadway stage (creating the role in *Dinner at Eight* later played onscreen by Jean Harlow) and returned to Hollywood. She was signed by Darryl F. Zanuck but was dropped after just two films. There also was a movie made in England; thereafter, she was usually down in the ranks of the supporting players.

If Hollywood gossip is to be believed, Wood's real life was many times more exciting than her "reel" one. She was regarded as a liberated woman, even by Hollywood standards, and had a string of affairs with such leading men as Franchot Tone, Robert Montgomery and William Powell. She married Percival Wren, Jr., a British diplomat who was assigned to the embassy in Tokyo prior to World War Two. (He was the son of novelist P. C. Wren, who wrote *Beau Geste*.) After they were divorced at the end of the War, she did some radio work in New York, eventually moving to Hollywood again where she became a costume designer.

FILMOGRAPHY

(as Helen Johnson)

1929
*Gold Diggers of Broadway

1930
Children of Pleasure
The Divorcée
Soldiers and Women
Sin Takes a Holiday

1931
It Pays to Advertise
The Vice Squad

(as Judith Wood)

Women Love Once
The Road to Reno

Girls About Town
Working Girls

1932
The Divorce Racket

1933
Hotel Variety
Advice to the Lovelorn

1934
Looking for Trouble
Crime Doctor
The Man Who Reclaimed His Head

1936
Riffraff

1937
Rhythm Racketeer (U.K.)

1941
They Met in Bombay

1949
Beyond the Forest

1950
The Asphalt Jungle

*Wood's participation in this film is uncertain.

Wray, Fay

(Vina Fay Wray); Cardston, Alberta, Canada, 1907–; 5'2"–5'3"; brown hair (sometimes blonde), blue-green eyes. *Wampas Baby Star:* 1926.

Fay Wray had the good fortune (or perhaps misfortune) to be a part of one of the iconographic images of 1930s cinema. And she had the "tallest, darkest leading man in Hollywood" to share it with her. It is the scene in which the giant gorilla King Kong places her character atop the Empire State Building. She was, to paraphrase the final words of the classic film, the beauty who killed the beast.

The 1933 picture assured for Wray a permanent place in film history, but it also practically ensured that she is remembered for little else. As dedicated fans of horror movies know, *King Kong* was only one of a string of films in which she was the most menaced actress of them all. *Doctor X, Mystery of the Wax Museum, The Vampire Bat* and *The Most Dangerous Game* also saw her threatened by unspeakable dangers.

If Fay Wray is now known only for her movie screaming, that is not a true picture of her career. She began as a teenage extra and then was cast in Hal Roach two-reelers and westerns. Her future seemed to be as a run-of-the-mill Universal ingenue when Erich von Stroheim selected her to be the leading lady in his last great silent effort, *The Wedding March*. Like most of the director's films it was tampered with post-production and was not successful. It did, however, bring the actress to the attention of Paramount moguls where she was signed to a contract.

There Wray was co-starred with Gary Cooper in an effort to recreate a kind of Charles Farrell–Janet Gaynor romantic duo. Their films together did not generate much heat. Director Josef von Sternberg used her in his first talkie *Thunderbolt*, and she went on to appear with other major male stars such as Emil Jannings, Ronald Colman, Spencer Tracy, Richard Barthelmess, William Powell, Fredric March, Richard Dix and Warner Baxter. She also played an occasional unsympathetic part, as in MGM's *Viva Villa* with Wallace Beery.

After her 1931 release from Paramount Fay Wray freelanced. She made some pictures in England in the mid–'30s, no doubt in hopes of giving her career a boost, but found upon her return that it had accomplished the opposite. She had been overtaken by a new crop of ingenues and her best screen days were now behind her, although she was seen on the screen until the early 1940s.

Some ten years later Wray returned to play character roles. Ever in the large ape's debt, her reentry into movies could well have come about because of the rerelease of *King Kong* around that time. She made stage appearances in New York and other cities, and did television in the 1950s, including the series *Pride of the Family*. She also turned her hand to writing plays, among which were *The Brown Danube* and *Angela Is 21* (later made into a film).

Fay Wray was three times wed, the first marriage being to writer John Monk Saunders. Her second marriage to writer Robert Riskin ended with his death as did her third, to prominent neurosurgeon Sanford Rothenberg, who had been one of Riskin's doctors. The marriages produced three children. Her final professional appearance, to date, was in a 1980 television play. She also wrote her autobiography *On the Other Hand*, the title being an allusion to the massive hand of that famous tall, dark leading man.

FILMOGRAPHY

Shorts

1923–1926?
Gasoline Love
What Price Goofy?
No Father to Guide Him
Don't Shoot
The Saddle Tramp

Features

1925
The Coast Patrol

1926
Lazy Lightning
The Man in the Saddle
The Wild Horse Stampede

1927
Loco Luck
A One Man Game
Spurs and Saddles

1928
Legion of the Condemned
The Street of Sin
The First Kiss
The Wedding March

1929
The Four Feathers
Thunderbolt
Pointed Heels

1930
Behind the Make-Up
The Texan
The Sea God
Paramount on Parade
Captain Thunder
The Border Legion

1931
The Finger Points
The Conquering Horde
Not Exactly Gentlemen (aka Three Rogues)
Dirigible
The Lawyer's Secret
The Unholy Garden

1932
Stowaway
Doctor X
The Most Dangerous Game

1933
The Vampire Bat
Mystery of the Wax Museum
King Kong
Below the Sea
Ann Carver's Profession
The Woman I Stole
The Big Brain
One Sunday Afternoon
Shanghai Madness
The Bowery
Master of Men

1934
Madame Spy
Once to Every Woman
The Countess of Monte Cristo
Viva Villa
The Affairs of Cellini
Black Moon
The Richest Girl in the World
Cheating Cheaters
Woman in the Dark
White Lies
Mills of the Gods

1935
Come Out of the Pantry (U.K.)
Alias Bulldog Drummond (aka Bulldog Jack) (U.K.)
The Clairvoyant (aka The Evil Mind) (U.K.)

1936
Roaming Lady
When Knights Were Bold (U.K.?)
They Met in a Taxi

1937
It Happened in Hollywood
Murder in Greenwich Village

1938
The Jury's Secret
Smashing the Spy Ring

1939
Navy Secrets

1940
Wildcat Bus

1941
Adam Had Four Sons
Melody for Three
1942
Not a Ladies Man
1944
This Is the Life

1953
Treasure of the Golden Condor
Small Town Girl
1955
The Cobweb
Queen Bee
1956
Hell on Frisco Bay

1957
Rock, Pretty Baby
Crime of Passion
Tammy and the Bachelor
1958
Summer Love
Dragstrip Riot

Young, Loretta

(Gretchen Jung, later Young); Salt Lake City, Utah, 1912/13–2000; 5'5½"; brown hair (sometimes blonde), blue-gray eyes. *Wampas Baby Star:* 1929.

The year she was selected as a Baby Star, Loretta Young was a callow ingenue whose journeyman acting ability gave little indication of the major star she would become. A resident of Los Angeles from early childhood, she joined her sisters Polly Ann and Elizabeth (Betty) Jane in occasional extra stints. Her first film appearance may have come at the age of four or so. She was rediscovered as a teenager, supposedly when substituting for Polly on a casting call.

By this time Betty Jane was making her mark in films as Sally Blane, also named a Wampas Baby in 1929. This is the only time sisters were so designated in the same year and they appeared together briefly singing and dancing in the "Meet My Sister" number in *The Show of Shows*. Young and her sisters, including half-sister Georgianna, were to be together again many years later in *The Story of Alexander Graham Bell*.

Loretta Young's breakthrough was her role with Lon Chaney in *Laugh, Clown, Laugh* in 1928. Although she was inexperienced and the director, Herbert Brenon, apparently gave her an extremely hard time, her performance was considered worthy enough. It was of course her beauty that shone from the screen; eyes like lamplights being her most striking feature. Her face was considered eminently photographable from any and every angle.

The timbre of Young's speaking voice was good and she transitioned to the talkies easily, often co-starring with Douglas Fairbanks, Jr., in her early sound films. The American Institute of Voice Teachers three times voted hers the finest female speaking voice in the cinema. She also made many radio appearances.

Young's first major studio was First National, later to be merged into Warner Bros. Her pictures there were generally run-of-the-mill and did little to raise her above the crowd of other leading ladies. It was her move to 20th Century about 1933 that paved the way to stardom. Although she was quoted as saying she wanted be a character actress, it was usually as a bland "window-dressing" heroine in romantic costume melodramas that she thrived. She once stated that her costumes often received the bulk of the good reviews.

Under Darryl F. Zanuck's aegis, Loretta Young made the move into romantic comedy, *Love Is News* being an early example. The apex of her prestigious starring career seemed to have occurred in the later 1930s. With her signing at Columbia in 1940 there was a general decline in her filmic fortunes that lasted throughout the World War II period. However, other triumphs were yet to come.

In 1947 Young made *The Farmer's Daughter*, complete with Swedish accent, and won that year's Oscar for Best Actress. (Ingrid Bergman had been the first choice for the role.) Follow-up films like *Come to the Stable* (another Oscar nomination for her role as a nun), *Rachel and the Stranger* and *The Bishop's Wife* cemented a solid "comeback."

Like most leading ladies flirting with the age of 40, Loretta Young soon did face the end of her starring career. She realized the relatively new medium of television lacked bankable stars (mainly because of Hollywood's opposition to it), and in 1953 the *Loretta Young Show* debuted. Although she was parodied for her clothes-horse appearances, particularly the swirling skirts, the show proved very successful. Three Emmys were the result, as well as a host of other prizes and awards.

There were over 300 shows produced, with Young starring in more than half of them. *The New Loretta Young Show* premiered in 1962 but did not meet with success and she busied herself with private good works for more than 20 years thereafter. In 1986 she was once again seen on the small screen in a made-for-television movie.

Loretta Young's grip on her private life was not as firm as that on her professional one. Her early marriage to actor Grant Withers ended in divorce, and the troubled lives of her three children have been well publicized. Her supposedly adopted daughter Judy Lewis — who took the surname of Young's second husband Tom Lewis — contends that she is actually her mother's natural daughter and the love child of none other than Clark Gable. Jean Louis, the Academy Award-winning costume designer, who fashioned many of her famous television outfits, was her third husband.

Despite her latter-day reputation as an iron butterfly, unflatteringly referred to by such names as "Gretch the Wretch" and "Attila the Nun," Young's place as an important leading lady speaks for itself. Although rarely respected for her acting abilities, the list of her co-stars reads like a Hollywood *Who's Who*: Gable, Spencer Tracy, Richard Barthelmess, George Arliss, Ronald Colman, Charles Boyer, Tyrone Power, Don Ameche, Ray Milland, Melvyn Douglas, Gary Cooper, James Cagney and Alan Ladd.

Filmography

1927
*Naughty but Nice

1928
The Whip Woman
Laugh, Clown, Laugh
The Head Man
The Magnificent Flirt

1929
The Girl in the Glass Cage
Fast Life
The Careless Age
Scarlet Seas
The Squall
The Forward Pass
The Show of Shows

1930
Loose Ankles
The Man from Blankley's
The Second Floor Mystery
Road to Paradise
Broken Dishes
Kismet
The Truth About Youth
The Devil to Pay

1931
Beau Ideal
Big Business Girl
Three Girls Lost
The Right of Way
Too Young to Marry
I Like Your Nerve
Platinum Blonde
The Ruling Voice

1932
The Hatchet Man
Play Girl
Taxi!
Week-end Marriage
Life Begins
They Call It Sin

1933
Employee's Entrance
Zoo in Budapest
The Devil's in Love
Heroes for Sale
She Had to Say Yes
The Life of Jimmy Dolan
Grand Slam
Man's Castle
Midnight Mary

1934
Born to Be Bad
The House of Rothschild
Bulldog Drummond Strikes Back
The White Parade
Caravan

1935
The Crusades
Clive of India
The Call of the Wild
Shanghai

1936
Private Number
Ramona
Ladies in Love
The Unguarded Hour

1937
Love Is News
Cafe Metropole
Love Under Fire
Wife, Doctor and Nurse
Second Honeymoon

1938
Four Men and a Prayer
Three Blind Mice
Suez
Kentucky

1939
The Story of Alexander Graham Bell
Wife, Husband and Friend
Eternally Yours

1940
The Doctor Takes a Wife
He Stayed for Breakfast

1941
Bedtime Story
The Men in Her Life
The Lady from Cheyenne
A Night to Remember

1943
China

1944
Ladies Courageous
And Now Tomorrow

1945
Along Came Jones

1946
The Stranger
The Perfect Marriage

1947
The Farmer's Daughter
The Bishop's Wife

1948

Rachel and the Stranger
The Accused

1949

Mother Is a Freshman
Come to the Stable

1950

Key to the City

1951

Half Angel
Cause for Alarm

1952

Because of You
Paula

1953

It Happens Every Thursday

Appendix A: Wampas "Drop-Outs"

Lynne (sometimes Lynn), **Sharon** (D'Auvergne, Sharon Lindsay); Weatherford, Texas, 1904/10–1963

At least one Los Angeles newspaper announced that Sharon Lynne was to be a 1929 Wampas Baby Star, and it ran her photograph with those of the others. Since no other evidence of her naming was uncovered, it may have been an error. Or there may have been a last minute decision to replace her, for reasons now unknown. It is even possible that she was only a runner-up. In the event, it was Caryl Lincoln, who was not mentioned in the story, who made the final list of 13 that year.

Lynne is best known to modern-day film buffs as the hard-boiled saloon owner Lola Finn (and wife of Jimmy Finlayson's character — an unlikely pair) in one of Laurel and Hardy's best-loved comedies, *Way Out West*. Especially memorable is the scene in which she unmercifully tickles the foolish Laurel to get him to surrender a valuable deed. The film came toward the end of her career; she was to make only two more.

Possessed of reddish-blonde tresses, Lynne had won a newspaper beauty contest and was awarded a job as an extra. She is thought to have appeared in some Harold Lloyd shorts and entered features in 1927, being particularly noticed in that year's *Clancy's Kosher Wedding*. It led to a long-term contract with the Fox studio in 1928. In the four years from 1927 to 1930, she made over 20 films.

As the "other woman" in the first Janet Gaynor–Charles Farrell talkie, *Sunny Side Up*, Lynne received very good notices, but after 1930 she made only eight films the rest of the decade. She returned in 1941 for a couple of "B" feature supporting parts. Among her pictures were *Jake the Plumber, Red Wine, Fox Movietone Follies of 1929, Lightnin', The Big Broadcast, Go Into Your Dance* and *Reg'lar Fellers*.

Miles, Lillian; Oskaloosa, Iowa, 1912?–

Previously a player in Midwestern stock companies, Lillian Miles entered pictures in 1932 and made fewer than a dozen films in a career that lasted, with interruptions, until 1938. She had been submitted as Columbia Pictures' candidate in the 1932 Wampas elections, but left the studio before the final selection was made. The studio's second choice, Toshia Mori, was then elected to be the first and only Asian-American Baby.

Miles went on to play the vaudeville circuit. Her films included *Man Against Woman*, *The Headline Woman*, *The Gay Divorcee*, *Dizzy Dames* and *The Mad Miss Manton*. She had a few "B" westerns to her credit as well.

Navelle, Jeanne, ?–1960?

Although described in contemporaneous accounts as a silent film actress, Jeanne Navelle does not seem to have had any credits in American films. She did perhaps appear in French motion pictures. After her naming to Wampas honors in 1927, it was reported that she had returned to France due to a nervous condition. She was replaced by Martha Sleeper, the daughter of an ex–Montana congressman and future Broadway luminary.

Appendix B: Presidents of Wampas

1922	Ray Leek
1923	Joseph Jackson
1924	Harry Wilson
1925	Harry Brand
1926	Pete Smith
1927	Ray Coffin
1928	Mark Larkin (resigned)
	Harold Hurley (resigned)
	Barrett Kiesling
1929	Harry Beall
1930	Joe Sherman
1931	John L. Johnston
1932	Frank Whitbeck
1933	George Landy

Appendix C: Wampas Baby Miscellany

Academy Award and Equivalent Nominations

Jean Arthur (Best Actress, 1943 — *The More the Merrier*)

*Mary Astor (Best Supporting Actress, 1941 — *The Great Lie*)

Joan Blondell (Best Supporting Actress, 1951 — *The Blue Veil*)

Joan Crawford (Best Actress, 1945 — **Mildred Pierce*; 1947 — *Possessed*; 1952 — *Sudden Fear*)

*Dolores Del Rio — Four Arieles (equivalent to the Mexican Academy Award)

Janet Gaynor (Best Actress, 1927–28 — **Seventh Heaven, Street Angel, Sunrise* [won for all three films]; 1937 — *A Star Is Born*)

Bessie Love (Best Actress, 1928–29 — *The Broadway Melody*)

*Ginger Rogers (Best Actress, 1940 — *Kitty Foyle*)

Gloria Stuart (Best Supporting Actress, 1997 — *Titanic*)

*Designates Winner or Winning Performance.

Authors

Mary Astor (autobiographies, novels)
Lina Basquette (autobiography, dog training)
Jean Carmen (fiction?)
Helen Ferguson (press agent career)
Bessie Love (play, autobiography)
Patsy Ruth Miller (autobiography, short stories, plays)
Colleen Moore (autobiography, doll house, investing tips)
Gloria Stuart (autobiography)
Fay Wray (autobiography, plays)

Children

As far as is known, Ethlyne Clair won the honor for most children with five.

Comebacks

The most notable comebacks were probably Joan Crawford (*Mildred Pierce*); Bessie Love (*The Broadway Melody*) and Gloria Stuart (*Titanic*).

Earliest Death

Lucille Ricksen died at the age of 16, a year after her Wampas designation. Two were in their 30s: Iris Stuart, about 33; Adamae Vaughn 37.

Earliest Appearance in Films

Dolores and Helene Costello began appearing in films as children about 1909.

Eye Color

Colleen Moore had one blue eye and one brown eye.

Fewest Films

Betty Arlen seems to have received no billing in films; Eleanor Holm and Margaret Leahy were billed in one each. All may have done uncredited bits.

First Names

Although there were some unique first names, several first names were widely shared. Seven Babies were called Dorothy: Devore, Drake, Gulliver, Layton, Mackaill, Revier and Wilson.

Sally came next with six: Blane, Eilers, Long, O'Neil, Phipps and Rand, as did Helen or Helene: Cohan, Costello, Ferguson, Foster, Lynch and Twelvetrees.

Five shared Mary; another five were Marion or Marian. There also were four Bettys and four Joans. Among other shared names were Eleanor or Elinor, Frances, Ruth, Evelyn or Evalyn, June, Jean, Anne or Ann, Pauline, Margaret and Gloria.

Foreign Born

Australia: Ena Gregory
Canada: Rita Carewe (?), Pauline Garon, Barbara Kent, Fay Wray
Japan: Toshia Mori
Mexico: Dolores Del Rio, Mona Rico, Lupe Velez
United Kingdom: Lillian Bond, Flora Bramley, Margaret Leahy, Dorothy Mackaill
West Indies: Marian Marsh

Height

Shortest: At an official 4'11", Anne Cornwall; Barbara Kent may have also been this height.
Tallest: At an official 5'7", Hazel Hayes, Gwen Lee and Iris Stuart. Judging from her appearance in her films it is possible that Gwen Lee was actually taller.

Longest Film Career

Bessie Love was in films about 68 years, making her first about 1915; her last in 1983. If Gloria Stuart makes films after the turn of the century, she could break this record. Her screen appearances began in 1932.

Husbands

Lina Basquette, married eight times to seven different men, wins the most married award. There were also "shared" husbands: Lowell Sherman was married to Pauline Garon and Helene Costello; Ross Forrester was married to Marion Aye and Pauline Garon; William Seiter wed both Laura La Plante and Marion Nixon.

Most Recent Film

Gloria Stuart

Oldest at Time of Selection

Given the uncertainty of birth dates, Lois Wilson might have been the oldest at 28 or so. Others in the running are Claire Windsor, Anne Cornwall and Kathryn McGuire.

Publicity Names

All-American Girl — Lucille Lund
Baby Tetrazzini — June Clyde
Belle of the Box Office — Dolores Costello
Cameo Girl — Mary Astor
Cinderella of Hollywood — Dorothy Wilson
Girl with a Million Faces — Iris Stuart
Girl with the Perfect Film Face — Margaret Leahy
Glad-Sad Girl — Pauline Starke
It Girl — Clara Bow
Joy Girl — Olive Borden
Kodak Girl — Eleanor Boardman
Little Brown Wren — Bessie Love
Love Insurance Girl — Sally Long
Most Photographed Girl in the World — Hazel Keener and Sally Long
Perfect American Beauty — Claire Windsor
Perfect Ingenue — Helen Twelvetrees
Post Toasties Girl — Anita Louise
Queen of Poverty Row — Dorothy Revier
Queen of the Underworld — Evelyn Brent
Screen Tragedy Girl — Lina Basquette
Sweetest Girl in Pictures — Mary Brian
Whoopee Lupe — Lupe Velez

Serials Queen

Although many Wampas Babies made serials, the honors go to Louise Lorraine with twelve to her credit

Sisters

Several sets of sisters were Wampas Baby Stars:
Laura La Plante (1924) — Violet Avon (1925)
Alberta Vaughn (1924) — Adamae Vaughn (1927)
Dolores Costello (1926) — Helene Costello (1927)
Marceline Day (1926) — Alice Day (1928)
Sally O'Neil (1926) — Molly O'Day (1928)
Sally Blane (1929) — Loretta Young (1929)

And for good measure, a pair of cousins: Olive Borden (1925) — Natalie Joyce (1925)

Songs

"Joan Crawford Has Risen from the Grave"; "The Rochelle Hudson Tango"; "Sweet Sue" (Sue Carol)

Suicides (Probable)

Marion Aye, Sidney Fox, Margaret Leahy, Helen Twelvetrees, Lupe Velez

Surnames

The most common surname was Lee. Three Baby Stars bore this name, Frances, Gwen and Lila. They were not related and in no case was it their birth name.

Youngest at the Time of Selection

Given the uncertainty of birth dates, the youngest would seem to be Lucille Ricksen, Gloria Grey and Anita Louise. Also in the running are Rochelle Hudson and Patricia Ellis.

APPENDIX D: RIVALS AND SUCCESSORS TO WAMPAS

The publicity value inherent in forecasting future stars was still appreciated by Hollywood after Wampas itself had ceased to exist. Into the 1950s, and possibly later, various studios, professional organizations and individuals were still trying to be prophets. Like the original Wampas Baby Stars, a few of the anointed actresses went on to major stardom, some attained respectable leading lady status without true stardom, and others were destined to be recalled only in the pages of books like this.

FOX DEBUTANTES (1931)

Some three years before Wampas breathed its last, Fox had opted out of the organization when none of its starlets were selected in the 1931 balloting. It modestly announced only three of its actresses as stars of the future, dubbing them "Fox Debutantes." They were Helen Mack, Conchita Montenegro and Linda Watkins. Only one actually would prove to have staying power.

Mack, Helen (Helen McDougal or McDougall); Rock Island, Illinois, 1913/14–1986. A child actress in small roles in silent movies, red-haired Helen Mack later became a popular leading lady in numerous movies from the early 1930s into the middle of the following decade. She also appeared on Broadway. Among her films as an adult were *Son of Kong*, *The Lemon Drop Kid* (1934 version), *Melody Cruise*, *His Girl Friday*, *The Milky Way*, *She*, *Divorce* and *Calling All Marines*. After her film days were over, she directed radio programs and wrote an unsuccessful Broadway play.

Montenegro, Conchita, San Sebastian, Spain, 1912?–. The major part of brunette Conchita Montenegro's Hollywood career was spent in making Spanish language versions of Hollywood-produced pictures from 1931 to 1935. Her occasional English language films included *The Cisco Kid*, *Strangers May Kiss*, *The Gay Caballero* and *Handy Andy*. After her return to Europe, she worked in the cinema of several countries.

She was married to actor-singer Raul Roulien of *Flying Down to Rio* fame.

Watkins, Linda, Boston, Massachusetts, 1908/09–1976. First a Broadway supporting actress and then a leading lady, Linda Watkins's few films in the 1930s included *Sob Sister, Charlie Chan's Chance, The Gay Caballero* and *Playthings of Desire*. The pretty blonde apparently preferred the stage and did not return to the screen until the 1950s in character parts. Among her later films were *Cash McCall, The Parent Trap* and *Good Neighbor Sam*. She also did numerous television guest roles.

Paramount Protégées (1934)

Because all the 1934 Wampas winners were deliberately chosen among freelance actresses, major studios such as Paramount were not long in putting forth lists of their own. The studio's selection proved quite prescient in one case; still others had worthwhile careers. They were Dorothy Dell, Frances Drake, Ida Lupino, Helen Mack (previously a Fox Debutante), Evelyn Venable and Elizabeth Young.

Dell, Dorothy (Dorothy Goff); Hattiesburg, Mississippi, 1914–1934. The promising career of Dorothy Dell, who had been both Miss America and Miss Universe, was cut short — almost before it had begun — by a fatal auto accident just after her 20th birthday. She had made just three features, one with Shirley Temple, and some Vitaphone shorts. She had also been seen in the Ziegfeld Follies. Her features, all released the year of her death, were *Little Miss Marker, Wharf Angel* and *Shoot the Works*.

Drake, Frances (Frances Dean); New York, New York, 1908/12–2000. A sultry, dark beauty, Frances Drake had been a dancer appearing in English movies before her Hollywood days, which began in the mid–'30s. Her name presumably was changed because of its similarity to that of 1931 Wampas Baby Frances Dee. Her first U.S. film, *Bolero*, featured her dancing skills. Among her more than 20 other pictures to 1942 were *Les Miserables, Mad Love, The Lone Wolf in Paris, Forsaking All Others, The Invisible Ray* and *I Take This Woman*. She joined the English nobility with her marriage to the brother of the Earl of Suffolk.

Lupino, Ida; London, England, 1914/18–1995. A member of the famed Lupino theatrical family, Ida Lupino appeared in the British cinema before making her American debut in 1934. Having made numerous films during the 1930s, she really hit her stride after being signed by Warner Bros. at the end of the decade. She sometimes played good-bad women or, occasionally, downright wicked ones. Among the films in which she appeared steadily for 20 years, and sporadically thereafter into the 1970s, were *Peter Ibbetson, Sea Devils, High Sierra, The Light That Failed, The Hard Way, Deep Valley, Devotion, While the City Sleeps* and *Junior Bonner*.

In the 1950s Lupino was, for a brief period, one of the few American women directing, as well as writing and producing, some films. Among them, her "B" thriller *The Hitch-Hiker* was praised. Later she did much television, including a comedy series co-starring her then-husband Howard Duff. She had previously been wed to British actor Louis Hayward.

Mack, Helen— See the Fox Debutantes (1931) above.

Venable, Evelyn; Cincinnati, Ohio, 1913–1993. Pretty brunette Evelyn Venable was a success not only as an actress but also in the profession she pursued thereafter. A former theater performer, and best known today for her role in 1934's *Death Takes a Holiday* (remade in 1998 as *Meet Joe Black*), she had come to pictures in 1933 and remained active until the end of the decade. She also was said to have been the model for Columbia Pictures' statue logo.

Among Venable's films were *Alice Adams, North of Nome, The Little Colonel, Heritage of the Desert, Racketeers in Exile, Happy Go Lucky* and *He Hired the Boss*, her last in 1943. She also co-starred with Will Rogers in two pictures.

After retiring from motion pictures, Venable returned to college in the 1950s to earn a master's degree, and spent many years teaching Greek and Latin at the University of California, Los Angeles. There she was known as Mrs. Mohr, having been the wife of well-known cameraman Hal Mohr.

Young, Elizabeth; New York, New York. Although once touted as a possible rival to Katharine Hepburn, Elizabeth Young had only a brief fling in films after appearing on Broadway. Her onscreen career lasted from 1933 to 1935 and apparently consisted of but four pictures: *Big Executive, Queen Christina, There's Always Tomorrow* and *East of Java*. She was married to the famous director and screenwriter Joseph Mankiewicz.

Paramount Protégées (1935)

Paramount prognosticated one more time, after the Wampas organization had ceased to exist, and all of their 1935 selections were winners. The future hopefuls this time were Wendy Barrie, Grace Bradley, Katherine DeMille, Gertrude Michael, Gail Patrick and Ann Sheridan.

Barrie, Wendy (Wendie, Wendy or Margaret Jenkin or Jenkins); Hong Kong, 1912–1978. In the early days of television, Wendy Barrie presented an eccentric persona that was far different from her conventional leading lady roles in the movies. She had made her screen debut in the U.K. about 1934 and gained notice as one of the monarch's six wives in *The Private Life of Henry the VIII*. Her American debut came in *It's a Small World* (1935), following which she appeared in more than 50 films. They included *Wings Over Honolulu, Five Came Back, Speed, College Scandal, Dead End, The Saint Takes Over* and *I Am the Law*.

Barrie was out of pictures by the mid-'40s, but after her success as an acerbic television talk show hostess she was cast in a few more movie cameo roles. The statuesque actress was also much seen in TV commercials and she played on Broadway.

Bradley, Grace; Brooklyn, New York, 1913–. The widow of actor William Boyd (perhaps better known as Hopalong Cassidy), blonde Grace Bradley had a ten year career before the cameras. Among her numerous motion pictures, beginning in 1933, were *Too Much Harmony, Redhead, Old Man Rhythm, Rose of the Rancho, Wake Up and Live, Sign of the Wolf* and *The McGuerins from Brooklyn*, her last. Her output declined dramatically after 1937.

DeMille, Katherine (Katherine Lester); Vancouver, British Columbia, 1911–1995. The adopted daughter of famed director Cecil B. DeMille, Katherine DeMille was a dark-eyed actress who looked like Hollywood's idea of a villainess and was often consigned to such portrayals. Starting out as an extra, she was in many films of the '30s and '40s, including some of her father's. Among them were *Call of the Wild, Belle of the Nineties, Viva Villa, Trapped in the Sky, Unconquered, Black Gold* and *The Crusades*. She was the wife of actor Anthony Quinn.

Michael, Gertrude; Talladega, Alabama, 1911–1964. Blonde Gertrude Michael was a leading lady in many pictures from 1932 through the '40s, and even appeared into the 1960s as a character player after overcoming her much-publicized battle with alcoholism. She was perhaps best known as the jewel thief title character of the Sophie Lang series. Among her films were *Sailor Be Good, Murder on the Blackboard, The Farmer's Daughter, Second Wife, Flamingo Road, Caged* and *Twist All Night*. She was also seen on the stage and television.

Patrick, Gail (Margaret Fitzpatrick); Birmingham, Alabama, 1911–1980. Tall, brunette Gail Patrick was a winner of one of the regional "Panther Girl" contests, as had been 1932 Wampas Baby Lona Andre. (Like Andre, she was not selected as *the* winner.) The publicity resulted in a career of more than 60 films (often as the "other woman") from 1932 to the later 1940s, including *Cradle Song, Artists and Models, My Man Godfrey, My Favorite Wife, The Hunchback of Notre Dame* and *Calendar Girl*. She then became an entertainment executive, producing radio shows and, most importantly, the long-running *Perry Mason* series on television.

Sheridan, Ann (Clara Lou Sheridan); Denton, Texas, 1915–1967. Willowy Ann Sheridan had been in movies from 1934 after winning a beauty contest. She possessed talent within a limited range, and had a melodiously low-pitched voice, but it was not until Warner Bros. publicists dubbed her the "Oomph Girl" that her career took off. Her major films came in the late 1930s and 1940s, among them *Kings Row, George Washington Slept Here, They Drive By Night, They Made Me a Criminal, Nora Prentiss* and *I Was a Male War Bride*.

Sheridan was never quite as big a star as her publicity seemed to indicate. By the 1950s she was onscreen only sporadically, and during the next decade was on television, including in a soap opera. Among her husbands were actors Edward Norris and George Brent.

Fox Nominees of 1934/35 (?)

The Fox studio tried again in the mid–1930s (probably 1934 or '35) to predict four more future stars, but did not continue its earlier practice of dubbing them "Fox Debutantes." They were simply named. It was a mixed bag; one was a superstar-to-be, and one fell into almost immediate obscurity. They were Barbara Blane, Rita Cansino (i.e., Rita Hayworth), Frances Grant and Rosina Lawrence.

Blane, Barbara (Barbara? Holmes); New Haven, Connecticut. After a minor career as a dancer and an actress in regional theater, Barbara Blane came to Hollywood but had supporting roles in only two 1936 films. They were *My Marriage* and *Satan Met a Lady*.

Grant, Frances, 1910?–1982. Frances Grant was primarily a leading lady of "B" westerns in the mid–'30s, including those of Gene Autry, Bob Steele and George O'Brien. Her relatively few movies included *Thunder Mountain*, *Red River Valley*, *Dancing Feet*, *Born to Fight* and *Top of the Town*.

Hayworth, Rita (Margarita Cansino); Brooklyn, New York, 1918/19–1987. Famed as a lushly beautiful red-haired sex symbol of the 1940s, the originally brunette Rita Hayworth began as a pre-teenage dancer with her family, the Cansinos. She made her first bit part appearances in films beginning in the mid–1930s, and until about 1941 was relatively little known. A massive publicity campaign and such films as *Blood and Sand*, *The Strawberry Blonde* and *You'll Never Get Rich* made her a star. By then her physical appearance had been completely made over.

Hayworth's major stardom came in the World War II period in a series of popular musicals with the likes of Fred Astaire and Gene Kelly, such as *Cover Girl*, *You Were Never Lovelier*, *My Gal Sal* and *Tonight and Every Night*. She also was the pin-up dream of millions of GIs with her famous provocatively posed nightgown picture. Post-war dramas like *Gilda* and *The Lady from Shanghai* continued her stardom for a while.

With the 1950s, Rita Hayworth's career began to founder. It was instead her stormy personal life that garnered headlines, with unhappy marriages to Orson Welles, Aly Khan and singer Dick Haymes. She turned to making pictures in Europe, eventually returning for a few '60s films in America. By that time her fabled beauty had faded and her mental health was soon to follow.

Lawrence, Rosina; Westboro, Ontario, 1913?–1997. The ingenue of *Way Out West*, one of Laurel and Hardy's best-loved comedies, Rosina Lawrence began as a vaudeville singer and dancer, and appeared in silent movies. She also was seen in Hal Roach comedies, playing the teacher in the Little Rascals series, including the Academy Award-winning short *Bored of Education*. Among her dozen or so features between 1935 and 1937 were *Charlie Chan's Secret*, *Music Is Magic*, *Mr. Cinderella*, *Pick a Star* and *$10 Raise*. She made her last film in Italy and married an Italian count who later became a New York City judge.

WARNER BROS. NOMINEES OF 1935

With Fox and Paramount in the forecasting business, could Warner Bros. be far behind? In 1935 the studio named a group of six starlets to be groomed for stardom in 1936–'37. Although they were not given a group name, a columnist dubbed them the "Scintillating Sextuplets." ("Sextet" would have been more accurate, but perhaps it was recognition of the frenzied publicity surrounding the birth of the Dionne Quintuplets.) One of the group was to be a shining star; some of the rest also had "legs." They were Dorothy Dare, Olivia De Havilland, Maxine Doyle, June Grabiner (i.e., June Travis), Nan Grey and June Martel.

Dare, Dorothy; Philadelphia, Pennsylvania, 1914?–. Red-haired Dorothy Dare, a former Ziegfeld Follies and musical comedy performer, made seven films during 1934 and '35, most of them musicals. Her last one came in 1937. Among them were *In Caliente*, *Gold Diggers of 1935*, *Sweet Adeline*, *Happiness Ahead* and *High Hat*. She also appeared in several Vitaphone shorts.

De Havilland, Olivia; Tokyo, Japan, 1916–. While still a teenager, Olivia de Havilland was discovered by theatrical impresario Max Reinhardt for his famed Hollywood Bowl production of *A Midsummer Night's Dream*. After she appeared in the Warner Bros.' filmed version, a long-term contract ensued. Usually playing innocent ingenues, she was cast in some of that studio's major films, among them *The Adventures of Robin Hood*, *Anthony Adverse*, *The Private Lives of Elizabeth and Essex* and *The Charge of the Light Brigade*. Swashbuckler Errol Flynn was a frequent co-star.

De Havilland's selection to play Melanie in *Gone with the Wind* was a major coup, but her discontent with subsequent roles back at Warners led to a lengthy suspension. There was a protracted court battle that she ultimately won, and in 1946 she scored the first of two Oscars for Best Actress in *To Each His Own*. The second was for 1949's *The Heiress*. Another of her deeply dramatic roles in the late 1940s was in *The Snake Pit*. Her screen career declined in the 1950s, although she still made occasional films interspersed with stage performances until the late '70s.

Doyle, Maxine; San Francisco, California, 1915–1973. From 1934 to 1938 Maxine Doyle was seen in such motion pictures as *Babbitt*, *Born to Gamble*, *It's Up to You* and *Thanks for Listening*. Previously, she had been a dancer, was in vaudeville with comic Charlie Murray, and did regional theater. She was also heard on the radio. As were those of many other fading ingenues, some of her later '30s films were "B" westerns like *Rio Grande Romance* and *Come On, Cowboys!* She was back in the mid–1940s, this time as a bit player, with a handful of pictures including the oaters *Overland Mail Robbery* and *Raiders of Sunset Pass*. She also made a couple of serials.

Grey (sometimes Gray), **Nan** (Eschal Miller); Houston, Texas, 1918–1993. After Olivia de Havilland, Nan Grey was perhaps the most successful of the Warners' "sextuplets." Although the pretty blonde made a splash as one of Deanna Durbin's sisters in 1937's *Three Smart Girls* and its sequel, she had been onscreen since 1934. Among her many earlier films were *Dracula's Daughter*, *Babbitt* and *Sutter's Gold*. She continued at the top until 1941 when she retired. Other pictures included *Under Age*, *Tower of London*, *The House of the Seven Gables* and *The*

Invisible Man Returns. She also did radio. Popular singer Frankie Laine was one of her husbands.

Martel, June (Martha Greif); Chicago, Illinois, 1909/14–1978. A redheaded former singer and dancer in vaudeville and on the stage, June Martel made fewer than a dozen generally minor pictures from her entrée in 1935 until 1938. Some were "B" westerns. Her films included *Arizona Mahoney, Forlorn River, Fighting Youth, Her Husband Lies* and, finally, *Santa Fe Stampede.*

Travis, June (June Grabiner); Chicago, Illinois, 1914–. The daughter of a Chicago White Sox baseball team vice president, June Travis was a busy leading lady in "B" pictures of the mid to late '30s. They included *Times Square Playboy, Go Chase Yourself, The Case of the Black Cat, Little Orphan Annie* and *Earthworm Tractors.* She later did much regional theater and returned to the screen for one last time in the early 1950s.

FLASHLIGHTERS (OR FLASHLIGHTERS) STARLETS (1936?)

The Hollywood Press Photographers Association also got into the act and gave its imprimatur to ten starlets, a few of whom enjoyed minor leading lady status. The most well-known nowadays is probably Cecilia Parker, because of her involvement in the "Andy Hardy" series. They were Helen Burgess, Frances Gifford, Kay Hughes, Janice Jarrett, Rosina Lawrence (who also had been a 1934/35 Fox nominee previously), Cecilia Parker, Barbara Pepper, Joan Perry, June Travis (previously a 1935 Warner Bros. nominee) and Helen Wood.

Burgess, Helen; Portland, Oregon, 1915/18–1937. When blonde Helen Burgess died of pneumonia, probably in her very early 20s, her promise remained unfulfilled. A player in regional theater and an unknown when Cecil B. DeMille discovered her, her first role was as Buffalo Bill's wife in *The Plainsman.* Placed under Paramount contract, her legacy was just four films, the others being *A Doctor's Diary, King of Gamblers* and *Night of Mystery.*

Gifford, Frances (Mary Frances Gifford); Long Beach, California, 1920?–1994. From 1937 and well into the next decade, Frances Gifford appeared in numerous films — both major and minor, including "B" westerns — and made her mark in the 1941 serial *Jungle Girl.* Other films included *Mr. Smith Goes to Washington, Cry Havoc, Luxury Liner, Thrill of a Romance, Riding High* and *Border Vigilantes.*

A serious automobile accident in 1948 nearly ended Gifford's career, although she appeared in two more films and did some television. A combination of factors led to an emotional breakdown in the mid–1950s, and the auburn-haired actress spent much of the next two decades in a mental hospital. She had been married to actor James Dunn.

Hughes, Kay. Kay Hughes had been in a few films before her selection as a Flashlighters Starlet, but the designation seems to have given her career a boost. She made about a dozen pictures in 1937; however, that year marked both her peak and her virtual disappearance from the screen. She (or another actress of the same name?) did make a few "B" westerns in the 1940s. Among her films were *Fighting Youth, Brides Are Like That, The Mandarin Mystery, Strike Me Pink* and *Enemy of the Law*.

Jarrett, Janice. There is no evidence that Jarrett appeared in any films, although there may have been some uncredited bits.

Lawrence, Rosina—See the Fox Nominees of 1934/35.

Parker, Cecilia (also billed as Cecelia); Fort William, Ontario, 1905/14–1993. Fondly remembered as older sister Marian Hardy in the lengthy "Andy Hardy" series at MGM, blonde Cecilia Parker was a stalwart of "B" westerns as well. From 1931's *Frankenstein* to the mid–1940s, she was onscreen in such films as *Young As You Feel, High School Girl, Ah, Wilderness!, The Hardys Ride High, The Painted Veil* and *Gun Justice*. She returned once, in 1958, for the nostalgic but ill-advised *Andy Hardy Comes Home*.

Pepper, Barbara; New York, New York, 1912/15–1969. Looking at the pudgy and coarse-featured actress in such TV shows as *I Love Lucy* and *Green Acres*, it was hard to imagine the beauteous blonde showgirl that Barbara Pepper had been some 20 years earlier. A "graduate" of such Broadway revues as the Ziegfeld Follies and a Goldwyn Girl of the early '30s, she played in numerous films until the 1960s, oft times in bits. Her motion pictures included *Our Daily Bread* (a King Vidor film in which she had the lead), *The Singing Vagabond, Dante's Inferno, Unmasked, Of Mice and Men* and *The Music Man*.

Perry, Joan (Elizabeth Miller); Pensacola, Florida, 1907/11–1996. Later better known as Joan Cohn, the wife of Columbia head Harry Cohn, Joan Perry appeared in pictures from 1935 to 1941. They included *Gallant Defender, Meet Nero Wolfe, Good Girls Go to Paris, The Case of the Missing Man* and *International Squadron*. Considered one of the most powerful women in Hollywood as Mrs. Cohn, she was later married to English actor Laurence Harvey.

Travis, June—See the Warner Bros. Nominees of 1935 above.

Wood, Helen; Clarksville, Tennessee, 1918?–1988. From 1935 to that decade's end, Helen Wood made such movies as *My Marriage, The Goose and the Gander, Champagne Charlie, Crack-Up* and *Almost a Gentleman* for 20th Century–Fox and other studios. She also was heard on the radio.

NOTE: *Not to be confused with the film and TV actress of same name who was active in the 1950s.*

THE BABY STARS OF 1940

The new decade opened with yet another coronation. The Motion Picture Publicists Association, probably a successor to Wampas, reinstituted both that organization's selection of 13 young women and the "Baby Star" designation. Winsome Joan Leslie stood out from the crowd, but some others became stalwarts of "B" quickies. They were Ella Bryan, Lucia Carroll, Peggy Diggins, Lorraine

Elliott, Jayne Hazard, Joan Leslie, Kay Leslie, Marilyn Merrick (i.e., Lynn Merrick), Gay Parkes, Lois Ranson, Sheila Ryan, Patricia Van Cleve and Tanya Widrin.

Bryan, Ella. There is no evidence that Bryan appeared in any films, although there may have been some uncredited bits.

Carroll, Lucia. Brunette Lucia Carroll made her screen debut about 1940 and appeared in approximately a dozen films before the end of 1941, rarely rising above the middle of the cast list. There is no record of any further films, apart from a final picture in 1947, but there may have been bit parts. Among her credits were *High Sierra*, *Wild Bill Hickok Rides*, *Santa Fe Trail*, *Manpower* and *Danger Street*.

Diggins, Peggy (Margaret Diggins); New York, New York, 1921–. Tall, and considered to be a beauty by no less an expert than the artist James Montgomery Flagg, Peggy Diggins's first credited role came in 1940. She went on to make films until about 1943, in the meantime being named one of Warner Bros.' "Navy Blues Sextette" (comprised of six starlets who appeared in that film and others). Other pictures included *Lady Gangster*, *The Man Who Came to Dinner*, *Truck Busters* and *You're in the Army Now*.

Elliott, Lorraine. Besides her bit in 1943's *Hello, Frisco, Hello*, Lorraine Elliott may have had other parts but they were possibly uncredited.

Hazard, Jayne, 1924?–. Blonde Jayne Hazard bounced between major and minor studios, usually in smallish roles, throughout much of the 1940s. She was one of "Powers' American Beauties" in *The Powers Girl* and also appeared in *Black Market Babies*, *The Lost Weekend*, *Strange Illusion*, *The Monster and the Girl* and *Daredevils of the Clouds*.

Leslie, Joan (Joan Brodel); Detroit, Michigan, 1925–. Under her real name, Joan Leslie appeared in films as a young girl from 1937 or so, one of her earliest being *Camille*. She had previously been part of a musical act with two of her sisters. An intelligent and versatile actress, although never a top star, she assumed her stage name as an adult and was in many important Warner Bros. films. Among her co-stars were James Cagney, Humphrey Bogart, Gary Cooper, Henry Fonda, Fred Astaire and Fred MacMurray.

After the mid–1940s, Leslie's pictures became less important and her film career petered out completely during the next decade. Her films included *Nancy Drew, Reporter*, *High Sierra*, *Rhapsody in Blue*, *Yankee Doodle Dandy*, *The Sky's the Limit*, *Born to Be Bad* and *Hell's Outpost*.

Leslie, Kay (Melba De Closs); Fresno, California. No relation to her better known namesake above, Kay Leslie had won a beauty contest that earned her a screen test. The strawberry blonde had previously appeared in local theater. She seems to have made but a handful of early '40s films, although there could have been additional bit parts. Among her known picture appearances were *The Invisible Woman*, *Spring Parade*, *Argentine Nights*, *The Texas Marshal* and *Where Did You Get That Girl?*

Merrick, Lynn (Marilyn Merrick); Fort Worth, Texas, 1920?–. Called the "Perfect Figure Girl," blonde Lynn Merrick made a few films under her real name, and a host of others using its shortened version. From 1940 to about 1947, she appeared in pictures such as *Sis Hopkins*, *The Gay Vagabond*, *Nine Girls*, *The Voice of the Whistler*, *The Blonde from Brooklyn* and *I Love Trouble*. The leading lady in some, she also was seen in support.

Merrick's marriages made more news than her career did. Her first husband, actor Conrad Nagel, was more than twice her age. She then wed Robert Goelet, heir to one of the country's largest fortunes, and his displeased parents threatened to disinherit him.

Parkes, Gay. There is no evidence that Parkes appeared in any films, although there may have been some uncredited bits.

Ranson, Lois; Los Angeles, California, 1921–. A former dancer, Ranson was discovered by 1928 Wampas Baby Star, and later agent, Sue Carol (Ladd). She was placed under contract to Republic where she played Betty Higgins in several films in the Higgins Family series. Among her motion pictures, from 1939 to 1943 were *Angels with Broken Wings*, *Money to Burn*, *Grandpa Goes to Town*, *The House of the Seven Gables* and *Under Texas Skies*, one of several "B" oaters.

Ryan, Sheila (also known as Betty McLaughlin, Katherine McLaughlin); Topeka, Kansas, 1921–1975. From 1939 to 1958, pretty brunette Sheila Ryan was one of the queens of "B" pictures, of which she made about 60, including numerous westerns. She, too, was discovered by former Wampas Baby Sue Carol (Ladd) and was soon dubbed the "Most Perfectly Beautiful Girl in Films." Her films included *Sun Valley Serenade*, *Something for the Boys*, *Getting Gertie's Garter*, *Mule Train*, *Fingerprints Don't Lie* and *Street of Darkness*. She was heard on the radio. She was married to three actors, cowboy hero Allan "Rocky" Lane, Edward Norris and Pat Buttram, one-time sidekick to Gene Autry.

Van Cleve, Patricia. Patricia Van Cleve was the niece of actress Marion Davies and wife of Arthur Lake, Dagwood Bumstead in the long-running Blondie series. She was heard on the radio version of *Blondie*, but does not seem to have made any films. More interesting to some was the speculation that she was not Davies's niece at all but was, in reality, the love child of Davies and her longtime paramour William Randolph Hearst. The gossip remains unproved.

Widrin, Tanya. There is no evidence that Widrin appeared in any films, although there may have been some uncredited bits.

THE STAR RING OF 1943 (1942?)

Universal Studio belatedly joined the drum-beaters of new talent and proved to be good at it. All six of their ladies had worthwhile careers. They were Louise Allbritton, Jennifer Holt, Elyse Knox, Marjorie Lord, Grace McDonald and Peggy Ryan.

Allbritton, Louise; Oklahoma City, Oklahoma, 1920–1979. Regally tall, blonde, and pretty, Louise Allbritton was later known as the wife of longtime CBS correspondent Charles Collingwood. She had a respectable enough career during the 1940s in second features, after stints in regional theater and on Broadway. A Universal contractee, among her films in many genres were *Parachute Nurse*, *Who Done It?*, *Son of Dracula*, *The Egg and I*, *Sitting Pretty* (the last two being among her few major productions), *Tangier* and *The Doolins of Oklahoma*. She was also seen on television.

Holt, Jennifer (Elizabeth Holt); Hollywood, California, 1920–1997. A daughter of the "industry"—her father was rugged leading man Jack Holt—Jennifer Holt had some stock experience before entering into a career as a "B" western leading lady. Like her older brother, Tim Holt, she was rarely allowed to stray far from the saddle. Among some 50 features and serials from 1941 to 1948 were *Beyond the Pecos*, *Hap Harrigan*, *Cowboy Buckaroo*, *Old Chisholm Trail*, *Deep in the Heart of Texas* and *Song of Old Wyoming*. One of her husbands had been actor William Bakewell.

Knox, Elyse (sometimes billed as Elise); Hartford, Connecticut, 1917/18–. Possessed of truly striking blonde beauty, Elyse Knox still was rarely able to rise above leads in lower-half-of-the-bill fare in the 1940s. The daughter of Franklin Roosevelt's Secretary of the Navy, Frank Knox, she began as a model and was signed by 20th Century–Fox. Her films included *Top Sergeant*, *Footlight Fever*, *A Wave, a WAC and a Marine*, *Linda Be Good*, *Army Wives* and *Tanks a Million*. She married football hero Tom Harmon; among their children were actor Mark Harmon and Kristin Harmon, who was wed to singer Rick Nelson.

Lord, Marjorie (Marjorie Wollenberg?); San Francisco, California, 1918?–. A versatile veteran of Broadway, movies and television, red-haired Marjorie Lord achieved fame in the latter medium as Danny Thomas's wife in his long-running sitcom. Her film career had been largely undistinguished following her signing by RKO in the mid–1930s, with such movies as *Air Hostess*, *Girls' School*, *Sherlock Holmes in Washington*, *New Orleans*, *Chain Gang* and *The Masked Raiders*. She was married to actor John Archer and is the mother of actress Anne Archer.

McDonald, Grace; Boston, Massachusetts, 1918?–1999. Although she was one of the pert singer-dancers much in evidence in Universal's wartime "B" musicals, Grace McDonald's career did not long outlast them. Sister of dancer Ray McDonald, with whom she did Broadway musicals, her films beginning in 1940 included *Dancing on a Dime*, *Give Out Sisters*, *What's Cookin'?*, *Strictly in the Groove* and *My Gal Loves Music*. There were also a few dramas, among them *Destiny* and *Gung Ho!*

Ryan, Peggy (Margaret Ryan); Long Beach, California, 1924–. Cute as a button, Peggy Ryan was a teenager when she entered pictures in 1937. Like her sister-in-law Grace McDonald, she also became a Universal wartime stalwart, known for her peppy dancing with partners such as husband-to-be Ray McDonald and Donald O'Connor. Her movies were such forgettable but fun fare as *The Merry Monahans, What's Cookin'?, Patrick the Great, Here Come the Coeds, Top Man* and *There's a Girl in My Heart*. By the early 1950s she was out of pictures, but later appeared on TV's *Hawaii Five-O* series.

THE WAMPAS BABY STARS OF 1956 (1955)

Although there was no extant Wampas organization — it had been defunct for some 20 years — its name was still obviously considered to be of value. Accounts differ somewhat about who the finalists were in this last major coronation of starlets, but definitely among them were Jewell Lain, Lita Milan, Ina Poindexter, Fay Spain, and Dell (or Del)-Fin Thursday.

Among the other possible winners were Phyllis Applegate, Roxanne Arlen, Jolene Brand, Mar Craig, Donna Cooke, Dee Davis, Barbara Jane Harris, Barbara Huffman, Evelyn Lovequist, Barbara Marks, Norma Nilsson, Violet Rensing, Dawn Richard and Doreen Stevens.

Others in the contest, but apparently out of the running, included Hedi Duval, June Gilmore, Marilyn Johnson, Myna Lundeen, Kathy Marlowe, Sydne Miller, Kay Twitchell, Audrey Vogel and Claire Weeks. Very few of the 1955 hopefuls made any mark whatever.

Arlen, Roxanne (Roxanne Giles); Detroit, Michigan, 1931/35–1989. Blonde (originally red-headed?) Roxanne Arlen could be described as a second-string sexpot in the era when Marilyn Monroe was the ideal of that type. She certainly was one of the more successful of the 1956 Babies, having done Broadway, films and television. Her films in the '50s to the mid–'60s included *The Loved One, Bachelor Flat, Miracle in the Rain, Battle Cry, Hot Rod Girl* and *Gypsy*.

Brand, Jolene (sometimes Joline). Brand's films included *Giant from the Unknown*, and she did series TV.

Craig, Mar; Durango, Colorado.

Davis, Dee; McCook, Nebraska.

Harris, Barbara Jane. Harris had been Miss California of 1955.

Lain, Jewell; Indianapolis, Indiana.

Lovequist, Evelyn; Chicago, Illinois. Among her '50s films were *Hot Stuff, The Las Vegas Story*, and *Two Tickets to Broadway*.

Milan, Lita (Iris Menshell); Brooklyn, New York, 1934?–. Dark, smoldering and sultry, Lita Milan was usually typecast in "exotic" Latin roles, although she was actually of Hungarian ancestry. In her dozen or so movies during the second half of the 1950s, many of them westerns, she co-starred with such leading men as Paul Newman and Anthony Quinn. She also appeared on television. Among her films were *The Left Handed Gun, The Ride Back, The Violent Men, I, Mobster* and *Never Love a Stranger*. Much publicity was engendered by her marriage to Rafael Trujillo, Jr., son of the Dominican Republic's dictator.

Nilsson, Norma. She played in movies as a child actress, and later appeared in *The Actress* and *The Green-Eyed Blonde.*

Poindexter, Ina; Covington, Indiana. She appeared in *Giant.*

Rensing, Violet. Violet Rensing's pictures included *The Singing Nun, When Hell Broke Loose, The Beast of Budapest* and *Desirée.*

Richard, Dawn. Richard was a Playboy Playmate of the Month in 1959 and she did many '50s TV shows. Among her films were *Legion of the Doomed, Live Fast, Die Young,* and *I Was a Teenage Werewolf.*

Spain, Fay; Phoenix, Arizona, 1933?–1983. A narrow-eyed blonde, Fay Spain had a somewhat hardened look that largely relegated her to "bad girl" roles. Apart from movies, she also did local theater, much television (in one show she was a lesbian murderess), and even played the Borscht Belt circuit in the Catskill Mountains. Her pictures from 1957 included *God's Little Acre, Al Capone, The Godfather, Part 2, The Beat Generation* and *Hercules and the Captive Women.*

Thursday, Dell-Fin (or Del-Fin), Honolulu, Hawaii. Thursday was a former Miss Hawaii.

There were still other attempts to interest the movie-going public in stars of the future. The studios, from time to time, continued to publicize both their male and female hopefuls. Beginning about 1946, the powerful columnist Hedda Hopper had made her own annual selections, perhaps aided by discreet studio input. In the 1950s the Make-Up and Hair Stylists of Hollywood issued their own prognostications. There were even balls held touting the stars of tomorrow that harked back to those of the Wampas glory days, though possibly less lavish.

To this day, there still continue to be publicity barrages that hype potential stars (who sometimes seem more like flavors of the month). With today's more sophisticated (or cynical) attitudes, it is unlikely that Wampas-type lists would impress picture-going audiences, or indeed even be attempted by the studios. Perhaps Wampas was, after all, better suited to a more naïve era, but the glamour that was Hollywood has unquestionably been dimmed.

SOURCES

FILMOGRAPHY

Filmographies for some Wampas Baby Stars are located at the Academy of Motion Picture Arts and Sciences, and may or may not have also appeared in published sources. The titles of sound shorts and silent one- and two-reelers are particularly difficult to find; some were uncovered in the Mack Sennett archives at the Academy.

Printed sources included:

The American Film Institute Catalog of Motion Pictures Produced in the United States. Berkeley, CA: University of California Press, 1988–
Fetrow, Alan. *Feature Films, 1940–1949.* Jefferson, NC: McFarland, 1994.
Fetrow, Alan. *Feature Films, 1950–1959.* Jefferson, NC: McFarland, 1999.
Maltin, Leonard. *The Great Movie Shorts.* New York, NY: Crown, 1972.

Also useful were the periodicals *Film Dope, Monthly Film Bulletin* and *Stars.*

BIOGRAPHICAL INFORMATION

Newspapers

Useful information was found in contemporaneous newspaper accounts, particularly in Hollywood's "local" papers, *The Los Angeles Times* and *The Los Angeles Herald.* Later years of the *Hollywood Reporter* and *Variety* were helpful as well. *The New York Times* also provided some data, and clippings from numerous other newspapers were in the files of various archives including the Academy of Motion Picture Arts and Sciences, the University of Southern California's Cinema-Television Library and the American Film Institute.

Periodicals

Although the "fan" magazines that flourished during the heyday of the Wampas Baby Stars contained mostly publicity puff pieces, there were occasional factual nuggets (such as real names) that were not found elsewhere. Among the contemporaneous (1922–1934) magazines consulted were *Modern Screen, Motion Picture, Motion Picture Classic, Movie Classic, Photoplay* and *Silver Screen.*

Among the more current periodicals which contained useful data were *American Classic Screen, Cinema Digest, Classic Images, Film Comment, Film Fan Monthly, Film Quarterly, Film Reader, Filmograph, Films and Filming, Films in Review, Focus on Film, Hollywood Studio Magazine, Journal of Popular Film and Television, Jump Cut, Premiere, Screen Greats, Sight and Sound, Silent Film Monthly, Silent Picture, Velvet Light Trap,* and *Wide Angle.*

Books

The 1920s and '30s produced many books that were, like the fan magazines, essentially puff pieces. They did, however, sometimes provide otherwise hard to find facts and photographs. Some of them are therefore included here.

Ankerich, Michael. *Broken Silence: Conversations with 23 Silent Film Stars.* Jefferson, NC: McFarland, 1993.

The Blue Book of the Screen. Edited by Ruth Wing. Hollywood, CA: The Blue Book of the Screen, Inc., 1920–1924.

Brundige, Harry. *Twinkle, Twinkle, Movie Star!* New York, NY: Garland, 1977. Reprint, originally published in 1930.

Current Biography. New York, NY: H. W. Wilson, 1940–

Fox Charles. *Famous Film Folk.* New York, NY: Doran, 1925.

_____. *Mirrors of Hollywood.* New York: Renard, 1925.

_____. *Who's Who on the Screen.* New York, NY: Gordon Press, 1976. Reprint, originally published in 1920.

How I Broke into the Movies. Edited by Hal Herman. Hollywood, CA: Herman, 1929.

Hughes, Elinor. *Famous Stars of Filmdom (Women).* Boston, MA: Page, 1931.

Hughes, Laurence. *The Truth About the Movies.* Hollywood, CA: Hollywood Publishers, 1924.

Kobal, John. *People Will Talk.* New York, NY: Knopf, 1985.

Parish, James R. *The RKO Gals.* New Rochelle, NY: Arlington House, 1974.

_____, and Ronald Bowers. *The MGM Stock Company.* New Rochelle, NY: Arlington House, 1973.

_____, and William Leonard. *Hollywood Players, the Thirties.* New Rochelle, NY: Arlington House, 1976.

Rainey, Buck. *Sweethearts of the Sage: Biographies and Filmographies of 258 Actresses Appearing in Western Movies.* Jefferson, NC: McFarland, 1992.

_____. *Those Fabulous Serial Heroines: Their Lives and Films.* Metuchen, NJ: Scarecrow, 1990.

The Real Stars. Edited by Leonard Maltin. New York, NY: Popular Library, 1979.

Reilly, Adam. *Harold Lloyd.* New York, NY: Macmillan, 1977.

Screen World (annual). New York, NY: Crown, 1966–

Slide, Anthony. *Idols of Silence.* South Brunswick, NJ: Barnes, 1976.

Trotta, Vincent and Cliff Lewis. *Screen Personalities.* New York: Grosset and Dunlap, 1933.

Wagner, Walter. *You Must Remember This.* New York, NY: Putnam, 1975.

Watters, James. *Return Engagement.* New York, NY: Potter, 1984.

Index

Las Abandonadas 73
The Ableminded Lady 81
Above Suspicion 62
Above the Clouds 173, 201
According to Hoyle 83
The Accused 73, 213
The Ace of Spades 135
Aching Youths 141
Acord, Art 93, 126
The Acquittal 206
Acquitted 131
Across the Continent 87
Across the Pacific 20
Across to Singapore 62
Act of Violence 18, 20
Action 85, 171
Action in the North Atlantic 199
The Actress 119, 234
Adam and Evil 119
Adam Had Four Sons 210
Adams, Albert 42
Adams, Maude 179
Adam's Eve 118
Adam's Rib 89
Adler, Buddy 128
Adorable 92
The Adorable Cheat 121
The Adorable Deceiver 194
Adrian, Gilbert 91
Advance to the Rear 29
Adventure 29, 185
Adventure in Manhattan 17
The Adventures and Emotions of Edgar Pomeroy 175
Adventures of Mazie 194
The Adventures of Prince Courageous 131

The Adventures of Robin Hood 128, 228
The Adventures of Tarzan 126, 127
Adventures of the Queen 187
The Adventurous Sex 35
Advice to the Lovelorn 26, 207
Affairs of a Gentleman 32, 53, 79
Affairs of Cappy Ricks 41
The Affairs of Cellini 209
Affinities 152
Afraid to Talk 86
After Marriage 134
After Midnight 119
After the Fog 93, 165
After the Show 121
After Tomorrow 158
Again, Pioneers 40
Against the Law 26
The Age for Love 204
The Age of Consent 201
The Age of Desire 165
Agee, James 70
Ah, Wilderness! 230
Ain't Love Funny? 194
The Air Circus 46
The Air Hawk 82
Air Hostess 114, 233
The Air Legion 182
Air Mail 31, 41, 187
The Air Mail Pilot 147
Air Police 76
Al Capone 234
The Alarm 116
Alban, John 89
The Albany Night Boat 33

Albright, Hardie 182
Alden, Joan *see* Mehaffey, Blanche
Alex the Great 21
Alexander Hamilton 51
Ali Baba Goes to Town 73
Alias Bulldog Drummond 209
Alias Mary Brown 185
Alias Mary Dow 78
Alias Mary Flynn 39
Alias Mary Smith 120, 147
Alias the Bad Man 82
Alias the Deacon 143
Alias the Doctor 145
Alias the Lone Wolf 204
Alice Adams 156, 225
Alice in Wonderland 199
Alimony 203
Alimony Madness 195
The All American 50, 187
All at Sea 76
All for Uncle 48
All Men Are Enemies 192
All Night Long 112
All Quiet on the Western Front 144
All Stuck Up 114
Allbritton, Louise 232, 233
Allen, Judith 14, 15
Allen, Robert (Bob) "Tex" 167
Allied 40
Alma de Gaucho 176
Almost a Gentleman 230
Almost Human 174
Aloha 94
Aloma of the South Seas 107
Along Came Jones 212

240 Index

Along Came Youth 36, 70
The Altar Stairs 127
Amateur Daddy 158
Amateur Night 131
The Amazing Exploits of the Clutching Hand 181
Amazing Mazie 194
The Amazing Mr. Williams 28
Ambassador 38
Ameche, Don 211
Amelita's Friend 24
The American 131
American Madness 64
American Manners 134
An American Tragedy 70, 167
The Ancient Mariner 35
And Now Tomorrow 109, 212
And So They Were Married 20
Anderson, La Una *see* Andre, Lona
Andre, Lona 11, 13–14, 226
Andy Hardy Comes Home 230
Angel Baby 29
Angela Is 21 208
Angel's Holiday 26
Angels with Broken Wings 232
The Angelus 19, 155
Ankles Preferred 53
Ann Carver's Profession 209
Anna Karenina 144
Annabelle's Affairs 26, 53
Annapolis Salute 103
Annie Laurie 20, 21
Another Man's Wife 121
Another Scandal 203
Anthony Adverse 129, 228
Any Number Can Play 20
Anybody's Blonde 173
Appel, Augusta *see* Lee, Lila
Applegate, Phyllis 234
Appointment for Love 97
April Fool 190
April Showers 152
Arbuckle, Roscoe "Fatty" 120
Archer, Ann 233
Archer, John 233
Arden, Eve 119
Arden, Joan 60
Are These Our Children? 104
Are We Civilized? 129
Are You Listening? 144, 154, 163
Argentine Nights 231
The Argument 185
The Argyle Case 122
Arizona 17, 50, 117
The Arizona Express 39, 55, 185
The Arizona Gunfighter 45
Arizona Mahoney 229
The Arizona Streak 193
The Arizona Sweepstakes 134
Arizona Terror 24
The Arizona Wildcat 66
Arlen, Bette 14

Arlen, Betty 8, 14, 220
Arlen, Judith 12, 14–15
Arlen, Richard 40, 168
Arlen, Roxanne 234
Arliss, George 78, 113, 211
Arm of the Law 24, 69, 173
Army Wives 233
Around the Bases 96
Around the World in 18 Days 116
Arsene Lupin 154
Artclass 25
Artcraft 54
Arthur, George K. 68
Arthur, Jean 9, 15–17, 219
Arthur Takes Over 88
Arthur's Deep Resolve 203
The Artist 194
Artists and Models 226
Artists and Models Abroad 53
The Aryan 131
Asher, Irving 115, 116
Ashes of Vengeance 87, 135
Asleep at the Switch 106
The Asphalt Jungle 207
Assistant Wives 141
Assorted Nuts 155
Astaire, Fred 71–72, 98, 176, 227, 231
Asther, Nils 153
Astor, Mary 8, 17–20, 51, 219, 221
At Scrogginses' Corner 59
At the Ridge 123
Atlantic Ferry 132
The Atom 185
Attorney for the Defense 39, 64
Aubrey, Jimmy 134
The Auction Block 30, 161
The Auctioneer 158
August Week-end 163
Auld Lang Syne 59
Auntie's Mistake 74
Autry, Gene 43, 227, 232
Autumn Leaves 63
Avalanche 101
The Avenger 173
Avenging Fangs 134
The Avenging Shadow 155
The Average Woman 89
Avery, Brock Van 65
Avery, Patricia 9, 20–21
The Aviator 150
Avon, Violet 8, 21, 116, 221
The Awful Goof 133
The Awful Truth 52, 53
Aye, Marion (Maryon) 7, 21–22, 89, 221
Ayres, Lew 177

Babbitt 118, 228
Babe Comes Home 180
Babies for Sale 105

Babies Welcome 74
The Baby Bandit 55
The Baby Cyclone 119
Baby Face Morgan 44
Baby Mine 127
Bachelor Bait 104
Bachelor Brides 81, 171
Bachelor Flat 234
The Bachelor Girl 125
Bachelor Mother 114, 177, 178
Bachelor of Arts 129
Bachelor's Affairs 144
Bachelor's Club 109
Bachelor's Paradise 161
Back Door to Heaven 80
Back from Shanghai 174
Back from the Front 116
Back Home and Broke 121
Back in Circulation 28
Back in the Saddle 199
Back Street 50, 123
Back to Life 149
Backstage 194
Bad Babies 168
Bad Boy 151, 201
Bad Company 192
Bad Girl 77
Bad Little Angel 204
The Bad Man 173
The Bad One 71, 72
Bad Sister 86
Badge of Honor 98
Baehr, Irving (Theodore) 167
Bag and Baggage 92, 95
Bakewell, William 233
Balalaika 53
Ball at Savoy 148
Bancroft, George 38
The Bandit of Sherwood Forest 129
The Bandit's Baby 85
Banks, Monty 15
Banyon 27
The Bar-C Mystery 199
Bardelys the Magnificent 30
Barefoot Boy 206
The Barefoot Contessa 132
The Bargain 114
The Barker 138, 139, 158
The Barkleys of Broadway 177, 178
Barnes, George 28
Barney, Howard 77
The Barrel Organ 59
Barrie, Wendy 225
The Barrier 69
Barrymore, Dolores 56
Barrymore, Drew 18, 43, 55, 56, 58, 68, 124, 144, 145, 150, 154, 175, 191, 196
Barrymore, John Drew 56
Barrymore, Lionel 54, 124
Bars of Hate 160

Barthelmass, Richard 23, 67, 89, 109, 130, 138, 145, 148, 158, 171, 208, 211
Bartholomew, Freddie 56
Bartman, Elizabeth see Francisco, Betty
Barton, Buzz 189
Bashful Suitor 19
Basquette (Baskett, Baskette), Lina (Lena) 9, 23–25, 66, 103, 219–221
Battle Beneath the Earth 132
Battle Cry 234
The Battle of the Sexes 64, 161
Battles, Stewart 161
The Battling Buckaroo 101
Battling Buddy 21
Battling Butler 160, 161
The Battling Orioles 146
Baxter, Warner 41–42, 92, 148, 164, 200, 208
Bayer, William 81
Be a Little Sport 80
Be Happy 19
Beach Babies 114
The Beach Club 106
Beahan, Charles 86
Beall, Harry 217
The Beast of Budapest 234
Beasts of Paradise 155
The Beat Generation 234
Beatty, Clyde 162
Beau Broadway 46
Beau Brummell 18, 19, 132
Beau Geste 41, 207
Beau Ideal 212
Beau Sabreur 39
The Beautiful and Damned 111
Beautiful but Dumb 150
The Beautiful Cheat 116
Beauty and Bullets 190
Beauty and the Boss 31, 145
Beauty Parlor 53, 110, 173
Beauty Shoppers 101
Because of You 71, 213
Beck, Helen see Rand, Sally
The Beckoning Trail 203
Becky 161
Becky Sharp 70, 90
Bedlam 174
Bedtime Story 54, 192, 212
Beery, Wallace 208
Before Dawn 201
Before Midnight 51
The Beggar Maid 19
Beggar's Holiday 162
Beginner's Luck 99
Behind Office Doors 19
Behind Prison Gates 199
Behind Stone Walls 47
Behind the Curtain 175
Behind the Front 41
Behind the Make-Up 209

Behind the Mask 50, 54, 64
Belcher, Ernest 103
Belden, Charles 143
Believe It or Not 153
Bell, Rex 35, 85, 180
Bella Donna 203
Belle of the Nineties 226
The Bells 191, 203
The Bells of St. Mary's 183
Bells of San Juan 111
Beloved 98, 187
The Beloved Brat 57
Beloved Enemy 154
The Beloved Rogue 68, 69
Below the Deadline 55, 109
Below the Line 142
Below the Sea 209
Ben-Hur 112
Benjamin, Joe 157
Bennett, Alex 118
Bennett, Charles 140
Bennett, Constance 160, 191
Bennett, Enid 118
Bennett, Marjorie 118
Benson at Calford 96
Berger, Henry 128
Bergerac, Jacques 177
Bergin, William 198
Bergman, Ingrid 211
Berkeley, Busby 27
Berlin, Irving 177
Bernardine 92
Berserk 63
Bertha, the Sewing Machine Girl 166
The Best Bad Man 35
The Best Man 190, 203
Best of Enemies 158
The Best of Everything 63
The Best People 155
The Best Place to Be 187
The Best Years of Our Lives 54
"Bette Davis Eyes" 61
The Better 'Ole 100, 101
Better Days 75
The Better Man 94
Better Movies 182
Better Times 107
The Better Way 172
Between Fighting Men 76, 98
Betty Co-Ed 155
Beutler, Byrnece see Phipps, Sally
Bevan, Billy 188, 193
Beware of Bachelors 84
Beware of Blondes 172
Beware of Married Men 84
Beware of the Bride 179
Beware of Widows 116
Beware Spooks! 44
Beyond the Forest 207
Beyond the Law 127
Beyond the Pecos 233

Beyond the Rainbow 34, 35
Beyond the Rockies 104
Beyond Victory 181
Biff Bang Buddy 16
The Big Brain 32, 209
The Big Broadcast 215
Big Business Girl 28, 212
The Big Cage 163
The Big Chance 30
The Big Charade 194
The Big City 69
Big City Blues 28, 76, 114
Big Daddy (aka *Paradise Road*) 29
Big Dan 157
The Big Diamond Robbery 137, 138
Big Ears 47
Big Executive 225
The Big Flash 99
Big Hearted 96
Big Hearted Herbert 79
The Big Hop 169
The Big Killing 41
The Big Land 200
Big Pal 107
The Big Party 46
The Big Race 140, 200
The Big Ranger 116
The Big Squirt 133
Big Stakes 81, 82
Big Timber 87
Big Time 76
Big Time Charlie 114
The Big Timer 64
Big Town 65
Big Town Ideas 116
Big Town Round-Up 116
Bigger and Better Blondes 16
A Bill of Divorcement 128
Billie 50
The Billion Dollar Scandal 64
Billy's Mother 59
Biograph 135
A Bird in the Hand 203
Bird of Paradise 71, 72
The Birth of a Baby 76
The Birth of a Nation 131, 183
The Birthday Gift 57
Bishop, Julie see Wells, Jacqueline
The Bishop Misbehaves 32
The Bishop of the Ozarks 163, 164
The Bishop's Wife 211, 212
A Bit of Heaven 121
Bits of Life 139
The Bitter Tea of General Yen 153
Biff Bang Buddy 16
Black Butterflies 121, 169
The Black Camel 77, 173
The Black Cat 133, 199

242 Index

Black Evidence 203
Black Feather 171
Black Fury 154
Black Gold 226
Black Lightning 35
Black Magic 76
The Black Mantilla 24
Black Market Babies 231
Black Moon 209
Black Oxen 93
The Black Pearl 122
The Black Room 145
The Black Sheep 59
Black Widow 178
Blake of Scotland Yard 95, 133
Blakely, James 43
Blane, Barbara 227
Blane, Sally 9, 25–27, 210, 220, 221
Blazing Days 94
Blazing Guns 181
The Blazing Trail 165
Blessed Event 41, 98
Blind Alleys Underworld 39
A Blind Bargain 124
Blisters Under the Skin 155
Blithe Spirit 64
The Block Signal 16
Block-Heads 79
Blond Cheat 32
Blonde Crazy 28
Blonde Fever 20
The Blonde from Brooklyn 232
Blondell, (Rose) Joan 9, 10, 27–29, 219
Blondes by Choice 206
Blondie 232
Blondie Johnson 28, 153
Blondie Meets the Boss 110
Blondie's Big Moment 129
Blood and Sand 120, 121, 227
Blood Money 70
The Blood Ruby 59
The Blood Ship 125
The Blot 206
Blow Your Own Horn 164
Blue, Monte 148
Blue Blood 147
The Blue Eagle 91
Blue Oyster Cult 61
Blue Skies 192
The Blue Streak 127
The Blue Veil 27, 29, 109, 219
Bluebeard's Eighth Wife 90, 199
Bluebeard's Seven Wives 203
Blues in the Night 54
Boardman, Eleanor 29–30, 221
The Boaster 95
Bobbed Hair 57
Body and Soul 123
The Body Punch 82
Boehling (Bolling), James 13
Bogart, Humphrey 138, 170, 231

The Bohemian Girl 199
Boiling Point 85
Bolero 170, 171, 224
Bombshell 183
Bond, Lillian (Lilian) 11, 31–32, 220
Bonny May 131
The Boob 62
Boobs in the Woods 112
The Bookworm Hero 96
The Boomerang 135
Borden, Olive 8, 32–33, 107, 221, 221
Border Brigands 14
The Border Cafe 190
The Border Cavalier 53, 167
Border Guns 147
The Border Legion 209
The Border River 38
Border Vigilantes 229
The Border Whirlwind 126
The Border Wildcat 138
Border Women 172
Bored of Education 227
Born Reckless 45, 53, 105
Born Rich 206
Born to Battle 16, 45
Born to Be Bad 212, 231
Born to Fight 227
Born to Gamble 204, 228
Born to the Saddle 155, 190
Born to the West 155
Born Yesterday 15
Borrowed Finery 127
Borrowed Hero 97
Borrowed Sunshine 135
Borrowed Wives 174
Borzage, Frank 77
Bote en Bote 143
A Bottle Baby 116
Bottoms Up 88
Boulder Dam 79
Bow, Clara 8, 27, 34–36, 52, 188, 221
The Bowery 209
Bowery Boys 43
Bowery Champs 40
The Boy Friend 69, 119
A Boy of the Streets 87
Boy, Oh Boy 119
A Boy Ten Feet Tall 64
Boyd, Betty 9, 36–37
Boyd, William 80, 225
Boyer, Charles 15, 211
Bradley, Grace 225
Brady, Alice 54
Bramley, Flora 9, 37, 220
Brand, Harry 217
Brand, Jolene (Joline) 234
The Brand Blotters 22
Brand of Courage 116
Brand of Cowardice 93
Branded Men 50, 143

Brass 83
The Brass Bottle 107, 108
The Brat 51, 160, 162
Braveheart 171
The Breaking Point 149
Breaking Records 96
Breaking the Ice 57
The Breath of Scandal 149
The Breath of the Gods 179
Breed of the West 82
Brenon, Herbert 210
Brent, Evelyn 7, 37–40, 221
Brent, George 78, 226
Brian, Mary 8, 40–41, 221
Brice, Fannie 102, 147
Brice, Monte 100
The Bride of Fancy 135
Bride of the Storm 57
The Bride Walks Out 156
The Bride Wore Red 62
Brides Are Like That 129, 230
The Bridge of Sighs 139
Brigham, Robert 135
Brigham Young — Frontiersman 20
Bright Eyes 204
Bright Lights 79, 139, 185
The Bright Shawl 19
Brilliant Marriage 144
Bringin' Home the Bacon 16
Broad Daylight 203
Broadway 39, 87
Broadway and Home 80
Broadway Babies 77
Broadway Bad 28, 87, 93, 178
Broadway Bill 81, 82, 99, 167
A Broadway Butterfly 74
A Broadway Cowboy 87
Broadway Daddies 77, 87, 125
Broadway Fever 161
Broadway Gondolier 28
Broadway Lady 39, 52
The Broadway Madonna 172
The Broadway Melody 130, 132, 162, 163, 219
Broadway Melody of 1936 14, 133
Broadway Nights 204
Broadway Scandals 66, 161
Broadway Through a Keyhole 64
Broadway's Like That 28
Brodel, Joan *see* Leslie, Joan
Broke Out 48
Broken Barriers 60, 174
The Broken Butterfly 185
Broken Chains 152, 206
The Broken Coin 99
Broken Dishes 212
Broken Dreams 183
The Broken Gate 16
Broken Hearts 121
Broken Hearts of Broadway 152
Broken Hearts of Hollywood 109, 149, 152

Broken Sabre 105
The Broken Violin 139
The Broken Wing 196
Broncho Billy and the Baby 166
The Broncho Buster 95
The Broncho Twister 60
Brook, Clive 38
Brooks, Walter 198
Brother of the Bear 19
Brotherly Love 16
Brothers Under the Skin 206
Brown, George 122
Brown, Harry Joe 77
Brown, Jacqueline *see* Wells, Jacqueline
Brown, Joe E. 78, 113
Brown, Nacio Herb 162
The Brown Danube 208
Brown of Harvard 41
Bruisers and Losers 155
Brust, C.K., Jr. 104
Bryan, Ella 230
Bryson, Betty 12, 41–42, 200
Bryson, Winifred 42, 200
The Buccaneer 25
The Buckaroo Kid 180
Bucking the Line 137
Bud and Ben Featurettes 82
Buffalo Bill, Jr. 15
Bugambilia 73
Buggs, Jack 177
The Bugle Call 206
Bull and Sand 106
The Bull Fighter 106
Bulldog Courage 131
Bulldog Drummond at Bay 129, 139
Bulldog Drummond Strikes Back 212
Bulldog Edition 114
Bulldog Jack 209
A Bullet for Joey 27
The Bullet Mark 136
Bullets or Ballots 28
Bunco Squad 90
Burgess, Helen 229
A Burglar for a Night 203
Burglar Proof 203
Burke, Kathleen 13
Burlesque 104, 130
Burning Daylight 83
Burning Sands 124
Burning the Wind 82
Burning Up 41
Burning Up Broadway 60
Burning Words 116
Burns, Neal 107
Burr 180
Bush Pilot 105
The Busher 152
The Bushranger 94
Busman's Honeymoon 64
Busses Roar 199

Bustin' Through 134
Busy Lizzie 141
Butter Fingers 106
Buttercups 59
Butterflies in the Rain 116
Butterfly 116
Button My Back 92
Buttram, Pat 232
Buffalo Bill on the U.P. Trail 138
By Appointment Only 69, 90, 162
By Candlelight 173
By the Governor's Order 59
By the Way 37
By Whose Hand? 198
By Your Leave 13, 158

Cactus Pictures 22
Cafe Metropole 212
Caged 109, 226
Cagney, James 27, 78, 113, 140, 145, 186, 211, 231
Cagney, William 140
Calaboose 41
Calendar Girl 226
Calford in the Movies 96
Calford on Horseback 96
Calford vs. Redskins 96
The Calgary Stampede 82, 94
Caliente Love 52
California 201
California or Bust 85
Call a Messenger 44
Call Her Savage 35, 36
Call It a Day 129
Call Northside 777 85
The Call of Courage 116
The Call of Home 169
The Call of the Canyon 203
Call of the Heart 147
Call of the Mate 172
The Call of the North 83
Call of the West 172
The Call of the Wild 212, 226
The Call of the Wilderness 141
The Callahans and the Murphys 161
Calling All Doctors 133
Calling All Marines 223
The Calling of Dan Matthews 103
Cameo Kirby 16
The Cameraman 68, 69
Camille 148, 149
Campbell, John 168
The Campus Carmen 77, 92
Campus Sweethearts 178
The Campus Vamp 77
The Canary Murder Case 15, 16
Candid Cameramaniacs 119
The Candy Kid 90
The Cannon Ball Express 106
Cansino, Rita 227

Cantor, Eddie 97, 163, 168, 197
The Canyon of Adventure 82
The Canyon of Light 93
Capital Punishment 35
Cappy Ricks Returns 204
Capra, Frank 15, 16, 152, 153
Captain Applejack 41
Captain Barnacle's Baby 59
Captain Barnacle's Legacy 57
Captain Barnacle's Messmate 59
Captain Blood 199
Captain Calamity 158
Captain Jack's Dilemma 57, 59
Captain Lash 206
The Captain of Koepenick 41
Captain of the Guard 115, 116
Captain Salvation 69, 185
Captain Swagger 46
Captain Thunder 209
Captured in Chinatown 181
Caravan 212
Carefree 178
The Careless Age 212
The Caretakers 63
Carew(e), Arthur Edmund 42
Carewe, Edwin 42, 71
Carewe, Rita 9, 42–43, 71, 220
Carewe, Violet *see* Carewe, Rita
Carey, Harry 80, 83
Carlisle (Carlyle), Mary 11, 43–44
Carmen, Jean 12, 44–45, 219
Carmen, Jeanne *see* Carmen, Jean
The Carnation Kid 118
Carnival 78, 167
Carnival Boat 178
Carnival Lady 140
Carnival Revue 99
Carny 170
Carol, Sue 9, 45–46, 221
Carolina 92
Carolyn of the Corners 131
Carroll, Earl 31
Carroll, Lucia 230, 231
La Casa Chica 73
Casa de Mujeres 73
Casanova Brown 129
Case, Allen 76
Case Dismissed 16
The Case of the Baby Sitter 14
The Case of the Black Cat 229
The Case of the Howling Dog 20
The Case of the Lucky Legs 79
The Case of the Missing Man 230
Casey at the Bat 26, 101, 188
Casey of the Coast Guard 84
Cash Customers 48
Cash McCall 224
Cass Timberlane 20
Cassavetes, John 27, 96

244 Index

Cassidy, Hopalong
Cassin, Billie *see* Crawford, Joan
The Cat and the Canary 115, 116
The Cat Creeps 192
Catlett, Walter 52
Catlow 132
The Cats' Meow 67
Caught 70
Caught in the End 174
Caught Short 120, 163
Cause for Alarm 213
Cause for Divorce 134
Cavalcade of the West 181
Celebrity 24
Center Door Fancy 28
Central Airport 78
Central Park 28, 79
Century 126
A Certain Young Man 69
Chain Gang 233
Chained 62
Chaliapin, Feodor 86
Chalk Marks 83
The Challenge of the Law 83
The Champ 29
Champagne Charlie 230
Champagne for Breakfast 43, 44, 122, 144
Champion, Marge 24
Chan, Charlie 153
Chance at Heaven 158, 178
Chaney, Lon 60, 68, 80, 120, 124, 148, 162, 164, 195, 210
Change of Heart 92, 178, 187
Channel Crossing 64
Chapburn, Jean 12
Chaplin, Charlie 126, 143, 145, 196, 205
Chaplin, Lita Grey 205
Chaplin, Sydney 100
The Charge of the Gauchos 125
The Charge of the Light Brigade 228
Charley's Aunt 51, 179
Charlie Chan at the Circus 153
Charlie Chan at Treasure Island 27
Charlie Chan Carries On 87
Charlie Chan in Paris 41, 42
Charlie Chan on Broadway 144, 153
Charlie Chan's Chance 158, 224
Charlie Chan's Courage 123
Charlie Chan's Secret 227
The Charm School 121
Chase, Charley 52, 68, 33, 41, 95
The Chaser 136
Chasing Rainbows 120, 132
Chasing Through Europe 46
Cheap Kisses 174
Cheaper by the Dozen 124

Cheaters 51, 84, 134, 139
Cheaters at Play 198
Cheating Blondes 97
Cheating Cheaters 209
Check and Double Check 46
Cheerful Givers 131, 185
Cherrill, Virginia 145
The Cherry Orchard 63
Chesterfield 23, 25, 67, 68, 114, 162, 171
Chevalier, Maurice 69, 191
Cheyenne 136
Cheyenne Autumn 72, 73
Chicken a la King 118
Chicken Every Sunday 202
Chickens Come Home 117
Chickie 48, 38, 39
The Chief 139
The Child Crusoes 57, 59
Children of Divorce 36, 188
Children of Dust 89
Children of Jazz 199
Children of Loneliness 45
Children of Pleasure 43, 207
The Children of Sanchez 73
Children of the Damned 132
Children of the Ritz 66, 138, 139
Chills and Fever 114
The Chimp 117, 182
China 212
China Bound 76
China Passage 53
China Seas 32
Chinatown After Dark 110
Chinatown Charlie 127
The Chinatown Mystery 99
Chinatown Squad 153
The Chinese Parrot 158
Chip of the Flying U 82
Chloe: Love Is Calling You 33, 160
Chop Suey 74
The Chorus Kid 82
Christie Pictures 14, 107, 150, 169, 173, 189
Christina 91
Christine of the Big Tops 89
Christmas Eve 29
Christmas in Connecticut 54
A Christmas Story 59
Christy, Ann 9, 46–47, 63, 110, 167, 201
The Church Across the Way 59
The Church Mouse 117
The Cincinnati Kid 29
Cinder Path 96
Cinderella Jones 199
The Circle 30, 62
Circumstantial Evidence 85, 173
The Circus Ace 108
Circus Blues 74
Circus Clown 79
The Circus Cowboy 157

Circus Jim 38
The Circus Kid 60
Circus Rookies 127
Circus Shadows 103, 173, 201
The Circus Show-Up 26
Circus Today 106
The Cisco Kid 223
City for Conquest 53
City Girl 134
City Lights 145
City Limits 26
The City of Masks 203
The City of Silent Men 203
The City of Stars 157
City Park 26, 120
La Ciudad de Carton 92
The Claim Jumper 22
Clair(e), Ethlyne 47–48, 219
Clair(e), Josephine 9
The Clairvoyant 79
Clancy of the Mounted 199
Clancy's Kosher Wedding 215
Clash of the Wolves 142
Classified 199
Claudia and David* 20
The Claw 206
The Clean Heart 21
Clearing the Range 77
Clearing the Trail 96
Cleopatra 107, 172
The Climax 55
Clive of India 212
The Cloud Dodger 95
The Cloud Rider 84
The Clown 172
Clowtman (Cloutman), Barbara *see* Kent, Barbara
The Clutching Hand 181
Clyde, Andy 36, 47
Clyde, June 11, 49–50, 221
Coast Guard 70
The Coast Patrol 209
The Cobweb 210
Cock o' the Walk 108, 126
Coco 177
Code of Honor 101
Code of the Air 143
The Code of the Scarlet 136
Code of the Sea 125
Cody, Bill 147, 189
Coffin, Ray 217
Cohan, George M. 50, 181
Cohan, Helen(e) 12, 50, 220
The Cohens and Kellys in Hollywood 50, 86, 187
The Cohens and the Kellys in Paris 46
Cohn, Harry 171, 230
Cohn, Jack 67
Cohn, Joan *see* Perry, Joan
Cold Nerve 94
Cold Steel 81
Cold Turkey 67

Colleen 28, 90
College 37, 54, 55
The College Boob 16
College Coquette 168, 169, 189
College Cuties 181
College Days 69, 112, 190
The College Hero 90
College Humor 13, 43, 44
The College Kiddo 106
College Love 96
College Lovers 158
College Rhythm 41
College Scandal 53, 225
The College Widow 57
The Collegians 26, 43
Collegiate 194
Collier, Constance 151
Collingwood, Charles 233
Collyer, Clayton (Bud) 51, 181
Collyer, Dan 51
Collyer, June 9, 51, 181
Colman, Ronald 40, 63, 208, 211
Columbia Pictures 15, 63, 99, 103, 122, 128, 137, 171, 191, 211, 216, 225
Come Across 24
Come Again Smith 203
Come Closer, Folks 146
Come On, Cowboys! 228
Come On Marines! 13
Come On Over 152
Come Out of the Pantry 209
Come to My House 33
Come to the Stable 211, 213
Coming Out Party 70
Coming Through 121
The Common Law 181
Common Property 152
Companionate Service 74
Compromise 89
Compson, Betty 80, 184
Compton, Joyce 8, 52–54
Compton, Olivia Joyce *see* Compton, Joyce
Comrades 60
Condemned Women 78
Coney Island 204
The Confession 179
Confessions of a Chorus Girl 118
Confessions of a Co-ed 183
Confessions of a Vice Baron 14
Confidential 114
A Connecticut Yankee in King Arthur's Court 184, 185
Connelly, Marc 105
The Conquering Horde 209
Conquest 204
Conspiracy 132
The Constant Woman 206
Contraband 203
Convention City 20, 28, 79
Convention Girl 162
Convicted Woman 105

Convoy 139
Cook, Clyde 193
Cook, Donald 114
Cook, Edward 180
Cooke, Donna 234
Cooper, Gary 15, 34, 38, 40, 150, 195, 202, 208, 211, 231
The Cop 125
The Copperhead 54, 55
Corbin, Virginia Lee 93
Cornwall, Anne 8, 37, 54–55, 220, 221
Coronado 199
Coroner Creek 78
Corporal Kate 174
The Corpse Came C.O.D. 29
Corruption 114, 120
Cortez, Natalie 38
Cortez, Ricardo 124
Costello, Dolores 8, 18, 55–57, 58, 59, 220, 221
Costello, Helen(e) 8, 9, 56, 58–60, 89, 220, 221
Costello, Maurice 55, 58
Counsel for Crime 199
Count Herzathy 112
The Count of Luxemburg 147, 190
The Count of Ten 169
Counterfeit 146
The Countess of Monte Cristo 209
The Country Beyond 33, 105
Country Fair 50
Country Gentlemen 53, 122
The County Fair 181
County Hospital 117
Courage 158
The Courage of Collins 85
The Courage of Marge O'Doone 185
Courage of Sorts 59
Court-Martial 101
The Courtship of Miles Standish 157
Cover Girl 123, 227
The Covered Wagon 202, 203
The Cowboy and the Bandit 147
The Cowboy and the Blonde 90
The Cowboy and the Flapper 172
The Cowboy and the Kid 173
Cowboy Buckaroo 233
The Cowboy Cop 16
The Cowboy Star 133
Crack-Up 230
Cradle Snatchers 77
Cradle Song 226
Craig, Colin 181
Craig, Mar 234
Craig's Wife 201
The Crash 204
Crashin' Thru Danger (aka

Crashing Through Danger, Crashing Thru Danger) 26
Crashing Broadway 101
Crashing Through 171
Crashing Thru 45
Crawford, Christina 61
Crawford, Joan 8, 60–63, 104, 119, 160, 162, 219
Crazy Like a Fox 182
Crazy to Marry 121
Crews, Laura Hope 151
The Cricket on the Hearth 82
Crime and Punishment 146
Crime Doctor 154, 207
The Crime of Doctor Forbes 187
Crime of Passion 210
The Crime of the Century 70
Crime on the Hill 26
The Criminal Code 63, 64
Criminals of the Air 133
Crimson Colors 96
Crinoline and Romance 87
Crofton, James 176
Cronin, Gladys *see* Christy, Ann
Cronk, Clara *see* Windsor, Claire
Crooked Alley 116
Crosby, Bing 43, 47, 143
The Crosby Case 198
The Cross Country Run 96
Cross Examination 26
Cross Streets 129, 206
The Crossroads of New York 137
The Crowd 29, 30, 77, 109
The Crowd Roars 28
Crowe, Elinor *see* Fair, Elinor
The Cruise of the Make-Believes 121
Crusade Against Rackets 14
The Crusader 39, 69, 83, 212, 226
Cruze, James 184
Cry Havoc 28, 229
The Crystal Cup 139
The Cuban Love Song 154, 196
La Cucaracha 73
The Cuckoos 49
Cukor, George 61, 191
Culpepper, Edward 177
Cummings, Constance 10, 63–64, 110, 201
Cummings, Robert 198
Cupid Forecloses 131
Cupid's Fireman 157
Cured in the Excitement 106
Curly Top 103, 104
Curtain at Eight 139, 181
The Curtain Falls 173
Custer, Bob 169
Custer's Last Stand 14, 97
Cutie 74
The Cyclist 194

246　Index

The Cyclone 152
Cyclone Cavalier 93
The Cyclone Kid 123
The Cyclone Rider 39
Cynthia 20

Dad Rudd, MP 198
Daddy Knows Best 52
Daddy Long Legs 92
Dade, Frances 10, 64–65
Daisy Kenyon 62
La Dame del Alba 73
Damaged Lives 69
Damaged Love 51
Dame Chance 106, 107
Die Dame Jewellen Hast 143
Dames 28
The Damned Don't Cry 63
Dance, Fools, Dance 62, 144
Dance, Girl, Dance 44, 114
Dance Hall 33
Dance Hall Hostess 195
Dance Madness 206
Dance Magic 185
The Dance of Life 172
The Dance of Love 24
Dance Team 77
The Dancer of Paris 139
Dancers in the Dark 123, 195
Dancing Dynamite 147
Dancing Feet 144, 227
Dancing Fools 48
Dancing Lady 62
Dancing Mothers 34, 35
Dancing on a Dime 233
Dancing Sweeties 46, 193
Dane, Karl 68
Danger Ahead 165
Danger Lights 17
Danger Patrol 78, 82, 103
Danger Quest 180
Danger Signal 54, 172
Danger Street 182, 231
Danger! Women at Work 41
Dangerous 89, 90
A Dangerous Adventure 164
A Dangerous Affair 26
The Dangerous Age 134
The Dangerous Blonde 116
Dangerous Blondes 129
The Dangerous Coward 108
Dangerous Curves 36, 52, 53
Dangerous Days 185
The Dangerous Flirt 39
Dangerous Innocence 116
Dangerous Lady 39
Dangerous Pastime 81
Dangerous Peach 141
Dangerous Pleasure 171, 172
Daniels, Bebe 157
Daniels, Thomas (John) 80
Dante's Inferno 95, 185, 230

Dantzler, Louise *see* Brian, Mary
Dare, Dorothy 228
The Dare-Devil 106
The Daredevil 112
Daredevils of the Clouds 231
Daredevil's Reward 108
Daring Danger 195
Daring Daughters 144, 145
The Daring Years 35
Dark Alibi 54
Dark Stairways 190
Dark Streets 122
Darkened Rooms 39, 101
The Darling of New York 87
Darmour 68
D'Arrast, Harry d'Abbadie 30
Dashing Thru 138
Dates for Two 48
Daughter Angele 185
Daughter of Shanghai 39
Daughter of the Dragon 65
A Daughter of the Poor 131
Daughter of the Tong 39
A Daughter of the Wolf 121
Daughters of Pleasure 35
Daughters of the Rich 179
Daughters of Today 149
D'Auvergne, Sharon Lindsay *see* Lynn(e), Sharon
D'Auvray, Joseph 193
Davies, Marion 232
Davis, Bette 18, 61, 70, 86, 89, 202
Davis, Dee 234
Davis, Mildred 167
Davy Crockett at the Fall of the Alamo 138
The Dawn of a Tomorrow 125
The Dawn of Understanding 131
Dawson, Doris 9, 66
Day, Alice 221
Day, Doris 115
Day, Marceline 8, 67, 68–69, 221
A Day at Santa Anita 28
The Day of Faith 9, 30, 66–68, 77
Daybreak 38, 154
Days of Daring 95
Daytime Wives 164
The Dazzling Coeds 96
Dead End 225
Dead Game 116
Dead Man's Curve 26
Dead Men Walk 44
Dean, James 104
Deans, Effingham S. 149
Dear Old Calford 96
Dear Old Darling 181
Death Flies East 167
Death in the Air 14
Death of a Salesman 130

Death Takes a Holiday 225
Deception 198
De Closs, Melba *see* Leslie, Kay
The Decoy 203
Dee, Frances 10, 69–71, 224
Deep in the Heart of Texas 233
Deep Valley 224
The Defense Rests 17
Defying the Law 94
De Havilland, Olivia 128, 228
del Barrio, Arturo 59
del Campo, Manuel 18
Delicious 92
Dell, Dorothy 224
Del Rio, Dolores 8, 27, 71–73, 138, 176, 195, 196, 219, 220
del Rio, Jaime 71
Deluge 204
DeMille, Cecil B. 23, 80, 89, 106, 120, 124, 169, 173, 202, 226, 229
DeMille, Katherine 225, 226
The Demon 190
Demos 38
Dempsey, Jack 23, 196
The Denial 175, 206
Denny, Reginald 115
The Denver Dude 146
Deputy Marshal 200
The Deputy's Double Cross 116
Derrick, George 100
Deseada 73
Desert Blossoms 83
The Desert Flower 94, 152
Desert Fury 20
Desert Guns 156
The Desert Outlaw 39
The Desert Pirate 190
Desert Valley 82
Deserted at the Altar 131
The Desert's Price 141
The Desert's Toll 112
Desirée 234
Desk Set 29
Desmond, William 87, 190
A Desperate Adventure 146
A Desperate Chance for Ellery Queen 32
Desperation 116
Destiny 233
Detectives 69
The Devil and Miss Jones 17
The Devil Is Driving 133, 204
Devil Monster 147
The Devil on Deck 143, 159
The Devil Pays 93
The Devil to Pay 212
A Devil with Women 176
The Devil's Cabaret 43
The Devil's Cage 90
The Devil's Cargo 105, 185
Devil's Chaplain 82
The Devil's Claim 152

The Devil's Dooryard 94
The Devil's Hairpin 20
The Devil's in Love 212
Devil's Island 158
Devil's Lottery 198
The Devil's Mask 129
The Devil's Masterpiece 82
The Devil's Parade 28
The Devil's Playground 73
The Devil's Skipper 135
Devil's Squadron 154
The Devil's Trademark 94
De Vito, Chester 96
De Voe, Daisy 35
Devore, Dorothy 7, 73–75, 220
Devotion 224
Diamond Handcuffs 30, 119
Diamond Jim 17
The Diamond Master 127
The Dictator 121
Diggins, Margaret (Peggy) 230, 231
Dillow, Barrett 45
Dillow, Jean Carmen *see* Carmen, Jean
Dinky 20
Dinner at Eight 154, 207
Dinty 152
Dirigible 209
Dirty Work 32
Discarded Lovers 198
Discontented Husbands 93
Disgraced 192
Disorderly Conduct 26, 77
Diversion 180
Divine Sinners 174
Divorce 223
Divorce in the Family 204
Divorce Made Easy 118
The Divorce Racket 33, 207
The Divorcée 207
Dix, Richard 15, 40, 124, 180, 201, 202, 208
The Dixie Handicap 206
Dizzy Dames 216
Do Children Count? 135
Do It Now 172
Do Your Duty 66
The Doctor 155
Doctor Bull 103, 104, 158
Dr. Jim 206
Doctor Rhythm 43, 44
The Doctor Takes a Wife 212
Dr. Terror's House of Horrors 105
Doctor X 208, 209
A Doctor's Diary 46, 229
Doctor's Orders 112
The Doctor's Secret 59
Dodging Danger 95
Dodsworth 17, 18, 20
A Dog of the Regiment 95, 96
Dogs of War 169

The Dolins of Oklahoma 233
The Dollar-a-Year Man 121
Domestic Meddlers 206
Don Coo Coo 194
Don Juan 18, 19, 60, 142
Don Juan Quilligan 29
Don Juan's Three Nights 87, 106, 112
Don Q 19
Don Quixote 86
Doña Perfecta 73
A Donde Van Nuestros Hijos 73
The Donovan Affair 81, 82, 172
Don't 161, 167
Don't Bet on Love 178
Don't Gamble with Strangers 55
Don't Get Personal 78, 133
Don't Shoot 209
The Door That Has No Key 38
Dorothy Vernon of Haddon Hall 199
Double Crossed 127
Double Crossroads 122
Double Daring 16
Double Dealing 83, 87
Double Harness 32
A Double Life 109
Double or Nothing 43, 44
Double Reward 22
Double Trouble 99
Double Wedding 120
Doubling with Danger 94
Doughboys 77
Douglas, Marian *see* Gregory, Ena
Douglas, Melvyn 186, 211
Dove, Billie 159
Down by the Rio Grande 172
Down the Stretch 79, 94, 158
Down to Earth 44
Down to the Sea in Ships 35
Down to Their Last Yacht 86, 163
Down with Husbands 118
Downstairs 154
Doyle, Maxine 228
Dracula 65
Dracula's Daughter 228
Drag 67, 68, 122
Dragnet 41
The Dragnet 39
The Drag-Net 158
Dragnet Patrol 174
Dragstrip Riot 210
Drake, Dorothy 12, 75, 220
Drake, Frances 224
Dramatic School 198
Dream House 47
A Dream of Egypt 24
Dream of Love 62
Dream Stuff 52
Dreamboat 178
Dress Parade 131

Dressed to Kill 19
Dressler, Marie 91, 162
The Dressmaker from Paris 33
The Drifters 203
Drifting Souls 204
Driftwood 69
Driven 81
Driven from Home 89
The Drivin' Fool 149
The Drop Kick 109, 110, 172, 194
Drug Store Cowboy 16
Drums of Jeopardy 51, 97
Drums of Love 165
The Drunkard 99
Dry and Thirsty 174
Dry Martini 19, 77
Duck Soup 106
The Dude Cowboy 37
The Dude Desperado 96
Dude Ranch 51
The Dude Wrangler 24
Duff, Howard 225
Dugan of the Badlands 147
Dugan of the Dugouts 90
The Duke Steps Out 62
Dulcy 55
The Dumb Girl of Portici 203
Dumbbells in Ermine 110
Dunaway, Faye 61
Duncan sisters 49
Dunn, James 13, 77, 159, 201, 229
Dunn, (Mary) Josephine 9, 76
Durand of the Bad Lands 157
Durant, Jack 159
Durante, Jimmy 196
Durbin, Deanna 228
Durham, Dick 82
Duval, Diane *see* Wells, Jacqueline
Duval, Hedi 234
Dynamite Denny 147
Dynamite Ranch 98
Dynamite Smith 125, 131

Eager Lips 89
The Eagle's Brood 173
The Eagle's Feather 81
Early to Wed 48
Earp, Virgil 47
Earp, Wyatt 47
Earthworm Tractors 229
The Easiest Way 163
East Is West 196
East of Broadway 87
East of Fifth Avenue 44
East of Java 153, 225
East Side of Heaven 28
East Side, West Side 51
Easy Going 85
Easy Going Gordon 138
Easy Living 17
Easy Millions 90

248 Index

The Easy Road 121
Easy to Cop 116
Easy to Love 20, 79
Easy to Make Money 179
Ebb Tide 25, 121, 124
Eclair Comedies 139
Edgar and the Teacher's Pet 175
Edgar Camps Out 175
Edgar Takes the Cake 175
Edgar's Jonah Day 175
Edgar's Little Saw 175
Edington, Harry 110
Educational Pictures 36, 98, 107, 141, 181
Edward and Mrs. Simpson 132
Edwards, Gus 94, 120
Edwards, Harry 38
The Egg and I 233
The Egg Crate Wallop 152
Egli, Joe 194
The Egyptian 88
Eight Cylinder Bull 16
Eight Girls in a Boat 201
"813" 116
Eilers, (Dorothea) Sally(e) 9, 77–78, 220
The Eleventh Commandment 145
Elinor Norton 123, 181, 182
Ella Cinders 150, 152
Elliott, Lorraine 230–231
Ellis, Patricia 11, 78–80, 83, 222
Ellis, Robert Reel 174
Ellis Island 53
Elmer and Elsie 134
Elmer the Great 79
Elmo the Fearless 127
Elsa Maxwell's Hotel for Women 53
Embarrassing Moments 158
Emergency Call 134, 195
Emergency Landing 39
Emma 110
Employee's Entrance 212
Empty Hands 108
Empty Hearts 35
The Enchanted Barn 131
The Enchanted Hill 41
The End of the Game 80, 203
The End of the Trail 80
The Enemies of Women 35
An Enemy of Man 172
Enemy of the Law 230
Enemy of Women 187
Enticement 19
Ericksen, Lucille *see* Ricksen, Lucille
Errol, Leon 13, 196
Erwin, Stuart 51
Escapade 26, 93
Escape from Crime 199
Escape to Paradise 53

Escovar, Louise *see* Lorraine, Louise
Essanay Studios 174
Eternal Love 175, 176
The Eternal Three 22, 92, 131, 134, 206
The Eternal Woman 33
Eternally Yours 212
Etta of the Footlights 57, 59
Evangeline 71, 72
Ever Since Eve 41
Everybody's Doing It 78
Everybody's Old Man 105
Everything But the Truth 55
Everything's Ducky 52
Everything's Rosie 129
Eve's Lover 35
The Evil Men Do 57
The Evil Mind 209
Ex-Bad Boy 17
Ex-Flame 158
The Ex-Mrs. Bradford 17, 122
The Exalted Flapper 46
Excess Baggage 76
Exchange of Wives 30
Excitement 116
Exit Smiling 127
Expensive Women 57
The Experiment 38
The Expert 204
Exposed 54, 110
Exposure 122
Extravagance 51, 120
Eyes of the Forest 185
Eyes of the Totem 55
Eyes of the Underworld 26
Eyes of Youth 185

The Face at the Window 139
A Face in the Fog 51
Face in the Sky 122, 158
Face to Face 155
Faces 96, 97
Faint Perfume 87
Fair, Elinor 8, 80–81
The Fair Cheat 139
Fair Enough 74
Fair Play 87
Fairbanks, Douglas 61, 78, 93, 106, 130, 168, 171, 210
Fairbanks, Douglas, Sr. 195
Faire, Virginia Brown(e) 7, 81–82
The Faker 125
The Fall of Babylon 185
The Fall of Eve 148, 150
Fallen Angel 37
Fallen Angels 143
The False Alarm 172
False Faces 53, 122
False Kisses 165
False Morals 190
Fame and Fortune 81

The Family Upstairs 199
The Famous Ferguson Case 28
The Famous Mrs. Fair 83
Famous Players 54
Fancy Baggage 84
Fangs of Justice 142
Fanny Foley Herself 104
The Far Cry 172
Farewell 96
The Farmer Takes a Wife 92
The Farmer's Daughter 109, 211, 212, 226
Farrell, Charles 90, 91, 208, 215
Fascinating Youth 35, 76, 121, 203
Fashion Madness 206
Fast and Fearless 16
Fast and Furious 109
Fast and Loose 144
Fast Company 39, 120
Fast Life 212
The Fast Male 194
Fast Work 142
The Fast Worker 116
The Fatal Plunge 116
The Fatal Warning 60
Fate of a Flirt 171, 172
Father and Son 172
Father's Close Shave 116
Fazenda, Louise 68
FBO 193
The Fearless Rider 109
Feet First 110
Feet of Clay 173, 174
Feet of Mud 112
Feldman, L.W. 164
Fellow Voyagers 57, 59
Female 204
Female on the Beach 63
Ferguson, Helen 7, 83–84, 219, 220
Ferris, Audrey 9, 84–85
Fessier, Michael 31
Fickle Women 107
Fields, W.C. 40, 103
Fiesta 20, 42
La Fiesta de Santa Barbara 43
Fifth Avenue 126
Fifth Avenue Girl 178
Fifth Avenue Models 87, 134, 165
Fifty Million Frenchmen 93, 114, 148, 198
Fifty Million Husbands 99
Fig Leaves 33
Fight and Win 92, 179
The Fight That Failed 155
A Fight to the Finish 133
Fightin' Mad 82
The Fightin' Redhead 190
The Fighting American 19
Fighting Back 116
The Fighting Blade 139
The Fighting Boob 147

The Fighting Buckaroo 126
Fighting Caballero 97
The Fighting Cheat 16
A Fighting Colleen 131
The Fighting Coward 19
The Fighting Eagle 171
The Fighting Edge 149
The Fighting Finish 96
The Fighting Fool 69
Fighting for Justice 53
Fighting for Victory 96
The Fighting Gentleman 76
The Fighting Guardsman 129
Fighting Hearts 194
The Fighting Lover 124
Fighting Mad 27
The Fighting Marshal 96
The Fighting Parson 69
The Fighting Peacemaker 191
The Fighting Ranger 173
The Fighting Sap 108
The Fighting Smile 16
Fighting Spirit 96
The Fighting Streak 149
Fighting the Flames 74
Fighting Thoroughbreds 44
Fighting Through 133
Fighting Thru 93
Fighting to Live 181
Fighting to Win 96
The Fighting Trooper 109
Fighting Youth 89, 229, 230
Figures Don't Lie 101, 113
File 113 113
Filling His Own Shoes 83
The Final Hour 25
A Final Reckoning 127
Finch, Gloria *see* Stuart, Gloria
Find Your Man 142
Finders Keepers 83, 85, 116
Fineman, Bernard 38
The Finger Points 209
Finger Prints 60
Fingerprints Don't Lie 232
Fingers of Fate 22
Finishing School 70, 178
Finkelstein, Harry 170
Finlayson, James 137, 215
Finn, Lola 215
Finnegan's Ball 146
Fire and Steel 135
The Fire Detective 136
The Fire Eater 127
The Fire Fighters 84
The Fire Trap 114
The Firebird 129
Fireman Save My Child 31, 76, 114
The Fires of Conscience 80
The Firing Line 55
The First Auto 149
First Division 138
The First Hundred Years 67, 106

The First Kiss 209
First Lady 129
First National Pictures 52, 67, 138, 150, 158, 159, 160, 175, 205, 210
The First Night 74, 109
The First Traveling Saleslady 179
The First Violin 59
The First Year 92
Fitzgerald, F. Scott 150
FitzGerald, John 148
Fitzmaurice, George 92
Fitzpatrick, Margaret *see* Patrick, Gail
Five Came Back 225
Five Star Final 145
Flagg, James Montgomery 136, 231
The Flame of Life 137
Flame of the Argentine 39
Flames of Treachery 203
Flaming Barriers 125
The Flaming Disc 127
Flaming Fathers 182
The Flaming Frontier 55, 112
Flaming Guns 98
The Flaming Hour 83
The Flaming Signal 69, 93
Flaming Star 72, 73
Flaming Waters 89
Flaming Youth 87, 150, 152
Flamingo Road 63, 226
Flapper Wives 174
Flashing Fangs 193
Flashing Oars 96
The Fleet's In 36, 110
Fleming, Victor 34
Flesh 154
Flesh and the Devil 109, 110
Flickering Youth 67
Flight 122
Flight into Nowhere 199
Flight to Fame 199
Flip Flops 194
Flirtation Walk 118
The Flirting Widow 37, 139
Flirting with Fate 103
Flirting with Love 152
Flirty Four Flushers 106
The Floating College 161
The Flood 30, 187
Flor Silvestre 73
Florida Special 78
The Florodora Girl 129
Flower of the North 185
Fluttering Hearts 182
Flyin' Thru 81
The Flying Buckaroo 190
Flying Down to Rio 71, 72, 98, 176, 178, 224
Flying Eagle 190
Flying Elephants 141
Flying Fate 195

The Flying Fleet 163
Flying High 96
The Flying Horseman 136
The Flying Irishman 53
Flying Luck 16
The Flying Mail 93
The Flying Torpedo 131
Flynn, Errol 228
Fog 41
Folies Bergeres de Paris 89, 90, 133
Follow the Fleet 178
Follow the Leader 144, 178
The Folly of Vanity 94
Fonda, Henry 177, 231
A Fool's Advice 98
Fools First 134, 206
Fools for Luck 26, 83
Fool's Gold 38
Fools' Highway 165
Fools in the Dark 149
Fools of Fashion 69
Fool's Paradise 124
Footlight Fever 233
Footlight Parade 28
Footlights and Fools 151, 152
Footloose Widows 125
For Beauty's Sake 204
For Big Stakes 149
For Heaven's Sake 29, 169
For Ladies Only 125, 141
For Love or Money 203, 204
For Sale 174, 206
For Sale a Bungalow 106
For Silvestre 72
For the Honor of the Family 57
For the Love of Mike 194
Forbidden Cargo 39
Forbidden Company 26, 76
Forbidden Hours 194
Forbidden Paradise 185
Forbidden Trail 198
Forced Landing 39
Ford, Harrison 194
Ford, John 160
A Foreign Affair 16, 17
Foreign Devils 206
The Foreign Legion 143
The Foreman Went to France 64
The Forest Runners 82
For(r)ester, Ross 22, 89221
Forever After 19
Forever Female 178
Forget-Me-Not 130, 131
Forgive and Forget 89
Forgotten 50, 113
Forgotten Babies 99
Forgotten Faces 41
The Forgotten Woman 185
Forgotten Women 93, 181
Forlorn River 229
Forsaking All Others 62, 152, 175, 224

Fortune, Louise *see* Lorraine, Louise
The Fortune Hunter 60
Fortune's Mask 149
Fortunes Turn 59
45 Calibre Echo 81
Forty-Five Minutes from Broadway 74
40-Horse Hawkins 55
42nd Street 79, 103, 176, 178
The Forward Pass 212
Foster, Helen 9, 85, 220
Foster, Lewis 201
Foster, Norman 26
Four Days' Wonder 183
Four Devils 91, 129
Four Faces West 70, 71
Four Fathers 116
The Four Feathers 209
Four Girls in White 45
The Four Horsemen of the Apocalypse 97, 110, 111
Four Men and a Prayer 25, 212
Four Sons 51
Four Walls 62
The Fourflusher 158
The Fourth Alarm 47
The Fourth Commandment 143
Fox 31, 32, 33, 40, 42, 52, 67, 77, 80, 86, 91, 103, 106, 140, 156, 160, 191, 193, 205, 215, 223, 224, 225, 226, 227, 230
Fox, Harry 38
Fox, Sidney 10, 86, 221
Fox Movietone Follies of 1929 46, 215
Foxe, Earle 164
The Frame-Up 199
Framed 39, 113, 155
Francisco, Betty 7, 86–87
Frankenstein 230
Free and Easy 120, 163
Free Lips 143
Free to Love 35
Freedom of the Press 69
Freeland, Thornton 49
The Freeze-Out 83
Freighters of Destiny 110
Fremault, Anita Louise *see* Louise, Anita
French Dressing 204
Frenzied Flames 82
The Freshman 108, 109, 167, 169
Freshman Love 79
The Freshman's Goat 181
Friendly Enemies 82
A Friendly Husband 194
Frisco Sally Levy 161
Frisco Waterfront 173, 192
From Broadway to Cheyenne 69, 120
From Headquarters 48
From Rags to Britches 106

From Soup to Nuts 141
The Front Page 41
The Frontiersman 127, 206
Frost, Art 48
Frozen River 190
The Fugitive 72, 73
Fugitive at Large 80
Fugitive from a Prison Camp 146
Full Confession 78
A Full House 203
Fun and Games 187
The Furies 204
The Furnace 87
Fury 120
Fury of the Jungle 153
Fury of the Wild 109

Gable, Clark 61, 138, 191, 211
Gabriel Over the White House 154
The Gaiety Girl 165
The Gaiety Girls 79
Gail, Jeanne *see* Gale, Jean
Gale, Jane 88
Gale, Jean 12, 88
Gale, Joan 88
Gale, June 88
Gallant Defender 230
The Galley Slave 59
The Galloping Ace 155
Galloping Fish 175
Galloping Fury 171
Galloping Gallagher 108
The Galloping Ghost 96, 120
Galloping On 16
Galloping Romeo 101
The Gamblers 83, 90, 204
Gambling Sex 98
Gambling Wives 87
The Gang Buster 17
Gang War 33
Garbo, Greta 29, 81, 109, 119, 143, 153, 162
Garmes, Lee 97
Garnett, Tay 149
Garon, (Marie) Pauline 7, 88–90, 220, 221
Gaslight Follies 36
Gasoline Gus 121
Gasoline Love 209
The Gate Crasher 150
Gates of Brass 203
The Gates of Doom 24
Gateway 109
The Gateway of the Moon 72
The Gaucho 195, 196
Gay and Devilish 124
The Gay Caballero 223, 224
The Gay Deceiver 69
The Gay Deception 70
The Gay Divorcee 177, 178, 216
The Gay Lord Waring 203
The Gay Retreat 87

The Gay Vagabond 232
Gayety 173
Gaynor, Janet 8, 42, 90–92, 103, 156, 208, 215, 219
Geared to Go 93
General Crack 107, 125, 158
General Custer at Little Big Horn 134
A Gentle Gangster 54
Gentle Julia 131
The Gentleman from America 127
Gentleman from Dixie 146
A Gentleman from Mississippi 38
Gentleman's Fate 163
Gentlemen of the Evening 114
Gentlemen Prefer Blondes 65, 189
George Runs Wild 48
George Washington Slept Here 226
George White's Scandals 56, 58, 88, 148, 153
Geraghty, Carmelita 8, 92–93
Geraghty, Thomas 92
Geraldine 156, 158
A Geranium 57, 59
Gershwin, George 177
Gershwin, Ira 198
Get-Rich-Quick Peggy 127
Get That Venus 17
Get Your Man 36, 76
Getting Gertie's Garter 171, 232
The Ghetto Shamrock 95
The Ghost Breaker 121
The Ghost City 85, 155, 190
The Ghost Patrol 131
The Ghost Talks 191, 192
Ghost Valley Raiders 14
The Ghost Walks 51
Giant 234
Giant from the Unknown 234
Gibbons, Cedric 72
Gibson, Hoot 25, 47, 69, 77, 81, 85, 87, 95, 100, 110, 115, 125, 126, 137, 148, 156, 180, 194
Giddy Gobblers 141
Gifford, Frances 229
The Gift of Gab 83, 187
Gigolettes of Paris 160
Gigolo 169, 171
Gilbert, Billy 79
Gilbert, John 29, 100, 109, 195–196
Gilbertini 14
Gilda 227
The Gilded Highway 74
Giles, Roxanne *see* Arlen, Roxanne
Gilmore, June 234
Gilmore, Warren 24
Gimbel, Benedict, Jr. 166

Gimme 30
The Gingham Girl 87, 109, 164, 204
Ginsberg the Great 84
The Girl and the Law 82
Girl Crazy 176
The Girl Dodger 74
The Girl Friend 167
The Girl from Avenue A 88
The Girl from Jones Beach 204
The Girl from Mexico 196, 197
The Girl from Scotland Yard 154
The Girl He Didn't Buy 90
The Girl I Loved 148, 149
A Girl in Every Port 108, 113, 123, 171
The Girl in 419 187
The Girl in Number 29 80
The Girl in Possession 117
The Girl in the Glass Cage 212
The Girl in the Pullman 138
The Girl in the Rain 55
The Girl in the Show 132
Girl in the Woods 54
Girl in 313 114, 199
Girl Missing 41
Girl o' My Dreams 43, 44, 163
A Girl of the Limberlost 95, 145, 163
Girl of the Port 161
Girl of the Rio 72
The Girl on the Barge 161
The Girl on the Front Page 187
The Girl on the Stairs 149
Girl Overboard 165, 187
Girl Shy 167, 169
Girl Trouble 101
The Girl Who Came Back 179
The Girl Who Ran Wild 175
Girls 166
Girls About Town 207
Girls Can Play 133, 199
Girls Demand Excitement 182
Girls Gone Wild 46
Girls Men Forget 149
Girls' School 233
Girls Under 21 105
Gish, Dorothy 15, 88, 202
Gish, Lillian 20, 88, 191, 202
Give Out Sisters 233
The Glad Rag Doll 57, 85
Glamour 64
Glamour for Sale 129
Glass Houses 134
The Glass Menagerie 130
Gleason, James 145
The Glimpses of the Moon 57
Glorious Betsy 56, 57
The Glorious Lady 38
The Glorious Trail 136
The Glory Trail 103
The Glove 29
Glyn, Elinor 34

Go Chase Yourself 229
The Go Getter 129
The Go-Getters 194
Go Into Your Dance 53, 215
Gobs of Fun 33
Gobs of Trouble 13
The Godfather, Part 2 234
The Godless Girl 23, 24, 36
God's Country and the Man 31
God's Gift to Women 28, 48, 117
God's Little Acre 234
Goelet, Robert 232
Goetten, Gisela *see* Marlowe, June
Goin' to Town 176
Going Crooked 131
Going Highbrow 90
Going Places 53, 129
Going Some 83
Going the Limit 126
Gold 68
Gold and the Girl 81
The Gold Diggers 55
Gold Diggers of Broadway 85, 207
Gold Diggers of 1933 27, 28, 103, 176, 178
Gold Diggers of 1935 186, 187, 228
Gold Diggers of 1937 28
Gold from Weepah 66
The Gold Hunters 138
Goldberg (Golden), Louis 14
The Golden Bed 46, 52, 173, 174, 199
Golden Dawn 107
Golden Earrings 124
The Golden Idiot 83
Goldie 24
Goldwyn, Samuel 65, 163, 174, 205
Golf Widows 112, 171, 174
Gone with the Wind 97, 128, 130, 172, 201, 228
Good as Gold 118
The Good Bad Boy 199
The Good Bad Man 131
Good Dame 99
Good Girls Go to Paris 28, 230
Good Men and True 182
Good Morning, Judge 96
Good Neighbor Sam 224
Good News 132
Good Sam 85
Good Sport 26, 53, 87
Good Time Charley 60, 107
Goodbye Again 28
Goodbye Darling 19
The Good-Bye Kiss 77, 93
Goodbye Legs 47
Goodbye My Fancy 63
The Goose and the Gander 230
The Gorgeous Hussy 62

The Gorilla 68, 122, 129, 173, 174
Gough, Lloyd 154
Grabiner, June 228
Graduation Daze 96
Graft 46, 93, 173
The Grain of Dust 206
Grand Canyon 54
Grand Hotel 43, 44, 62
Grand Larceny 206
Grand Old Girl 44
The Grand Parade 192
Grand Slam 212
Grandpa Goes to Town 232
Grange, Harold (Red) 168
Granger, Dorothy 12
Grant, Cary 15, 40, 177
Grant, Frances 227
Graves, Ralph 67, 188
The Gray Brother 83
Grease 29
The Great Alone 95
The Great Circus Mystery (serial) 127
The Great Divide 139
The Great Gabbo 184
The Great Gambini 146
The Great Gamble 116
The Great Gatsby 93, 202, 203
Great God Gold 183
The Great Hospital Mystery 14, 26
The Great Hotel Murder 42, 44
The Great Jewel Robber 109
The Great Lie 18, 20, 219
The Great Lover 31
The Great Meadow 30, 129
The Great Sensation 89
The Great Victory 83
Greater Than a Crown 57
Greater Than Love 87
The Greatest Thing in the World 59
Greathouse, Clyde 76
The Greeks Had a Word for Them 28
Green Acres 230
The Green-Eyed Blonde 234
Green Eyes 173
The Green Goddess 36
Green Light 129
Greene, Gladys *see* Arthur, Jean
The Greene Murder Case 17
Greenough, Thurkel "Turk" 170
Gregory, Ena 8, 93–94, 220
Gregory, Paul 91
Greif, Martha *see* Martel, June
Grey (Gray), Gloria 8, 94–95, 222
Grey, Nan 228
Grey, Zane 202

Gribbon, Harry 193
Grief Street 110
Griffith, Corinne 205
Griffith, D.W. 17, 76, 129, 150, 183, 195
Grinning Guns 94
The Grip of the Yukon 143
Grit, Black Oxen 35
Grogan's Foundling 59
The Groom Wore Spurs 178
Grumpy 65
Guard That Girl 110
Guardians of the Wild 48
The Guiding Light 181
A Guilty Conscience 87
The Guilty Generation 64, 197
Gulliver, Dorothy 9, 95–97, 220
Gulliver's Travels 132
Gun Gospel 82
Gun Justice 230
Gun Law 36, 48
Gun Play 181
Gun Smoke 41, 181
Gung Ho! 233
Guns Don't Argue! 45
Gunsmoke 16
Gunsmoke Ranch 45
Gus Arnheim Orchestra 24
Gypsy 55, 234
Gypsy Colt 71
Gypsy Melody 197

Hagerman, Arthur 136
Haines, William 137, 160, 162
Hal Coslow, the Broadway Minstrel 49
Hal Roach Studios 79
Half a Chance 135
Half a Sinner 26
Half Angel 70, 213
Half Marriage 26, 33
The Half-Back of Notre Dame 106
The Half-Naked Truth 196
Half-Way to Heaven 17
Hall, Ruth 11, 97–98
Hallam, Ray 24
Halverstadt, Constance *see* Cummings, Constance
Hamilton, Lloyd 98–99, 125, 141
Handcuffed 82
Handle with Care 140, 149
Hands Off 85
Hands Up! 151, 157
Handy Andy 44, 223
Hangman's House 51
Hannam, Edna *see* Marion, Edna
Hansen (Hanson), George 146
The Hansom Cabman 69
Hap Harrigan 233
Happiness Ahead 152, 228
Happiness C.O.D. 14

Happy Days 92
Happy Go Lucky 225
Happy Land 71
Happy Landing 199
The Happy Warrior 33
Hard-Boiled Haggerty 159
Hard Boiled Hampton 114
Hard Fists 127
Hard Hittin' Hamilton 108
The Hard Hombre 24
Hard to Get 139
Hard to Handle 41
The Hard Way 199, 224
Hardboiled 161
Harding, Ann 207
Hardy, Marian 230
Hardy, Oliver 79, 117, 141, 195, 215, 227
The Hardys Ride High 230
A Harem Knight 106
Hargrave, Homer 151
Hargreaves, Richard 83
Harlow 179
Harlow, Jean 35, 207
Harmon, Kristin 233
Harmon, Mark 233
Harmon, Tom 233
Harmon of Michigan 129
Harned, Alfred 166
Harold and Maude 91
Harold Teen 41, 79, 104
A Harp in Hock 131
Harper's Bazaar 30
Harriet Craig 63
Harris, Barbara Jane 234
Harron, Robert 150
Hart, William S. 130, 148, 179
Hartung, George 14
The Harvest of Hate 85
The Harvester 53, 113, 191
Harvey, Laurence 230
Has Anybody Here Seen Kelly? 132
Has the World Gone Mad! 81
Hat Check Girl 53, 77, 178
The Hatchet Man 153, 212
Haunted 114
A Haunted Heiress 141
The Haunted Homestead 21
Haunted Honeymoon 64, 146
Haunted Island 85
Havana Widows 28
Having Wonderful Time 178
Hawaii Five-O 139, 234
Hawaiian Buckaroo 114
Hawaiian Nights 44
Hawks, Howard 18, 131
Hawks, Kenneth 18
Hawks, William 131
Hawthorne of the U.S.A. 121
Hayakawa, Sessue 130, 150
Hayes, Hazel 12, 98, 220
Hayes, Rutherford B. 143

Hayes, Teddy 24
Haymes, Dick 227
Hayward, Louis 225
Hayworth, Rita 227
Hazard, Jayne 231
Hazardous Valley 82
Hazel from Hollywood 74
He Hired the Boss 225
He Knew Women 65
He Stayed for Breakfast 212
He Was Her Man 28
He Who Gets Rapped 194
He Wrote a Book 203
The Head Man 212
Head Winds 149
Headin' West 127
Headline Hunters 200
Headline Shooter 70
The Headline Woman 216
Heads We Go 64
The Healer 154
Healthy, Wealthy and Dumb 45, 133
Hearst, Randolph 232
The Heart of Broadway 90
The Heart of Jim Brice 57, 59
The Heart of Maryland 56, 57, 58, 60
The Heart of New York 98
The Heart of the Yukon 55
The Heart of Youth 121
Heart Punch 181
Heart to Heart 19
Heart Trouble 66
Heartbeat 178
Heartbroken Shep 59
Heartless Husbands 95
Hearts and Hoofs 176
Hearts in Exile 57
Hearts of Oak 174, 185
Heaven on Earth 119, 129
Heermance, Dorothea *see* Collyer, June
The Heiress 228
The Heiress at Coffee Dan's 131
Held for Ransom 147
Held to Answer 39
Helen's Babies 35
Hell-Bent fer Heaven 149
Hell Bent for Frisco 174
Hell Bent for Love 32
The Hell Diggers 203
Hell Harbor 196
Hell on Frisco Bay 210
Hell-Ship Morgan 135
Hell-to-Pay Austin 131
Hello Cheyenne 123
Hello, Dolly! 177
Hello, Everybody! 26
Hello, Frisco, Hello 231
Hello, Lafayette 16
Hello Sister 33
Hello, Sister! 140

Index 253

Hello Television 47
Hello Trouble 25
Hell's Angels 145
Hell's 400 69
Hell's Harbor 97
Hell's Headquarters 198
Hell's Highway 104
Hell's Hole 111
Hell's Outpost 231
Hell's Valley 82
Hellship Bronson 85
Help! Help! Police 38
Henderson, Clifford 145
Henry, Buck 189
Hepburn, Katharine 225
Her Big Night 116
Her Bridal Nightmare 151
Her Chance 203
Her Crowning Glory 59
Her Daily Dozen 141
Her Father Said No 41
Her First Elopement 155
Her First Romance 199
Her Forgotten Past 110
Her Gilded Cage 55
Her Great Adventure 131
Her Husband Lies 229
Her Husband's Secret 149
Her Husband's Women 203
Her Imaginary Lover 117
Her Mad Night 44
Her Majesty Love 97
Her Man 99, 191, 192
Her Night of Nights 87
Her Resale Value 49, 50
Her Sister's Children 57, 59
Her Splendid Folly 31, 32, 118
Her Summer Hero 26, 190
Her Wedding Night 36, 113
Her Wild Oat 107, 119, 152
Hercules and the Captive Women 234
Here Come the Brides 27
Here Come the Coeds 234
Here Comes Elmer 187
Here Comes the Groom 79
Here Comes the Navy 187
Here's Flash Casey 140
Here's to Romance 129
Heritage of the Desert 26, 225
The Hero 179
Hero for a Day 129
A Hero for a Night 149
A Hero on Horseback 48
Heroes for Sale 212
Heroes in Blue 171
Heroes of the Flames 182
Heroes of the Night 158
Heroes of the West 199
Hey! Hey! Cowboy 112
Hey Rube! 48
Hi'Ya Chum 50
Hiatt, Ruth 8, 98–99

Hickville to Broadway 155
The Hidden Hand 199
The Hidden Way 95
Hiers, Walter 189
Higgins, Kenneth 133
High and Handsome 179
The High and the Mighty 200
The High Flyer 180
High Flyers 197
High Gear 144
High Hat 14, 41, 228
High Pressure 31, 39, 114
High School Girl 230
High School Hero 166
High Sierra 224, 231
High Society Blues 53, 92
High Speed 93
High Stakes 154
High Steppers 19, 43, 72
High Tide 199
Highway Patrol 199
Hill, Doris 9, 100–101
The Hill Billy 175
Hillman, Edward 157
Hindman, Albert 193
The Hindoo Charm 57, 59
Hines, Johnny 124, 138
Hinshaw, Lonsdale 47
A Hint to Brides 189
Hired Wife 160
His Big Minute 136
His Brother's Blood 22
His Captive Woman 66, 139
His Children's Children 139
His Darker Self 126
His Dog 169, 171
His First Flame 99, 113
His Forgotten Wife 108
His Girl Friday 223
His Glorious Night 100, 101
His Greatest Gamble 201
His Hidden Talent 174
His Last Race 185
His Majesty Bunker Bean 74
His Majesty the Outlaw 21
His Marriage Wow 112
His New Mama 67, 106
His New York Wife 68
His Nibs 152
His People 82, 146
His Private Secretary 113, 114
His Robe of Honor 203
His Secretary 119
His Tiger Lady 39
Historia de una Mala Mujer 73
History Is Made at Night 17
Hit the Deck 49
Hitch-Hike to Happiness 54
Hitch Hike to Heaven 163
The Hitch-Hiker 224
Hitler, Adolf 23
Hogan's Alley 149
Hold 'Em Navy! 44

Hold 'Em Yale 79
Hold Everything 161, 172
Hold Me Tight 50, 78
Hold Your Breath 74
Hold Your Man 115, 116
Holiday 19
Holiday, Judy 15
Hollywood 19, 29, 56, 121, 124, 203
Hollywood and Vine 50
Hollywood Aristocrats 23
Hollywood Boulevard 201
Hollywood Canteen 42, 62, 199
The Hollywood Gad-About 19
Hollywood Hoodlum 50
Hollywood Hotel 190
Hollywood on Parade 114, 169
Hollywood on Parade, no. 9 13, 31, 43, 79, 97, 102, 117, 140, 187, 201
Hollywood Party 44, 50, 183, 197
The Hollywood Revue 130
The Hollywood Revue of 1929 62, 120, 132, 163
Hollywood Round-up 192
Holm, Eleanor 10, 11, 101–102, 117, 220
Holmes, Inez 27
Holmes, Taylor 83
Holt, Jack 171, 233
Holt, Jennifer 232, 233
Holt, Tim 233
Holt of the Secret Service 39
A Holy Terror 77
Hombres in Mi Vida 196
Home James 116
The Home Maker 199
Home on the Range 39
Home Talent 137
Homeward Bound 121
The Homicide Squad 41
Honesty — The Best Policy 185
Honeymoon Deferred 53
The Honeymoon Express 60
Honeymoon Flats 96
Honeymoon Lane 51
Hong, Chai 126
Honky Tonk 85, 122
Honolulu Lu 197
Honor Among Lovers 178
Honor Bound 134
Honor of the Press 96
The Hooded Falcon 171
Hoofbeats of Vengeance 85
Hoop-la 36
A Hoosier Romance 151
Hopalong Cassidy Returns 39
Hope 19
Hope, Bob 143
The Hope Diamond Mystery 179
Hopper, Hedda 100, 235
Horse Shoes 16
A Horseman of the Plains 26

254 Index

Horseplay 133
Horseshoe Luck 155
Horton, Edward Everett 115, 148, 202
Horton, Juanita *see* Love, Bessie
Hot Cha 196
Hot Curves 67, 68
Hot Heels 150
Hot Pepper 31, 196
Hot Rod Girl 234
Hot Saturday 31
Hot Stuff 66, 234
Hot Water 144, 167, 169
Hotel Anchovy 101
Hotel Continental 44
Hotel Haywire 44
Hotel Variety 33, 170, 171, 207
The Hottentot 150
Houdini, Harry 143
The Hound of Silver Creek 95
House, Herschel 162
House of Errors 146
The House of Glass 143
The House of Rothschild 212
The House of Shame 82
The House of the Seven Gables 228, 232
The House of Youth 95, 125
The House That Jazz Built 134
The Housekeeper's Daughter 32
Hovey, Ann 12, 102–103
How Baxter Butted In 74
How Cissy Made Good 57, 60
How Could You, Caroline? 131
How Could You, Jean? 144
How Do You Do? 206
How to Educate a Wife 87
How to Handle Women 21, 158
How to Watch Football 52
How Women Can Make Money in the Stock Market 151
Howey, Walter 150
Hoxie, Jack 36, 67, 93, 95, 137, 190
Hubbard, Chester 127
Huddle 183
Hudson, Rochelle 10, 103–105, 222
Huffman, Barbara 234
Hughes, Kay 229
Hughes, Lloyd 18, 87, 164
Hula 36
Hulda the Silent 203
Human Hearts 165
Human Wreckage 130, 131, 175
Humanity 140
Hume, Cyril 75
Humes, Fred 166
Humoresque 62
The Hunchback of Notre Dame 148, 149, 226

The Hunger 132
Hungry Hearts 83
Hunt, Eleanor *see* Compton, Joyce
Hunted Men 44
Huntington, Archer 84
Huntington, Collis P. 84
The Huntress 152
Hurley, Harold 217
Hurlock, Madeline 8, 105–106
The Hurricane 20
Hurricane Horseman 16
The Hurricane Kid 21, 157
Husband Hunters 16, 190
Husbands for Rent 60, 134
Husey, Robert 103
Hush, Hush 20
Hush, Hush Sweet Charlotte 20
Huston, John 18
Huston, Walter 63
Hyatt, Ruth *see* Hiatt, Ruth
Hyland, Dick 104

I Am a Fugitive from a Chain Gang 26
I Am a Thief 20
I Am the Law 225
I Can't Escape 122
I Escaped from the Gestapo 41
I Give My Love 129
I Hate Women 50
I Have Lived 163
I Like It That Way 145, 187
I Like Your Nerve 212
I Live Again 132
I Live for Love 72
I Live My Life 62, 109
I Love Lucy 230
I Love Trouble 232
I Love You Again 109
I, Monster 234
I Never Sang for My Father 202
I Saw What You Did 63
I Take This Oath 53
I Take This Woman 53, 224
I Think They Call Him John 132
I Walked with a Zombie 70, 71
I Want a Divorce 28
I Was a Male War Bride 226
I Was a Prisoner on Devil's Island 78
I Was a Teenage Werewolf 234
I Was Framed 199
Ibanez, Vicente Blanco 97
The Ice Follies of 1939 62
Icebound 174, 203
Ichioka, Toshia *see* Mori, Toshia
Idaho Kid 181
Ida's Christmas 57
Idea Girl 199
Idiot's Delight 144
The Idle Rich 132

Idle Tongues 175
If I Had a Million 53, 70
If I Were King 70
If Marriage Fails 125
If Women Only Knew 121
If You Believe It, It's So 185
If You Could Only Cook 17
I'll Be Seeing You 178
I'll Name the Murderer 181
I'll Never Forget What's 'Is Name 132
I'll Show You the Town 157
I'll Tell the World 187
Illegal Traffic 44
Illicit 198
Illicit Millie 28
Illusion 51
I'm a Father 167
I'm Still Alive 192
The Image of Kate 19
Imitation of Life 53, 104
The Impatient Years 17
The Imposter 39
In Bad the Sailor 106
In Caliente 72, 228
In Early Arizona 97
In High Gear 134
In Line of Duty 46
In Love with Life 122
In Old Arizona 134
In Old California 84
In Old Cheyenne 96
In Old Kentucky 60, 201
In Old Montana 45
In Old Santa Fe 114
In Person 178
In Spite of Danger 145
In the Cool of the Day 64
In the Garden Fair 59
In the Glitter Palace 187
In the Headlines 90, 158
In the Knicker Time 194
In the Money 204
In the Next Room 68
In the Palace of the King 94, 185
In the Shadow 57
In This Our Life 20
In Walked Charley 199
Ince, Thomas 136
Incident 54
The Incredible Charlie Carewe 19
The Incredible Journey of Doctor Meg Laurel 187
The Indestructible Wife 55
Indiscreet 110
Inez from Hollywood 19
Inherit the Wind 55
The Inner Man 139
Innocent's Progress 185
Inside Information 44, 181
Inspiration 120, 144, 153, 154
Interference 38, 39

International House 13
International Settlement 73
International Squadron 199, 230
The Intimate Stranger 64
Into No Man's Land 135
Into the Blue 64
Into the River 38
Intolerance 7, 130, 131, 183, 185
Introduce Me 55
The Intruder 120, 122
Invincible 38, 68, 161, 205
The Invisible Man 186, 187
The Invisible Man Returns 229
The Invisible Ray 224
The Invisible Woman 231
Irene 22, 150, 152
Irish Eyes 185
Irish Fantasy 85
Irish Hearts 112
Irish Luck 203
The Iron Man 155, 190
The Iron Mask 171, 172
Iron Master 122
The Iron Woman 38
Is Everybody Happy? 68
Is Matrimony a Failure? 121, 203
Is My Face Red? 192
Is That Nice? 101
Is There Justice? 85, 147
Isadora 132
Isham, Colonel Ralph 50
Island in the Sky 187
Island of Doomed Men 105
Island of Lost Souls 13
Isle of Doubt 139
The Isle of Hope 84
Isn't It Romantic 55
It 36
It Can Be Done 46, 81
It Could Happen to You 187
It Couldn't Have Happened 39
It Had to Be You 178
It Had to Happen 90
It Happened in Hollywood 133, 209
It Happens Every Thursday 213
It Must Be Love 152
It Never Rains 86
It Pays to Advertise 203, 207
It's a Great Feeling 63
It's a Small World 225
It's a Wonderful Life 88
It's Great to Be Alive 42, 144, 187
It's in the Air 44
It's the Old Army Game 76
It's Tough to Be Famous 31, 41
It's Up to You 228
I've Been Around 104
I've Got Your Number 28

The Jackpot 124
Jackson, Ethel Shannon *see* Shannon, Ethel
Jackson, Joseph 179, 217
The Jade Box 127
The Jade Cup 39
Jake the Plumber 215
Jane Eyre 64, 70
Jannings, Emil 15, 38, 86, 208
Jarrett, Arthur 101
Jarrett, Janice 229, 230
Java Head 124
Jaws of Steel 84
The Jazz Age 68, 69
Jazz Heaven 161
Jazz Mad 158
The Jazz Singer 76, 84
Jazzland 174
Jealous Husbands 92
Jealousy 155
The Jean Arthur Show 16
Jelks, Catherine *see* Meredith, Joan
Jenkin(s), Margaret *see* Barrie, Wendy
Jennie Gerhardt 19
Jet Pilot 54
Jewell, Lain 234
Jewish Prudence 182
Jiggs and the Social Lion 116
Jiggs in Society 116
Jim the Conqueror 81
Jimmie's Millions 87
Jimmy's Two Toots 181
"Joan Crawford Has Risen from the Grave" 61
Joan of Arc 109
Joan the Woman 106
Joanna 43, 72, 138, 139
John and Julie 64
John Petticoats 179
John Smith 19
Johnny Guitar 63
Johnson, Charles 172
Johnson, Helen *see* Wood, Judith
Johnson, Marilyn 234
Johnston, John L. 217
Johnston, Julanne (Julianne) 8, 106–107
The Johnstown Flood 90, 91
Jolson, Al 76
The Jolson Story 32
Jones, Buck 67, 81, 83, 87, 100, 107, 108, 110, 122, 125, 136, 156, 168, 180, 190, 197, 201
Josselyn's Wife 93
Journal of a Crime 98, 103
Journey into Fear 72, 73
Journey Together 132
The Joy Girl 33
Joy Street 166
Joyce, Natalie 8, 32, 107–108, 221
Judge, Neoma 12
Judge Priest 104, 129

Judgment of the Storm 175
June Moon 63, 70
Jung, Elizabeth Jane *see* Blane, Sally
Jung, Gretchen *see* Young, Loretta
Jung, Shia *see* Mori, Toshia
Jung, Toshia Mori *see* Mori, Toshia
Jungle Bride 162, 163
Jungle Girl 229
Jungle Jim 39
The Jungle Mystery 93
Junior Bonner 224
Junior Luck 96
Junior Miss 202
The Junior Year 96
Jurgens, Helen *see* Twelvetrees, Helen
The Jury's Secret 209
Just a Gigolo 31
Just a Woman 172, 206
Just Another Blonde 139
Just Imagine 176
Just Like Heaven 129
Just Married 121, 189
Just Off Broadway 47, 157
Just Pals 83
Just Speeding 99
Just the Type 48
The Juvenile Dancer Supreme 24
A Juvenile Love Affair 57

Kane, Diana 202
Kansas City Princess 28
The Kansas Terrors 199
Karloff, Boris 145
Kathleen 162
Kathleen Mavourneen 161
Keaton, Buster 13, 37, 54, 68, 77, 111, 117, 118, 136, 160, 162
Keefe, Lenore 12
Keefer, Allan 46
Keener, Hazel 8, 108–109, 221
Keep 'Em Rolling 70
Keep 'Em Slugging 144
Keep Smiling 55, 187
The Keeper of the Bees 35, 181
Keeping Company 114
Kellar, Audrey *see* Ferris, Audrey
Kelly, Gene 227
Kenaston, James 159
Kennedy, Joseph P. 193
The Kennel Murder Case 20
Kent 85, 180
Kent, Barbara 8, 9, 47, 63, 109–110, 201, 220, 220
Kentucky 155, 212
Kentucky Kernels 44
Kept Husbands 139
Kerrigan, J. Warren 201
Key, Francis Scott 110

Key, Kathleen 7, 110–112
Key to the City 213
Khan, Aly 227
The Kibitzer 41
Kick In 36
Kicking Through 96
Kid Boots 36, 112
The Kid Brother 167, 169
The Kid from Kokomo 28
The Kid from Spain 97, 98
Kid Galahad 53
Kid Gloves 204
The Kid Sister 47, 126
Kiddin' Katie 74
Kiener, Harry 147
Kiesling, Barrett 217
The Kill-Joy 135
Killer at Large 41, 109
Kilties 74
Kind Lady 44
The King and the Chorus Girl 28
King Cowboy 26
King for a Night 192
King Kelly of the U.S.A. 53
King Kong 97, 208, 209
King Leary 194
The King Murder 69, 173
King of Gamblers 39, 229
King of Hockey 90
The King of Jazz 115, 116
The King of Kings 124, 125, 171
King of the Campus 96
King of the Jungle 70, 126
King of the Kongo 124, 125
King of the Saddle 147
King of the Turf 57, 149
The King on Main Street 130, 131
The Kingdom Within 185
The King's Command 190
Kings Row 226
The King's Vacation 79
Kingsley, Sue *see* Weeks, Barbara
Kingston, Natalie 9, 112–113
Kirkwood, James 120, 121
Kirkwood, James, Jr. 121
Kismet 80, 212
Kiss and Make-Up 15, 42, 45, 50, 75, 88, 98, 103, 133, 148, 163, 199, 200
A Kiss Before Dying 20
The Kiss Before the Mirror 187
Kiss Me Again 35, 51
Kiss of Araby 206
Kitty Foyle 177, 178, 219
Kitty from Killarney 67
Klein, Arthur 69
Klondike Annie 111, 112
Klowtman, Barbara *see* Kent, Barbara
Knapp, Evalyn (Evelyn) 11, 113–114
The Knife 55

The Knight Before Christmas 155
Knock on Any Door 55
Knockout Kisses 52
The Knockout Man 127
Knockout Reilly 41
Knox, Elyse 232, 233
Knox, Frank 233
Kohner, Paul 165
Kohner, Susan 165
Kona Coast 29
Konga, the Wild Stallion 105
Kongo 196
Kornman, Mary 12
Kosher Kitty Kelly 22
Krauth, Violet *see* Marsh, Marian

La La Lucille 55
La Buna, Virginia *see* Faire, Virginia Brown(e)
La Cava, Gregory 196, 200
Ladd, Alan 46, 211
Ladd, David 46
Ladd, Sue Carol 232
Laddie 187
Ladies at Ease 90
Ladies Courageous 212
Ladies Crave Excitement 114
Ladies Day 197
Ladies in Love 68, 92, 212
Ladies Love Brutes 18, 19
Ladies Must Love 44, 162
Ladies Night in a Turkish Bath 139
Ladies of the Mob 36, 134
Ladies Prefer Brunettes 155
Lady and Gent 53
Lady Be Careful 44
Lady Be Good 139
Lady Behave! 78
Lady Chatterley's Lover 132
The Lady Escapes 187
Lady for a Night 28
The Lady from Cheyenne 212
Lady from Nowhere 20, 68
The Lady from Shanghai 227
Lady Gangster 199, 231
The Lady in Scarlet 173
Lady in the Dark 177, 178
Lady in the Morgue 79
The Lady Objects 144, 187
A Lady of Chance 119
The Lady of Lyons 155
Lady of Secrets 146
Lady of the Night 62, 119
Lady of the Pavements 195, 196
Lady Robinhood 37, 39
A Lady Takes a Chance 17, 54
Lady Tubbs 129
Laemmle, Carl 190
Laemmle, Carl, Jr. 67, 75, 86
Lahr, Bert 104
Lain, Jewell 234

Lake, Arthur 232
Lalla, Fred 170
Lanahan, Kathleen "Kitty" *see* Key, Kathleen
Lancer Spy 73
The Land of Missing Men 123
Landis, Cullen 137, 171
Landy, George 137, 217
Lane, Allan "Rocky" 232
Lane, Lupino 136
Langdon, Harry 66, 67, 68, 99, 108, 112, 136, 141, 188
Langdon's Legacy 203
Langhanke, Lucille 17
Langtry, Lily 31
La Plant(e), Violet *see* Avon, Violet
La Plante (La Plant), Laura 7, 21, 115–117, 157, 221
The Laramie Kid 195
The Lariat Kid 47
Larkin, Mark 217
La Roque, Rod 137, 168
The Las Vegas Story 234
The Lash 19, 158
The Last Act 206
The Last Command 39
The Last Dance 174
The Last Days of Pompeii 201
The Last Edition 193
The Last Frontier 96
The Last Lap 96
The Last Man 64
The Last Man on Earth 22, 164
The Last of His Face 155
The Last of Mrs. Cheyney 62
The Last of the Duanes 157
Last of the Lone Wolf 150
Last of the Redmen 199
The Last Parade 64
The Last Performance 165
The Last Ride 82, 173
The Last Trail 93
The Last Train from Madrid 39, 154
The Last Warning 53, 115, 116
Laugh and Get Rich 103, 104
Laugh, Clown, Laugh 119, 210, 212
Laughing at Death 108
Laughing at Life 98, 204
Laughing at Trouble 204
Laughing Boy 196, 197
Laughing Irish Eyes 114
Laughing Sinners 62
Laughter and Tears 38
Laughter in Hell 187
Laughton, Charles 186
Laurel, Stan 68, 79, 117, 141, 195, 215, 227
The Law Divine 38
The Law Forbids 81
The Law of 45s 160

The Law of the North 74
Law of the Plains 108
The Law of the Range 62
Law of the Sea 26
The Law Rustlers 94
The Law West of Tombstone 39
Lawful Cheaters 35
Lawful Larceny 57
Lawless Border 160
The Lawless Woman 120, 174
Lawrence, Rosina 227, 229, 230
Lawyer Man 28
The Lawyer's Secret 17, 209
Layton, Dorothy 11, 117, 220
Lazy Lightning 209
Leahy, Margaret 7, 117, 220, 220, 221, 221
The Leather Pushers 26, 144
Leave It to Me 33
Le Blanc, George 59
Lederer, Evelyn *see* Carol, Sue
Lee, Frances 9, 118, 222
Lee, Gwen 9, 119–120, 220, 222
Lee, Lila 7, 94, 120–122, 222
Leek, Ray 217
The Left Handed Gun 234
Leftover Ladies 173
Leftwich, Alexander 78
Leftwich, Patricia *see* Ellis, Patricia
The Legend of Lizzie Borden 187
Legion of the Condemned 209
Legion of the Doomed 234
Legionnaires in Paris 127
The Lemon Drop Kid 223
Lena Rivers 53
Lend Me Your Husband 128
Leni, Paul 115
The Leopard Lady 125
Le Pinski (Lepinski), Gwendolyn *see* Lee, Gwen
Leslie, Joan 230, 231
Leslie, Kay 231
Lester, Katherine *see* DeMille, Katherine
Le Sueur, Lucille *see* Crawford, Joan
Let 'Em Have It 53
Let 'Er Buck 157
Let 'Er Go Gallegher 81
Let 'Er Run 74
Let Us Be Gay 77
Let's Be Ritzy 13, 79
Let's Face It 54
Let's Get Married 203
Let's Make Music 53
Letters 89
Letty Lynton 62
Levant, Oscar 88
Levy, Benn 63
Lewis, Connie 202
Lewis, Eugene 76
Lewis, Judy 211

Lewis, Tom 211
Lewton, Val 38, 70
Liberman, Harry 99
Liberty 38, 138
Life Begins 212
Life Begins at 40 104
Life Begins in College 144, 187
Life Hesitates at 40 52
The Life Line 185
The Life of Jimmy Dolan 212
The Life of Riley 143
The Life of Vergie Winters 123, 159, 160
A Life on Film 19
Life Returns 204
Life's Greatest Problem 83
Life's Greatest Question 172
Lifting the Ban of Coventry 59
Light Fingers 172
A Light in the Window 21
The Light of Western Stars 41
The Light That Failed 125, 224
The Lighter That Failed 141
Lightnin' 50, 53, 215
Lightnin' Smith's Return 109
Lightning 168
Lightning Bill 16
The Lightning Express 127
The Lightning Rider 82
Lightning Romance 179
The Lightning Slider 194
Lights of New York 58, 60
Like, Ralph 146
Lilac Time 137, 138, 150, 152
Lilies of the Field 36
The Lily 87, 93
The Limited Mail 174
Limousine Love 141
Lina, DeMille's Godless Girl 24
Lincoln, Caryl 9, 122–124, 215
Lincoln, Elmo 125, 125
Linda 85
Linda Be Good 54, 233
Linder, Max 167
The Lineup 158
Linton, Mildred *see* Morley, Karen
Lions' Whiskers 106
Listen, Darling 20
The Little Accident 26, 144, 163
The Little Adventuress 174, 199
The Little Boss 131
Little Caesar 121
The Little Church Around the Corner 185, 206
The Little Colonel 225
Little Daddy 142
The Little Defender 131
The Little French Girl 41
The Little Giant 19, 103
The Little Girl Next Door 185
The Little Irish Girl 57
Little Johnny Jones 68

A Little Journey 206
The Little Knight 131
Little Laurette *see* Arlen, Judith
Little Lord Fauntleroy 57
Little Mariana's Triumph 24
Little Mickey Grogan 169
Little Miss Bluffit 155
Little Miss Marker 224
Little Miss Roughneck 199
The Little Missionary 135
Little Mister Jim 117
Little Orphan Annie 229
Little Orphant Annie 152
Little Papa 99
The Little Princess 129
Little Red Riding Hood 127
The Little Reformer 131
Little Robinson Crusoe 95
Little Rube 74
The Little Shepherd of Kingdom Come 66, 159, 185
Little Shoes 135
A Little Sister of Everybody 131
The Little Snob 118
The Little White Girl 135
The Little Wild Girl 122
The Little Wildcat 66, 84
Little Women 20, 70, 128
The Little Yellow House 182
The Littlest Rebel 154
Live and Let Live 134
Live Fast, Die Young 234
Live, Love and Learn 94
The Live Wire 195
Lizzie 29
Lloyd, Harold 47, 63, 108, 110, 148, 167, 168, 201, 215
The Local Bad Man 26
Local Boy Makes Good 97
Loco Luck 209
The Lodge in the Wilderness 190
Logan, Jacqueline 7, 124–125
Lohman, Walter 45
Lombard, Carole 138, 170
London After Midnight 69
London Scrapbook 131
The Lone Chance 39
Lone Cowboy 122
The Lone Defender 143
The Lone Eagle 110
The Lone Rider 174
Lone Star Pioneers 97
The Lone Star Ranger 46
Lone Trail 82
The Lone Wolf in Paris 224
The Lone Wolf Returns 119
The Lone Wolf Takes a Chance 114
Lonely Wives 117, 150
Lonesome 109, 110
The Lonesome Trail 82
Long, Sally 8, 125–126, 220, 221

Long Day's Journey into Night 63
Long Fliv the King 182
The Long Long Trail 77, 137, 138
The Look Out Girl 125
Look Your Best 152
Looking for Trouble 64, 69, 207
Loos, Anita 189
Loose Ankles 212
Lord, Marjorie 232, 233
Lord Byron of Broadway 120, 180
Loretta Young Show 211
Lorraine, Louise 7, 126–127, 222
Lorraine of the Lions 149
Loss of Innocence 132
Lost and Found 31
Lost and Found on a South Sea Island 185
Lost Angel 185
Lost at Sea 112
Lost at the Front 113
The Lost Battalion 83
Lost in Limehouse 116
Lost in the Stratosphere 13, 51, 90
A Lost Lady 142
The Lost Princess 80
The Lost Romance 203
Lost Sheep 86
The Lost Son 145
The Lost Special 123
The Lost Squadron 19
The Lost Weekend 231
The Lost World 130, 131
The Lost Zeppelin 137, 138
The Lotus Eater 152
Lotus Lady 87
The Loudspeaker 199
Louis, Jean 211
Louise, Anita 10, 128–129, 221, 222
Louisiana Purchase 79
Love, Bessie 7, 129–132, 162, 219, 220, 221
Love Affair 138, 139
Love Among the Millionaires 36
Love and Kisses 67
Love and Learn 134
Love at Second Sight 145
Love Before Breakfast 53, 193
Love Begins at Twenty 79
Love Bound 68
Love Business 142
The Love Captive 163, 187
The Love Doctor 51
Love 'Em and Leave 'Em 39
The Love Gamble 89
Love in a Police Station 106
Love in Exile 44
Love in High Gear 194, 195
Love in the Desert 33
Love Insurance 203

Love Is a Racket 70
Love Is Like That 104, 173
Love Is Love 80
Love Is News 211, 212
Love, Laugh and Live 122
The Love Letter 188
Love Letters 129
Love Makes 'Em Wild 113, 166
Love Me and the World Is Mine 165
Love Me Forever 167
Love Nest 124
The Love of Sunya 89
Love on a Budget 53
Love on the Run 62
The Love Piker 87
The Love Pirate 138
The Love Racket 68, 139
The Love Thrill 116
Love Thy Neighbor 65
The Love Toy 60
The Love Trap 116
Love Under Fire 212
The Loved One 234
The Lovelorn 159, 160, 161
Lovequist, Evelyn 234
Lover Come Back 63, 64
A Lover's Oath 112
Love's Blindness 185
Love's Greatest Mistake 39, 76
Loves of an Actress 135
The Loves of Carmen 72
Love's Whirlpool 121
Lovey Mary 130, 131
Lovin' the Ladies 204
Loving Lies 39
Loy, Myrna 84
Lubin 14, 98
Lubitsch, Ernst 148, 175
The Luck of the Foolish 69, 106
The Luck of the Irish 206
Lucky Boy 119
Lucky Devils 104, 201
Lucky Larrigan 85
Lucky Partners 178
Lucky Star 91, 95
Lucky Stars 112
Lucky Terror 14
Lugosi, Bela 34, 65, 86
Lukas, Paul 78
Lulu's Doctor 57, 59
The Lunatic at Large 139
Lund, Lucille 12, 133, 221
Lundeen, Myna 234
Lupino, Ida 224
Lupino, Stanley 148
The Lure of Heart's Desire 38
Luxury Liner 229
Lynch, Helen(e) 7, 134–135, 220
Lynn(e), Sharon 9, 122, 215
Lyon, Ben 157
Lytell, Bert 38, 205

M 155
MacDonald, Jeannette 83
Mack, Helen 223, 224, 225
Mackaill, Dorothy 8, 138–139, 158, 220
MacMurray, Fred 231
The Mad Empress 39
The Mad Genius 145
Mad Hour 161
Mad Love 224
The Mad Miss Manton 216
The Mad Parade 39, 50, 69
The Mad Racer 16
Madam Satan 15, 43, 87, 107, 135, 182
Madame Bo-Peep 185
Madame Du Barry 72, 129
Madame Racketeer 114
Madame Spy 209
Made on Broadway 78
Madison Square Garden 53, 158
Madness of Youth 107
The Madonna of Avenue A 57
Madonna of the Streets 39, 76
The Magic Box 132
The Magic Garden 155
Maginot, Paul 151
The Magnificent Ambersons 56, 57, 59
The Magnificent Brute 74
The Magnificent Doll 178
The Magnificent Flirt 212
Magnificent Obsession 53, 156
Mahin, John Lee 149
Maid o' the Storm 203
Maid to Order 36
Maigne, Charles 54
The Mailman 182
The Main Event 174, 199
Main Street Lawyer 129
Majestic 23, 40
The Major and the Minor 177, 178
Make Me a Star 28
Maker of Men 144
Making Good 96
The Making of O'Malley 139
Making the Grade 83
Malay Nights 93
Male and Female 120, 121
Mallory, Patricia "Boots" 11, 140
Maloney, Duane *see* Thompson, Duane
La Malquerida 73
The Maltese Falcon 17, 18, 20
Mamba 30
Mame 177
Man About Town 31, 154
Man Against Woman 216
The Man and the Moment 120
Man Bait 87, 171
A Man Betrayed 70
Man Crazy 139

Index 259

The Man from Blankley's 212
The Man from Brodney's 111
The Man from Dakota 73
The Man from Glengarry 89
Man from God's Country 172
Man from Monterey 98
The Man from Nevada 108
Man from New Mexico 123
A Man from Wyoming 51
The Man I Love 41
The Man in Hobbles 121
Man in the Attic 32
The Man in the Moonlight 152
The Man in the Saddle 126, 209
The Man in the Shadow 135
The Man in the Trunk 144
A Man Must Live 125
Man of Action 123
Man of Iron 20
A Man of Nerve 16
A Man of Sentiment 145
Man of the Moment 117
The Man on the Box 60
The Man on the Flying Trapeze 41
Man Power 41
Man-Proof 120
Man to Man 197
Man Trouble 139
The Man Upstairs 74
Man vs. Woman 74
The Man Who Came Back 92, 139
The Man Who Came to Dinner 45, 231
The Man Who Dared: An Imaginative Biography 144
The Man Who Fights Alone 203
The Man Who Laughs 165
The Man Who Lived Twice 146
The Man Who Played God 19
The Man Who Reclaimed His Head 207
The Man Who Woke Up 185
The Man with Two Faces 20
The Man Without a Conscience 142
Man Without a Country 184, 185
Man, Woman and Wife 158, 185
Mancuso, Frank 24
The Mandarin Mystery 230
Manhattan 125
Manhattan Butterfly 93
A Manhattan Knight 89
Manhattan Monkey Business 52
Manhattan Parade 31, 98
Manhattan Tower 41
Mankiewicz, Josef 225
Mannequin 57, 62, 120
Mannix 128
Manpower 53, 231
Man's Castle 212

A Man's Fight 203
A Man's Game 114
A Man's Land 181
Man's Law and God's 179
A Man's Man 76, 203
Manslaughter 203
Mantrap 34, 36
Many Happy Returns 144
March, Fredric 34, 208
Marching to Georgie 118
Maria Candelaria 72, 73
Marie Antoinette 129
Marion, Edna 8, 141
Mark of the Frog 155
Marks, Barbara 234
Marley, Peverell 24
Marlie the Killer 147
Marlowe, June 8, 141–143
Marlowe, Kathy 234
Marriage 136
The Marriage Bargain 122
Marriage by Contract 148, 150
The Marriage Circus 106
The Marriage Maker 19
The Marriage Market 89
Marriage on Approval 110
The Marriage Playground 41, 129
The Married Flapper 108, 175
Married in Haste 80
Married in Hollywood 95
Married on the Wing 203
Married to a Mormon 38
Marry in Haste 172
Marsh, Joan 10, 143, 144
Marsh, Marian 10, 143, 144–146, 220
Marshall, Herbert 140
Marshall, William 177
Martel, June 228, 229
The Martyr Sex 172
Marx, Zeppo 97
Marx Brothers 97, 187
Mary of the Movies 131
Mary Stevens M.D. 103
Masciotra, Pierre 99
Mascot Pictures 12, 14, 75
The Mask of Fu Manchu 154
The Mask of Lopez 108
Masked 82
The Masked Menace 16
The Masked Raiders 233
Mason, Carol *see* Todd, Lola
Mason, LeRoy 42
Mason, Rita *see* Carewe, Rita
Mass Appeal 187
Master of Men 209
A Master Stroke 179
The Master Sweeper 114
Mata Hari 154
Matching Wits 116
Matchmaking Mammas 77
Mather, A. Wiley 74

The Matinee Idol 131
The Mating Call 39, 85
Matrimonial Maneuvers 59
Maugham, Somerset 170
Maybe It's Love 187
Mayer, Louis B. 184
Mayfair 205
Mayfair Girl 26
Maynard, Ken 49, 65, 69, 81, 97, 100, 136, 201
Maytime 35, 87, 179, 199
The Maze 32
Mazie's Married 194
McAl(l)ister, Mary 8, 9, 135
McCann, Frances *see* Stuart, Iris
McConnell, Gladys 9, 136
McCormack, John 98, 151
McCoy, Tim 69, 93, 100, 122, 180, 197
McCrea, Jody 70
McCrea, Joel 70, 71, 180
McDonald, Grace 232, 233
McDonald, Ray 233, 234
McDougal(l), Helen *see* Mack, Helen
The McGuerins from Brooklyn 226
McGuire (Maguire), Kathryn 7, 136–138, 221
McGuire of the Mounted 127
McKee, Raymond 99, 188
McKinnon, Bert 188
McLaglen, Victor 201
McLaughlin, Betty *see* Ryan, Sheila
McLaughlin, Katherine *see* Ryan, Sheila
McMath, Virginia *see* Rogers, Ginger
Me and My Pal 169
Me, Gangster 51
The Meanest Man in the World 22, 134
The Measure of a Man 135
Medinille y Grau, Jose 179
Meet Boston Blackie 105
Meet Corliss Archer 40
Meet Joe Black 225
Meet Me in St. Louis 17, 20
Meet Nero Wolfe 230
Meet the Baron 120
Meet the Prince 131
Meet the Stewarts 70
Meet the Wife 117, 144
Meeting of the Ways 57, 59
Mehaffey, Blanche (aka Joan Alden and Janet Morgan) 8, 146–147
Meighan, Thomas 38, 80, 120, 124, 202
Meiklejohn, Elizabeth *see* Bryson, Betty

260 Index

Melody Cruise 45, 223
Melody for Three 210
Melody for Two 79
Melody Lane 76
The Melody Man 68
Memories That Haunt 59
Memory Lane 30
Men Are Like That 101, 117
Men in Black 99
Men in Her Life 196, 197, 212
Men Must Fight 44
Men of Action 109
Men of America 201
Men of Chance 19
Men of Daring 94
Men of the Hour 167
Men of the Sky 198
Men Without Law 93
Men Without Souls 105
Mendes, Lothar 139
Menjou, Adolphe 38, 78
Menshell, Iris see Milan, Lita
Meredith, Joan 8, 147
Meredith, Lu Ann (Lu-Anne) 12, 147–148
Merely Mary Ann 92
Merrick, Marilyn (Lynn) 231, 232
The Merry Monahans 234
The Merry Monarch 86
The Merry Widow 13, 90, 123, 201
Merry-Go-Round 165
Metro 29, 175
Mexican Spitfire 197
Mexican Spitfire at Sea 197
Mexican Spitfire Out West 197
Mexican Spitfire Sees a Ghost 197
Mexican Spitfire's Baby 197
Mexican Spitfire's Blessed Event 197
Mexican Spitfire's Elephant 197
MGM 9, 18, 20, 27, 29, 31, 31, 43, 59, 60, 61, 68, 72, 76, 91, 92, 110, 111, 119, 127, 130, 143, 151, 153, 160, 162, 180, 184, 191, 200, 205, 207, 208
Michael, Gertrude 225, 226
The Middle Watch 125
The Midlanders 131
Midnight 18, 20, 86, 134
Midnight Club 81, 107
Midnight Daddies 108
Midnight Faces 138
The Midnight Flyer 74
The Midnight Girl 121
The Midnight Kiss 91, 136
Midnight Lady 24
Midnight Madness 125
Midnight Mary 183, 212
Midnight Molly 37, 39
Midnight Morals 120, 195

Midnight Mystery 49
The Midnight Raiders 127
The Midnight Son 155
The Midnight Sun 116
The Midnight Taxi 60
The Midnight Watch 135
Midshipman Jack 45
Midstream 205, 206
Midsummer Madness 87, 121, 203
A Midsummer Night's Dream 57, 59, 128, 129, 228
The Mighty 172
The Mighty Barnum 104
Mighty Joe Young 54
Mighty Lak' a Rose 139
Mike 161
Milan, Lita 234
The Mild West 33
Mildred Pierce 54, 61, 62, 219
The Mile-a-Minute Man 82
Mile-a-Minute Mary 74
Miles, Lillian 10, 152, 216
The Milkman 55, 109
The Milky Way 201, 223
Milland, Ray 211
Miller, Elizabeth see Perry, Joan
Miller, Eschal 228
Miller, Neil 139
Miller, Patsy Ruth 7, 148–150, 219
Miller, Sydne 234
Millie 93, 129, 191, 192
A Million Bid 57
The Million Dollar Collar 166, 167
The Million Dollar Handicap 174
The Million Dollar Hotel 188
Million Dollar Mystery 121
Million Dollar Ransom 44, 53
A Million for Love 76
The Millionaire 114
The Millionaire Cowboy 95
Millionaires 60
The Millionaire's Double 38
Mills of the Gods 209
The Mind Reader 64
Mindell, Robert 104
The Mine with the Iron Door 139
Minnie 134
Miracle in the Rain 234
The Miracle Man 80
Miracle on Main Street 75
The Miracle Rider 88
Miranda, Carmen 195
Misbehaving Ladies 122
Les Misérables 104, 224
Miss Hobbs 107
A Miss in the Dark 194
Miss Information 202, 203
Miss Lulu Bett 83, 202, 203
Miss Pacific Fleet 28

Miss Pinkerton 28, 98
Missing Daughters 105, 146, 184, 185
The Missing Link 99
The Mississippi Gambler 93
Mr. Billings Spends His Dime 124
Mr. Bolter's Niece 59
Mr. Broadway 76, 196
Mr. Cinderella 227
Mr. Deeds Goes to Town 15, 17
Mr. Dynamite 53
Mr. Moto Takes a Chance 105
Mr. Muggs Steps Out 144
Mr. Scoutmaster 71
Mr. Skitch 104
Mr. Smith Goes to Washington 17, 55, 114, 201, 229
Mr. Wong, Detective 39
Mix, Art 31
Mix, Tom 25, 32, 92, 107, 110, 115, 122, 137, 148, 150, 156, 196
Moby-Dick 56
Model Wife 28
A Modern Hero 36
Modern Mothers 110
Moeller, John 33
Mohr, Hal 225
Mollison, Henry 24
Molly and Me 194
Molly O' 124
Mommie Dearest 61
Mommy Angel 45
The Money Kings 57
Money Talks 112, 206
Money to Burn 74, 232
Monkey Business 97, 167, 178
The Monkey Talks 33
Monogram 23, 38, 40, 103, 114, 140, 145, 161, 162, 171, 180, 191, 205
Monsieur Beaucaire 203
The Monster and the Girl 231
The Monster of Piedras Blancas 45
The Monster Walks 173, 174
Montana Bill 22
The Montana Kid 101
Montana Moon 62
Monte Carlo Nights 41
Monte Cristo 82
Montenegro, Conchita 223
Montgomery, Earl 174
Montgomery, Robert 207
Moon Over Her Shoulder 53
Moonlight and Cactus 127
Moonlight and Pretzels 41
Moore, Colleen 7, 106, 137, 150–152, 219, 220
Morals for Women 50, 132
The Morals of Hilda 203
The Morals of Marcus 197
Moran, Lee 193

Moran, Polly 162
More, Robert, Jr. 47
More Pay — Less Work 41
More Than a Miracle 73
More Than a Secretary 17
The More the Merrier 17, 219
Moreno, Antonio 66
Morgan, Janet *see* Mehaffey, Blanche
Morgan, Jean(ne) 144
Morgan, Marilyn *see* Marsh, Marian
Morgan, Marion 163
Mori, Toni *see* Mori, Toshia
Mori, Toshia (Toshiye) 10, 11, 152–153, 216, 220
Morley, Karen 10, 153–155
Morning Glory 107
Morrill, Captain John 143
Morris, Glenn 102
Morris, Margaret 8, 155–156
Morrison, Kathleen *see* Moore, Colleen
Morse, Hollingsworth 77
A Most Dangerous Game 208, 209
The Most Immoral Lady 76
The Most Precious Thing in Life 17, 129
The Moth 162
The Mother 155
Mother Didn't Tell Me 124
Mother Is a Freshman 213
Mother's Cry 114
Mother's Millions 65
Moulders of Men 155
Mountains of Manhattan 75
Mounted Fury 24, 147
The Mounted Stranger 127
Mousey 132
The Mouthpiece 86
Movie Crazy 63, 64
Movie Mad 74
Mule Train 232
Mulhall, Jack 138
Muni, Paul 78
Munson, Ona 172
Murder at Dawn 76
Murder at the Vanities 13
Murder by Invitation 109, 146
Murder by Television 51
Murder by the Clock 162
Murder in Greenwich Village 209
Murder in the Music Hall 199
Murder in the Private Car 44
The Murder of Dr. Harrigan 20
Murder on the Blackboard 226
Murder on the Campus 98
Murder on the Roof 82, 172
Murder, She Wrote 186
Murder Will Out 122

Murder with Pictures 53
The Murders in the Rue Morgue 86, 141
Murphy, John 121
Murray, Charlie 137, 228
Murray, Mae 184
The Music Goes Round 104
Music Is Magic 227
The Music Man 230
The Music Master 128
Must We Marry? 90
The Mutiny of the Elsinore 83
My Baby Doll 141
My Best Girl 92, 93
My Bill 129
My Blue Heaven 88
My Dear Miss Aldrich 120
My Favorite Wife 226
My Favorite Year 187
My Friend Flicka 128
My Friend from India 81
My Gal Loves Music 233
My Gal Sal 227
My Hero 198
My Hollywood 149
My Home Town 21
My Husband's Wives 39
My Lady Friends 134
My Lady o' the Pines 19
My Lady of Whims 35, 93
My Lady's Lips 35
My Life with Caroline 176
My Man 149
My Man Godfrey 226
My Marriage 227, 230
My Neighbor's Wife 84
My Own Pal 33, 134
My Past 28, 198
My Son Is a Criminal 199
My Son Is Guilty 199
My Story 19
My Weakness 140, 198
My Wild Irish Rose 185
My Woman 192
The Mysterious Dr. Fu Manchu 17
The Mysterious Lodger 59
The Mysterious Rider 13
The Mysterious Stranger 93, 190
The Mysterious Witness 81
The Mystery of the Golden Eye 40
The Mystery of the Leaping Fish 131
Mystery of the Stolen Child 59
Mystery of the Wax Museum 208, 209
Mystery Pilot 138
Mystery Ranch 87
The Mystery Rider 164
Mystery Train 69
The Mystery Trooper 147

Nagel, Conrad 232
Name the Man 149
Name the Woman 107
Nameless Men 171, 206
Nana 196, 197
Nancy Drew, Reporter 231
The Narrow Corner 79
The Narrow Street 74
Nation Aflame 122
Naughty 90
Naughty Baby 66, 108
Naughty but Nice 137, 138, 152, 212
Naughty Mary Brown 74
Naughty Nanette 85
Navelle, Jeanne 8, 182, 216
The Navigator 136, 138
Navy Blues 41, 163
Navy Secrets 209
Nazimova, Alla 148
Near the Rainbow's End 127
Near the Trail's End 181, 182
Neck and Neck 174
The Ne'er-Do-Well 121
Negrette, Dolores Asunsolo Lopez *see* Del Rio, Dolores
Neighbor's Wives 139
Nellie, the Beautiful Cloak Model 205, 206
Nelson, Rick 233
Never Love a Stranger 234
Never Say Die 83
Never the Twain Shall Meet 154
The New Adventures of Terrance O'Rourke 203
New Brooms 131
The New Klondike 121
The New Loretta Young Show 211
New Orleans 233
New Year's Eve 19
New York 204
New Yorker 24
Newell, Blair 186–187
Newlin, Jacqueline Alice *see* Day, Alice
Newlin, Marceline *see* Day, Marceline
The Newlyweds' Advice 48
The Newlyweds' Angel Child 48
The Newlyweds' Anniversary 48
The Newlyweds Build 48
The Newlyweds Camp Out 48
The Newlyweds' Christmas Party 48
The Newlyweds' Court Trouble 48
The Newlyweds' Excuse 48
The Newlyweds' False Alarm 48
The Newlyweds' Friends 48
The Newlyweds' Happy Day 48
The Newlyweds' Hard Luck 48
The Newlyweds' Holiday 48

The Newlyweds' Imagination 48
The Newlyweds in Society 48
The Newlyweds Lose Snookums 48
The Newlyweds' Mistake 48
The Newlyweds Need Help 48
The Newlyweds' Neighbor 48
The Newlyweds' Pets 48
The Newlyweds Quarantined 48
The Newlyweds' Shopping Tour 48
The Newlyweds' Success 48
The Newlyweds' Surprise 48
The Newlyweds' Trouble 48
Newlyweds Unwelcome 48
The Newlyweds' Visit 48
Newman, Paul 234
The News Parade 166
The Next Corner 139
Next to No Time 132
Niagara Falls 180
Nice Women 70, 86
Nifties of 1923 23
Night After Night 64
Night and Day 54
A Night at the Movies 119
A Night at the Ritz 79
Night Beat 150
The Night Before Christmas 59
Night Cargo 199
The Night Club 174
Night Club Scandal 39
Night Court 44, 163
The Night Cry 142
The Night Flyer 169
A Night for Crime 25
A Night in a Dormitory 178
Night Life 21, 68
Night Life in Hollywood 131
Night Life in Reno 93
Night Life of the Gods 148
The Night Mayor 114, 198
Night Nurse 28
The Night of June 13 70, 122
The Night of Love 113, 171
A Night of Mystery 39, 229
Night of Terror 26
Night Parade 96
Night Ride 110
The Night Rider 81
A Night to Remember 212
The Night Walker 105
The Night Watch 95
Night Work 99
Night World 173
Nightmare Alley 27, 29
Nilsson, Norma 234, 235
Nina, the Flower Girl 131
Nine and Three-Fifths Seconds 84
Nine Girls 129, 232
The Ninety and Nine 152
El Nino y la Niebla 73

Nip and Tuck 194
The Nitwits 39
Nixon, Marion (Marian) 8, 116, 156–158, 221
Nixon, Pat 128
Nixon, Richard 128
No Babies Wanted 75
No Blondes Allowed 48
No Father to Guide Him 209
No Greater Glory 204
The No-Gun Man 95
No Highway in the Sky 132
No Limit 36
No Living Witness 110, 173
No Man of Her Own 138, 139
No Man's Gold 22
No Man's Law 110
No More Children 31
No More Ladies 62
No More Women 26
No Other Woman 72
No Place to Go 19
No Time to Marry 20
Noah's Ark 56, 57
Nobody's Children 204
Nocturne 32
A Noise in Newboro 87
Noisy Neighbors 194
Nolan, Frank 94
None But the Brave 166
None Shall Escape 123
Noonan, Suzanne see O'Day, Molly
Noonan, Virginia see O'Neil, Sally
The Noose 23, 24
Nora Prentiss 226
Norris, Edward 13, 226, 232
North of Arizona 147
North of Hudson Bay 111
North of Nevada 108
North of Nome 225
North of Shanghai 85, 97
North of 36 203
Northern Pursuit 199
Not a Ladies Man 210
Not Exactly Gentlemen 53, 209
Not Quite Decent 51
Nothing Like It 74
Nothing to Wear 125
Notorious but Nice 104, 145
The Notorious Sophie Lang 193
Novarro, Ramon 68, 162
Now I'll Tell 192, 198
Nowhere to Go 132
The Nth Commandment 152
Numbered Women 26
Nurse from Brooklyn 78
The Nurse's Secret 199
Nye, Caroll 134

Oakie, Jack 119
Obey the Law 204

Object — Alimony 93, 204
O'Brien, George 33, 201, 227
O'Brien, Patricia see Ellis, Patricia
Occasionally Yours 80
The O'Conners 19
O'Connor, Donald 234
O'Day, Molly (Mollie) 9, 158–160, 161, 221
Of Human Bondage 70
Of Mice and Men 230
Off the Record 28
Office Blues 178
The Office Wife 28, 138, 139
The Officer and the Lady 105
Officer Jim 95
Officer 13 122
Oh, Baby! 180
Oh, Doctor! 19, 134
Oh, Kay! 107, 152
Oh! Mabel 48
Oh, Men! Oh, Women! 179
Oh, My Nerves 99
Oh, What a Nurse! 149
Okay America 123
Old Age Handicap 194
Old Chisholm Trail 233
Old Clothes 62
The Old Dark House 31, 186, 187
The Old Doll 59
Old Dynamite 116
An Old Fashioned Boy 179
An Old Fashioned Young Man 151
The Old Fool 87
An Old Gypsy Custom 36
Old Home Week 121
The Old Homestead 44
Old Man Rhythm 110, 226
The Old Nest 175
Old San Francisco 57
The Old Soak 142
An Old Sweetheart of Mine 109
The Old Swimmin' Hole 115, 116
The Old Wyoming Trail 198
Oliver Twist 110
Olivier, Sir Laurence 63
Olmsted (Olmstead), Gertrude 165
Olmsted, Mason 36
Olsen's Big Moment 198
The Olympic Hero 107
O'Maley, George 79
Omar the Tentmaker 82, 149
On Again — Off Again 103
On Guard 96
On Her Majesty's Secret Service 132
On Probation 87, 134
On Special Duty 95
On Such a Night 154
On the Go 85
On the Level 135

On the Other Hand 209
On the Side Lines 96
On the Stroke of Twelve 143
On Trial 135, 204
On with the Show 161
On Your Back 181
On Your Toes 109
Once a Gentleman 167, 204
Once a Sinner 26, 139
Once and Forever 149
Once in a Lifetime 78, 86, 166
Once to Every Bachelor 158
Once to Every Woman 44, 209
Once Upon a Honeymoon 178
Once Upon a Time 73
One Clear Call 206
One Dollar Bid 203
One Frightened Night 44, 114
One Glorious Day 121
One Glorious Scrap 96
One Glove Wilson 22
One Good Turn 59
One Hour Late 192
One Hour of Love 109, 125, 190
One Hour with You 76
One in a Million 120, 201
One Increasing Purpose 121
A One Man Game 209
One Man Justice 198
One Man Trail 94
One Man's Journey 70
One Mile from Heaven 26
One Million in Jewels 81
One Minute to Play 135
One More Spring 92
One Run Elmer 13
One Stormy Knight 74
One Sunday Afternoon 209
One Way Passage 97, 98
The One Way Trail 101
One Wild Time 96
The One Woman Idea 69, 166
One Year Later 41, 90
One Year to Live 139
O'Neil, Isabel(le) 159, 160
O'Neil (O'Neill), Sally 8, 159, 160–162, 220, 221
O'Neil, Sue *see* O'Day, Molly
O'Neill, Eugene 63, 190
Only Angels Have Wings 17
Only Saps Work 41
Only the Brave 41
The Only Thing 30, 62
Only 38 55, 202, 203
Only Yesterday 50, 53, 113, 123
Opening Night 27, 29, 206
The Opposite Sex 29
Orchids and Ermine 119, 152
The Oregon Trail 127
Oriente y Occidente 196
The Orphan 194
O'Shaughnessy, Brigid 18
The Other Kind of Love 171, 172

The Other Man's Wife 38
Other Men's Women (aka *Steel Highway*) 19, 28
The Other Side 134
The Other Woman 59
La Otra 73
Otra Día Veremos la Resurección de las Mariposas Disecadas 73
Our Betters 129
Our Blushing Brides 62, 120, 163, 182
Our Daily Bread 154, 230
Our Dancing Daughters 60, 62, 162, 163
Our Gang 12
Our Leading Citizen 203
Our Modern Maidens 62, 76, 163
Our Relations 14
Out All Night 158
Out of Luck 116
Out of the Ruins 158
Out of the Storm 125
Outcast 154
The Outlaw 127
The Outlaw Dog 85
Outlaw Justice 97
The Outlaw Tamer 147
Outlawed 26
Outside These Walls 57
The Outsider 125
Over, Charles, Jr. 36
Over a Garden Wall 145
Over the Garden Wall 131
Over the Hill 77
The Overland Limited 33
Overland Mail Robbery 228

The Pace That Thrills 19
Pack Up Your Troubles 117
Paddling Coeds 96
Paddy, the Next Best Thing 92
The Pagan Lady 38, 39, 120
Page, Anita 9, 130, 162–163
Page Miss Glory 20
Pages of Life 38
Paid 60, 62, 120
Paid to Dance 199
Paid to Love 77
Paint and Powder 164
The Painted Desert 191, 192
Painted Faces 85, 96
The Painted Flapper 89
The Painted Lady 139, 175
Painted People 152
Painted Ponies 48
Painted Post 113
The Painted Stallion 44, 45
The Painted Veil 153, 230
Painting the Town 149
Pajamas 33
Pal o' Mine 89
The Palm Beach Story 18, 20

Palmy Days 198
Palooka 44, 197
Pals 127
Pals First 71, 72
Pals of the Prairie 108
Panama Flo 192
Panama Lady 39
Pangborn, Franklin 52
Panic on the Air 133
Pants 135
Parachute Nurse 85, 233
Parade of the West 136
Paradise for Three 20
Paradise Island 36, 69
Paradise Park 24, 25
Paralta 201
Paramount 13, 15, 25, 34, 34, 35, 37, 38, 40, 43, 44, 46, 51, 52, 70, 70, 76, 81, 89, 91, 100, 119, 173, 176, 180, 186, 188, 198, 200, 201, 202, 205, 207, 208, 224, 225, 227, 229
Paramount on Parade 17, 36, 39, 41, 209
Pardon Me 142
Pardon My Sarong 14
Pardon Us 143
The Parent Trap 224
Paris 62
Paris at Midnight 41
Paris Bound 93
Paris Honeymoon 198
Parisian Love 35, 109
A Parisian Romance 53, 181
Parked in the Park 174
Parker, Cecilia (Cecelia) 229, 230
Parker, Lewis 197
Parkes, Gay 231, 232
Parlor, Bedroom and Bath 77
Paroled from the Big House 45, 120
Parrish, Dillwyn 163
Parrish, Gigi (Gi-Gi) 12, 163
Partners in Crime 41
Party Husband 139, 197
Party Wire 17
Pass the Gravy 182
Passionate Youth 89, 93
Passport to Paradise 147
The Past of Mary Holmes 17, 104
The Patent Leather Kid 158, 159
The Path She Chose 55
Pathé 32, 176, 191, 193
Patrick, Gail 225, 226
Patrick the Great 71, 234
Patterson, Harold 139
Patton, Richard 13
Paula 213
Pavlova, Anna 23
The Pawn 45
The Pay-Off 39, 158
Payment on Demand 71

Payne, Conrad 192
The Payoff 79
PDC/Majestic 138
El Pecado de una Madre 73
Peacock Feathers 125
Peck, Lydell 91
The Pecos Dandy 97
Pegeen 131
Peine, Jack 121
Pelayo, William 172
The Penal Code 50
Penguin Pool Murder 104
Penny Arcade 27
Penny of Top Hill Trail 131
Penrod 24
Penrod and Sam 165
Penthouse 183
Penthouse Party 39
The People's Enemy 122
Pepper, Barbara 229, 230
Pepper, Jack 177
Perdue, Derelys 7, 163–164
The Perfect Clown 147
A Perfect Crime 124
The Perfect Crime 136
The Perfect Flapper 152
The Perfect Marriage 212
The Perfect Specimen 28
Perfect Strangers 178
The Perils of Pauline 113, 114
Perils of the Yukon 116
Perrin, Jack 80, 85, 141
Perry, Joan 229, 230
Perry Mason 226
Personal Maid's Secret 129
Personality Kid 129, 156
Persons in Hiding 192
The Persuader 54
The Pet Shop 114
Pete and Gladys 52
Peter Ibbetson 224
Peter Pan 15, 40, 41, 81, 82
Phantom 165
The Phantom Broadcast 90
The Phantom Express 25, 26, 179
Phantom Justice 138
The Phantom of Crestwood 129, 154
The Phantom of Santa Fe 93
The Phantom of the Forest 87
Phantom of the Hills 22
The Phantom of the North 112
The Phantom of the Opera 164, 165
Phantom of the Range 190
Phantom of the Turf 60
The Phantom of the West 96
Phantom Thunderbolt 65, 118
Philbin, Mary 7, 164–165
Phipps, Sally 9, 166, 220
Phyllis of the Follies 68, 190
The Phynx 29
Pick a Star 53, 198, 227

Pick-Up 31, 117
Pickford, Mary 24, 91, 92, 93, 130, 143, 152, 160
Picking Peaches 194
Picture Brides 139
The Picture of Dorian Gray 32
Picture Snatcher 79
Pied Piper Malone 203
Pierce, Evelyn 8, 166–167
Pilgrimage 158
Pilgrimage Play 75
Pillow to Post 54
The Pirate 194
Pirate of Panama 113
Pirate Party on Catalina Island 146
Pirate Treasure 133
Pirates Beware 36
Pirates of the Skies 105
Pirates of Tripoli 32
The Pit 38
Pitfalls of a Big City 106
A Place Called Saturday 19
Plain Clothes 112
The Plainsman 14, 17, 229
The Plastic Age 35, 119
Platinum Blonde 212
Play Girl 212
Play Square 116
Playboy of Paris 69–70
Playing with Fire 38, 137
Playing with Souls 19, 125
Playmates 196, 197
Playthings of Desire 76, 160, 224
Pleasure 24, 65
Pleasure Before Business 82
The Pleasure Buyers 142
The Pleasure Garden 93
Pleasures of the Rich 107
The Plumber and the Lady 52
The Plumber's Daughter 67
The Plunderer 39
Plunging Hoofs 109
The Pocatello Kid 69
Poindexter, Ina 234, 235
Pointed Heels 209
Points West 194
Poisoned Paradise — The Forbidden Story of Monte Carlo 35
Poker Faces 116, 172
Police Bullets 144
Police Car 17 114
Politics 144, 154
Polly Ann 131
Polly Put the Kettle On 24
Pollyanna 132
Pomares, Anita *see* Page, Anita
Ponjola 33
The Pool of Flame 203
Poor Aubrey 83
Poor Girls 172
Poor Little Rich Boy 88
Poor Little Rich Girl 187

Poor Men's Wives 87
The Poor Nut 16
Poppy 103, 105
Popular Science #J-7-3 43
Port of Hate 153
The Port of Missing Girls 113
Porter, Cole 177
Portland Expose 45
Ports of Call 109
Possessed 61, 62, 219
Postal Inspector 79
Powder and Smoke 146
Powder My Back 84
Powdered Chickens 141
Powdersmoke Range 140
Powell, Dick 28, 40, 78, 180, 186
Powell, James 145
Powell, William 15, 124, 177, 180, 207, 208
Power 125
Power, Tyrone 211
The Power and the Glory 151, 152
The Power and the Prize 20
The Power of Silence 94
The Power of the Press 169
The Power Within 89
The Powerful Eye 16
The Powers Girl 231
The Prairie Wife 74, 109
PRC 49, 103
Preferred Pictures 34
Prepared to Die 94
The President's Mystery 39
Presley, Elvis 72
Prestige 93
Pretty Clothes 168, 169
Pretty Ladies 62, 119
The Price of a Party 19
The Price of Fear 190
The Price of Her Soul 80
The Price of Honor 172
The Price Woman Pays 203
Pride and Prejudice 155
The Pride of Pawnee 48
Pride of the Family 208
The Pride of the Legion 26, 110
Pride of the Navy 105
The Primrose Path 35, 85, 178
The Prince Chap 121
The Prince of Hearts 109
The Prince of Tempters 41
The Princess from Hoboken 146
The Princess on Broadway 89
Princess O'Rourke 199
Principal 114
The Printer's Devil 138
Prinz, Le Roy 42
Prison Camp 146
Prison Nurse 146
Prison Shadows 133
The Prisoner of Shark Island 186, 187

Prisoner of Swing 19
The Prisoner of Zenda 18, 20
Prisoners 107
Prisoners of the Pines 203
Private Affairs 87
The Private Affairs of Bel Ami 71
Private Detective 62 103
Private Izzy Murphy 149
Private Jones 187
The Private Life of Henry the VIII 225
The Private Lives of Elizabeth and Essex 228
Private Number 212
Private Scandal 41, 158
Probation 26
Proctor, Jack 96
The Prodigal Bridegroom 106
Prodigal Daughters 173, 174
The Prodigal Son 145
Professional Soldier 187
Professional Sweetheart 178, 201
Progressive Pictures 31
Promise Her Anything 132
The Property Man 169
Prosperity 163
Proud Flesh 30, 62
Prowlers of the Night 110
Public Defender 104
Public Enemy 28
Public Ghost No. 1 52
Public Hero No. 1 17, 60
The Public Menace 17
Public Opinion 204
Puppy Love 121
Puritan Passions 19
Purple Dawn 131
Pursuit 78
Put 'Em Up 95
Putting It On 31
Putting on Airs 141
Puzzled by Crosswords 141
Pye, Merrill 21

The Quaker Mother 59
Quebec 149, 150
Queen Bee 63, 210
Queen Christina 225
Queen High 178
Queen o' Diamonds 39
Queen of Broadway 105
Queen of the Chorus 82, 87
Queen of the Night Clubs 122
Queen of the Northwoods 47, 48
The Question of Today 84
Quick Let's Get Married 179
Quick Millions 77
Quick Trigger Lee 123
Quick Triggers 164
Quinn, Anthony 234
The Quitter 172, 198

A Race for Life 81, 82
Race Suicide 14
Rachel and the Stranger 211, 213
Racing Blood 55
Racing Luck 83, 109
Racing Romance 82
A Racing Romeo 169
Racing Youth 50
The Racket 109
Racketeers in Exile 225
The Radio King 127
Radio Kisses 43
Radio Patrol 50, 122
Raffles 65
Raffles, the Amateur Cracksman 38
Raft, George 159, 170
Rafter Romance 178
Rags to Riches 44
Ragtime 132
Rah, Rah, Rah! 74
The Raiders 206
Raiders of Sunset Pass 228
Raiders of the South 40
Rain 60, 62, 1707
The Rainbow Man 158
Rainbow Over Broadway 143, 144
Rainbow Riders 82
The Rainbow Trail 55
Rains, Claude 15, 186
Ralston (Raulston), Jobyna 7, 47, 63, 110, 167–169, 201
The Ramblin' Ghost 21
The Ramblin' Kid 116
The Rambling Ranger 96
Ramona 43, 71, 72, 212
Rand, Sally 8, 9, 169–171, 220
Randy Rides Alone 195
Range Courage 95
The Range Fighter 74
Range Law 65
The Range of Fear 164
Range Warfare 133
The Ranger and the Lady 199
Ranger of the Big Pines 60
Ranger of the North 24
Ranger's Code 101
Ransom 204
Ranson, Lois 231, 232
Ranson's Folly 139
The Rapids 19
Rascals 105
Raspberry Romance 106
Rasputin and the Empress 183
Rawhide 114
Ray, Charles 115, 148, 150, 179, 189
Raymond, Gene 176
Reaching for the Moon 153
Readin' and Writin' 142
Readin', 'Ritin, 'Rithmetic 141

Rebecca of Sunnybrook Farm 156, 158, 187
Rebel Without a Cause 104, 105
Reckless 109
Reckless Courage 85
The Reckless Hour 28, 139
The Reckless Way 158
The Reckoning 26
Recompense 82
Red Clay 69, 191
Red Courage 165
The Red Dance 72, 172
Red Dust 18, 19
Red Hair 36
Red Headed Woman 35
Red Hot Leather 94
Red Hot Rhythm 76
Red Hot Speed 68
Red Hot Tires 20, 149
Red Lips 158
The Red Mill 77
The Red Rider 135, 181
Red Riders of Canada 150
Red River Valley 227
The Red Sword 158
The Red Warning 95
Red Wine 51, 215
The Redeeming Sin 57
Redemption 30
Redfern, Ruth *see* Hiatt, Ruth
Redhead 226
Redhead from Manhattan 197
Reds 132
Reducing 77, 163
The Reel Virginian 112
Reeves, Bob 22
A Reformed Santa Claus 57
Regan, John 58
The Regenerates 185
Regeneration 59
Reggie Mixes In 131
Reg'lar Fellers 215
A Regular Fellow 41
Reid, Wallace 87, 120, 202
Reinhardt, Max 228
The Relay 96
El Relicario 171
Remember 191
Remember Last Night? 64, 78
Remember When? 112
Remembrance 149, 175
Remington 40
The Rendezvous 111, 175
Rendezvous with Annie 54
Renegade Holmes, M.D. 69
Reno 53, 111, 129
Rensing, Violet 234, 235
Rent Free 121
Reportaje 73
Reported Missing 89
Republic 44, 191
The Restless Sex 74
Restless Youth 69

Resurreción 196
Resurrection 43, 72, 196
Retreat, Hell! 129
The Return of Casey Jones 98
The Return of Dr. Fu Manchu 17
The Return of Jimmy Valentine 204
The Return of Peter Grimm 91
The Return of the Riddle Rider 191
Return of the Terror 20
Return to Peyton Place 20
Reunion 105
Reunion in France 62
Reunion in Reno 71
Revelation 112
Revenge 42, 43, 72
Revenge at Monte Carlo 51, 97
Revenge Is Sweet 197
Revier, Dorothy 8, 171–173, 220, 221
Revier, Harry 172
Reynolds, Vera (Norma?) 8, 173–174
Rhapsody in Blue 198, 199, 231
Rhythm in the Clouds 53, 79
Rhythm on the Range 183
Rhythm Racketeer 207
Rich Man's Folly 70
Rich Men's Wives 206
Richard, Dawn 234, 235
The Richest Girl in the World 209
Richman, Harry 34
Ricksen (Rickson), Lucille 8, 174–175, 220, 222
Rico, Mona 9, 175–176, 220
Riddle Ranch 142, 143
The Ride Back 234
Ride Beyond Vengeance 29
Ride for Your Life 116
Ride Him Cowboy 98
Rider of Death Valley 204
Rider of the Plains 31
Riders of the North 147
Riders of the Purple Sage 157
Riders Up 179
Ridin' Gents 101
Ridin' Thru 99
Riding for Fame 48
Riding High 229
Riding Rivals 16
Riding to Fame 136
Riding with Death 87
Riffraff 59, 60, 207
Riggs, Betty *see* Brent, Evelyn
Riggs, Mary Elizabeth *see* Brent, Evelyn
The Right of the Strongest 83
The Right of Way 212
The Right Way 83
Riley, Lewis 72
Riley of the Rainbow Division 90

Ring Madness 13
Rinty of the Desert 84
Rio Blanco 73
Rio Grande Romance 133, 228
Rio Rattler 181
Rio Rita 31
Rip Van Winkle 59
Ripley, Robert 153
Riskin, Robert 208
Risky Business 174
The Ritz 132
The Rivals 96
River of Romance 41, 51, 113
The River Woman 124, 125
River's End 114
RKO 40, 66, 70, 71, 77, 103, 140, 176, 180, 191, 192, 200, 233
Roach, Hal 32, 44, 90, 117, 158, 169, 195, 227
The Road Through the Dark 80
The Road to Life 181
The Road to Paradise 203, 212
The Road to Reno 207
Road to Rio 88
The Road to Romance 69
The Road to Ruin 85
The Road to Singapore 145
The Road to Yesterday 169, 171, 173, 174
Road to Zanzibar 143, 144
Roadhouse Queen 52
Roaming Lady 209
Roar of the Dragon 153
Roar of the Press 114
A Roaring Adventure 135
Roaring Ranch 77
Roaring Rider 16
Roberta 178
Robin Hood of Monterey 40
Robinson, Edward G. 15, 113, 145
Rock, Pretty Baby 210
The Rodeo 99
Rogell, Albert 93
Rogers, Charles "Buddy" 40, 76
Rogers, Ginger 10, 11, 72, 98, 176–179, 219
Rogers, Lela 177
Rogers, Will 50, 77, 103, 201, 225
Rogers St. John, Adela 23
Rogue of the Rio Grande 93
Le Roi Pausole 86
Rolled Stockings 26
Rolling Home 157
A Roman Scandal 151, 163, 187
The Roman Spring of Mrs. Stone 132
Romance and Riches 41
Romance in Manhattan 178
Romance in the Rain 87
Romance of the Underworld 19, 134

Romance of the West 141
Romance on the Run 79
The Romance Promoters 83
Romance Ranch 82
Romance Rides the Range 181
The Romantic Age 194
Romantic Rogue 94
A Romany Rose 24
Romeo and Juliet 112
Romero, Ramon 94
Rookies 69, 127
The Rookie's Return 111
Rooney, Pat, III 66
Roosevelt, Buddy 15, 21
Roosevelt, Franklyn 233
Rose, Billy 102
Rose-Marie 62
Rose o' the River 121
The Rose of Kildare 94
The Rose of Paris 165, 172
Rose of the Golden West 19
Rose of the Rio Grande 25
Rose of the Tancho 226
Rose of the World 89, 149
Rose of Washington Square 53
Rosen, Matty 88
Rosher, Charles 143
Rosher, Dorothy *see* Marsh, Joan
Rosita 92, 157
Ross, Frank 16
Rothenberg, Sanford 208
Rough and Ready 94
Rough House Rosie 36, 101
The Rough Riders 19
Rough Shod 83
Rough Waters 168, 169
Roughly Speaking 54
The Roughneck 22, 55
Rovin' Tumbleweeds 44
Roxie Hart 178
The Royal Bed 19, 90
The Royal Family of Broadway 41, 78
The Royal Fourflusher 66
A Royal Romance 36, 185
A Royal Scandal 37
Rubber Racketeers 105
Rubber Tires 131
Rugged Water 203
Ruggles of Red Gap 203
Rule 'Em and Weep 180
The Ruling Voice 212
The Rummy 185
The Runaround 41
The Runaway 36
The Runaway Bride 19
The Runaway Express 146
Runnin' Straight 82
Running Wild 41, 96
Rupert of Hentzau 206
Russell, William 83
Rust, David 106

Rustlers of Red Dog 53
Rustlin' 155
Rustling a Bride 121
Rusty Rides Alone 198
Ruth, Babe 179
Rutherford, Ann 14
Rutherford, Laurette *see* Arlen, Judith
Ryan, Peggy 232, 233
Ryan, Sheila 231, 232

Sabre Jet 200
The Sacred Flame 122
The Saddle Buster 85
The Saddle Hawk 157
The Saddle Tramp 209
Sadie Goes to Heaven 135
Sadie McKee 62
Safe in Hell 139
Safety in Numbers 76
Sagebrush Politics 31
Sailor Be Good 226
Sailor Izzy Murphy 84
Sailors Beware 196
Sailor's Holiday 77, 108
Sailor's Luck 78
Sailors' Wives 19
St. Denis, Ruth 106
St. Elmo 131
Saint Joan 63
The St. Louis Kid 79
The Saint Takes Over 225
Sally 52, 152
Sally, Irene and Mary 62, 160, 161
Sally of the Scandals 132
Sally of the Subway 147, 173
Sally's Shoulders 204
Salomy Jane 124
Salute 53
Salvation Nell 162, 184, 185
Sammy Going South 64
Samson and Delilah 37, 155
Samson at Calford 96
Sandra 48
Sands of Iwo Jima 200
Santa Fe Stampede 229
Santa Fe Trail 231
The Sap 135, 150
The Sap from Syracuse 178
A Saphead's Sacrifice 174
Satan and the Woman 206
Satan in Sables 89
Satan Met a Lady 227
Saturday Afternoon 99
The Saturday Night Kid 17, 36
Saturday's Heroes 146
Saturday's Millions 44, 133
Saunders, John Monk 208
The Savage 151
The Savage Girl 104
Saved by Radio 124
Saving Sister Susie 74

The Sawdust Ring 131
Say It in French 44
Say It with Songs 158
Scandal 116
The Scarecrow 19
Scared to Death 54
Scareheads 199
Scarface 154
The Scarlet Arrow 109
The Scarlet Empress 81, 107
The Scarlet Letter 152
Scarlet Pages 84, 158
Scarlet River 104, 201
Scarlet Saint 19
Scarlet Seas 212
The Scarlet Streak 190
A Scarlet Weekend 173
The Scarlet West 35, 84
Scattergood Meets Broadway 53
Schilling, Marion *see* Shilling, Marion
School for Girls 13, 86, 198, 204
School's Out 142
Schulberg, B.P. (Bud) 34
Schwartz, Jean 125
Scotland Yard 32
Scott, Albert 145, 151
Scott, Randolph 196
The Scoundrel 183
Scrappily Married 13, 74
Screen Snapshots 41, 203
Screen Snapshots no. 8 131
Screencraft 161
The Sea Beast 56, 57
Sea Devils 159, 224
A Sea Dog's Tale 106
Sea Ghost 117
The Sea God 209
The Sea Hawk 110, 112
The Sea Lion 131
Sea Racketeers 53
Sea Shore Shapes 127
The Sea Tiger 19
Sealed Lips 50, 172
Second Choice 48, 57
Second Fiddle 19
The Second Floor Mystery 212
Second Hand Wife 19
Second Honeymoon 76, 212
Second Wife 122, 226
The Secret Garden 121
Secret Menace 82
Secret of the Blue Room 187
Secret Orders 39
Secret Service in Darkest Africa 144
Secret Sinners 46
The Secret Studio 33
The Secret Witness 50
Secrets 67
Secrets of the French Police 104
The Secrets of Wu Sin 153, 173, 204

See America Thirst 132
See You in Jail 68
Seed 65, 202, 204
Seeds of Vengeance 185
Seeing It Through 107
Seiter, William 115, 157, 221
Self-Defense 110, 205, 206
A Self-Made Failure 149
Sellers, Peter 64
La Selva de Fuego 73
Selznick, David O. 91
Sennett, Mack 32, 36, 47, 52, 66, 67, 68, 77, 92, 99, 105, 112, 136, 143, 169, 173, 188
Sennett, Will 42
Señor Daredevil 74
Señora Ama 73
La Señorita de Chicago 176
Serenade 24
Servants Entrance 92
Seven Chances 16
Seven Different Ways 179
Seven Keys to Baldpate 87
Seven Sinners 64
The Seventh Day 55
Seventh Heaven 90, 91, 219
The Seventh Victim 38, 39
The Shadow of the Eagle 96
The Shadow of the East 39
The Shadow of the Law 35, 180
Shadowed 129
Shadows of Paris 174
Shadows of Sing Sing 41
Shadows of the Night 127
Shadows of the North 82
The Shakedown 110
Shakespeare, William 64
Shall We Dance 90, 178
The Shamrock Handicap 91
Shane 16, 17
Shanghai 212
Shanghai Bound 41
Shanghai Lady 176
Shanghai Madness 209
Shanghai Rose 99
Shanghaied 149
Shanghaied Love 26
Shanghaied Lovers 67
Shannon, Ethel 7, 179–180
The Shannons of Broadway 165
Sharp Shooters 119
She 223
She Asked for It 53
She Couldn't Say No 77
She Done Him Wrong 104
She Gets Her Man 192
She Goes to War 30
She Had to Choose 26
She Had to Eat 105
She Had to Say Yes 212
She Knew All the Answers 185
She Made Her Bed 78
She Married an Artist 199

She Never Knew 59
She Was a Lady 192, 198
She Wrote the Book 187
Shearer, Norma 60, 119
Sheekman, Arthur 187
Sheer Luck 169
The Sheik 149
The Shepherd of the Hills 94, 159
Sheridan, Ann 225, 226
Sheridan, Clara Lou *see* Sheridan, Ann
Sherlock, Jr. 136, 138
Sherlock Holmes in Washington 233
Sherlock's Home 194
Sherman, Joe 217
Sherman, Lowell 58, 89, 221
Sherwood, George 184
Sherwood, Robert E. 105
She's a Sheik 76
She's My Weakness 46
The Shield of Honor 96
Shilling, Marion 10, 180–181
Shine On Harvest Moon 42
The Shining Hour 62
Shipmates 144
Ships of the Night 125
Shipwrecked Among the Animals 194
Shiver My Timbers 142
Shockley, Marian (Marion) 11, 51, 181–182
Shod with Fire 83
Shoes 24
The Shoes That Danced 185
Shoop, General Clarence 198
The Shoot 'Em Up Kid 96
Shoot the Works 224
Shootdown 188
Shootin' for Love 116
Shootin' Irons 26
The Shooting of Dan McGrew 38
Shop Angel 181
Shore Leave 138, 139
Short Skirts 94
A Shot in the Dark 181
Should a Girl Marry? 85
Should Husbands Do Housework? 116
Should Husbands Marry? 67
Should Ladies Behave 44
Should Married Men Go Home? 141
Show Boat 115, 116
Show Folks 23, 24
Show Girl 119
The Show of Shows 25, 26, 48, 56, 57, 58, 60, 67, 68, 68, 69, 77, 90, 107, 118, 122, 125, 150, 158, 159, 160, 161, 193, 194, 204, 210, 212
The Show Off 203, 204
Show Them No Mercy! 104

The Showdown 39, 134
A Shriek in the Night 178
The Shriek of Araby 138
Shulman, Harry 31
The Shuttle of Life 38
Sic 'Em 87
Sic-Em 87
Side Show 114
Side Street 49
Side Streets 79
Sidewalks of New York 163
The Sign of the Claw 180
Sign of the Wolf 82, 226
Silence 174
The Silent Accuser 30
The Silent Avenger 190
The Silent Battle 203
The Silent Call 137
The Silent Code 147
The Silent Flyer 127
The Silent Guardian 127
The Silent Lover 112
The Silent Power 180
The Silent Rider 146
Silent Star 151
The Silent Stranger 108
The Silent Watcher 131
Silent Witness 39
Silk Stocking Sal 37, 39
Silk Stockings 116
Silks and Saddles 158
Sills, Milton 110, 124
The Silver Cord 70
The Silver Horde 17, 39
Silver Skates 54
The Silver Slave 84
Silver Spurs 54
The Silver Streak 26, 66
Sin 155
The Sin of Madelon Claudet 154
The Sin Ship 19
The Sin Sister 76
Sin Takes a Holiday 207
Sin Town 81
Sinews of Steel 194
Sing as You Swing 148
Sing Me a Love Song 79
Sing Sing Nights 140
Sing, Sinner, Sing 53
Singed 135
Singer Jim McKee 149
The Singing Fool 76, 134
The Singing Nun 234
The Singing Vagabond 230
A Single Man 69
Single-Handed Saunders 156
Sinister Hands 85
Sinner's Holiday 28, 114
Sinners in Love 33
Sinners in Silk 30
Sinner's Parade 141, 172
Sins of the Fathers 16
Sin's Pay Day 173

Sioux Blood 94
The Siren 172
Sirens of the Sea 26
Sis Hopkins 232
A Sister of Six 130, 131
Sister to Judas 206
Sisters 159, 160, 161
The Sisters 129
Sitting on the Moon 53
Sitting Pretty 178, 233
Six Cylinder Love 86
Six Lessons from Madame La Zonga 197
Sixteen Fathoms Deep 162
The Sixth Commandment 128
Sixty Cents an Hour 124
The $64,000 Question 24
Skin Deep 68
Skinner Steps Out 141
Skinner's Big Idea 182
Skinner's Dress Suit 116
Skip the Maloo! 199
Skull and Crown 160
Sky Bride 70
The Sky Hawk 53
Sky Liner 105
Sky Murder 52, 53
The Sky Pilot 152
The Sky Raider 125
Sky Raiders 69
The Sky Skidder 85
The Sky Spider 147
Skybound 14
The Sky's the Limit 231
Skyscraper 46, 194
Skyscraper Souls 163
Slave Girl 143
Slave of Desire 131
The Slaver 93
Slaves in Bondage 14
Slaves of Beauty 46
Sleeper, Martha 8, 9, 182–183, 191, 216
The Sleeping Cutie 194
Slide, Kelly, Slide 161
Sliding Home 96
Slightly Married 114
Slightly Scarlet 39
Slightly Used 77, 84
Slim Fingers 190
Slippy McGee 152
The Small Bachelor 93, 110
Small Town Boy 53
Small Town Girl 92, 210
The Small Town Guy 83
A Small Town Princess 106
A Small Town Romeo 194
Smart Money 114
The Smart Set 68
Smart Woman 19
Smarty 28
Smashing the Spy Ring 209
Smile, Brother, Smile 139

Smile Please 194
Smilin' at Trouble 134
Smilin' Guns 147
Smiling Irish Eyes 87, 107, 151, 152
The Smiling Terror 164
Smith Baby's Happy Birthday 99
Smith's Army Life 99
Smith's Baby 99
Smith's Candy Shop 99
Smith's Catalina Rowboat Race 99
Smith's Cook 99
Smith's Cousin 99
Smith's Customer 99
Smith's Farm Days 99
Smith's Fishing Trip 99
Smith's Holiday 99
Smith's Kindergarten 99
Smith's Landlord 99
Smith's Modiste Shop 99
Smith's New Home 99
Smith's Pets 99
Smith's Picnic 99
Smith's Pony 99
Smith's Restaurant 99
Smith's Surprise 99
Smith's Uncle 99
Smith's Vacation 99
Smith's Visitor 99
Smith, Elizabeth *see* Boyd, Betty
Smith, Pete 217
Smith, Sydney 31
Smoky Trails 45
Smooth as Satin 37, 39
The Smooth Guy 114
Smouldering Fires 115, 116, 134
Smuggled Cargo 105
The Snake Pit 228
Sneakers 74
Sneezing Beezers 106
The Snob Buster 95
Snookums Asleep 48
Snookums' Buggy Ride 48
Snookums Cleans Up 48
Snookums Disappears 48
Snookums' Merry Christmas 48
Snookums' Outing 48
Snookums' Playmates 48
Snookums' Tooth 48
Snowblind 185
Snowed Under 79
Snyder, George 114
So Big 150, 152
So Ends Our Night 70
So Long, Letty 85, 150, 152
So Proudly We Hail 109
So This Is Marriage 30
So This Is Paris 149
The Soap Suds Lady 67
Sob Sister 159, 224
The Social Buccaneer 175

The Social Highwayman 74
The Social Lion 33, 41
Social Register 152
Society Fever 181, 204
Society Sailors 116
Soft Cushions 46
Soft Living 53
Soldier Man 112
Soldiers and Women 207
Soldiers of Fortune 185
Soldiers of the Storm 163, 198
Sombras de Gloria 176
Some Good in All 57
Some Mother's Boy 169
Some Pun'kins 190
Some Steamer Scooping 57, 59
Somebody Lied 16
Somebody's Mother 138
Someone to Love 41
Something for the Boys 232
Son of Dracula 233
A Son of His Father 131
Son of Kong 223
A Son of the Immortals 203
A Son of the North 82
A Son of the Sahara 206
The Son of Wallingford 194
Son of Zorro 19
The Song and Dance Man 131
Song of Old Wyoming 233
Song of the Caballero 101
Song of the Eagle 41
Song of the Saddle 90
Song of the Trail 39
Sonia 38, 167
Sonny 89
Sono-Art 23
Sons o' Guns 28
Sons of the Saddle 101
The Sophomore 161
Sorrell and Son 37
The Sorrows of Satan 76
Sorry, Wrong Number 54
So's Your Old Man 194
Sothern, E.H. 179
The Soul Market 38
Soul of the Slums 147
The Soul of Youth 121
Soul-Fire 130, 131
Souls at Sea 25, 70
Souls for Sables 206
Souls for Sale 30, 131, 149, 206
South of Panama 93
South of the Rio Grande 101
South Sea Love 149
A Southern Yankee 54
The Southerner 55
Spain, Fay 234, 235
Spangles 158
The Spanish Cape Mystery 192
The Spanish Jade 38
Speakeasy 134
Special Delivery 169

Spector, Theodore 33
Le Spectre Vert 90
Speed 89, 194, 225
Speed Demon 144
The Speed Limit 180
Speed Limited 39
Speed to Spare 201
Speed Wild 179
Speed Wings 114
Speeding Through 134
Speeding Youth 96
Speedway 163
Speedy 47
Spell of the Circus 195
The Spell of the Yukon 38
Spendthrift 40, 41
The Spider 123
The Spirit of Notre Dame 26
The Spirit of the U.S.A. 95
The Spirit of the West 101
The Spirit of Youth 87, 129
The Spitfire 89, 183
Splash Mates 96
Splashing Through 96
The Splendid Crime 55
The Splendid Road 69, 89
Spook Ranch 84
The Sport Parade 145
Sporting Courage 96
Sporting Life 94, 157
Sporting Love 148
Sporting Youth 115, 116
Spradling, Fred 87
Sprigg, Rodney 142
Spring Fever 16, 62
Spring Madness 53, 199
Spring Parade 231
Spring Reunion 117
Spurs and Saddles 209
Spy Train 39
The Squall 212
Square Shooter 199
Square Shoulders 129
The Squaw Man 30, 31, 196
The Squealer 172
Stacked Cards 138
Stage Door 45, 177, 178
Stage Door Canteen 181, 182
Stage Struck 28, 40, 129
Stage to Tucson 78
Stairs of Sand 16
Stand and Deliver 196
Stand-In 28
Stand Up and Cheer! 97, 122
Stanwyck, Barbara 83, 123
Star for a Night 53
A Star Is Born 88, 91, 92, 219
Star of Midnight 178
Star Witness 26
Stardust 197
Stark Mad 125
Starke, Pauline 7, 183–185, 221
Starrett, Charles 197

Stars Over Broadway 180
Start Cheering 133
State Fair 78, 92
State Trooper 114, 198
State's Attorney 192
Stay Away, Joe 29
Steady Company 50
Steel Against the Sky 199
Steel Preferred 174
Steele, Alfred 61
Steele, Bob 85, 100, 107, 181, 227
Stella Maris 165
Stelling, Howard 182
Step Lively, Jeeves! 79
Steppin' Out 172
Stepping Along 41
Stepping Out 31
Stepping Sisters 107, 198
Stern Brothers 141
Stevens, Byron 123
Stevens, Doreen 234
Stewart, James 15, 61, 177
Stewart, Roy 137
The Still Alarm 141
The Sting of Stings 141
Stocks and Blondes 125
The Stolen Jools 62
Stolen Love 69, 134
Stolen Pleasures 172
The Stolen Ranch 127
Stolen Sweets 26
Stone, Lewis 200
Stone of Silver Creek 181
Stool Pigeon 33
Stop Flirting 179
Stop That Man 110
The Stork Pays Off 105
The Storm 196
Storm Over Bengal 105
Storm Warning 178
Stormswept 82
The Story of Alexander Graham Bell 26, 210, 212
The Story of Dr. Wassell 109
The Story of Esther Costello 50, 63, 132
The Story of Louis Pasteur 129
The Story of Vernon and Irene Castle 178
Stout Hearts and Willing Hands 116
Stowaway 87, 209
Straight from Paris 87
Straight from the Heart 20
Straight from the Shoulder 83
Straight Is the Way 154
Straightaway 46
Strait-Jacket 63, 104, 105
Stranded 79, 131
Stranded in Paris 188
Strange Adventure 49, 50
Strange Cargo 62

The Strange Case of Clara Deane 70
Strange Conquest 199
Strange Illusion 78, 231
Strange Justice 145
The Strange Love of Molly Louvain 114
The Stranger 212
Stranger in My Arms 20
The Stranger's Banquet 29, 30, 175, 206
Strangers May Kiss 223
Strangers May Marry 154
Strangers on a Honeymoon 64
The Strawberry Blonde 227
Strawberry Roan 98
The Streak of Yellow 22
Street Angel 91, 113, 219
Street of Chance 17, 87
Street of Darkness 232
The Street of Forgotten Men 41, 128
The Street of Sin 209
Street of Women 187
A Streetcar Named Desire 192
The Streets of New York 139
Streets of Shanghai 153, 185
Strictly Business 124
Strictly Dishonorable 86
Strictly Dynamite 45, 158, 197
Strictly in the Groove 233
Strictly Modern 106, 107, 139
Strike Me Pink 78, 196, 230
Strings of Steel 96
The Stronger Sex 118
The Stronger Will 42, 43
The Stu Erwin Show 51
Stuart, Gloria 10, 11, 186–188, 219, 220, 221
Stuart, Iris 9, 188, 220, 221
Stuart, Nick 46
The Studio Murder Mystery 101
A Study in Scarlet 50
Submarine 172
Subway Sadie 139
Success 19
Success at Any Price 152
A Successful Calamity 19, 114
Such a Little Pirate 121
Such Women Are Dangerous 104
Sudden Bill Dorn 39
Sudden Fear 61, 63, 219
Sued for Libel 32
Suez 212
Sugar Daddies 141
Suicide Fleet 178
Summer Love 210
Summerville, Slim 15, 188
Sun-Up 184, 185
Sun Valley Serenade 232
Sunday, Bloody Sunday 132
Sundaying in Fairview 83
Sundown 131

Sundown Rider 198
Sundown Trail 181
Sunny Side Up 91, 171, 174, 215
Sunny Skies 69
Sunrise 77, 90, 91, 219
Sunrise Trail 147
The Sunset Derby 19
Sunset Murder Case 171
The Sunset Strip Case (aka The Sunset Murder Case) 14, 45, 170, 171
Sunset Trail 99
Superspeed 44
Support Your Local Gunfighter 29
Supreme 23
The Supreme Test 95, 172
Surrender 165
Susan and God 62
Sutter's Gold 228
Svengali 144, 145
The Swamp 131
Swanson, Gloria 105, 173
Sweeping Against the Winds 112
Sweepings 187
Sweepstake Annie 158
Sweepstakes 158
Sweet Adeline 228
Sweet Charlotte 20
Sweet Daddies 169
Sweet Kitty Bellairs 51
A Sweet Pickle 67
Sweet Sixteen 85
The Sweetheart of Sigma Chi 44
Sweethearts of the U.S.A. 97
Sweethearts on Parade 181, 182
Sweetie 127
The Swell(ed) Head 131
Swell-Head 110
The Swellhead 113, 180
Swim, Girl, Swim 76
Swing High 192
Swing Out the Blues 54, 85
Swing Time 178
Swiss Miss 140
The Sword of Valor 172
Sybil 38
Symphony of Living 39, 163
Syncopating Sue 53
Synthetic Sin 107, 137, 138, 152
System 114

The Tabasco Kid 118
A Tailor Made Man 124, 144, 183
Take a Chance 13, 32, 144
Take It from Me 146
Take Me Home 101
Take the Heir 75
Taking a Chance 191
Taking the Count 48
Taking Things Easy 116
Talbot, James 94

Talent Scout 28
Tales of Manhattan 178
Talk of the Devil 78
The Talk of the Town 17
Talking Screen Snapshots 180
Talmadge, Norma 67, 117
Talmadge, Richard 137, 189
The Taming of the West 69
Tammy and the Bachelor 210
Tangier 233
Tangled Destinies 101, 174
Tangled Fortunes 123
Tango 158
Tanks a Million 233
Tanned Legs 26, 49, 172
Tarkington, Booth 174
Tarnished Angel 78
Tarzan the Fearless 199
Tarzan the Mighty 112, 113
Tarzan the Tiger 112, 113
Tarzan's Revenge 102
Tashman, Lilyan 119
Taxi! 212
The Taxi Dancer 62
Taxi, Mister 14
Taxi Talks 114
Taxi! Taxi! 158
Taxi 13 182
Taxi Troubles 99
Taylor, Ellis 54
Taylor, Howard, Jr. 117
Taylor, Ruth 9, 188–189
Tea for Toomey 194
Tea — With a Kick 107, 108
Teacher's Pet 142
Tearin' Loose 16
Tearing Through 138
The Teaser 116
Ted Husing's Sports Thrills, no. 1 102
Tee for Two 67
Teenage Rebel 179
The Telegraph Trail 69
The Telephone 57
Tell It to Sweeney 101
Tell It to the Marines 30
Telling the World 163
Temple, Shirley 103, 186, 224
Temple of Venus 16, 67, 165
Temple Tower 69
Temptation 203
Temptations of a Shop Girl 89, 90
Temptation's Workshop 85
The Temptress 81, 82
Ten Cents a Dance 26, 183
Ten Days 109
$10 Raise 154, 227
Tender Comrade 178
The Tender Years 88
The Tenderfoot 178
A Tenderfoot Hero 95
Tenderloin 57, 166, 167

The Tenth Woman 142
Terror by Night 50
Terror Island 121
Terry, Philip 61
Tess of the Storm Country 50, 92
Tex Takes a Holiday 82
The Texan 209
The Texas Bearcat 169, 171
The Texas Marshal 231
Texas Ranger 93
The Texas Streak 146
Texas Tornado 101
The Texas Trail 179
Thank You 125
Thanks for Listening 228
Thanks for the Buggy Ride 116
That Certain Woman 129
That Flannigan Girl 149
That Forsyte Woman 32
That Gang of Mine 109
That I May Live 105
That Model from Paris 69
That Wild West 172
That Wonderful Urge 124
That's Gratitude 44
That's My Baby 155
That's My Boy 104
That's My Daddy 110
Thayer, Julia *see* Carmen, Jean
Their Hour 143
Their Mad Moment 139
Theodora Goes Wild 146
There Goes My Girl 156
There Goes the Bride 182
There Must Be a Pony 121
There You Are! 119
There's a Girl in My Heart 234
There's a Will 48
There's Always a Woman 20, 28
There's Always Tomorrow 204, 225
There's That Woman Again 133
These Glamour Girls 129
These Thirty Years 118
They All Kissed the Bride 62
They Call It Sin 212
They Drive By Night 53, 226
They Learned About Women 132
They Made Her a Spy 78
They Made Me a Criminal 226
They Met in a Taxi 209
They Met in Bombay 207
They Won't Believe Me 55
A Thief in the Dark 101, 119
A Thief in the Night 57
The Thief of Bagdad 106, 107
The Things I Had to Learn 83
The Third Alarm 129
The Third Degree 57
13 Washington Square 85
The Thirteenth Guest 178
The Thirteenth Hour 155
36 Hours to Kill 187

This Could Be the Night 29
This England 64
This Happy Feeling 20
This Is the Army 57
This Is the Life 26, 210
This Is Your Life 121
This Man Is Mine 64
This Modern Age 62
This Reckless Age 44, 70
This Side of Heaven 44
This Sporting Age 114
This Thing Called Love 93, 189
This Was Burlesque 170
This Way Please 48
This Woman 35
This Woman Is Dangerous 63
Thomas, Danny 233
Thomas, John 194
Thomas, Olive 163
Thompson, Duane 8, 189–190
Thompson, Harold 104
Thomson, Fred 85, 108, 190
The Thoroughbred 82, 90, 192
Thorpe, Franklyn 18
Those We Love 19
Those Who Dance 122, 131, 175
Those Who Judge 149
Thou Art the Man 144, 203
Thousands Cheer 20
The Threat 200
Three Ages 117, 118
Three Bad Men 33
Three Blind Mice 212
The Three-Cornered Hat (aka *It Happened in Spain*) 30
Three Cornered Moon 144
Three Dumb Clucks 133
Three Foolish Weeks 106
Three Girls About Town 28
Three Girls Lost 53, 144, 212
365 Nights in Hollywood 42
Three in Exile 127
Three Loves Has Nancy 92
Three Married Men 41
Three Men on a Horse 28
Three Miles Up 48
The Three Musketeers 98, 187
Three-Must-Get-Theres 167, 169
Three of a Kind 114
3 on a Honeymoon 78, 123
Three on a Limb 13
Three on a Match 28, 79
Three-Ring Marriage 19
Three Rogues 209
The 3 Sisters 51, 53
Three Smart Girls 228
Three Stooges 44, 99, 133
Three Weekends 36
Three Weeks in Paris 74, 134
Three Who Paid 131
Three Wise Crooks 39
Three Wise Fools 30
Three X Gordon 203

Three's a Crowd 136
Three's Company 64
The Thrill Chaser 116, 165
The Thrill Hunter 138, 173
Thrill of a Romance 229
Thrill of Youth 50
The Thrill Seekers 95, 126
Thrilling Youth 95
Through the Back Door 81
Through the Breakers 108
Through the Dark 93, 152
Through Thick and Thin 180
Thunder Below 176
Thunder Birds 54
Thunder in the Night 112, 154
Thunder Mountain 227
Thunder Over Texas 181
Thunderbolt 208, 209
Thundergate 82
Thundergod 121, 134
The Thundering Herd 203
Thundering Romance 16
Thundering Through 16
Thursday, Dell-Fin (Del-Fin) 234, 235
Tibbetts, Merna *see* Lee, Frances
Ticket to a Crime 204
Tiffany 23, 67, 68
Tiffany-Stahl 205
Tiger Rose 196
The Tiger's Shadow 136
Tight Spot 178
The Tight Squeeze 114
The Tigress 172
Tillie and Gus 199
Tillie's Punctured Romance 101
Timber War 133
The Timber Wolf 81, 82
Time Out for Murder 187
Times Square 68, 108
Times Square Lady 192
Times Square Playboy 229
The Timid Terror 101
The Timid Young Man 13
Tin Hats 206
Tin Pan Alley 80
Tinkle, Sybil *see* Borden, Olive
The Tip-Off 178, 190
Tip-Off Girls 39, 43, 44
The Tired Business Man 146
Titanic 10, 186, 188, 219
To a Finish 83
To Each His Own 228
To Have and to Hold 55, 92
To Hollywood — With Love 130–131
To Please One Woman 206
To the Death 38
To the Last Man 203
The Toast of New York 53, 156
Today 141

Today We Live 62
Todd, Lola 8, 190–191
Todd, Mike 28
Todd Thelma 190
The Toilers 169
Tom and His Pals 101, 134
Tom, Dick and Harry 177, 178
Tom Tilling's Baby 59
Tomasini, George 40
The Tomboy 74, 134
Tomorrow's Youth 183
Tone, Franchot 61, 207
Tongues of Flame 131
Tonight and Every Night 227
Tonight at Twelve 174
Tony Runs Wild 125
Too Busy to Work 158
Too Many Crooks 87
Too Many Husbands 17
Too Many Women 54
Too Much Burglar 57, 59
Too Much Harmony 226
Too Much Johnson 203
Too Tough to Kill 162
Too Wise Wives 206
Too Young to Love 132
Too Young to Marry 212
Toomey, Regis 162
Top Hat 178
Top Man 234
The Top o' the Morning 179
Top of the Town 53, 227
Top Sergeant 233
Top Sergeant Mulligan 121
Top Speed 176
Topper 206
Topper Returns 28
Topsy and Eva 49
Torch Song 63
Torchy Mixes In 139
Torchy Raises the Auntie 181
Torchy Rolls His Own 181
Torchy Turns the Trick 181
Torchy Turns Turtle 181
Torchy's Busy Day 181
Torchy's Kidd Coup 181
Torchy's Loud Spooker 181
Torchy's Millions 139
Torchy's Night Cap 181
Torchy's Promotion 139
Torero! 73
Torment 131
Torpedo Boat 44
Torture Ship 199
Touch and Go 132
Touchdown Army 44
The Tough Guy 190
Tovarich 129
Tower of London 228
The Town Scandal 155
The Toy Maker 57
Tracked 122, 123
Tracked by the Police 81, 82

Tracked in the Snow Country 142
Tracy, Spencer 61, 77, 151, 191, 208, 211
Tracy Rides 82
Trade Winds 53
A Tragedy at Midnight 32, 97
The Tragedy of Youth 150
The Trail of '98 72
The Trail of the Wolf 116
Trailin' Trouble 14
Trailing North 101
Trails of Peril 82
Tramp, Tramp, Tramp 62
Trapped 81
Trapped by Television 20, 53
Trapped by the Mormons 38
Trapped in the Sky 226
Travelin' Fast 16
Traveling Husbands 39, 64, 120
Traveling Saleslady 28, 118
Travis, June 228, 229, 230
A Treacherous Rival 116
Treason 203
Treasure of the Golden Condor 210
A Tree Grows in Brooklyn 27, 28
Trem Carr 85
Trent's Last Case 69
Tri-Art Studio 17
Trial Marriage 77
The Trial of Vivienne Ware 31
Triangle 130, 183
Trick for Trick 26
The Trigger Trail 127
Trigger Tricks 77
Trimmed 149
Trimmed in Gold 106
Trimmed in Scarlet 175
A Trip to Chinatown 136
Triple Justice 55
Trog 63
Trojan 68
Troopers Three 96
Tropical Nights 150
The Trouble Shooter 112
The Trouble with Father 51
The Troublesome Stepdaughters 57, 59
The Trouper 165
Truck Busters 231
True as Steel 30
True Blue 127
True Confession 55
True to the Navy 36
Trujillo, Rafael, Jr. 234
The Trumpet Blows 53
The Truth About Youth 212
The Truthful Sex 147
Tryon, Glenn 148
Tuhey (Tuey), Leo 125
The Turmoil 30, 89
The Turn of a Card 80, 203

Index 273

Turnabout 20, 53
Twelve Miles Out 62, 119
Twelvetrees, Clark(e) 191
Twelvetrees, Helen 9, 191–192, 220, 221
Twentieth Century 163
20th Century–Fox 43, 59, 88, 91, 128, 186, 210, 230, 233
$20 a Week 120, 173, 185
Twenty Million Sweethearts 178
Twenty-One 139
Twilight Trail 155
Twin Beds 150
Twinkletoes 107, 152
Twist All Night 226
Twist of Fate 178
Twisted Triggers 16
Twitchell, Kay 234
Two Arabian Nights 19
Two Can Play 35
Two-Fisted Jones 138
Two Fisted Justice 198
Two Fisted Law 68
Two Fisted Sheriff 198
Two Flaming Youths 41
Two Girls on Broadway 28
2 Girls Wanted 91
Two Heads on a Pillow 13
Two in a Taxi 129
Two Kinds of Women 76
Two Little Girls in Blue 167
Two Sinners 183
Two Tars 55
Two Tickets to Broadway 234
Two Weeks Off 139
Two Weeks to Live 114
Two Wise Maids 122
Two Women and Two Men 59
The Two Worlds of Jennie Logan 187
Two's Company 41
Tyler, Tom 15, 31, 47, 81, 107, 122, 180, 189, 193

Unashamed 192
Unconquered 226
Under a Texas Moon 36
Under Age 110, 228
Under 18 53, 145, 163
Under Fire 16
Under Montana Skies 96
Under Northern Lights 82
Under Texas Skies 113, 232
Under the Black Eagle 69
Under the Pampas Moon 13
Under the Rouge 93
Under the Tonto Rim 41
Under Western Skies 55, 112
Under Your Spell 53
Undercurrent 109
The Understanding Heart 62
Undertow 85
Underworld 37, 134

Undressed 82
Uneasy Payments 87, 194
The Uneven Road 135
Unfinished Business 50
The Unfortunate Bride 122
The Unguarded Hour 212
Unguarded Women 19
The Unholy Garden 209
Unholy Love 53, 122
The Unholy Night 90
The Unholy Three 120, 122
Union Depot 28, 31, 98
United Artists 175, 195
United States Smith 121
Universal (studio) 7, 21, 23, 31, 40, 47, 49, 54, 67, 73, 75, 81, 86, 95, 96, 115, 126, 143, 156, 165, 175, 186, 189, 190, 193, 205, 232, 233
The Unknown 60, 62, 155
Unknown Blonde 173
Unknown Dangers 95
The Unknown Purple 83
Unknown Woman 145
Unmarried 192, 230
Untamed 55, 62, 109, 120, 185
Untamed Justice 82
The Untamed Lady 128
Untamed Youth 45, 164
Until they Get Me 185
The Unwritten Law 41
Up and at 'Em 190
Up in Arms 74
Up in Mary's Attic 94
Up in the Air About Mary 127
Up Pops the Devil 53
The Upland Rider 94
Upper World 178
Upperworld 20
Upstage 119
Use Your Feet 96

Vacation Love 36
The Vagabond Lover 25, 26
Vagabond Luck 80
The Vagabond Trail 157
Valentino, Rudolph 120, 165, 171, 202
Valenzuela, Maria Enriqueta *see* Rico, Mona
Vallee, Rudy 25
The Valley of Hate 83, 134
Valley of the Lawless 53
The Valley of the Rogues 127
The Vampire Bat 208, 209
Vampyres 132
Van Cleve, Patricia 231, 232
Vandraegen, Daniel 200
The Vanishing American 203
The Vanishing Frontier 114
Vanishing Hoofs 109
The Vanishing Pioneer 26
The Vanishing Rider 47, 48

Vanities 31
Vanity Fair 30, 110
Vanity's Price 175
Varsity 41
The Varsity Drag 96
Vaughn, Adamae 9, 192–193, 220, 221
Vaughn, Alberta 8, 192, 193–195, 221
Velegra (Velagra), Doris (Dorothy, Dorethea) *see* Revier, Dorothy
Velez, Lupe 9, 195–197, 220, 221
Venable, Evelyn 224, 225
Vengeance 133, 172
Vengeance of the Deep 82
The Vengeance Trail 22
Venus Makes Trouble 79
Venus of Venice 93, 107
The Verdict 127
The Vermilion Pencil 131
Vernon, Bobby 118
The Very Idea 26
Via Pony Express 69, 101
The Vice Squad 207
Vidor, Charles 154
Vidor, King 29–30, 151, 230
Viennese Nights 68
The Vigilantes 99
The Viking 185
The Village Blacksmith 131
The Villain Still Pursued Her 53, 129
Villalobos, Guadalupe Velez *see* Velez, Lupe
The Violation of Sarah McDavid 187
The Violent Men 234
The Virgin 172
Virgin Lips 33
The Virginian 41
Virtue Is a Dirty Word 24
The Virtuous Husband 17
Visions of Spain 24
Vitagraph 55, 58, 130, 134, 193
Vitaphone 49, 100, 202, 224, 228
Viva Villa 208, 209, 226
Vivacious Lady 178
Vogel, Audrey 234
Voice of Hollywood 96
Voice of the City 190
The Voice of the Storm 182
The Voice of the Whistler 232
The Volga Boatman 80, 81
von Sternberg, Josef 37, 208
von Stroheim, Erich 140, 165, 208
Vruwinck, Dr. John 56
Vultures and Doves 57

Wages for Wives 125
The Wages of Sin 147

274 Index

The Wagon Show 94
Wagon Train 38
Wagons Westward 129
Wait for Me 80
Wake Up and Live 226
Wales, Wally 15
Walking Back 46
Walking Down Broadway 140
The Wall Flower 116, 152
The Wall Street Whiz 69
Wallace, Mary *see* Drake, Dorothy
Wallflowers 16, 191
Walloping Wallace 21
Walls of Gold 78, 104
Walthall, Henry B. 21
Wandering Girls 172
Wandering Husbands 121
Wandering Waistlines 106
Wandering Willies 99
The Waning Sex 135
Wannenwetsch, Dorothy *see* Layton, Dorothy
Wanted 22
Wanted — A Grandmother 57, 59
Wanted: Jane Turner 156, 187
Wanted by the Police 114
War Correspondent 122
War Drums 45
The War Horse 191
War Nurse 163, 182
War of the Range 123
War Paint 185
Ware, Irene 12
Warming Up 16
Warner, Jack 145
Warner, Sam 23
Warner Bros. 27, 31, 40, 56, 58, 61, 68, 72, 73, 76, 78, 101, 113, 115, 128, 138, 141, 148, 156, 166, 176, 179, 188, 197, 198, 202, 210, 224, 226, 227, 228, 229, 230, 231
The Warning 172
The Warrior's Husband 120
Washburn, Bryant 83
The Washington Masquerade 154
Washington Merry-Go-Round 64
Wasted Lives 87
Watch Him Step 179
Watch Your Step 149
The Water Hole 47
Water Wagons 106
Waterfront 139
Waterhole No. 3 29
Watkins, Linda 223, 224
Watling, Belle 172
Wattles, Buddy 189
A Wave, a WAC and a Marine 78, 233
Way Down East 104

Way Down South 26
The Way of a Girl 30
The Way of All Men 172
The Way of the Strong 68
Way Out West 215, 227
Wayne, John 15, 49, 69, 81, 97, 194
We Americans 37, 76, 150
We Have Our Moments 53, 78
We Moderns 152
The Weak and the Wicked 132
A Weak-End Party 22
The Weaker Vessel 24
The Weakness of Strength 38
Weber, Lois 205
Wedding Bill$ 188
The Wedding March 208, 209
Wedding Present 204
Wedding Rings 33, 204
Wednesday at the Ritz 114
Wednesday's Child 154
Wee Lady Betty 131
Week End Millionaire 41
Weekend at the Waldorf 178
Week-end Marriage 212
Weeks, Barbara 10, 197–198
Weeks, Claire 234
Weissmuller, Johnny 102, 196
Welcome Danger 110
Welcome Granger 194
Welcome Home 155, 203
Welcome Stranger 82
Weld, John 163
Welles, Orson 56, 72, 227
Wellman, William 168
Wells, Jacqueline 12, 198–200
Wells, Ted 189
Wells Fargo 70, 109
We're in the Money 28
We're Not Married 178
We're Rich Again 144, 158
West, Mae 111
West Meets East 22
West of Broadway 120
West of Chicago 111
West of the Divide 82
West of the Pecos 183
West Point 62
Western Bullets Are Blank 45
Western Limited 182
Western Pluck 69
The Western Rover 94
The Western Way 22
The Western Whirlwind 22
The Westerner 31, 32, 85, 181
Westmore, Ern(est) 47–48
Westward Ho 39
Westward Passage 53
Westward the Women 200
Wet Paint 60, 112
The Wet Parade 144
Wharf Angel 224
The Wharf Rat 185

What a Man 129
What a Party! 48
What Becomes of the Children? 143, 144
What Do Men Want? 206
What Every Girl Should Know 93, 149
What Every Woman Knows 203
What Fools Men 52
What Happened to Jones 157
What Men Want 93, 110, 185
What Price Gloria? 194
What Price Glory? 71, 72
What Price Goofy? 209
What Price Hollywood? 94, 191
What Price Vengeance 133
What Shall I Do? 139
What Women Did for Me 196
Whatever Happened to Baby Jane? 61, 63
What's a Wife Worth? 134
What's Cookin'? 233, 234
What's Worth While? 206
What's Your Hurry? 203
Wheel of Chance 24
Wheeler 196
Wheelock, Thomas 18
Whelan, Thomas 102
When a Dog Loves 85
When a Man Loves 56, 57
When a Man Sees Red 173
When a Man's a Fan 155
When a Man's a Man 142, 201
When a Man's a Prince 106
When a Queen Loved O'Rourk 203
When Danger Calls 126
When Dawn Came 152
When Dreams Come True 60
When G-Men Step In 199
When Hell Broke Loose 234
When Husbands Flirt 172
When Knights Were Bold 209
When Ladies Meet 62
When My Baby Smiles at Me 85
When Odds Are Even 74
When Sally's Irish Rose 194
When Strangers Marry 31, 32
When Strangers Meet 198
When the Devil Laughed 82
When the Door Opened 125
When the Wife's Away 171, 172
When's Your Birthday? 146
Where Did You Get That Girl? 231
Where East Is East 195, 196
Where Is My Mother? 135
Where Is My Wandering Boy This Evening? 106
Where Is My Wandering Boy Tonight? 111, 149
Where Is This West? 165
Where Sinners Meet 200

Index   275

Where the Worst Begins 164
Where Was I? 89, 157
Where's There's a Bill 155
While London Sleeps 60
While the City Sleeps 163, 224
While the Patient Slept 79
The Whip 139
The Whip Woman 107, 212
Whirlpool 17, 122, 148
The Whispered Name 203
Whispering Enemies 57
Whispering Sage 108, 109
Whispering Whiskers 106
Whispering Winds 150
The Whistler 187
Whitbeck, Frank 217
Whitcomb, Jon 40
White, George 88, 140
White, Jack 99, 184
White, Pearl 113
White and Unmarried 124
The White Black Sheep 149
The White Cockatoo 90
White Collars 22
The White Desert 206
White Eagle 198
White Flannels 82
White Hands 81
White Lies 209
White Mice 125
The White Outlaw 69
The White Parade 52, 53, 201, 212
The White Renegade 147
The White Sheep 146
White Shoulders 19
Who Cares 74
Who Done It? 233
Who Killed Aunt Maggie? 53
The Whole Town's Talking 15, 17, 72
Whom the Gods Destroy 81, 87
Whom the Gods Would Destroy 185
Whoopee! 145, 197
Who's Afraid of Virginia Woolf? 63
Who's Hooligan? 194
Who's Your Neighbor? 38
Who's Your Servant? 203
Whose Wife? 48
Whosoever Shall Offend 135
Why Be Good? 152
Why Bring That Up? 39, 134
Why Get Married? 83
Why Girls Go Back Home 149
Why Leave Home? 46
Why Sailors Go Wrong 166
Why Smith Left Home 203
Why Worry? 167, 169
Wickedness Preferred 135
Wide Open 150
Wide Open Town 39

The Widow from Chicago 55, 87
The Widow from Monte Carlo 73
The Widow in Scarlet 173
Widow's Might 117
Widrin, Tanya 231, 232
Wife Against Wife 185
Wife, Doctor and Nurse 212
Wife, Husband and Friend 212
Wife of the Centaur 30, 87
Wife Savers 26
The Wife Who Wasn't Wanted 81, 142
The Wild Affair 132
Wild Beauty 143
Wild Bill Hickok Rides 199, 231
Wild Blood 48
Wild Boys of the Road 103, 104
Wild Company 53
The Wild Girl 127
The Wild Goose Chaser 106
Wild Horse 195
Wild Horse Mesa 26, 155
The Wild Horse Stampede 209
The Wild Party 34, 36, 52, 53, 69, 172
Wild West 84
Wild West Romance 123
The Wild West Show 96
Wildcat Bus 209
Wildcat Saunders 147
Wildcats 187
The Wilderness Trail 152
Will Success Spoil Rock Hunter? 29
Williams, Alma Inez *see* Devore, Dorothy
Williams, Guinn "Big Boy" 197
Williams, Katherine 12, 41, 200
Williamson, Ethlyne *see* Clair(e), Ethlyne
Wilson, Carey 92
Wilson, Dorothy 11, 200–201, 220, 221
Wilson, Harry 22, 217
Wilson, Lois 7, 201–204, 221
Wilson, William Howard 46
Wilson or the Kaiser... 83
Win That Girl 46
Windsor, Claire 7, 204–206, 221
Windsor, William 205
The Windy Hill 149
Wine 35
The Wine of Youth 16, 30, 89
Winged Hoofs 95
Wings 36, 64, 168, 169
Wings of the Storm 82
Wings Over Honolulu 53, 225
The Winking Idol 96
Winner Take All 158, 187
Winners of the Wilderness 62, 127
The Winning Five 96

The Winning Goal 96
The Winning Point 96
The Winning Punch 96
Winston, William 124
Winter Has Come 74
Wise Girls 180
Wise Guy 19
The Wise Virgin 149
The Wise Wife 125
The Wishing Ring Man 131
With Stanley in Africa 127
Withers, Grant 211
Within the Law 83
Within the Rock 85, 122
Without Benefit of Clergy 81, 82
Without Children 39
Without Compromise 203
Without Mercy 174
Without Orders 78
Wizard of the Saddle 190
The Wolf Dog 140
Wolf Fangs 122, 123
The Wolf Hunters 82
Wolf Song 195, 196
Wolf's Clothing 149
Wolves of the City 26
Wolves of the Sea 45
The Woman Accused 13
A Woman Against the World 171
Woman Against Woman 20
The Woman Between 90, 129
The Woman from Hell 19
Woman Hungry 122
The Woman I Love 155
The Woman I Stole 209
Woman in the Dark 209
The Woman Inside 29
A Woman Is the Judge 105
A Woman of Affairs 128
Woman of Bronze 137, 138
A Woman of Experience 192
A Woman of the World 146
The Woman on the Jury 131
Woman-Proof 19, 121, 174
Woman Trap 39
Woman Unafraid 13, 198
The Woman Who Came Back 88
The Woman Who Was Forgotten 136
Woman Wise 51, 105
Womanhandled 155
A Woman's Face 61, 62
Woman's Law 84
A Woman's Woman 139
The Women 32, 61, 62
Women Are Like That 53
Women Go on Forever 158
Women Love Diamonds 119, 184, 185
Women Love Once 30, 207
Women Men Marry 26
Women of All Nations 53
Women They Talk About 84

Women Without Names 135
Women's Wares 39
Women's Weapons 144
Won in the Clouds 85
Won Ton Ton, the Dog Who Saved Hollywood 29, 95
Wonder Bar 72, 90
Wonder of Women 129
Wood, Helen 229, 230
Wood, Judith 10, 206–207
Woody, Frank 192
Woolsey 196
Words and Music 69, 192
Words and Music By— 80
Working Girls 70, 195, 206, 207
The World Changes 19, 79
The World Gone Mad 39, 41
The World to Live In 55
The World's Champion 203
Worne, Howard "Duke" 82
Worth, Barbara *see* Keener, Hazel
Wray, (Vina) Fay 8, 208–210, 219, 220
Wrecking Crew 39
Wren, P.C. 207
Wren, Percival, Jr. 207
The Wright Idea 127
The Wrong Mr. Wright 75
The Wrongdoers 55

X Marks the Spot 26

The Yankee Clipper 80, 81
The Yankee Consul 149
Yankee Doodle Dandy 231
A Yankee Princess 131
The Yankee Senor 33
Ybanez, Ruth *see* Hall, Ruth
Yellow Fingers 33
Yes, We Have No Bonanza 45
You and Me 53
You Came Along 199
You Can't Beat the Law 87, 121
You Can't Fool Your Wife 89
You Can't Take It with You 17
You Said a Mouthful 178
You Were Never Lovelier 227
You'll Never Get Rich 227
Young, Clara Kimball 80, 137
Young, Elizabeth (Betty) 210, 224, 225
Young, Elizabeth Jane *see* Blane, Sally
Young, Georgianna 210
Young, Loretta (Gretchen) 9, 25, 83, 103, 210–213, 221
Young, Polly Ann 25, 210
Young and Beautiful 15, 42, 45, 75, 88, 98, 103, 133, 148, 200
Young April 131
Young As You Feel 230
Young Bill Hickok 199
Young Blood 85
Young Bride 192

Young Donovan's Kid 181
Young Eagles 17
Young Ideas 20, 116, 175
The Young in Heart 92
Young Man of Manhattan 176, 178
Young Mother Hubbard 135
Young Mrs. Winthrop 144
Young Nowheres 158
The Young Painter 19
Youngblood Hawke 20
The Younger Generation 24, 107
Your Uncle Dudley 204
You're in the Army Now 231
You're Telling Me! 144
You're the One 14
Yours for the Asking 57
Youth on Parole 146
Youth's Gamble 155
Yukon Jake 112

La Zandunga 197
Zanuck, Darryl F. 47, 88, 91, 103, 207, 211
Ziegfeld, Florenz 23, 25, 125, 166, 196, 197, 224, 230
Ziegfeld, Zoe 138
Ziegfeld Girl 54
Zombie 184
Zoo in Budapest 212
Zorro Rides Again 175, 176
Zuckerman, Paul 189

www.ingramcontent.com/pod-product-compliance
Lightning Source LLC
Chambersburg PA
CBHW081544300426
44116CB00015B/2753